Computer Communications and Networks

The **Computer Communications and Networks** series is a range of textbooks, monographs and handbooks. It sets out to provide students, researchers and non-specialists alike with a sure grounding in current knowledge, together with comprehensible access to the latest developments in computer communications and networking.

Emphasis is placed on clear and explanatory styles that support a tutorial approach, so that even the most complex of topics is presented in a lucid and intelligible manner.

Also in this series:

An Information Security Handbook
John M.D. Hunter
1-85233-180-1

Multimedia Internet Broadcasting: Quality, Technology and Interface
Andy Sloane and Dave Lawrence (Eds)
1-85233-283-2

The Quintessential PIC® Microcontroller
Sid Katzen
1-85233-309-X

Information Assurance: Surviving in the Information Environment
Andrew Blyth and Gerald L. Kovacich
1-85233-326-X

UMTS: Origins, Architecture and the Standard
Pierre Lescuyer (Translation Editor: Frank Bott)
1-85233-676-5

Designing Software for the Mobile Context: A Practitioner's Guide
Roman Longoria
1-85233-785-0

OSS for Telecom Networks
Kundan Misra
1-85233-808-3

The Quintessential PIC® Microcontroller 2nd edition
Sid Katzen
1-85233-942-X

From P2P to Web Services and Grids: Peers in a Client/Server World
Ian J. Taylor
1-85233-869-5

Alan Steventon and Steve Wright (Eds)

Intelligent Spaces

The Application of Pervasive ICT

 Springer

Alan Steventon, BSc, MTech, PhD,
CPhys, MInstP
Judal Associates Ltd, UK

Steve Wright, MA, PhD, CEng, MIEE
BT Group, Ipswich, UK

Series editor
Professor A.J. Sammes, BSc, MPhil, PhD, FBCS, CEng
CISM Group, Cranfield University, RMCS, Shrivenham, Swindon SN6 8LA,
UK

British Library Cataloguing in Publication Data
A catalogue record for this book is available from the British Library

Library of Congress Control Number: 2 0 0 5 9 2 9 8 6 6

Computer Communications and Networks ISSN 1617-7975
ISBN-10: 1-84628-002-8   Printed on acid-free paper
ISBN-13: 978-1-84628-002-3

Printed in the United States of America (EB)

9 8 7 6 5 4 3 2 1

Springer Science+Business Media

springeronline.com

Contents

Contributors

M O Ahmed, Department of Computer Science, University College London

J Allen, Natural Language Research, BT, Adastral Park

S Appleby, Multimedia Coding Research, BT, Adastral Park

B Azvine, Intelligent Systems Research, BT, Adastral Park

A Bamidele, Department of Computer Science, University College London

G Bilchev, Web Research, BT, Adastral Park

E Bonsma, Nature Inspired Computing, BT, Adastral Park

P A Bowman, Customer Networks Research, BT, Adastral Park

R Briscoe, Networks Research, BT, Adastral Park

S Brown, Technology for Business, BT, Adastral Park

P Bull, Networks Research, BT, Adastral Park

J Bulman, Broadband Applications Research, BT, Adastral Park

T Burbridge, Networks Research, BT, Adastral Park

V Callaghan, Computer Science Department, University of Essex

J Chin, Computer Science Department, University of Essex

G Churcher, Web Research, BT, Adastral Park

G Clarke, Computer Science Department, University of Essex

M Colley, Computer Science Department, University of Essex

B Crabtree, Broadband Applications, BT, Adastral Park

F Doctor, Computer Science Department, University of Essex

R Ellis, Chimera, University of Essex

P Garner, Pervasive ICT Research, BT, Adastral Park

R Ghanea Hercock, Future Technology, BT, Adastral Park

A Gower, Broadband Applications Research, BT, Adastral Park

H Hagras, Computer Science Department, University of Essex

S Hailes, Department of Computer Science, University College London

J Hart, School of Geography, University of Southampton

D J T Heatley, Pervasive ICT Research, BT, Adastral Park

N Hine, Applied Computing, University of Dundee

C Hoile, Future Technology, BT, Adastral Park

D A M Holm, Strategic Analysis, BT, Adastral Park

N Hristov, Influx Technology Ltd

H Jovanovic, PHB Automation, Zagreb

R S Kalawsky, Department of Computer Science, University of Loughborough

N Kaveh, Future Technology, BT, Adastral Park

J L Landabaso, Technical University of Catalunya, Spain

B-S Lee, Research Fellow, BT, Adastral Park

B Lei, Visual Information Processing, BT, Adastral Park

R Limb, Customer Networks Research, BT, Adastral Park

D Luckett, Strategic Projects, BT, London

M H Lyons, Strategic Analysis and Research, BT, Adastral Park

B MacDonald, Consultant

B Majeed, Intelligent Systems Research, BT, Adastral Park

D Marston, deceased, formerly Web Research, BT, Adastral Park

K Martinez, School of Electronics and Computer Science, University of Southampton

D Molnar, University of California, Berkeley, USA

J Morphett, Media Business Development, BT, Adastral Park

D D Nauck, Intelligent Systems Research, BT, Adastral Park

I Neild, Disruptive Technology Research, BT, Adastral Park

S Nicolas, formerly Future Technology, BT, Adastral Park

A Oldroyd, Future Applications and Services, BT, Adastral Park

R Ong, Department of Engineering, University of Leicester

O K Oyekoya, Department of Computer Science, University College London

R Payne, Mobility Research, BT, Adastral Park

E Peytchev, School of Computing and Mathematics, Nottingham Trent University

J M M Potter, Strategic Analysis and Research, BT, Adastral Park

A Riddoch, School of Electronics and Computer Science, University of Southampton

C Roadknight, Customer Networks Research, BT, Adastral Park

F Saffre, Future Research, BT, Adastral Park

A Seleznyov, Department of Computer Science, University College London

M Shackleton, Future Technology, BT, Adastral Park

A Sixsmith, Department of Primary Care, University of Liverpool

A Soppera, Software Research, BT, Adastral Park

F W Stentiford, Electrical and Engineering Department, University College London

A Steventon, Research Consultant

J Sutton, Multimedia Research, BT, Adastral Park

R Tateson, Future Technology, BT, Adastral Park

S Thompson, Intelligent Systems Research, BT, Adastral Park

R Venousiou, Strategic Analysis and Research, BT, Adastral Park

N Wall, Shadow Creek Consulting Ltd

S Wright, Strategic Research, BT, Adastral Park

L-Q Xu, Visual Information Processing, BT, Adastral Park

Introduction

This book sets out a vision of pervasive IT through intelligent spaces and describes some of the progress that has been made towards its realisation.

The context for intelligent spaces (or iSpaces) is the world where information and communication technology (ICT) disappears as it becomes embedded into physical objects and the spaces in which we live and work. The ultimate vision is that this embedded technology provides us with intelligent and contextually relevant support, augmenting our lives and our experience of the physical world in a benign and non-intrusive manner.

The enormous advances in hardware, system design, and software that are being achieved enable this vision. In particular, the performance advances and cost reductions in hardware components — processors, memory, storage, and communications — are making it possible to embed intelligence and communications ability into lower cost objects. The Internet is a living experiment in building complex, distributed systems on a global scale. In software, there have been solid advances in creating systems that can deal with complexities on the scale required to interact with human activity, in limited domains at least.

The ultimate vision is challenging, and there are many obstacles to its realisation. There are several technical barriers, especially in the creation of intelligent software, but there are also social and economic barriers. We can already see the first deployments of this technology in domains where the benefits are substantial. It is not clear, however, whether there are sufficient value points and benefits to support the fully pervasive and synergistic infrastructure of the iSpace vision.

An iSpace consists essentially of three components:

- the physical world in which users exist, in their relevant context;

- the interface between the digital world and the physical world — this contains embedded sensors to gather parameters, labels to identify objects, actuators to control things/appliances in the physical world, together with support software to facilitate non-intrusive two-way communication across the interface;

- the digital world in which digital knowledge and intelligent systems are available to influence and support actions in the physical world.

This volume opens with three general chapters. Firstly an overview, by the editors, to describe the broader topic, followed by Lyons et al, in Chapter 2, who describe the impact of iSpaces on businesses and the way people will work. This is followed, in Chapter 3, by Thompson and Azvine, who identify what intelligent systems research is needed to prevent users being overwhelmed by the complexity of the systems with which they will be asked to interact.

Physical World — Applications, Benefits, and Concerns
There follows a set of chapters describing several different iSpace application areas. Firstly, Luckett, in Chapter 4, describes the use of such technologies for supply chain

and production improvements, where application has advanced to the stage of commercial trials. Next, Brown et al, in Chapter 5, describe monitoring the well-being of people in need of care in their own home. The first systems for well-being monitoring have also undergone trials, and the chapter describes research on the next generation of more intelligent systems. The following three chapters describe the conversion of the home to an intelligent space (Bull et al in Chapter 6), an intelligent co-operative vehicle highway system (Bilchev et al in Chapter 7), and mixed-reality systems where the real and digital multimedia worlds can be merged to augment user experiences (Bulman et al in Chapter 8). Martinez et al, in Chapter 9 on glacial iSpaces, emphasise that the technology is applicable to hostile environments where humans rarely go but where we want to know what is happening.

These are just a few example application areas selected from the almost limitless possibilities where the technology could have a significant impact.

There are, however, concerns about trust, privacy, and security in these systems. Selezynov et al, in Chapter 10, define realistic models of digital trust that are capable of dealing with the uncertainties inherent in the environment to help engender trust. Then Sopppera and Burbridge, in Chapter 11, describe privacy issues, including legal and technical aspects, and offer a privacy management system for iSpace devices. In Chapter 12, the same authors describe the issues and approaches to satisfying the needs for privacy in the application of radio frequency ID (RFID) technologies, such as those introduced in Chapter 4.

The Interface — Observing Human Activity

In order that the relevant parameters can be gathered to make applications truly beneficial there is a need for a wide range of high-performance and low-cost hardware technology to form the interface between the real and digital worlds. Payne and Macdonald, in Chapter 13, analyse the massive advances and ongoing trends that have occurred in the hardware area, covering silicon, batteries, displays, wireless connectivity, etc. They conclude that there is still some way to go to achieve the full vision, but that enough progress has been made to have real impact in the immediate future. Heatley et al, in Chapter 14, show how large amounts of information can already be gathered from very simple sensors, e.g. attaching a microphone to the water pipe can lead to inferences of many household activities to feed data to a homecare application.

Xu et al, in Chapter 15, tackle the issue of automating visual events detection-and-behaviour analysis for advanced visual surveillance systems. Extracting behaviour from such sensors would considerably empower iSpace technology. The iSpaces can also allow the inference of interests a user might have and hence help retrieve contextually relevant information to support the user. Bamidele et al, in Chapter 16, do this by using a visual attention algorithm to drive content-based image retrieval, while Oyekoya and Stentiford, in Chapter 17, describe how they track eye-gaze direction to infer what a user is interested in, for image retrieval purposes.

Digital Infrastructure — Architectures and Intelligence

The realisation of iSpaces as an application of pervasive ICT will radically increase the number of intelligent, communicating objects in the world. The complex and dynamic nature of these systems will require new approaches to system design and implementation. For example, the Internet provides the glue for iSpaces, combining wire and radio links, but will it cope with the future scale, dynamics, and heterogeneity? Briscoe, in Chapter 18, concludes that the Internet was well conceived for this sort of usage, but that a number of issues will arise and will need attention. Three further chapters consider aspects of the digital infrastructure. Firstly, Shackleton et al, in Chapter 19, consider self-managing, self-repairing systems that can be easily deployed; secondly, Saffre et al, in Chapter 20, consider the design of scale-free networks; thirdly Ghanea-Hercock et al, in Chapter 21, consider the implementation of a service-oriented architecture in a heterogeneous world.

The networks gather the data from the interface elements and present them for intelligent analysis, according to the requirements of the applications. Some of these aspects are tackled by the final three chapters. Nauck et al, in Chapter 22, describe their development of a system that abstracts required information from an iSpace and provides the data for automatic intelligent data analysis, which is then used for a homecare application. One significant problem is that of inferring users' needs from observations of their behaviour. Allen et al, in Chapter 23, have developed the xAssist framework as a vehicle to experiment with such an inferencing process. Both these chapters seek to create software that explicitly infers intent or needs, whereas Callaghan et al, in the final chapter, discuss a solution based on the use of embedded agents to enable emergent intelligent behaviour by predominantly implicit processes.

Towards the Vision

This book provides an overall vision of intelligent spaces, where they are expected to provide benefits, and what many of the social and technical issues are that must be solved before widespread adoption. However, it is clear that before this vision can be fully realised there are many other technical, social, economic, and business issues to be solved. *En route* to the full vision there are many more constrained visions that can provide valuable benefits to users and useful business opportunities. The technologies are now ready for the development and implementation of such spaces. It is hoped that the content of this book will help readers to imagine and then create a future in which iSpaces become widely implemented.

Steve Wright
Head of Strategic Research
Research and Venturing, BT CTO

Alan Steventon
Research Consultant

1

Intelligent Spaces — The Vision, the Opportunities, and the Barriers

S Wright and A Steventon

1.1   A Vision of Intelligent Spaces

The objective of this book is to explore the vision of a world where information and communication technology (ICT) moves from the PC on the desktop out into the physical world and becomes pervasive. In this world of pervasive ICT, physical objects and spaces are linked to the digital world, and information about the physical world can be used to augment human functionality and experience. The world about us can appear to have intelligence embedded in it, as it seeks to support our human activities. This vision is similar to that described by Weiser [1] and others [2–5], though we prefer to use the term 'intelligent spaces', or iSpaces, to emphasise our initial focus on bounded applications.

We have built on the vision developed in the earlier work [1] and used it to drive our research programme within BT. We are not unique in this; for example, a very similar vision ('ambient intelligence') has been used to drive research within the EU 6th Framework programme [5]. It is emerging as a realisable vision because of major developments in technology in a number of areas. These developments (which are described in more detail below, and in the following chapters) are bringing ICT into the physical world through the following capabilities.

- Embed digital links into the physical world

    We are able to link the physical and digital worlds. For example, static information or identity can be embedded into real world objects, such as radio frequency ID (RFID) tags. Additionally, increasingly sophisticated sensor systems are being developed, and dynamic parameters or events in the physical world can be converted into digital information.

- Communicate physical state everywhere

    We can embed wireless communications into even small physical components. State or events from the physical world can be communicated locally and globally. Increasingly, this will give us global access to rich, diverse, and dynamic data about the physical world around us.

- Process and mine data

    We are already generating vast amounts of data from the digital world. We will be adding increasing amounts of dynamic data about the real world. This can have immense benefits, but only in so far as we are able to extract meaning and draw intelligent and sensitive inferences from it.

Taken together, these provide powerful new capabilities to system designers and can be used to improve our abilities to sense, and make sense of, the physical world about us, and to use this knowledge to augment our capabilities as we deal with this world, or to augment our experience of it. This is illustrated in Fig. 1.1, which represents a system that is able to sense a number of parameters of the physical world, draw some inferences from this data, and recommend (or even take) an action in the physical world.

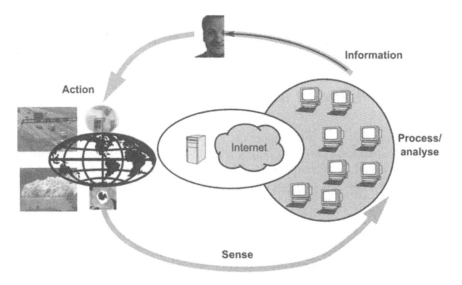

Fig. 1.1   Schematic of generic iSpace system.

Over the next two decades the tens of billions of embedded processors that already exist will grow to trillions. Many will acquire a communications capability, which most commonly will be short-range wireless. Many will connect to the Internet, either directly or via intermediaries, resulting in a trillion globally communicative intelligent objects by 2020. These will provide a wide range of information and sensory data about the physical world. An application will have the ability to gather information from appropriate sources that help it achieve its objectives. The application can then provide information or control signals to achieve the desired actions. This technology could have a significant beneficial impact on virtually every area of human endeavour, provided it is designed and implemented in a way that takes account of the needs of users and society.

The iSpace technology concept is that of 'the disappearing computer' — where the computational demands of the system are utterly non-intrusive and interfaces are so intuitive they are unperceived. In practice, this means the system and its interfaces mediate interactions with humans passively, but of course can be driven or overridden by humans directly. Because the technology can accept, interpret, or infer in a highly personalised and contextualised manner, it can assist virtually everyone by taking into account their abilities, and hence take us closer to universal digital access.

This is a grand and benefcent vision, but it is also a vision that can excite polarised reactions. There are many people who have concerns over increasing technology-driven intrusion and control in our lives, with the associated threats to civil liberties and personal privacy. There are causes for legitimate concern here (though it must be said that the level of public concern often outstrips the reality, both of the technological capability and of the business intent). In some of the areas where this technology could be applied, society will have to work through the trade-offs between costs and benefits, either in the market-place or through the legislative process.

1.2 Applications

On the whole, our observation is that the vision described above is not a distant and dystopian world. It is a world that is coming into being step by step, and it is moving forward fastest in those areas where the benefits clearly outweigh the costs, and where there is strong value for all the actors in the value chain (or the value net). We will illustrate this by describing a number of example applications, both current and potential.

1.2.1 Example Applications

Supply Chain
RFID tags are digital labels that can be attached to components, to give them a digital identity that can be simply read at various stages in the supply chain [6] (see also Chapter 4). It is an application with high value to participants in the supply chain, where it has the potential to improve efficiency. It is already being applied widely to aggregations of goods down to the pallet level. Just recently, a number of important retailers have announced to their suppliers their intent to introduce this in the retail context. The objective is to improve retail efficiency, both in staff time and in better stock control and less lost sales.

Environmental Monitoring
This technology will enable the monitoring of environmental variables at a much higher precision and granularity than by existing techniques. Early research examples of this are being applied to coastal erosion, flooding, and glacial movement [7, 8] (see also Chapter 9). The availability of richer and more precise data may well strain existing models and theories for these (or related) processes. In turn, one can imagine the consequences of improved predictive capability on agriculture, government regulation, and the insurance industry.

Leisure Experiences
Several very interesting experiments use this technology to create richer and more responsive museum or city guides [9, 10]. In the right situations and with the right content, these are proving to be very successful. Moreover, the same or similar systems can be used to create new classes of leisure experiences (situated games, for example), and artistic creations. This is an area of application where we can expect to see some exciting developments and experiments.

Healthcare

There are several potential applications in healthcare, and the most developed are in the monitoring of the state of health of patients with some illness or disability, either for diagnostic or for preventative purposes. For example, there is a high level of interest in continuous monitoring of frail, elderly patients, to allow them to continue to live in their own homes, and so greatly reducing the cost of care (for further details, see Chapter 5).

There are many other opportunities to support healthcare professionals in various activities, with the aspirational goal of creating an intelligent hospital [11].

Emergency Response

In emergency situations, lives can be saved if the right information can be delivered at exactly the right time (accidents, rescues, medical aid). This may be route-finding or diagnostic guidance, or warning of hazards. It will be important to deliver the information so that it does not distract or intrude.

Intelligent Car

To give an introductory example of what is achievable today, consider the technology in the high-end car. It is probably the nearest we have currently to an iSpace, with over 100 silicon chips providing engine, control, safety, and occupant information systems. It is currently a nearly closed system with extensive on-board communication between the 100 chips, but only radio, mobile telephone, and navigation or tracking systems extending significantly beyond the vehicle. The automobile manufacturers have very carefully designed and evolved many features to augment the driver's experience and not supplant it, resulting not only in high levels of acceptability, but also in a highly desirable product sold at a premium. Our vision is that many other spaces could eventually acquire similar levels of in-built intelligence, and the application areas will move to increasingly pervasive scenarios. The care in design, user awareness, and market development shown by car manufacturers will undoubtedly be needed in other application areas if they are to be successful.

1.2.2   A Framework for Applications

This set of example applications covers a wide area, in terms of their characteristics, but they all fit in with the model described earlier in Fig. 1.1. We have also found the model shown in Fig. 1.2 a useful way of distinguishing between the different types of application.

At one extreme (A), there are the applications where the advantage comes from the improved and fine-grained monitoring of the real world (supply chain, environmental monitoring). Pervasive ICT, through cheap embedded tagging, tracking, or sensing, will enable businesses to monitor assets and processes at a precision and granularity that was not previously possible, and in real time. Benefit flows from the availability of this data, and from our ability to mine and interpret it. In most cases, this means that the data must all be brought together for mining and interpretation, if only virtually, in a centralised architecture. In general, it is in these types of application where there is most concern over privacy of personal data.

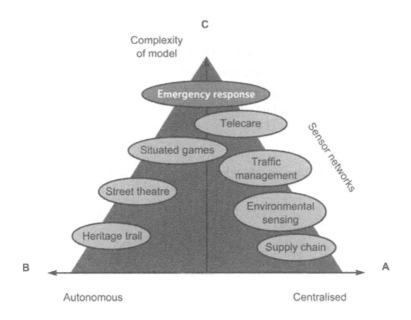

Fig. 1.2   Schematic showing the degrees of autonomy and complexity
of iSpace application areas.

At another extreme (B), there are a class of applications where benefit flows from the availability of local information, extra information from the digital world about the user's physical context.

These are exemplified by, for example, heritage guides or augmented art/museum experiences. These can often be implemented with an autonomous architecture, where users can gain access to the information or experience without necessarily revealing their context to anyone else.

These are both interesting classes of the application of pervasive ICT, and one can point to the first, real emerging applications of both classes. Even in their most basic form, these are applications that support or augment our experience of the world, or our productivity, and they are first steps towards the creation of intelligent spaces. We believe that the most compelling and valuable examples of intelligent spaces may arise towards point (C), as we develop richer and more subtle ways of capturing and modelling human interaction with the physical world, and as we find the right form of interaction between man and machine, between autonomous action and global inference.

Systems of this form are exemplified by current research to support emergency response teams and even combat troops, in stressful and life-threatening situations (as described above).

We are convinced iSpace technology is now at the take-off stage due to advances in the capabilities and the cost reductions of all the relevant technologies, combined with a clearer understanding of the research and development needed to solve some of the gaps. We are now able to visualise integrated solutions to a range of real-world applications, despite the incredible complexity of the systems.

1.3 Technology Capabilities

A generic application as exemplified by the previous outlines of an iCar will be a complex, dynamic, and usually heterogeneous integration of:

- hardware — labels, sensors, actuators, processors;
- software — generic systems, artificial intelligence, software learning and analysis systems, application-specific systems;
- domain models;
- communications systems.

A representative system architecture for an iSpace is shown schematically in Fig. 1.3.

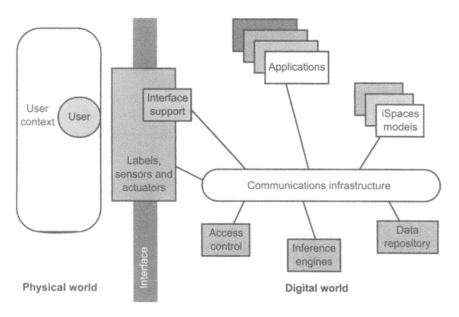

Fig. 1.3   Generic iSpace architecture showing hardware and software functionalities needed.

We will refer to three classes of physical entity in the world of iSpaces, and we can use Fig. 1.4 to describe them more precisely.

- Interfaces — labels, sensors, and actuators

  These are components that link the physical and digital worlds. The simplest example might be a switch, or a keyboard, but this class would also include a video camera, for example.

- iSpaces — intelligent spaces

  A collection of labels, sensors, and actuators with some processing intelligence associated with them, which together form a system able to sense a number of parameters of the physical world, draw some inferences from this data, and recommend (or even take) an action in the physical world. We think of an iSpace

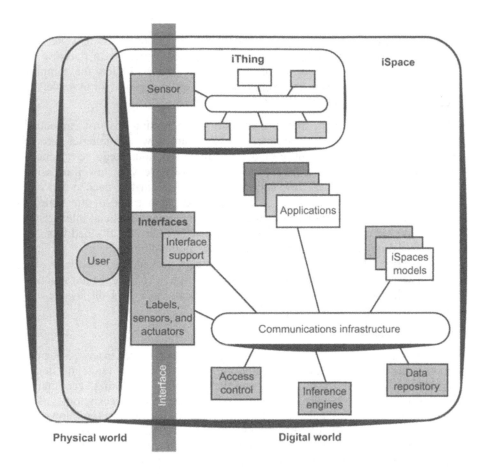

Fig. 1.4   The components of an intelligent space.

as a complete system, containing some kind of model of the 'space', and a set of applications that improve our abilities to sense and make sense of the physical world about us, and use this knowledge to augment our capabilities as we deal with this world, or to augment our experience of it.

- iThings — intelligent things

  Some of the components of the iSpace will be realised in physical entities in the iSpace, and some of the components may be implemented on remote infrastructure. We use the term iThings to mean what it says — intelligent subsystems of an iSpace that are in the iSpace.

1.3.1   Hardware Advances

A range of the enabling hardware advances are described in Chapter 13. The most salient aspects are described ahead.

- Cheap, powerful chips, embedded silicon, a continuing route to cost reduction

  The continuing increase of chip power described by Moore's law (Chapter 13) will allow increasingly complex processing, to analyse data or to optimise an automatic recommendation or action. In particular, this will allow the complex analysis of video and image data from embedded image sensors (for more details see Chapters 15, 16, and 17).

  However, the advances in silicon also result in decreasing costs of embedded chips at low computational complexity. There are new technologies, at the research stages, where current printable electronic functions could be enhanced by printable active devices [12]. These may only have very low processing power, and operate at very low speed, but that is all that is needed for vast numbers of the components within iSpaces. Thus, at one end of the scale, a billion transistor chips enabling advances in modelling and artificial intelligence will be in production by 2007, and at the other chips (already attached to some retail goods) might become ultra-low cost, ultra-high volume silicon or through direct printing. The printing of electronics on labels, packages, and fabrics is still at the research stage but maintains the existing evolution path for the introduction of embedded intelligence to ever lower-value items, including disposable and consumable ones.

- Miniaturisation

  The miniaturisation of chips, smart sensors, and, to a lesser extent, actuators enables the easier attachment of smart features to a wide range of items. Smallness allows not just invisibility and the possibility of making ever smaller items smart, but also increasingly simpler or easier attachment technologies. The attachment processes themselves are a significant cost deterrent for low-cost consumer goods. Self-adhesive labels should not only carry barcode-type identifiers or RFID tags, but also sensors to track product history or state (undesirable moisture, low/high temperatures, decay, etc), intelligence, and communicability. The Smart Dust concept at UC Berkeley is an excellent example of this [3]; see also Pister's views of the impact of smart dust technology by 2010 and 2020 [13].

- Power sourcing

  Power sourcing has been improved through four main routes [13]:

  — the ever shorter transistor gates driving Moore's law also drive voltage and power reductions in the basic circuits — this really is a win/win situation;

  — there have been huge advances in actively managing the powering of individual chips, or parts of a chip, so unused circuitry is only powered when needed;

  — battery technology has improved dramatically;

  — power scavenging techniques are advancing and extending rapidly beyond just solar powering — this category could also include techniques where a read request signal also provides the required power to trigger the response, passive RFID tags and optically read sensors being examples, but one can anticipate further extensions of this approach.

1.3.2   Universal Connectivity

iSpaces take advantage of whatever communications links are readily available, and will undoubtedly cause considerable increase in both the complexity of communications and alter the communications traffic patterns/statistics, causing new communications network issues (see Chapter 18 for more details). They will benefit from the increasing ability of linking a diverse range of tetherless links (radio, optical, acoustic) to fixed infrastructure via a highly heterogeneous set of technologies and protocols. The links will include everything from very short range to global links.

- Web presence

  The universal connectivity will allow and include a Web presence to virtually any device, anywhere, providing universal access to information and resources.

- Grid technology

  For many applications, distributed, embedded, or networked processors will cope with the iSpace demands; however, the iSpace applications could involve very large numbers of inputs each requiring very large amounts of on-line computation. This includes health systems, health research systems, safety systems, etc. Grid technology seems eminently suitable to tackle this sort of problem.

1.3.3   Software Techniques

It is clear that there is an extensive requirement for complex and very advanced software to satisfy the functions needed in Fig. 1.1. Fortunately, many of the advances driven by the needs of current information technologies, such as knowledge management, speech recognition and synthesis, image analysis, video analysis, data mining, intelligent data analysis, data fusion, scheduling, computational linguistics, etc, will provide a strong basis for iSpace solutions. Also, those technologies are being pushed ever closer to the levels of computational understanding that are necessary for natural human interaction. For example, soft computing [14, 15] is enabling digital technology to cope with human types of imprecision, vagueness, and ambiguity. Thus the software stage already provides many tools that will enable the creation of true solutions to selected examples of the iSpace vision. However, the fuller range of applications will need ongoing research to integrate many different elements of these technologies into viable systems and also to meet the many new challenges.

1.4   Roadmap to the Vision

We have described the ultimate vision of an intelligent space, where the world around us provides us with intelligent and contextually relevant support. The intent is to bring ICT out into the real world, to improve our lives. It is a challenging vision, and there are many barriers on the path to its realisation. Many of these barriers are technical, but there are also many significant (and perhaps rather more challenging) human and economic barriers. We can group these under the following headings.

• Where is the value?

Where are the compelling products and services that are enabled by this technology and that will generate significant revenue in the world?

• Can we deliver this value?

Can we develop appropriate ambient interfaces that allow us to access environmentally embedded intelligence? Can we develop appropriately rich models that allow us to augment human capability in anything more than trivial and limited examples? Are we prepared to delegate control to inanimate intelligence? Are we prepared to expose our actions and desires to an impersonal infrastructure?

• How do we deliver the value?

How does the infrastructure come into being, and how is it supported? What are the sustainable ecosystems that will deliver these services?

These are quite challenging questions, and there is no obvious and compelling 'killer application' with enough value to drive the investment required for a pervasive infrastructure. On the other hand, there is a set of trials and implementations taking place that suggest that the value is there, in a number of specific application areas.

For example, a number of organisations are running trials on the use of RFID for asset tracking, especially for supply chain management for the retail industry (see Fig. 1.5) [16]. The belief is that these investments will pay for themselves through efficiencies and increased turnover (reduction in sales lost through poor stock control). This is an example of a centralised system of pervasive monitoring, and, since it is restricted to the supply chain itself, it does not threaten personal privacy.

Similarly, there have been a number of trials and experiments on heritage and museum guides.

As the capability of hand-held devices and mobile bandwidth has improved, the utility and user value has tended to increase significantly, especially when due attention is paid to the quality of the content [17, 18]. One can envisage more personalised and interactive forms of guides, the creation of new situated events and experiences, as well as new generations of situated gaming. We expect to see continuing development in the evolution of intelligent spaces for new leisure and artistic activities, accelerated by the increasing availability of mobile broadband access to the Internet through WiFi access points.

There are a number of other pervasive sensor networks that generate valuable information without raising concerns over individual privacy, generally because the information that is currently collected is anonymous, and the value is in the aggregate information. The best example is traffic information, where the aggregate information from a private network of roadside sensors is a platform for a portfolio of travel services [19].

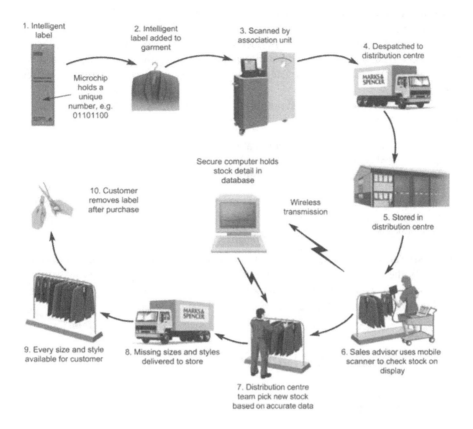

Fig. 1.5   Trial system for the use of RFID labels to improve the retail supply chain [15].

The question is whether these will remain as separate and disconnected application areas, or whether they can provide a platform for wider developments. Will the vision of intelligent spaces only drive the creation of a few valuable 'stove-pipe' applications, or it will it evolve into a pervasive, heterogeneous infrastructure, supporting a rich set of wealth-creating applications?

One potential evolution path can be illustrated by a specific example — traffic information. As well as aggregate traffic information, we also have the capability to monitor or track individual vehicles, through a number of technologies. There is a system to enforce congestion charging in London; and European governments will soon be introducing systems to enforce lorry road usage charging (LRUC) [20]. Each of these is a 'stove-pipe' solution, introduced and justified by a specific revenue stream, but each can also create a great deal of information that, in aggregate, or with appropriate privacy controls, could be a platform for a rich set of travel-related services. Taking LRUC as an example, a system could be introduced simply as a tax revenue collection system. On the other hand, if it were implemented as an open information system, so that the collected information could be used by third parties (with appropriate controls and revenue sharing) to create added value travel services, it is likely to have a much bigger impact on road network efficiency and the UK economy.

We believe that this is a good example of a way in which intelligent spaces and services can be created. Each time that a local or national government or authority introduces an ICT system, especially one with a strong pervasive component, it is often an opportunity to create an open information system, and a service platform for added value, and this could be encouraged through appropriate government policy [21].

This discussion suggests the evolution path, or roadmap, that iSpace technology could follow:

- domain-specific solutions — application of the technology in a number of valuable applications (supply chain, traffic management, leisure, etc), and proprietary or standards-defined systems;

- open systems — selective opening of interfaces in some applications, to allow third parties to create a richer set of services (an explosion of competing architectures and interface definitions);

- pervasive and heterogeneous — on the one hand, competition and standardisation simplify the landscape, while on the other hand, there is a profusion of devices/ appliances/services/applications/markets; iThings need to become much smarter and more adaptive with major issues of complexity being trust and dependability.

1.5   Research Challenges

1.5.1   Current Research Issues

A good view of the research focused on the current generation of 'stove-pipe' solutions can be seen in the DTI-supported 'Next Wave Markets and Technologies' programme [22]. In this programme, there are a number of research centres, each focused on one specific 'stove-pipe' application area. Clearly, there are research challenges in each area associated with the 'where and how' of delivering value.

There are also some specific issues that are quite common across most centres:

- sensing and collecting meaningful data on 'human' activities;
- model building for real-world activity;
- data analysis;
- application of software agent technology;
- middleware;
- appropriate unintrusive interfaces;
- security, privacy, and trust;
- human factors and social impact;
- low-power nodes;
- dynamic communications networks;
- development of complex market nets.

This is all work that is still in progress, but the sense that seems to be emerging is that there are no major technology 'show stoppers' to realising the iSpaces vision, at least as disconnected 'stove-pipe' solutions in a number of application areas. Of course, there are many areas where developments and improvements in hardware and software technology would have a major impact on utility, usability, and value.

1.5.2   Research Issues for Pervasive Deployment

On the other hand, many research issues need to be addressed before we could contemplate the implementation of a pervasive, heterogeneous, and open ICT system of any complexity or scale. There are major challenges in all of the components of the system and also in the overall system architecture and structure. Some of the major issues are discussed in more detail below.

Architectures and Interfaces

A world of pervasive ICT is a world of billions of connected devices, interacting in dynamic and yet-to-be-defined ways, with each other and with the physical world. We are only now at the prototype stage for the implementation of individual 'stove-pipe' applications. At some stage on the roadmap, as we move to a more open system model, the issues of interworking and open interfaces will need to be considered. Some issues are likely to go beyond the scope of current approaches, for example, in Web services. An example would be the limited computational ability of some iThings (see Chapter 11 for more details).

Complexity and Scale

Pervasive systems will need to cope with new dimensions of scale, complexity, heterogeneity, and dynamics and be driven by the combinations and permutations of software and assets being integrated for each specific implementation (including for one-shot usage, hence on-demand software creation).

It is anticipated that increasing demand for personalised/contextualised service offerings will also lead to the need for much more dynamic system functionality. From a user's perspective this will require new system solutions that are able to 'hide' all the complexity and dynamics but are still capable of responding 'on demand'. In principle, the Open Services Gateway Initiative (OSGi) is addressing aspects of this problem, but the solutions may prove to be too static and specialised for an environment where all users, in their context/time/space, could potentially have a unique range of dynamic profiles.

A number of interesting developments based on nature-inspired techniques (Chapters 19 and 20 provide more details) demonstrate greater robustness against heterogeneity and dynamics, including errors, faults, and the consequences of malicious behaviour. Self-organising systems can acquire a variety of valuable properties, which will facilitate the establishment of individual iSpaces over periods of time and varieties of usage, and reduce the impact of scale.

Communications Systems

It is envisaged that iSpaces will be interconnected by a very diverse range of communications technologies, usually provided by many different suppliers and evolving over lengthy timelines. Thus there will be a large number of systems and protocols, and different communications instances could use widely varying stacks of actual systems or protocols with the type driven by geography, context, application, and time. In addition, the communications load itself is likely to have traffic patterns and traffic statistics very different from what present-day systems are designed for, and will continue to change as the popularity of dominant applications evolves. There will be an increase in the number of tiny packets of information used for data gathering from elementary sensors (door open, room temperature, water level, pressure sensors, etc) and an increase in various types of video monitoring data streams and data streams for complex human-centric modelling. Thus the sheer scale, complexity, heterogeneity, and dynamics of future demands on networks will stress current technology. Chapter 18 points out that the Internet architecture took the more obvious aspects into account when it was established to provide 'IP over everything'. It analyses the issues raised by the needs of sensor networks and finds a number of underlying issues in the areas of naming and addressing, routing, traffic profiles, and security that need further research.

Human Interfaces

We need major advances to realise the true vision of computational understanding, and in all human modalities. Although current software capabilities can provide very exciting functionality to iSpaces, there is the desire for much greater capability, to increase the accuracy of a space's response to inputs, to improve the usability, and to reduce any interface demands on humans.

Major advances are needed not just in text, speech, and vision, but eventually in all human modalities, to realise the true vision of computational understanding. There is also the need for some degree of synthesis in each modality. The need is for invisible interfaces wherever possible, i.e. any system interactions are either totally unobtrusive or easily visible and intuitive. However, although this is an important and desirable 'wish list', current capabilities are not yet sufficient to initiate the full vision.

Although there have been useful advances in communicating using the other human senses, especially the tactile sense, they are still very under-researched and could significantly improve the sense of presence. This is especially so for the large proportion of the population who suffer from various sensory impairments. Advances in the iSpace technology should be capable of improving accessibility in quite dramatic ways.

Security, Privacy, and Trust

Traditional security systems rely upon physical security, user authentication, and access control for their protection, but iSpaces are dynamic aggregations of large numbers of elementary transducers with very limited computational power, together with more powerful embedded or explicit processors. Many nodes will be in physically insecure places, making them vulnerable to assault. The information gathered will often be trivial on its own, but could become personally sensitive or commercially valuable when correlated with other distributed information sources. The logical and geographically distributed nature, combined with the heterogeneity of systems and component types, makes it unfeasible to guarantee security.

However, applications will generate a widely diverse range of requirements for security, and satisfying them needs ongoing research focus. Chapter 18 discusses several aspects, including verifiable location, tamper resistance of hardware with limited computational power, and key management for cryptography schemes, and goes on to describe some solutions.

Trust needs assurances about the content of data, the reliability of the source, and the purpose for which information is used. Trust is needed between individuals and organisations who want to co-operate for any purpose. It has been defined as '... a measure of willingness of a responder to satisfy an inquiry of a requestor for an action that may place all involved parties at risk of harm ...'. Trust is threatened by loss of privacy and lack of integrity. There is an additional impact if the association of devices and information is undermined.

The heterogeneity, distributed nature, and dynamics in iSpaces generate considerable need for the development of a new understanding of trust and new flexible techniques to enable it. Chapter 10 discusses these issues in some detail and presents a conceptual description of a distributed access control system aimed at automation of a trust establishment process.

Privacy (as relating to information) has been defined as '... the claims of individuals, groups or institutions to determine for themselves when, how and to what extent information about them is communicated to the others' [23]. Invasions of privacy can be against (or by) individuals or corporations, e.g. criminal activity, industrial espionage. Currently iSpaces are only designed to protect privacy, e.g. by notifying users of the intent to gather information, offering them the choice to decline, or giving them access to information gathered, if the designers have had the forethought to build it into the system. Open systems will need to develop new techniques, individually or collectively, to comply with something like the principles of fair information practice along the lines of the iThings equivalent of the EU Data Protection Directive 95/46/EC. The many privacy issues raised by pervasive networks are discussed in detail in Chapter 11, and, more particularly, RFID-based systems in Chapter 12.

Accessibility

A utopian perception of iSpace technology is that it could satisfy the needs of everyone, regardless of ability or inability. Although this is false, the technology, if developed in a user-centric manner with comprehensive contextualisation capabilities, will indeed extend the accessibility to a much broader range of users than any existing technologies to date. The concept is that of 'the disappearing computer', i.e. where the computational demands of the system are utterly non-intrusive and interfaces are so intuitive they are there and real but unperceived. In practice, this means the system and its interfaces require passive interactions with humans or interactions using our evolved, not learned, capabilities, e.g. vision, sound.

It is possible that extensive anthropomorphisation of entities, e.g. by use of software agents to represent physical objects and information, will produce the desired effect. However, this assumes willingness of humans to adapt and accept the changes. Even without such willingness, lower levels of iSpace complexity will still open the benefits to a much wider range of people.

1.6   Summary

Our vision of intelligent spaces is more than the evolution of many, disparate stove-piped solutions. It is seen as an integration of many subsystems having the capabilities to gather information unobtrusively and to infer and fulfil the contextually specific needs of humans. Cost reductions and performance enhancements in the hardware and the software suggest this could be a viable vision. The application opportunities are huge and cover virtually every area of human endeavour. However, the benefits are generally seen as spread across many aspects, and finding killer applications in such a dilute benefit-space will need imagination. The complexity of the systems will also raise the barriers to market entry, because the systems frequently need a complex and extensive system roll-out before the benefits materialise. Fortunately, there are some applications where initial benefits can accrue gradually, leading to an iSpace evolution roadmap that will provide growth opportunities in time.

The technology issues are perceived as solvable. The market and business issues will be demanding, but the technology is already being introduced in pilot deployments. It can be of huge benefit to a wide range of people and can offer very significant improvements in the quality of life of many, including those with a restricted quality of life through age, infirmity, or disability. However, like most technologies, it can be abused, and issues of privacy, confidentiality, trust, and reliability will need debating, so that the right controls and freedoms are developed.

The time is now right to develop practical and useful iSpaces and apply them where the benefits outweigh the disadvantages. These are likely to range from initially simple, but large-scale, implementations, such as RFID-based systems for supply chain/retail improvements to localised systems for aiding and automating some aspects of care provision, where the personal interactions are much more computationally complex and the privacy issues can be controlled.

References

1. Weiser M. The Computer for the Twenty-First Century. Scientific American, 1991:256:3:94–104.

2. MIT Project Oxygen — http://oxygen.lcs.mit.edu/

3. Endeavour — http://endeavour.cs.berkeley.edu/

4. CITRIS — http://www.citris.berkeley.edu/

5. Ambient Intelligence — http://www.cordis.lu/ist/istag.htm

6. RFID Journal — http://www.rfidjournal.com/

7. Envisense Centre — http//envisense.org/

8. MWTN — http://www.nextwave.org.uk/

9. Equator Project — http://www.equator.ac.uk/

10. City and Buildings Centre — http://www.nextwave.org.uk/centres/buildings.htm

11. UbiCare Project — http://www.ubicare.org/index.shtml

12. PolymerVision — http://www.polymervision.nl/

13. Pister K — http://robotics.eecs.berkeley.edu./~pister/SmartDust/

14. Zadeh L. The Roles of Fuzzy Logic and Soft Computing in the Conception, Design and Deployment of Intelligent Systems. BT Technol J, 1996:14:4:32–36.

15. Azvine B et al. Soft Computing — A Tool for Building Intelligent Systems. BT Technol J, 1996:14:4:37–45.

16. James Stafford (Marks & Spencer) from MWTN Centre for Information on the Move — http://www.ipi-uk.com/cims.htm

17. Fleck M et al. From Informing to Remembering: Deploying a Ubiquitous System in an Interactive Science Museum. IEEE Pervasive Computing, April-June 2002:1:2:13–21.

18. Node explore — http://www.nodeexplore.com/

19. Trafficmaster — http://www.trafficmaster.co.uk/

20. HM Customs and Excise — http://www.hmce.gov.uk/business/othertaxes/lruc.htm

21. Department of Trade & Industry — http://www.dti.gov.uk/innovationreport/innovation-report-full.pdf

22. Department of Trade & Industry — http://www.nextwave.org.uk/

23. Westin A. Privacy and Freedom. Atheneum, New York, 1967.

2

The Socio-Economic Impact of Pervasive Computing — Intelligent Spaces and the Organisation of Business

M H Lyons, R Ellis, J M M Potter, D A M Holm, and R Venousiou

2.1   Introduction

This chapter is based on work carried out for the Eurescom project P1302 — PROFIT (Potential Profit Opportunities in the Future Ambient Intelligence World). The vision driving iSpaces is described in many different ways, e.g. ubiquitous computing [1], pervasive computing [2], ambient intelligence [3]. Based largely on expected developments in information and communications technology, it has three main aspects:

- pervasive communications;
- ubiquitous sensors and actuators;
- embedded intelligence.

How these capabilities can be exploited for the benefit of both individuals and businesses is the key challenge of the iSpace vision. The different descriptions referred to above emphasise the three characteristic capabilities to varying extents. Ubiquitous computing, as its name implies, concentrates very much on the embedded intelligence of technology. Its emphasis on 'calming' human-centred technology is highly dependent on intelligent systems providing intuitive interfaces and appropriate information to the user in such a way that the underlying technology becomes invisible. Ambient intelligence and iSpaces build on this vision, to include the sensor and actuator networks that enable a continuous interaction between individuals and their environment — and all these visions assume some degree of communication between individual devices, between devices and humans, and between humans.

Thus, an iSpace is an environment that responds and adapts intelligently to the presence of the individuals within it and anticipates requirements, including the need to communicate and interact with other iSpaces. The pervasive communications strand is similar to ideas of seamless, mobile, and broadband communications networks that are seen as the prime enabler of the information society. The concept of an iSpace emphasises an aspect often neglected in discussions of pervasive computing or pervasive ICT — the notion of boundaries. Spaces are bounded both physically and logically; access to these spaces may be restricted to particular people, or at particular times. However, a key feature of iSpace technology is its ability to extend information horizons — potentially to a global level. Like PCs in today's Internet, iSpaces will be interlinked to enable interactions between anyone (or anything) connected to them, regardless of physical location. One challenge for the technology, therefore, will be to protect those spaces from intrusive and unauthorised access by others.

2.2   Commercial Opportunities

The development of iSpaces will create a system of trillions of interconnected entities, ranging from the most humble object to the most complex. Each entity will have both communications and computing capabilities. They will be able to communicate information, interpret it, and process it. This vision leads us to envisage new ways of creating value and organising businesses.

New business (value creation) opportunities may arise through the development of new infrastructures (such as sensor nets), new operating systems (already a key battleground [4]), and a wide range of applications including intelligent management systems to support both businesses and individuals. A Eurescom survey [5] of iSpace and ambient intelligence scenarios [3, 6, 7] identified a number of key application areas:

- communications/messaging;
- leisure/entertainment;
- collaboration/teleworking;
- e-Government;
- safety-/location-based;
- live independently/health;
- financial security/financial services;
- data across the Web/information services;
- quality of life/monitoring;
- education.

Some specific applications described in the scenarios included:

- 'Digital Me' — a device for controlling access by voice at a particular time, and could decide which calls to ignore;
- identity verification — a device-verifying identity and unifying identity-related information;
- taste and preference adaptor — a device altering things to your own tastes and preferences, e.g. room lighting, news, TV programmes;
- guardian angel — a device to 'look after them', e.g. telling people when they are ill or stressed, remembering where things have been left, stop them when running a bath that is too hot;
- device as 'agent' — a device that acts as an individual's agent, e.g. ordering groceries, looking for and ordering cheaper insurance.

All these applications depend on embedded intelligence and at least local (within a room or house) communication, but the use made of sensors/actuators or global communications varies widely. A crucial concept is 'context-awareness' — the idea that the intelligence within the iSpace is such that it can act (both proactively and reactively) to humans in an appropriate manner, i.e. in a way that reflects the current mood, activity, role, etc, of one or more individuals.

The wide range of potential applications reflects the pervasive nature of the underlying technologies, but will also present problems for companies seeking to exploit the opportunities. As Odlyzko [8] points out, the spread of pervasive computing or iSpace technologies will '... ignite an explosion of innovation that will destroy any stability that might exist'. In this dynamic environment '... new players and new business ideas will be emerging constantly .... no company will be certain of its commercial environment, even in the short-term. If companies are to succeed in the long-term they will need to be constantly innovating' [9]. But eventually, user expectations will start to stabilise and more permanent business forms will emerge.

Although there are many visions of end-user applications, there has been much less attention on the impact of iSpaces on companies. Yet iSpace technologies will have a profound effect, not only on the products and services offered, but also on the way companies are organised and managed. The following sections look at three areas in particular:

- many of the new iSpace applications will be complex services involving several companies working together — this will continue to drive the development of new organisational forms and strategic approaches;

- the rapidly changing market environment and the need for constant innovation will force successful companies to adopt management structures and systems that favour flexibility and adaptiveness;

- the adoption of iSpace technologies by companies will change the way people work — in particular, iSpaces will encourage a merging of home, work, and public spaces.

2.3 New Organisational Forms — The Emerging Value Nets

2.3.1 Value Chains and Value Nets

Following Porter's generic framework [10], much strategic thinking still focuses on the product with competitive strategies being based on cost leadership, product differentiation, and focus. The value chain model can be used to analyse the processes in a product delivery from inbound logistics through to sales and marketing. Upstream suppliers provide inputs, add value, and pass down the chain to the next actor — similar to an assembly-line metaphor. The aim of the value chain is to promote a best-product strategy; a profit margin will result if costs are low. This approach assumes product definitions and customer needs are stable and well understood; strategic effort to increase operational effectiveness is key to this best-product paradigm.

However, in the emerging iSpace market, neither products nor customer expectations are fixed, posing a challenge to the simple concept of a supplier adding value to a physical component and passing on to the next downstream actor in the chain.

In a volatile, competitive environment, strategy is no longer a matter of positioning a fixed set of activities along a physical value chain — the focus is the value-creating system itself. This includes not only the suppliers, partners, and allies, but also the customers who together co-produce value to allow an ever-improving fit between supplier competencies and customer needs. Value occurs in complex value networks rather than in sequential chains (see Fig. 2.1).

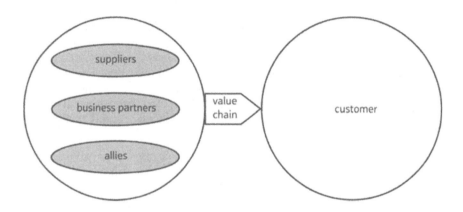

Fig. 2.1   Supplier 'system' allowing the customer to add value.

In many cases the operational boundaries between supplier environment and customer can be thought of in terms of three main components — content, infrastructure, and context. This provides a useful simplification when dealing with virtual value chains [11] — value may be extracted by disaggregating some or all of these components.

A value chain, has three principal roles — the enterprise creating value, the customer, and the supplier. The enterprise buys goods and services from its suppliers and assembles them to produce new goods and services to meet the needs of the customer (who may also be other businesses).

A value network (Fig. 2.2) includes additional actors — intermediaries and complementors. The intermediary performs on behalf of the enterprise a function (typically sales, fulfilment, or information and communication) which is a part of the enterprise's operational requirements. The complementor provides additional products and services to extend the capabilities of the value network.

Moving towards a more holistic view, the value network must operate with the efficiency of a self-contained enterprise, which requires managing the network on a process rather than an organisational basis. This places great importance on the core enterprise, which is no longer just one actor in a chain but the central point of execution and responsible for the whole value network. This includes the operational platform and infrastructure by which the other business partners can collaborate to deliver goods and services. Such value networks will lead to the development of new strategies for competing in emerging iSpace markets.

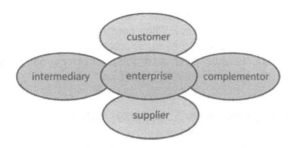

Fig. 2.2   Actors in a typical value net (Tele-Management Forum).

2.3.2   Strategies for Competitive Advantage

The emerging market for iSpace applications is characterised by:

- the constant innovation of new products and services;
- rapidly evolving customer needs, often as a response to new products and service offerings;
- complex supply systems (value nets) that involve several companies working together to deliver the end-user application.

The delta model developed by Hax and Wilde [12] captures these three aspects and is helpful in further strategic analysis (see Fig. 2.3) [5, 13]. Porter's models [10] are built on product economics — a best-product concept, which defines differentiation, cost, and focus as shown on the right-hand side of the triangle in Fig. 2.3. But the delta model indicates that competition can also be thought of in terms of two other dimensions:

- customer economics — products 'locked' to customers;
- system economics — products 'locked' to customers and complementors.

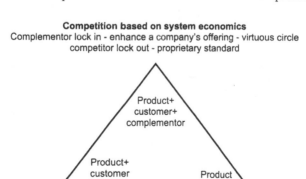

Fig. 2.3   The delta model [12].

The 'best-product' value chain approach concentrates on the internal operation of the firm and its operational efficiency. The concept of a value net is more outward looking, bringing in the concepts of external actors and co-operation. A degree of lock-in between products, customers, and complementors, not seen in the best-product paradigm, is a characteristic of the value net.

Competition Based on Customer Economics — Customer Targeting

If operational efficiency was the keyword of the best-product paradigm, then customer targeting is the keyword here. As an example, the amazon.com business model is shown in Fig. 2.4. Amazon relies on the centralised or intermediate server acting as a hub for transactions. The actors in this case are simply a supplier, a customer, and the centralised Amazon portal. The portal intercepts the business processes between provider and customer. In the parlance of the delta model, Amazon comes under the category of 'horizontal breadth' and is positioned on the customer economics/system economics axis. Examples such as Disney and McDonalds are termed as 'redefining the customer experience' and positioned on the customer economics/product economics axis.

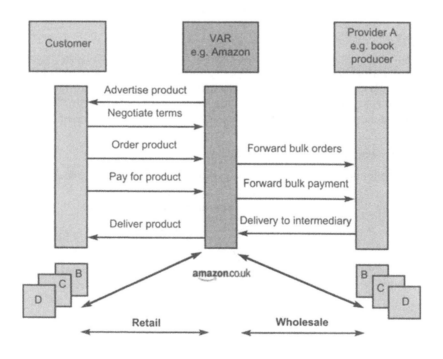

Fig. 2.4   Amazon business model.

Competition Based on System Economics — Innovation

The key characteristic in this space is that companies claim to be the *de facto* standard in the industry [14, 15] and act as the core enterprise of the value network — this is the highest value space. The keyword is innovation — the existence of network externalities [16] generates a virtuous circle in which users are locked into the dominant system. Complementors are locked to products, which in turn are locked to customers. Microsoft, Intel, and partners are classic examples of system-based economics. Microsoft has dominated the desktop market for years. The high user-base of Microsoft products, and the advantages of portability this gives users, have effectively locked competitors out. Other notable examples of business models exploiting system-based competition are eBay and i-mode.

NTT DoCoMo owns the i-mode standard, and this enables competition based on system economics. In the i-mode model, DoCoMo advertises the service in return for a 9% commission for deals negotiated using the i-mode platform. There is very little for the central server to do other than vet content from providers (Fig. 2.5). Content providers and customers trade freely between themselves; content providers self-organise, akin to a peer-to-peer model. Thus, Japanese banks self-organised to provide a coherent customer service. No trading agreements are in place between the content providers and DoCoMo, yet the existence of the content providers itself generates up to 20% more telephone calls [17]. The i-mode example is particularly interesting as it begins to demonstrate the characteristics of a complex ecosystem — i-mode exhibits the last vestiges of the 'centralised' model before migrating to peer-to-peer and demonstrates self-organising properties in terms of the behaviour of content providers.

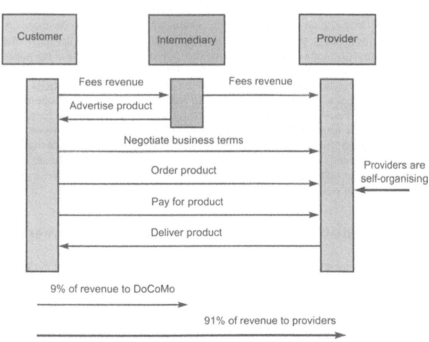

Fig. 2.5   i-mode business model.

Regulation

A feature of system economics is that the virtuous circle created by network externalities can result in one company dominating the market. As Microsoft has found, this raises questions about the need for regulatory intervention, as it is assumed that market dominance will encourage anti-competitive practices. Active regulation can serve as a barrier to competition based on 'system lock-in'. This will be one of the most difficult issues that telcos will face in the new economy, if they seek to compete by controlling a key part of the system. Yet, such control may be necessary to justify the potentially enormous capital investments required in providing high-bandwidth fibre services on a ubiquitous basis. This regulatory limit on the nature of competition will serve to limit the profitability of telcos. The only telco that appears to have circumvented this is NTT DoCoMo, with the i-mode service. NTT DoCoMo has an extremely powerful advantage, as the company owns the i-mode standard, and owning a proprietary standard enables the company to dictate specifications to providers and operators. In Europe, operators do not control the rights to mobile Internet standards in the same way. From the delta model perspective, rather than competing in terms of system economics, most other wireless carriers are presently moving along the horizontal axis in the direction from product economics towards customer economics.

2.4   Creating the Adaptive Company

The dynamic nature of the future market, and the complex relationships this will generate, imply that the days of mechanistic command and control in business are limited. The enterprise should build relationships with customers, suppliers, and even competitors to create a powerful value net. Often, there will be advantages from co-operating with potential competitors, as joint development plans can lead to bigger returns. Relationships also need to be built with organisations that complement what we do. The most valuable resource today is the combined knowledge of the team. For example, it is advantageous for software and hardware developers to work together, as seen in the case of Microsoft, Intel, and partners. Effective knowledge management will be the key to harnessing the opportunities that complexity brings. The approach for future iSpace business models should be to create networks that respond to the environment and that have the freedom to evolve as self-organising systems.

2.4.1   Controlling the Work or Controlling the Worker?

The need for organisations to be flexible has implications for the way iSpace technologies will be used in future companies. Current ICT systems include enterprise resource planning (ERP), supply chain management (SCM), customer relations management (CRM), and employee relationship management (ERM). The capabilities of these systems will be greatly enhanced by iSpace technologies — much greater information on process performance and status will be gathered in real time, leading to greater control of both processes and service. By taking over much of the routine information transfer and recording, and ensuring process information is delivered to individuals in a timely and controlled way, these systems could both improve efficiency and reduce information overload. However, these same systems will involve the monitoring and storage of far larger amounts of information about individuals than is currently possible. Used inappropriately, they could give rise to unacceptable levels of monitoring of both consumers and employees, resulting in consumer suspicion and causing stress in employees [18]. Furthermore, if system design emphasises efficiency, then the resultant levels of monitoring and control may work against the need for flexibility and self-organisation, inhibiting the innovation essential for survival in an increasingly competitive environment.

DeTienne, in a largely optimistic article [19], saw the use of ICT systems as a means to provide support and coaching for the users — by monitoring and providing feedback on performance, ICT systems can help both individuals and teams to improve. Monitoring programmes can ensure that successful strategies discovered by one team member can be shared with others. For example, Fastline's fast tracker enables co-workers to monitor each other's Web surfing, helping them to discover the best practices of successful co-workers. Context-sensitive support can ensure appropriate information is delivered to an individual, thus relieving them of the need to remember vast amounts of detail which may only be used occasionally. Work-flow systems can 'talk' employees through complex procedures, thus helping workers to concentrate on key issues. In these examples, the emphasis is on providing support and feedback to individual workers, rather than assessment and control.

Unfortunately, DeTienne [19] contains a number of examples (often in call centre environments) where existing systems were used primarily as means of control, to impose compliance and uniformity on the workforce. Common criticisms of the then-current monitoring systems were that they were only used to speed up work and that there was too much emphasis on quantity of work rather than quality. Ten years later, little seems to have changed. Head [20] suggests that if anything, the situation has worsened — for many workers, the introduction of advanced ICT-based management systems (such as ERP or CRM) has led to a deskilling of the work, strictly enforced work practices, and constant, real-time monitoring of performance.

Given that the emerging ICT and iSpace technologies can be used either to control employees or to support adaptive responses through coaching and appropriate information access, it is worth considering why the trend seems to be so firmly towards control at present. There appear to be four drivers:

- the technology needed to monitor and control is, in general, simpler and largely in place — in contrast, coaching systems require a higher level of intelligence that has yet to be developed;

- the emergence of a 'risk society' [21] in which institutions use surveillance as a means of managing risk — information collected about individuals and their activities is compared with standard profiles (good, bad, trustworthy, untrustworthy) to decide how to deal with those individuals;

- ERP and CRM systems, etc, offer the potential to replace (costly) experts with expert systems and (cheaper) unskilled people [20];

- finally, there is the attitude of managers — '... most business people, without knowing it, see the service world through the lenses of manufacturing goggles ... they are influenced by historical traditions in business training, strategy techniques and organisational theory, all rooted in manufacturing' [22], chief among these traditions being the manufacturing production line and scientific management, with their emphasis on standardised procedures, measurement and control.

A more holistic view of a company's operations may be necessary — rules and procedures tend to grow over time, in response to specific failures, or to meet growing regulatory and legal requirements. The more these are automated, the less freedom individuals have to ignore them. A different view of the workplace [23] described it as a bundle of services, noting that 'employee self-service is an emerging and rapidly evolving set of applications.' If the iOffice and other work-related systems are to live up to the promise of supporting flexible and adaptive organisations by helping and coaching individuals, then the use and control of the key tools must move towards the workers, rather than remain with the employer [24].

2.5   Changing the Way We Work

2.5.1   Field Work — the Home–Work Interface

Many of the iSpace scenarios are technology-driven and in most (though not all) cases there is an emphasis on efficiency in terms of using time, interactions with others, etc, as effectively as possible. The interface of personal activities and work activities are a key element of many scenarios. However, some of the visions (e.g. the 'road warriors' travelling the globe, but simultaneously in contact with both work and home) describe a life-style that is alien to many, and one not sought after nor attractive to the majority. The frenetic juggling of multiple interactions described in some scenarios is a marked contrast to the vision of 'calming technology' described by Weiser [1] and a reminder that the way the technology is used depends on a wide range of social, political, and economic factors.

In an attempt to build a more realistic scenario, work has been undertaken to study how ICT supports both the maintenance of work–home boundaries and the integration of these domains, with a view to understanding the likely impact of iSpace technologies [25]. One of the main impacts of ICT has been a marked increase in the number of people working from home for at least part of the time. For example, data from the e-Living project show that in the UK approximately 8% of people use the Internet to work from home, while a further 12% work at home using a PC. Understanding how people use the current generation of ICT to mediate between the home and work roles provides clues as to how iSpaces may be used in the future.

The survey was carried out by means of over 30 interviews with a range of people working both in small businesses and in corporations. The small businesses included a number of 'life-style businesses' where the main driver was quality of life rather than profit maximisation. People had very different views about the extent to which they wanted to merge the work and home roles. Some, particularly small businesses, saw it as part of their service to be available at any time. Other people, more often life-style (hobby) businesses and corporate employees, sought to maintain a clear separation between work and home. Both groups, however, used ICT to control the degree to which work and home activities were integrated. Few people maintained a strict work and home separation; work activities would be done in the home, and home activities could be done at work.

As well as current technologies, interviewees were asked about their feelings towards proposed iSpace applications (see Section 2.2) in order to gain some insight into customer acceptance of these services. Overall, the responses were largely negative. This may in part reflect a suspicion of new technology and bad experiences with existing technology, but the concerns expressed were common to most interviewees across Europe and indicate the issues that need to be solved if the technology is to be widely accepted.

The main advantages of the iSpace technologies were seen to be in automating the mundane (reducing the time spent on routine and trivial activities) and helping people to be more in control of their lives. In fact, the concept of control is central to much of the debate, as most of the perceived problems and disadvantages of the iSpace technologies are also related to issues of control. Negative responses to technology included the following:

- privacy concerns — how to control access to, and the use made of, the (very personal) data gathered by iSpace applications;

- a concern that some of the devices would take over (the device controlling the human rather than vice versa), e.g. the 'guardian angel' might prevent people from undertaking activities it (the device) considered dangerous or the taste and preference adaptor would not recognise changes in taste, thus inhibiting spontaneity;

- a concern that choices made by an agent, or advice provided by the taste and preference adaptor, might not be independent, but influenced by the provider of such services — again this is an issue of who is ultimately in control of the technology;

- there was a concern about the risk of identity theft in an environment where transactions are being made remotely, and possibly without direct intervention by the individual;

- there was considerable scepticism about the ability of the applications to cope with the variability and unpredictability of human behaviour;

- finally, there was a concern about our becoming overly dependent on technology — although a valid concern, it is the one most affected by unfamiliarity, and therefore, as applications become more widespread and are found to be reliable, this concern should fade.

In general, then, the interviews highlighted two areas of concern. One is that of control — who controls the technology, who controls the data or information generated by the technology, and to what extent the user is being controlled by someone or something else. This is not primarily a technology issue, but a result of institutional factors including social and corporate norms, the legal framework, and economic drivers.

A second, related, concern is a scepticism about whether the technology is capable of the level of intelligence needed to filter incoming communications (Digital Me), adapt to changing tastes and preferences, or act as an autonomous agent, for example.

2.5.2   Institutional Issues and Control

In the context of the work–home interface, several issues of control need to be considered:

- the extent to which employees are in control of when and how they work;
- the extent to which the users have control over the data generated within an iSpace, particularly in their own home;
- the extent to which users want to be in direct control of the system, or are willing to trust the system.

Controlling Home–Work Boundaries

Prior to the industrial revolution, most craft workers worked at home, and life and work was an integrated whole. The introduction of factories and, later, office work led to a very clear separation between work and home life, with firm boundaries being set in both time (working hours) and space (work location separated from home). ICT has enabled more workers to re-integrate their work and home lives, leading to a blurring of the work–home boundary. There is no doubt that many people find it advantageous to be able to spend more time at home, working. The greater flexibility in both time and place of work gives individuals the freedom to juggle home and work responsibilities — all the more important in a world where most men and women work, and care of children or elderly relatives has to be shared. Growing use of the Internet for a variety of commercial transactions also enables people to sort out home issues (e.g. purchasing or paying bills) in the work environment.

Flexible working practices can be of benefit to both employees and employers. Thus, a survey within BT found that the ability to work flexibly helped to retain staff. However, the Eurescom survey showed that most people, especially those working for a corporate employer, still wished to maintain a distinction between work and home. An application such as 'Digital Me', which could automatically screen and prioritise calls (a task often achieved currently by the use of CLI or an answerphone), was seen as offering a useful service although there was considerable scepticism over whether such a system could work in practice.

The concern to maintain some distinction between work and home raises issues about who controls the boundaries. For the most part, interviewees were either self-employed or creative knowledge workers — groups that could reasonably exercise some control over these boundaries. Significantly, it was profit-making small businesses that were least inclined to impose a strict separation between home and work. While this was usually expressed as a matter of personal choice, it is also the case that such businesses may feel unable to restrict their work time for fear of damaging reputation and customer relationships.

A consequence of working from home is that the iOffice is extended into the home. As noted in Chapter 1, employees are more acquiescent to corporate 'Big Brother' in the iOffice. However, will this aquiescence extend to extensive monitoring in the home environment? And where are the boundaries drawn when personal and work life merge? Workplace monitoring is already widespread and likely to increase in scope [26–28]. If, for employees, the prime benefit of home working is greater flexibility in when or how they work, then systems that impose rigid working practices on individuals will undermine both the benefits of, and enthusiasm for, home working.

Within the corporate sphere, the ability to maintain a separation between work and home depends very much on the norms of both the corporation and wider society. In the USA, where a high priority is placed on the demands of the economy, separating home and work life has become problematic for many workers — 'the long arm of the job has reached into employees' homes, their nights, their weekends, and their vacations, as technology designed to make work less onerous has made it more pervasive' [29]. Quoting a book by Jill Andresky Fraser, Beatty [29] describes how work is encroaching into the time people spend at home: 'What Fraser calls "job spill" is the dirty little secret behind many a corporation's thriving bottom line. Half of all households own pagers and half of those who own pagers have been beeped during a vacation' [30]. It is important to recognise that the driver for these trends is not the technology — much of which, as Beatty notes, was developed to make life easier — but the extreme competitiveness of the US commercial environment, which forces firms to find new ways to increase productivity and reduce costs.

It does not have to be like this, but it is important for both companies and employees to have a clear understanding of expectations. For example, Microsoft UK recently introduced advanced technology (smart phones, tablet PCs, and broadband at home). However, a survey conducted with the Work Foundation found strong '... demand for an "agreed etiquette" and "clarity of expectations" from Microsoft's management as to when work ended and their home life began'. Staff felt stressed by the '... ambiguous expectations about how available they should be, ... given that the technology enabled them to work 24 hours a day'. In response, Microsoft '... issued guidance to all its UK staff on when they should turn off their mobile phones and disconnect from the Internet at home, following a six-month trial of the latest mobile technology...' [31] and saw clear benefits from the experiment. After an initial drop, due to a learning curve, the company saw an increase in the productivity of its workers.

Microsoft UK is not the only example of good practice. BT has for many years promoted teleworking, both for its own staff and for its customers. All the authors of this chapter work from home at least part of the time and have benefited from the greater flexibility and productivity offered by teleworking.

Ownership and Control of Information — a Key Issue

There is a widespread concern about the implications of ICT for the privacy of consumers [26] that is thought to be slowing the development of eCommerce. Concern is likely to increase in the future — an announcement that Benetton intended to sew RFID tags into its clothing range caused a deluge of complaints by customers and the project's being postponed [32]. The development of iSpaces greatly increases the extent of monitoring and surveillance. 'This will be possible not only because this intelligent environment will be able to detect what people are doing in their everyday lives ... but also because it will connect and search isolated databases containing personal information' [33]. Thus it will be increasingly difficult for people to find a space where they have 'the right to be left alone' — one of the earliest definitions of privacy. The issue is not monitoring *per se*, but rather the use made of the monitoring taking place, by whom and the extent to which an individual can control this monitoring. But such monitoring is an integral part of iSpaces, without which the vision of an intelligent, responsive, and adaptive environment is not feasible.

Fortunately, the same technology that is reducing the cost of data gathering and collection also offers greater control of information by the individual. Agent-based approaches are being developed such as the P3P [34], which enables an individual's computer agents to seek Web sites for business, having specified what types of privacy policy are acceptable, or should be avoided. Such systems enable individuals to establish an optimal level of privacy at minimal cost in terms of time and money — a clear case of 'automating the mundane'. They will also be able to monitor and track the usage of personal information by those gathering it. This transparency in usage also acts as a check on abuse of privacy [35].

Control of Services

Interviewees were very concerned that the advice and actions taken by intelligent systems should be independent of any third party. This was particularly the case for services offering medical or health support and advice. There is clearly an issue of trust here — many of the iSpace systems are designed to learn individual preferences and will, after an initial period, act in the interests of their user. However, those users must feel confident that the device is not being manipulated by other organisations, and providers of intelligent devices and services need to be sensitive to customer expectations. Failure to do so can have serious consequences, as TiVo discovered. TiVo is a personal video recorder (PVR) that will automatically scan programme listings and record on to a hard disk everything for which it is programmed.

This is another example of technology 'automating the mundane' and PVRs have been sold on the basis that customers have control over what they watch and when they watch it. The machines can also be used to monitor viewing habits. This latter facility could be useful in letting the machine learn users' tastes and suggest other programmes they may be interested in.

However, the machines can also be remotely set to record specific programmes. In 2002, this facility was used to record for all subscribers a BBC sitcom 'Dossa and Joe'. The idea was to try using the machines to market new TV programmes; no one was forced to watch the programme, but some people might be tempted to try it. The response from TiVo subscribers was fury, much of it related to the fact that they were not given any option over whether or not to record the programme [36]; viewers perceived it as an invasion of privacy.

2.6   Summary

The development of iSpace technologies will have a radical impact on the commercial relationships between companies and the way individuals interact with these companies, both as consumers and as employees. Successful companies will exploit not only the new commercial opportunities offered by iSpaces, but also the technology within their own organisation.

The dynamic market-place created by emerging technologies will have an impact on the way companies are structured, with a shift from a linear value chain of suppliers and customers to more complex value nets that incorporate complementors and aggregators. Commercial relationships will become more complex and dynamic, requiring companies to move away from a command and control approach towards one that emphasises flexibility and adaptiveness. iSpace technologies will be adopted in the workplace; they offer greater flexibility both in where people work and in how they work. Where individuals have retained overall control of the technology (as at Microsoft), such flexibility has been shown to improve productivity and can improve employee retention.

Although individuals can see potential benefits from proposed iSpace services, there is considerable concern about privacy issues and the question of who is in control of the technology. Intelligent systems can help with both the privacy and control issues, but this depends very much on the trust people place in their suppliers. Service providers will need to be sensitive to these concerns and ensure their actions do not breach customer expectations. A key issue is the question of control — some degree of end-user control over the way the systems use information and interact with individuals will be essential if iSpaces are to be accepted both in the home and at work.

References

1. Weiser M. The Computer for the 21st Century. Scientific American, 1991:94–104 — http://www.ubiq.com/hypertext/weiser/SciAmDraft3

2. Pervasive Computing. Special Issue. IBM Systems J, 1999:38:4 — http://www.research.ibm.com/journal/sj38-4.html

3. ISTAG. ISTAG Scenarios for Ambient Intelligence in 2010. EU, 2001 — http://www.cordis.lu/ist/istag-reports.htm

4. Santo B. Embedded Battle Royal. IEE Spectrum, 2001:38:12:36–41.

5. Potter J M M (editor). Strategic Business Models for the New Economy. Eurescom Deliverable D3, Project P1302, 2004 — http://www.eurescom.de/public/projects/P1300-series/P1302

6. WWRI. Towards Technologies, Systems and Networks Beyond 3G: Work Package 1 — Sector Analysis: Scenarios for the Wireless Telecoms Market, 2002 — custom@analysys.com

7. MIT. Pervasive, Human-Centered Computing: MIT Project Oxygen. Brochure, 2000 — http://oxygen.lcs.mit.edu/publications/Oxygen.pdf

8. Odlyzko A. The Visible Problems of the Invisible Computer: A Skeptical Look at Information Appliances. First Monday, 1999:4:9 — http://www.firstmonday.org/issues/issue4_9/odlyzko/index.html

9. Pearson I, Lyons M H and Greenop D. Cyberspace — From Order to Chaos and Back. The Journal (IBTEJ), 2000:87–96.

10. Porter M E. Competitive Advantage: Creating and Sustaining Superior Performance. The Free Press, New York, 1985.

11. Rayport J F and Sviokla J J. Exploiting the Virtual Value Chain. Harvard Business Review, 1995:75–85.

12. Hax A C and Wilde D L. The Delta Model: Adaptive Management for a Changing World, Sloan Management Review, 1999.

13. Lyons M H (editor). Strategic Study into the Impacts of a Multi-Network Infrastructure. Eurescom Deliverable 1, Project P841, 1998.

14. Rumelt R P. How Much Does Industry Matter? Strategic Management J, 1991:12:3:167–185.

15. McGahan M and Porter M E. How Much Does Industry Matter Really? Strategic Management J, 1997:18:15–30.

16. Lyons M H. Information, Networks and Economics. The Journal (IBTEJ), 2000:40–44.

17. Natsuno T. i-mode Strategy. Wiley, Chichester, UK, 2000.

18. Smith M J et al. Electronic Performance Monitoring and Job Stress in Telecommunications Jobs. Univ Wisconsin–Madison, Dept Industrial Engineering and Communications Workers of America, TeleManagement Forum. Enhanced Telecom Operations Map (eTOM): The Business Process Framework. Version 3.0, June 2002.

19. DeTienne K B. Big Brother or Friendly Coach. The Futurist, 1993:33–37.

20. Head S. The New Ruthless Economy: Work and Power in the Digital Age. OUP, Oxford, 2003.

21. Regan P M. Privacy as a Common Good in the Digital World. Information, Communication and Society, 2002:5:3:382–405.

22. Reichfield F and Markey Jr R G. Loyalty and Learning: Overcoming Corporate Learning Disabilities. Bain and Company Essays, 2003.

23. Bell M et al. The Agile Workplace: Supporting People and Their Work. Gartner and MIT, 2001 — http://www4.gartner.com/1_researchanalysis/focus_areas/special/agile_workforce/agile.jsp

24. Lyons M H. Insights from Complexity: Organisational Change and Systems Modelling. In: Pidd M (editor). Systems Modelling: Theory and Practice. John Wiley, Chichester, 2004.

25. Ellis R (editor). Work/Home Boundaries and User Perceptions of AmI: Key Issues and Implications for Business. Eurescom Deliverable D4, Project P1302, 2004 — http://www.eurescom.de/public/projects/P1300-series/P1302

26. Pearson I D and Lyons M H. Business 2010: Mapping the New Commercial Landscape. Spiro, London, 2003.

27. Schulman A. The Extent of Systematic Monitoring of Employee E-mail and Internet Usage. Privacy Foundation, 2001.

28. Hazards. Hazards Magazine, 2004 — http://www/hazards.org/privacy

29. Beatty J. White Collar Sweatshop: Politics and Prose Column. Atlantic Unbound, 2001 — http://www.theatlantic.com/unbound/polipro/pp2001-06-07.htm

30. Fraser J A. White-Collar Sweatshop: The Deterioration of Work and Its Rewards in Corporate America. In: Beatty J (editor). White Collar Sweatshop: Politics and Prose Column. Atlantic Unbound, 2001.

31. When It's OK to Switch off — Microsoft Rewrites Its Rulebook for the 'Always on' Generation. Daily Telegraph, 2003.

32. Shabi R. The Card up Their Sleeve. The Guardian, July 2003 — http://www. guardian.co.uk/weekend/story/0,3605,999866,00.html

33. IPTS. Security and Privacy for the Citizen in the Post-September 11 Digital Age: A Prospective Overview. European Commission Inst Prospective Technological Studies, 2003 — http://www.jrc.es/home/publications/publication.cfm?pub=1118

34. Dyson E. Privacy Protections: The Intersection of Protocols and Policy, May 2004 — http://www.research.ibm.com/iac/transcripts/internet-privacy-symp/estherdyson.html

35. Brin D. The Transparent Society: Will Technology Force Us to Choose Between Privacy and Freedom? Perseus Publishing, 1998.

36. Wells M. Big Brother: Watchers and the Watched. The Guardian, September 2003 — http://www.guardian.co.uk/bigbrother/privacy/yourlife/story/0,12384,785843,00.htm

3

No Pervasive Computing
Without Intelligent Systems

S G Thompson and B Azvine

3.1   Introduction

It is interesting to think about the technologies that have become part of our everyday lives and compare their invention and development with those that have fallen by the wayside. Examples of failed technologies such as electrical cars and satellite mobile telephones are not uncommon, but more interestingly numerous other technologies such as instant messaging, text messaging, and b2c eCommerce have moved through the cycle of initial rejection, adoption by a new user community, and adaptation to its needs, despite the early scepticism of many users and commentators.

Because of the current power and low cost of computing devices and the development of techniques for manufacturing low-cost sensor and actuator technology, many see the proliferation of active, intelligent computing networks as inevitable. Pervasive information and computing technology (PICT) is envisioned as cutting across user groups and contexts in a way that only a few foundational technologies ever have done. Significantly, it is expected that PICT technology will become part of people's everyday lives, making our experience of computation similar to our experience of electrical power. If this vision is to be realised, pervasive computing must present itself as useful to all user groups in all circumstances — but does this mean that pervasive computing will be somehow exempt from the normal processes of technology development?

Moore [1] introduces the concept of the chasm — a gap in the technology adoption life cycle between the adoption of a technology by early adopters and mass-market pragmatists. The chasm is the time between the technology message being successfully transmitted to its targets and the time for the social agents of change in the early adopter community to do their work in persuading the mass market of the technology's usefulness [2]. Yet, for many of the pervasive computing products to come about, the mass market will have to adopt them. How will early adopters be able to persuade the wider world of the usefulness of pervasive computing without being able to demonstrate these goods?

The stage of development of any technology determines to a large extent its market. Tidd et al [3] refer to the three generations of innovation:

- in the first generation (technology push), R&D personnel identify new business opportunities created by the developed technology — at this stage market is limited and fragmented, and the best prospect for commercialisation is to find niche segments with high profit margins;

- in the second generation (market pull), marketing managers direct R&D staff into appropriate development work — the market could be either niche or mass, but it is different to the first stage because there is a degree of match between market need and the technology, which is often the main problem to overcome in the technology push approach;

- the third generation (close coupling) encourages marketing and R&D personnel to work together to identify opportunities, clearly the ideal situation — however, it suffers from a number of practical problems such as culture mismatch, lack of skills to understand each other's contribution, and organisational problems.

Pervasive ICT technology is currently somewhere between the first generation and the second (see Fig. 3.1). So far the majority of products have targeted niche markets consisting mainly of innovators and early adopters. Market acceptance of a technology depends to a large extent on its position within the new technology life cycle. How can pervasive computing simultaneously broaden its appeal and bridge the adoption gap? Pervasive computing must be constructed so as to be as accessible as possible— all barriers to adoption must be removed. Critically the early adopters of pervasive computing must be given applications with demonstrable utility that do not rest on the requirement that everyone else in their community also has access to the technology. In this chapter we argue that intelligent systems can be used to achieve both of these aims.

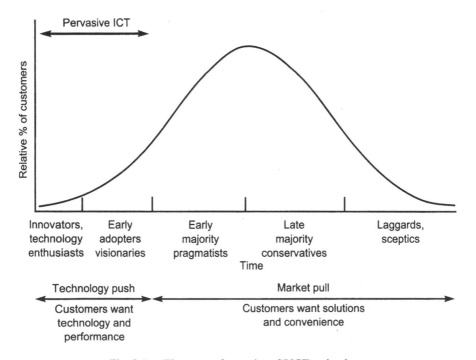

Fig. 3.1   The stage of maturity of PICT technology.

In Section 3.2 we develop a straw-man scenario to illustrate the types of difficulty that PICT technology faces if it were introduced today. Our intention is to show how narrow the appeal of such devices is likely to be and how much work users will be compelled to do to use them if they are not properly supported with intelligent systems.

In Sections 3.3, 3.4, and 3.5 we provide a tour of the current state of the art in relevant areas of intelligent systems research as we understand it at the time of writing. The areas we think pertinent are the following:

- autonomous agents, for reducing the load on users, bridging between devices, and automating repetitive tasks;

- soft computing enabling humans to conceptualise and cope with computer interfaces;

- machine learning to provide computing devices with the capacity to adapt to human requirements and needs.

Section 3.6 summarises how these technologies will bridge/enable PICT technology and remedy the deficiencies highlighted in our scenario.

3.2   Needs Identification

3.2.1   Opening Scenario — A Typical Day in Disubiquatopia

As sun breaks over Disubiqatopia (one of the new towns built by the government in response to the housing crisis in mid-21st century Britain), James and Alison are woken in the morning by their household Vibro^{TM} alarm; shaken from their beds they stumble about the house retrieving smashed ornaments. The ornaments insist that they can be repaired and the bin refuses to accept them; so they end up in a heap next to the bin, muttering complaints to anyone who passes.

The milk in the fridge has passed its use by date over night. It was perfectly fine when James used it to make tea the evening before, but overnight the processor in the carton has dyed the milk purple and screeches an alarm when James picks it up. This wouldn't be a big problem, but James is a podiatrist and is wearing his white scrubs. A quick change later and James would be ready to go again but to top everything off the resulting spillage causes the fridge to refuse to allow itself to be closed, and the cleaning robots get in Alison's way as she is drying her hair, causing her to stub her toe and causing James' stock to fall still further.

Chastened and hungry, James leaves the house and gets into the car. The car doesn't want to go anywhere, because it knows that James hasn't got all the items that are required for a proper day out; 20 minutes later James has located the survival blanket, personal alarm, tool-kit, map, satellite tracker, watch, torch, mobile phone, recovery contact card, and reflective jacket required by his insurance policy and is finally ready to go. The car consents to start and the day is set fair.

Meanwhile Alison is running into trouble of her own. Her job as a probation officer involves her meeting a large number of clients every day. Today, in the pervasive computing world, this is not possible. Firstly, the events of the morning have thrown her biometrics out and she can't get her diary to authenticate her. Because she can't get the diary to authenticate her, she can't initialise her day; because of this her clients can't access the building and they start queuing outside.

Two of them take exception to one another and a nasty fight breaks out. The rest of the queue are most entertained and this breaks the ice sufficiently to form a new drug distribution system for Alison's area. Later the coffee machine refuses to vend to Alison, because the probation service system has decided that she is having a day off. Not only that but the HR computer has docked her a day's pay and made a note on her work file for absenteeism.

James meanwhile has arrived at work. He turns on his clinic and sees that all his instruments have cleaned and organised themselves as they were programmed to do. Unfortunately, something appears to have gone wrong in the cycle and half the instruments are indicating that they aren't properly cleaned. Obviously it is impossible for James to use a non-sterile instrument, and other practitioners are dependent on James to clear his clinic in a timely way, so he presses on doing the best he can with the limited tools he has available for the day. At the end of the day he is finally able to find time to get his support services to come up and look at the cleaning cycle, but they instantly identify the problem as not being with the cleaning cycle at all, but rather with the indicators on a number of devices that have begun to interact in a strange way to give erroneous error messages. A few clicks later and all the devices are registering sterile status. James is left to reflect what sort of impact a reduced technical support budget might have on the pay and conditions of clinicians.

After calming down James struggles back home to find a distraught Alison sitting in a dark and freezing house. The ornaments that were smashed by the Vibro^{TM} alarm in the morning have communicated their distress to the house proper, which has decided that because significant damage has been sustained and not corrected in the prescribed period it should enter a safe mode. Of course this involved killing all power and closing the heating system down. James has the reboot code, but repeated attempts fail to get the thing to restart and a call to the house system administration in China coincides with the West Coast wake-up busy period. Finally, cold, hungry, and miserable, James casts around for a solution to his problems. The house manuals (carefully stored under the stairs) run to 40 ring-bound A4 folders of basically unintelligible jargon so midnight finds James and Alison huddled around the embers of their fire, waiting until morning comes so they can hunt again, just like millions of human couples from ages past. Alison's last thought before she drifts off is that at least the house shut down means that the Vibro^{TM} alarm won't go off in the morning.

3.2.2   Identified Needs

This scenario visits a world in which the seven challenges of ubiquitous computing [4] have not been surmounted:

- being able to cope with the gradual accretion of new devices in a space;
- facilitating impromptu interoperability;
- managing environments without systems administrators or support;
- dealing with devices designed for domestic environments;
- accounting for the social impact of new, ubiquitous computing devices;
- ensuring reliability to support user trust;
- encountering inference in the face of ambiguity.

No such environment is tolerable; others have noted that society is constantly walking a tightrope between liberty and responsibility on the one hand and control and strictures on the other. Surely no one will accept the kind of impositions imposed on the victims of our vision. It is easy to imagine pervasive computing following the path that has led human cloning, for example, to become ethically unacceptable and banned in our society.

From our scenario it is apparent that future pervasive computing environments could:

- potentially overwhelm their users with information — in the scenario above James is confronted with a clinic full of instruments complaining about various spurious faults, while James understandably ignores the detail and pushes on with what seems like the most important task in his agenda;

- frustrate their access to goods, services, and information that they should rightfully be able to use — Alison wants to get a drink from the vending machine, but, because her work systems have failed to validate her, she cannot even have her afternoon cup of tea;

- pester them unnecessarily and require constant hands-on control — James wants to go to work, but the car refuses to start and requires the presence of a host of other devices (James has to guess which ones) before moving.

The problem is that in the pervasive computing environment we have envisioned all the benefits of the systems installed are accrued by the businesses and governments that have installed them. Normal users have no tools with which to fight the new and frightening technology which takes over their lives.

To overcome these difficulties, and to provide users with the tools that they want to use in any context, three challenges must be met:

- understandability — PICT technology must be transparent to users and must have interfaces that are intuitive for humans;

- integration — PICT technologies must work together and work with, and not against, the users;

- adaptivity — PICT technology must be personalised to users to prevent them from constantly requiring intervention.

3.3 Problems from Ubiquitous Computing — Solutions from Intelligent Systems Research

Intelligent systems research is the study of computer systems that are created in order to solve problems using techniques inspired by human problem-solving methods. These systems are used in situations where normal computational techniques break down because of the impossibility of exhaustively checking sets of possible solutions that can be astronomically large. For example, a car can require several thousand components, each of which can be supplied by 10 or so different suppliers; sometimes a particular supplier can supply just a single part, sometimes the supplier may supply hundreds of parts, and discounting can be dependent on the types of bundles that are agreed. These different factors are compounded together to create what is known as a combinatorial problem; these combinatorial problems are what computers are very bad at resolving, and yet humans seem to manage quite well. Intelligent systems research aims to bridge this gap in performance.

The challenges of pervasive computing that we have identified fall into this gap, and it seems reasonable to speculate that their solutions may be the domain of intelligent systems research. We can identify three techniques that can be applied to the three general problems noted above.

3.3.1   Component Integration — Autonomous Intelligent Agents and the Semantic Web

Systems integration is an expensive and problematic part of developing any computer system; it is also an expensive overhead on the running costs of any real deployed computer system.

Two forces are responsible for a significant part of this cost. Computers are situated in a real world in which changing requirements impose adjustments to their interfaces and operational characteristics. In addition, computer systems are the result of a business process driven by immediately identifiable and tangible business requirements — users value tangible short-term functionality, rather than intangible long-term life-cycle cost implications. These twin forces result in the cycle of specification drift, requirement change, rework, update, modification, patch, and bug fix, with which all practitioners are familiar. One response to these facts is to design software that is predicated on change and able to cope with it. Autonomous agents are one approach to this challenge, and it is clear that they will play a pivotal role in fulfilling the vision of pervasive computing.

> 'An [autonomous] agent is a computer system that is situated in some environment and that is capable of autonomous action in this environment in order to meet its design objectives.' [5]

Agents are computer programs that act to achieve their goals in their environment. Their environment can, and will, include interactions with other agents. In this way, system development is reduced to the creation of independent components that mediate with one another at run time to decide on their priorities and to resolve contradictions and conflicts.

These are fine ideas, but what are the concrete abilities that enable their implementation? Three fundamental ideas have been developed to support the instantiation of agents.

3.3.2   Goal-Directed Behaviour

Agents are able to be programmed to execute goals within the environment that they find themselves. These goals may be instantaneous in nature (create session from point A to point B) or they may be persistent (ensure that traffic never exceeds 85% capacity on route X). An agent resolves its goals into actions by a process of symbolic deduction; it matches the goals that it sees to actions that it knows it is allowed to take (see Fig. 3.2).

Logical conditions (represented by stars, squares, circles, and triangles) form the goal. These conditions can be assertions such as, 'The purchase order is completed and signed by all required authorities for its value'. The agent breaks the goal into its constituent parts according to preprogrammed decomposition rules, e.g. 'create purchase order', and 'get director's sign-off'. These elements are then matched to the effects (right-hand side of Fig. 3.2) of each action available to the agent. Actions may be programmed into the agent, or they may be discovered from registrations that other agents make in directories. The agent can deduce the order in which actions must be executed and therefore is able to form a schedule of the actions that must be executed to achieve its goal.

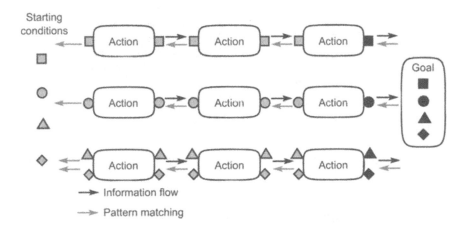

Fig. 3.2   Plan construction.

In the example given above, the agent's goal is established or created by a user (for example, the buyer) creating a job for it. In the case of agents with persistent goals, they can use a 'perceive, reason, act' cycle to determine the actions that should be taken, as shown in Fig. 3.3.

3.3.3   Negotiation

As we noted above, one of the issues with open systems is that components not specifically designed to work together can sometimes suffer from interactions over resources. Agent technologists have dealt with this issue by devising systems that can negotiate for resources in a rational fashion.

Implementation of this ability rests on the insights of game theory [6], in particular, the insight that rational entities that co-operate in certain systems can do better over the long term (or even the short term) than entities that do not know how to co-operate; and that there are certain ways of behaving that will always be successful in a properly defined system, even in the face of deceptive or un-cooperative competitors. Of course, this is common sense; after all, human societies are uniformly underpinned by systems of laws and penalties that determine the rational behaviour of the participants, and most people know that being nice to others brings long-term rewards. But more specific examples are required to

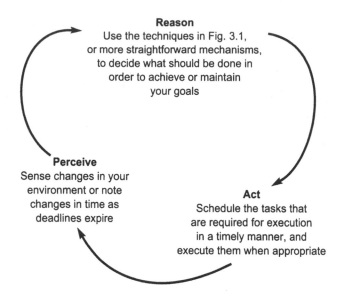

Fig. 3.3   The 'perceive, reason, act' cycle, implemented in some agent systems.

illustrate why this can be useful in the context of developing ubiquitous computing systems.

3.3.4   Ontologies and Semantics

Recently a great deal of attention has been focused on the development of the so-called Semantic Web. The objective of these efforts is to provide an Internet that consists of data and resources that can be logically integrated and manipulated much more easily than is the case with the original infrastructure. The technological requirement to achieve this is either to provide algorithms that can interpret resources that are described in terms of natural languages, or to provide content providers with attractive, easy-to-use mechanisms that enable them to provide the data required to structure resources for manipulation.

The first approach (providing algorithms that can manipulate resources in terms of natural language) is widely considered to be intractable at the time of this writing. Current natural language understanding systems are constrained to limited domains and tend to be deceived by subtleties of grammar and meaning. The second approach has gained considerable favour with researchers and has resulted in the development of the OWL language and its subset, OWL-S.

OWL is a language for defining the relationship between terms based on a formal system of description logics. It provides the building blocks for 'ontologies', which are precise definitions of the relationships between terms in particular domains. For example: 'employee works_at place_of_work'. The 'semantics' of an ontology depend on the shared meanings of the building blocks defined by the standards and their consistent use by the ontology's developers.

As yet, it is not clear that the use of ontologies of this sort will provide the required functionality to enable the development of a competent Semantic Web. In particular, it is not clear that:

- the current languages are easy enough for widespread adoption by mainstream developers;

- the reasoning systems that can utilise the ontologies developed will provide significant functionality;

- applications of the technology will be compelling and valuable enough to drive its productisation and adoption;

- business models for the maintenance and distribution of ontologies, and/or the proper intellectual property laws to permit their use actually exist.

In addition, it is noticeable how similar some of these ideas are to the premises of the 'expert systems' movement in the 1980s; in that case it was hoped that, by raising the level of conceptualisation required by computer programmers to the 'knowledge level', it would be possible to reduce systems development times and improve the quality of the delivered software.

The expert systems movement floundered both on the difficulty of training programmers to use the technology and on the difficulty of maintaining and managing the resulting systems. A key failure of the movement was the failure to be able to properly measure and communicate the impact of adoption of the technology that it proposed. These barriers will have to be overcome by the Semantic Web community if their technology is to be successful.

Agent systems are a key application mechanism for Semantic Web technologies. The original Semantic Web vision [7] featured agents as active integrators of data, facilitating their users' days by moving appointments and delivering information just in time for use. However, not all agent-based systems make use of OWL or similar languages; many agents operate with the assumption that they are functioning in a closed world of known systems that share common data formats underpinned with tacit assumptions of semantics.

Projects that have studied agent systems in open worlds, such as the Internet, include Agentcities [8], which made extensive use of the DAML-Oil language, which was developed into OWL by the W3C.

3.3.5 Application of Agent Technology to Support Integration in Ubiquitous Computing

All of these ideas have been developed over a long period — in particular, the concepts were first proposed as long ago as 1992 [9]; however, while agents have been used in particular commercial applications [10, 11], to date they have not been widely implemented in mainstream software development practices for several reasons. As we briefly described above, the modelling of the knowledge in the system and the testing and understanding of the system by domain engineers, in particular, is less intuitive than straightforward implementations that require intervention by users.

However, the agent research community, and its sister community investigating the Semantic Web, represent the research efforts by computer scientists to solve the problems of developing and integrating computer programs that can operate in open environments in the face of incomplete knowledge.

3.4   Component Understandability — Soft Computing

We have already stated the importance of intelligence in PICT. Real-world problems are typically ill-defined, are difficult to model and have large-scale solution spaces [12]. In these cases precise models are impractical, too expensive, or non-existent. Therefore, there is a need for approximate modelling techniques capable of handling imperfect and sometimes conflicting information. Soft computing (SC) offers a framework for integrating such techniques [13, 14].

Learning and adaptation are important features of SC techniques. Fuzzy and probabilistic techniques can be used as the basic mechanism for implementing the reflexive and deliberative functions. Approximate reasoning is required in the user model where the information from the user is incomplete, uncertain, or vague. Evolutionary computing can be used to learn both structure and parameters of the models in the HCIS architecture. Neuro-fuzzy techniques take advantage of efficient neural network learning algorithms to learn fuzzy rules and adjust their parameters [15]. In the next section we will give specific examples of the application of SC in PICT.

3.4.1   Application of Soft Computing in PICT

Fuzzy set theory has been used to deal with the vagueness of natural language in human–machine communication. Farreny and Prade [16] introduced possibility and necessity measures to query knowledge bases, so that objects that possibly satisfy a request and those that more or less certainly satisfy a query can be easily retrieved. In other applications, a request is transformed progressively using synonymous requests until it can be directly answered from the knowledge base [17]. In this process, the words or expressions that have similar meaning according to a fuzzy measure are used to find an answer more or less appropriate to the initial query. Similarly, in a dialogue with a robot, commands such as pick up the small box on the dark seat can be interpreted by soft computing techniques. Wahlster has simulated a language generation module that uses fuzzy descriptions [18]. There are applications of fuzzy techniques to speech recognition systems where a phonetic fuzzy recogniser has been used to enhance the recognition capabilities of an acoustic-phonetic-type speech recognition system [19]. It is important to note that soft computing techniques only deal with the vagueness aspect of natural language, and there are many other non-trivial problems in natural language systems.

Mitaim and Kosko [20] have proposed a neural fuzzy system that can learn a user profile in the form of fuzzy if–then rules to be used within a smart software agent. Their work addresses two issues:

- how soft computing can be used to learn what one likes and dislikes;

- how soft computing can be used to search databases on one's behalf.

They have shown how neural-fuzzy function approximators can help both in learning a user preference map and in choosing preferred search objects. Active research issues are accelerating the learning process and reducing the number of required user interactions.

Soft computing has been used in intelligent retrieval systems to model, using fuzzy linguistic terms, the relevance of index terms to documents using rules such as:

> If the frequency of term *t* in document *d* is high and the frequency of *t* in the archive is low, then *t* is very significant in *d*. [21]

The retrieval activity for vague queries can be seen as a decision-making process in which the alternatives are vaguely characterised. The decision process ranks the alternatives according to their possibility and necessity in satisfying the criteria [22]. A framework based on fuzzy pattern matching has been successfully applied to flexible queries in uncertain or imprecise databases [23].

Finally, soft computing techniques have been used at the human interface to enhance the recognition capabilities of computers. Kitzaki et al have developed a human–computer interaction model based on facial expressions, situations, and emotions [24].

3.4.2   Flexible Human Interfaces

Advances in the fields of vision, speech recognition, text to speech, and graphical interfaces would greatly enhance the flexibility and the range of capabilities of existing user interfaces. Intelligent interfaces can fuse multi-modal information and use their task-specific knowledge to overcome the limitations of single modalities. Experiments have shown that speech recognition accuracy improves dramatically by simplifying words used during dialogue, e.g. instead of give me more information about object 02134, we can say tell me more about this, where this refers to a graphical representation of object 02134 on the screen at which the user is looking [25]. From the human point of view, the flexibility of a system can be measured in terms of naturalness of interactions.

There are situations in which pointing or gestures are more natural ways of specifying a query than natural language, for example, in direct manipulation of objects or selecting an object out of many represented on the screen. Handling the inherent flexibility within natural language is also an important issue in PICT. Humans express the same meaning in many different ways, e.g. the playback message on an answering machine. Given a system that performs relatively few functions (e.g. an automated telephone answering system), increased flexibility of the system means a many-to-few mapping of possible queries to system functions. When dealing with more complicated interaction, this mapping becomes non-trivial as the number of possible queries increases exponentially. Natural language understanding systems try to use the meaning of a sentence to simplify this task. The so-called 'do what I mean' (DWIM) interfaces are one way to address this issue. Another, more challenging problem with natural language is the ambiguity, i.e. multiple possible interpretations. Resolving such ambiguities by simultaneous parallel evaluation or by engaging in clarification dialogue is another way to make existing systems more flexible.

3.5   Component Adaptivity — Machine Learning

What should the PICT systems do if no goal within an acceptable set of goals can be achieved? This could occur if the initial goal is ambiguous or if the goals fail. User interaction is necessary in such situations. PICT should have the capability to acquire, represent, and utilise new knowledge based on observing the user in order to learn from experience. Learning is essential to keep an accurate up-to-date model of the system and the world. Deliberative functions such as planning, and reflexive functions such as pattern recognition, can be learnt through observations.

Learning and adaptivity are two closely related concepts. Adaptivity is the ability to change behaviour in the face of change, whereas learning is the ability to improve performance in the face of new information. Equipping computers to adapt and learn has been the focus of the machine learning community in intelligent systems research. The fruits of these studies have included the data-mining technologies that enable Google to discover pages that are of interest to users from its massive database [26].

In the domain of pervasive computing, components face two challenges that must be overcome to make them useful. Firstly, they must be able to perform in the case of ambiguity, which in the context of computation means that you must be able to make decisions over data that appeared to be the same to your programmer. Secondly, they must be able to function reliably over long periods of time, which for a computation entity translates into being able to make decisions over data that were not anticipated by your programmer.

Machine learning techniques can be divided into supervised and unsupervised techniques. Supervised learning is the ability to form a classification algorithm (a classifier) which can be executed to provide a labelling (a classification) for a piece of data if given ready-labelled examples to work from. For example, I can provide the data set:

> {*car, Ford, red, four, four, five*}
> {*bike, Yamaha, red, two, zero, two*}
> {*car, GM, black, four, four, five*}
> {*bike, Kawasaki, blue, two, zero, two*}
> {*car, Toyota, yellow, four, two, two*}

and induce that the sets 'car' and 'bike' are discriminated on the basis of the number of wheels or the number of doors that they possess. Colour is irrelevant, manufacturer is irrelevant, and the number of passengers that can be carried is irrelevant. The quality of the classifier that is learned is dependent on the examples presented; in this case the presence of a sports car made in Japan provides the information that you cannot separate the sets on the basis of the number of passengers that can be carried. However, classifiers can be learned (using the appropriate algorithms) from data presented in any order, positive examples only or negative examples only. Well-known supervised learning techniques include inductive logic programming [27], top-down induction of decision trees [28], back propagation in perceptrons [29], and support vector machines (sometimes called kernel learning algorithms) [30].

Unsupervised learning algorithms are able to build models of the data that they encounter in order to make decisions from them. For example, we may want to incrementally build a model, forming expectations of the items that are presented until an anomaly that does not conform to the model or requires the model to be extensively revised presents itself. Using the example above, we could construct a model that expects cars to have four doors and be able to carry five passengers. When the sports car was encountered, it would not fit the model in any way and we could use that fact to announce that something of interest had been observed. Numerous unsupervised learning algorithms have been developed, including Bayesian networks [31], hidden Markov models [32], and Q-learning [33].

3.5.1 Supervised Learning in Pervasive Computing Environments

The likeliest application of supervised learning in the context of PICT is the employment of user feedback episodes to modify behaviour. Requiring users to 'supervise' their systems by telling them what they have done correctly and incorrectly could be just as intrusive as systems that do not have any learning component, so it will be important to ensure that feedback mechanisms are discrete and have a parasitic relationship with applications. Examples of how this can be achieved are the modification of diary appointments by users (numbers of cancellations, rebookings), the repositioning and reconfiguration rates for widgets on the user interface, and the retrieval of non-spam mail from discarded mailboxes. In these cases, users are monitored to discover when they 'repair' decisions that the system has erroneously made on their behalf, and this information is fed back into the decision-making routine to improve future performance.

By utilising these techniques, users can, over time, 'program' their environments to fit more closely with their particular needs. Of course, the users cannot be expected to explicitly program the environment in the sense of providing streams of logical statements for the machines to reason over. Supervised learning, in the setting of pervasive computing, is a mechanism that allows the user to program machines by correcting their behaviour in the way that we 'program' small children and pets by telling them to change how they act.

3.5.2 Unsupervised Learning in Pervasive Computing Environments

In some circumstances feedback is not derived from monitoring human users or sucked parasitically from their interaction with applications; instead it can be derived from interactions solely with the environment or with other computational entities within it.

These mechanisms can be used to manage change in PICT environments. For example, the mechanism of 'trail following' has previously been used to manage the dynamic routing of packets in IP networks [34] in order to respond to disruption of the network or peaks in traffic patterns. Another example of this kind of learning is the maintenance of quality-of-service records in agent market-places [35] in which one agent monitors the compliance to contract of other agents and provides a reference point for agents that wish to determine how likely it is that offered contracts will be adhered to. This kind of system allows prices and expectations to be modified over time according to the experiences that the community of participants have had.

3.6   Summary

Pervasive ICT is a vision of computational entities permeating everyday life. In order for them to be a boon and not a burden, we must equip them with mechanisms that allow them (not us) to bridge the gap between the computed world and the inferred world of humans (and our pets). In this chapter we have shown how three technologies from intelligent systems research can be used to build these bridges:

- intelligent agents can be used as delegates for routine decision-making tasks and to deal with other entities with diverse agendas and needs;

- soft computing and smart interfaces can be used to paper over mismatches between human and machine perception;

- machine learning can be used to repair machine behaviour to conform with human use of them in a real and dynamic environment.

We highlighted three key problems in the Disubiquatopia scenario for James and Alison that we described in Section 3.2:

- users (specifically James in the scenario) were overwhelmed with information, but intelligent agents can be used to filter and manage these information streams — routing information only to those who need it, when they need it;

- machines operating to strict, crisp rules frustrate users, like Alison, who know that they should be able to do something that they are being prevented from doing — but soft computing techniques can narrow the gap between human expectations and machine actions;

- machines that have no ability to adapt to their users' requirements need constant instruction and correction, and impose a burden on their users, as when James has to conform to a vehicle engineer's expectation of what he should bring with him on a long distance trip, even though the car goes to work via the same route every morning and every evening and is never more than an hour from home — machine learning can help machines to adapt to the actual circumstances in which they are deployed, and to the actual users who are interacting with them.

In our introduction we described what the experience of living with pervasive ICT could be like if these technologies were not available. Obviously this was a false prospectus; no society or individual would tolerate the introduction of devices of the sort that we imagined. Many persuasive arguments make us believe that pervasive ICT technologies will be propelled into use in the near future, changing demographics, social structures, and expectations — all of which seem likely to provide compelling cases to drive adoption. But unless the first wave of devices and applications in the pervasive ICT world fit into the human world and fit in with human expectations and are immediately compelling, easy to use, and easy to live with, pervasive ICT will simply not happen, and one path for the future of our society will be closed off. The intelligent systems technology we have described is a way of making the first wave of pervasive ICT easy to live with.

Given that, we feel that it is possible to offer an alternative vision of how a world pervaded by computation, and computational intelligence, will look.

3.6.1 Closing Scenario — a Typical Day in Eastbourne in 2020

As sun breaks over Eastbourne (a nice, normal town on the south coast of Britain built by Victorian thrill seekers) James and Alison are woken in the morning — their household playing a tune selected from their music collection on the basis of their recent listening habits, the weather forecast, how much alcohol was consumed in the household the night before, and what their diaries hold for the day.

The house runs the grocery ordering for James and Alison, so the fridge is well stocked. It also knows that James is working, so there are clean scrubs ready and waiting. Best of all, it informs Alison that it has worked out a window in her diary with the hairdressers and she's got an appointment at lunchtime.

James gets into his car, which drives him to work, taking a negotiated route, away from school-run routes and away from particular choke points, which prevents unnecessary traffic build-ups for the particular time of morning. The car is very happy this morning because the intricate game of bluff and double bluff, that a coalition of commuters has been playing with some school-run mums' cars (and which James' car has bought into), has paid off and it'll get James to work 10 minutes early. A small triumph perhaps, but small things please small minds and thankfully the car isn't all that bright.

Alison's diary has learned that early in the week her pupils tend to dilate a bit more slowly than normal, which would normally put her out of the recognition range for such high confidentiality workers, but it uses its ontology to interface with the security hub and check that it's OK to let her access, presenting evidence of the past variations to get verification. One of Alison's clients wants to change his appointment because of a family crisis. Alison's diary would normally refuse the change (the client is on a court order and so must comply with Alison's time-table) but wants to allow it here because the client's diary is presenting evidence from an accredited medical source that the failed appointment is unavoidable. The client proposes that the appointment could be made at lunchtime, but Alison's diary knows that she has a hair appointment so refuses to allow it. It reasons that although the management meeting is half an hour long it's probable that enough of the afternoon's appointments will be quicker than the allotted slots to make the management slot a client-facing candidate. It negotiates with Alison's colleagues' diaries and agreement is reached that there is a high probability that all users will accept a reschedule and that the overall working pattern of the team would be best served by the change. Alison is presented with a short note on the changes for her day when she logs on; she glances at them confident that they'll be right and clicks OK.

James's work agent is rather different in character to Alison's. Its duties include looking after the clinic's appointing system, but it also works to bring together summaries of information from a huge range of up-to-date sources around the world, to give James a bang up-to-date opinion on his patients' conditions. It also ensures that all the instruments that are likely to be required are available and that they are set to the correct configurations for the required work.

James arrives home to find that dinner is on; being a smart cookie he's programmed his diary to inform him whenever his wife has had a haircut and so he's got an appropriate compliment ready even though he's exhausted from the day's work. The evening passes with entertainment prepared by the house computer with an eye to the fact that it's a Monday night and everyone is likely to be a bit tired and an easy-to-prepare meal has been laid in by the house to provide an energy boost. Their house has a fireplace, but cleaning it is too much like hard work, so midnight doesn't find James and Alison in front of an open hearth; instead they are safely tucked up in bed, dreamily unconcerned that they are immersed and surrounded by computers possessed of a very non-human intelligence.

Not all the thinking entities in the house are so senescent. In the garage their car has discovered a rare database of chess games and is wondering if it can find a new ploy to use in its endless battle with the school-run mums.

References

1. Moore G A. Crossing the Chasm. Harper Business, New York, 1991.

2. North D C. The New Institutional Economics and Development. Working Paper, Washington University, St. Louis, 1993 — http://www.econ.iastate.edu/tesfatsi/NewInstE .North.pdf

3. Tidd J, Bessant J and Pavitt K. Managing Innovation: Integrating Technological, Market and Organisational Change. John Wiley & Sons, Chichester, Second edition, 2000:288.

4. Edwards W and Grinter R. At Home with Ubiquitous Computing: Seven Challenges. Proceedings of the Conference on Ubiquitous Computing, 2002:256–272.

5. Wooldridge M and Jennings N. Intelligent Agents: Theory and Practice. The Knowledge Engineering Review, 1995:10:2:115–152.

6. Rosenchein J S and Zlotkin G. Rules of Encounter: Designing Conventions for Automated Negotiation Among Computers. MIT Press, July 1994.

7. Berners Lee L. Design Issues: Architectural and Philosophical Points — http:// www.w3.org/DesignIssues/Overview.html

8. Thompson S G, Willmott S and Bonnefoy D. Creating Bespoke Applications on Demand from the Agentcities Test-bed. BT Technol J, October 2003:21:4:153–161.

9. Rao A S and Georgeff M. An Abstract Architecture for Rational Agents. In: Fikes R and Sandewall E (editors). Proceedings of Knowledge Representation and Reasoning (KR&R-91), 1991:439–449.

10. Jennings N R and Wittig T. ARCHON: Theory and Practice. In: Avouris N M and Gasser L (editors). Distributed Artificial Intelligence: Theory and Praxis. Kluwer Academic Publishers, 1992:179–195.

11. Bussmann S and Schild K. Self-organising Manufacturing Control: An Industrial Application of Agent Technology. Proceedings of the Fourth International Conference on Multi-Agent Systems, ICMAS, 2000.

12. Bonissone P P. Soft Computing: The Convergence of Emerging Reasoning Technologies. Journal of Research in Soft Computing, 1997:1:1.

13. Azvine B, Azarmi N and Tsui K C. Soft Computing — A Tool for Building Intelligent Systems. BT Technol J, October 1996:14:4:37–45.

14. Zadeh L A. Soft Computing and Fuzzy Logic. IEEE Software, 1994:11:6:48–58.

15. Nauck D and Kruse R. Neuro-fuzzy systems. In: Ruspini E, Bonissone P, and Pedrycz W (editors). Handbook on Fuzzy Computation. Oxford University Press/Institute of Physics Publishing, 1998.

16. Farreny H and Prade H. Dealing with the Vagueness of Natural Languages in Man-Machine Communication, Applications of Fuzzy Set Theory. In: Karwowski W and Mital A (editors). Human Factors. Elsevier, 1986.

17. Kayser D. An Experiment in Knowledge Representation. Proceedings of the European Conference on Artificial Intelligence, 1982.

18. Wahlster W. Implementing Fuzziness in Dialogue Systems. Empirical Semantics, Brockmeyer Bochum, 1981:1.

19. Bertelli F, Borrometi L, and Cuce A. Phonemes Fuzzy Characterization in Speech Recognition Systems. In: Applications of Soft Computing. Proceedings of SPIE, July 1997:3165:305–310.

20. Mitaim S and Kosko B. Fuzzy Function Approximation and Intelligent Agents. In: Applications of Soft Computing. Proceedings of SPIE, July 1997:3165:2–13.

21. Kraft D H, Bordogna G, and Pasi G. An Extended Fuzzy Linguistic Approach to Generalize Boolean Information Retrieval. Journal of Information Sciences, 1994:2:3: 119–134.

22. Bordogna G and Pasi G. Multi-Criteria Decision Making in Information Retrieval. Proceedings of the 3rd International Conference on Current Issues in Fuzzy Technologies '93, Roncegno, Trento, Italy, June 1993.

23. Bose P and Prade H. An Introduction to the Fuzzy Set and Possibility Theory-based Treatment of Flexible Queries and Uncertain or Imprecise Databases. In: Motro A and Smet P (editors). Uncertainty Management in Information Systems. Kluwer Academic Publishers, 1997.

24. Kitazaki S and Onisawa T. Communication Model Considering Facial Expressions and Situations. Proceedings FUZZ-IEEE '98, IEEE World Congress on Computational Intelligence, Alaska, 1998.

25. Azvine B and Wobcke W. Human Centred Systems and Soft Computing. BT Technol J, July 1998:16:3:125–133.

26. Brin S and Page L. The Anatomy of a Large-Scale Hypertextual {Web} Search Engine. Computer Networks and ISDN Systems, 2001:30:1-7:107–117.

27. Muggleton S. Inverse Entailment and Progol. New Generation Computing Journal, 1995:13:245–286.

28. Quinlan R. C4.5: Programs for Machine Learning. Morgan Kaufmann, 1993.

29. Rumelhart D E, Hinton G E and Willams R J. Learning Representations by Backpropagation. Nature, October 1986:323:533–536.

30. Schölkoph B, Burges C and Vapuik B. Extracting Support Data for a Given Task. In: Fayyad U M and Uthurusamy R (editors). Proceedings of 1st International Conference on Knowledge Discovery and Data Mining. AAAI Press, Menlo Park, CA, 1995:252–257.

31. Charniak E. Bayesian Networks Without Tears. AI Magazine, 1991:12:4:50–63.

32. Rabiner L R and Juang B H. An Introduction to Hidden Markov Models. IEEE ASSP Magazine, 1986:4–5.

33. Watkins J C H and Dayan P. Technical Note q-learning. Machine Learning, 1992:8:279–292.

34. Appleby S and Steward S. Mobile Software Agents for Control in Telecommunications Networks. BT Technol J, April 1994:12:2:104–113.

35. Norman T J et al. CONOISE: Agent-Based Formation of Virtual Organisations. Research and Development in Intelligent Systems XX, Proceedings of AI2003, the Twenty-third International Conference on Innovative Techniques and Applications of Artificial Intelligence, 2003:353–366.

4

The Supply Chain

D Luckett

4.1   Introduction and Background to RFID

This is not a technical exposition about radio frequency identification (RFID), but as 'RFID' means different things to different people, it is worth spending some time at the start explaining the technology. Most of the retail push is centred on low-cost, 'passive' tags. 'Passive' and 'active' relate to whether the tag has a power source actually on the tag (active), or whether it draws power from a reader when in range and then uses this to send back a response (passive). Unless stated otherwise, this chapter relates to passive tags. Figure 4.1 shows a typical passive tag.

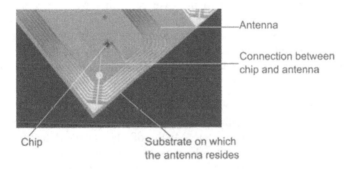

Fig. 4.1   Elements of standard passive RFID tag source.

It can be frustratingly difficult to get straightforward answers to the common questions that always get asked about RFID tagging. Many factors can affect an RFID solution; the most important is interference from the physical environment in which it is placed.[1] Avoiding the 'how long is a piece of string' response, some standard 'retail' answers are outlined ahead.

---

[1] It is also possible in the future that 'interference' in the form of spurious or 'spammed' reads will be deliberately generated by 'blockage tags' (e.g. http://www.rsasecurity.com/rsalabs/node.asp?id=2030) by consumers wishing to ensure privacy. It is also likely in the future (not from RSA Security!) that some form of 'RFID Denial of Service' attack will emerge, for example, as a way of disrupting RFID-based security/asset management systems.

- How much do the tags cost?[2]

  Today, a range of 10–30 pence per tag would be typical. However, the price is incredibly volume dependent — if Coca-Cola wanted to place an order for several billion tags, no doubt they would be pressing hard for the Auto-ID Center's aspirational cost of 5 US cents per tag.

- How big are the tags?

  The tags tend to be a few square inches. The 'spy chips the size of a grain of sand' headlines are misleading as they refer to the chips and ignore the much bigger components such as the antenna that also make up the complete tag (see Fig. 4.1).

- What are the read ranges and accuracy rates of the tags?

  Read ranges vary depending on local frequency regulations and solution technical design. Typical US ranges in operational settings tend to be 1–2 m; however, with lower power allowances in the UK, the range would be likely to be below 1 m, although this is highly variable. It is also possible to design antennas that can improve range and accuracy. Accuracy (i.e. whether a tag is read or not) varies greatly depending on how close multiple tags are placed to each other, the type of item tagged (metal, water, etc), and many other factors. Accuracy of 95+% reads is typical in real-world settings, but rotating the items slightly, reducing the speed of pass, or moving the reader, etc, can usually improve this figure to an acceptable level (usually >99.5%).

  Solutions can also be designed to increase reliability by simply not allowing items to proceed if there is no read or by picking items up further down the line, etc. Early hype from some hardware vendors over 'miniature tags guaranteed to produce accurate reads from several metres away' simply produced disappointed customers and unnecessarily worried privacy advocates. In the real world, RFID is often not an exact science.

- How much data can you fit on a tag?

  Tags can be designed to be either read-only or read/write with memory. Adding additional memory increases cost. Much of the retail industry has been concentrating on low-cost, read-only tags that contain only the unique serial number of the item. In this scenario, any additional data would be held centrally on a database. Some of the most innovative work on tagging is exploring embedding sensors such as thermometers which can record temperatures of the items and store it on the tag memory.[3]

  As with all technology, there is a trade-off between a number of variables. In the case of RFID, the trick is optimising the combination of:

---

[2] While this is the most common first question, it is also a red herring. Fixating on the cost of the tag often makes people lose focus on both the potential benefits of deployment and also on other costs such as the data management and the cost of applying the tag to the item. Initial work with one manufacturer showed that applying tags on the production line would involve slowing it down by 30%, which was not an option.

[3] This could be especially useful for vaccines. At the moment, some food 'chill chains' are monitored using thermochromatic inks that change colour when temperatures exceed set parameters. Some vaccines could survive for limited times outside thresholds as long as they were subsequently chilled. A sensor that constantly monitors temperature and records it on the tag memory would offer the required level of sophistication for the audit trail. This means vaccines would not be discarded unnecessarily because inks have changed colour.

- price — not just tags and fixing the tags to the item, but also readers and the data architecture of the overall solution (why tag things to collect data you'll never be able to exploit?);

- size — the tags must be capable of being securely attached to the final item;

- performance — read range, ability to work next to metal, water, etc;

- storage — is there only a need for a write-once serial number (the electronic bar code) or is there a requirement for more memory?

Now we can examine why the technology may be of use in supply chains.

4.2   Retail/Supply Chain

The 'Holy Grail' of supply chains has long been complete forward and backward visibility of information (Fig. 4.2). From manufacturers wishing to perform product recalls once the items have left the retailer, to recyclers interested in which raw materials were used to make the item, there are technical and regulatory barriers that prevent end-to-end information sharing. Even where the regulatory barriers can be overcome (for example, by consumer opt-in), current printed retail bar codes do not allow the granularity of information required to provide the holistic view in Fig. 4.2. This holistic view could also be important when tracking parallel or 'grey' markets (e.g. for ensuring excise/tax compliance on alcohol).[4]

The key to barcode proliferation has been a global, standards-based approach under the aegis of EAN International and the UCC (European Article Numbering and the Uniform Code Council [1]). The same approach is also being applied to RFID with the recent creation of EPC Global [2] (a not-for-profit joint venture between the UCC and the Auto-ID Center).

Bar codes have many advantages, not least of which is that they are effectively free to produce as part of printed packaging. However, they also have their limitations. A supply chain based on bar codes is essentially a manual system, relying on humans to do their part and scan accurately at various points. It also provides a simple 'moment in time' snapshot, indicating that the goods were in a certain place at a certain time. This is not an accurate, constantly updated view of the real world. A more fundamental limitation of current retail bar codes is the inability to distinguish unique products. One bottle of water will have the same bar code as the next bottle of water — checking that bar code will not identify which unique bottle of water is being read. This would be useful, for example, when recalling products.

In many cases, supply chains have now been optimised as far as bar codes (and other 'manual technologies') will allow. However, retailers and manufacturers still feel there is potential for improvement, but they would need information that is accurate, constantly updated, and granular to a point where uniqueness can be identified. That is why, in 1999, at a 30th birthday party for the bar code, the Auto-ID Center was founded. In its four years of operation (it officially closed in October 2003), it raised over US$15m in research funds and recruited over 100 sponsors, who represented sales in excess of 40% of the retail market globally. In addition to technology companies such as BT, NTT, IBM, and Accenture, it attracted some of

---

[4] For more information, see UK Home Office trials: 'The Chipping of Goods Initiative' — http://www.chippingofgoods.org.uk/

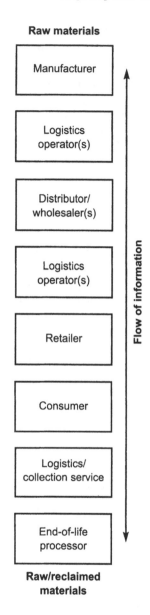

Fig. 4.2   End-to-end information flow in the supply chain.

the biggest names in retail and logistics (Wal-Mart, Tesco, Metro AG, Ahold, Unilever, Procter & Gamble, Gillette, US Department of Defense, etc).

The mission of the Auto-ID Center will be familiar to anyone interested in 'pervasive computing'. The vision was to 'change the world by merging bits and atoms'. The goal was to connect the physical and virtual worlds by bringing together supply chains (atoms) and computers (bits) using low-cost, reliable RFID tags to allow a real-time, real-world view that was both accurate and granular enough to identify unique items, not just product types.

Taking this vision to its ultimate conclusion where every product is tagged at individual item (or even component) level, the volume of data generated in this new world would be huge. Two of the larger Center sponsors (Coca-Cola and the US Postal Service) each have some 200 billion items a year flowing through their supply chains. Table 4.1 shows the results of a 2002 survey of a small section of just 14 sponsors' projected tag volumes. Even with a conservative assumption of only five events needing to be recorded per item, it does not take long before storage requirements start to quickly mount up.

Table 4.1   Survey of projected tag volumes of a small cross-section
of Auto-ID Center's sponsors.

End user	Estimated number of units in supply chain (billions)
CHEP	0.2
Johnson & Johnson consumer goods division	3.0
Kimberly Clark	10.0
WESTVACO	10.0
The Gillette Company	11.0
YFY	15.0
Tesco	15.0
The Procter & Gamble Company	20.0
Unilever	20.0
Philip Morris Group	25.0
Wal-Mart	30.0
International Paper	53.0
Coca-Cola	200.0
Subtotal	412.2
(Adjust for double counting @ 15%)	−61.8
United States Postal Service	205.0
Total including USPS	555.3

The exact reasons for RFID deployment will depend on the business case justifications of each company, but will usually be one or more of:

- operational improvements — removing manual checks, reconciliations in depots or store back doors, tracking and elimination of mistakes such as mis-routed items, etc;

- audit trails — especially for product recalls in high value or high potential impact industries, such as healthcare and pharmaceuticals;

- manufacturing/inventory efficiencies — greater automation in manufacturing processes, reduced stock holding due to quicker response capabilities, etc;

- security — in the Metro Future Store in Germany, for example, the smart shelf RFID implementation has also been designed to work with their security gates at the shop exit; it is also possible to use the unique serial numbers to track counterfeit items such as drugs or cosmetics and/or grey markets.

It is also possible that, in the future, tagging may play a part in areas such as recycling and returns handling/refunds, etc. However, both of these assume that goods are tagged at item level (rather than tagging cases or pallets) and that consumers will be happy to have the tags left active beyond the point of purchase.

Despite some widely publicised trials of RFID tags being used on individual items (e.g. Tesco and Gillette with razor blades in Cambridge and the Tesco DVD trials at Sandhurst), the business cases for item-level tagging remain unproven for many companies — especially on lower-value items. Simply, the costs of the tags and associated infrastructure are still greater than the anticipated benefits. However, recently several major retailers and government agencies (including Wal-Mart, Tesco, and the US Department of Defense) have announced that they expect their suppliers to be 'EPC compliant' [5] (i.e. using RFID tags) at case level within the next 2 to 3 years. [6]

One effect of the shift of focus from item-level tagging to pallet/case level has been to partially calm the privacy debate (see Section 4.3), as RFID is now seen as an internal supply chain solution, rather than something directly affecting consumers.

This raises the interesting question of who should pay for the tags. Arguably, everyone in the supply chain will see some benefit when the goods are tagged. The manufacturers will have potential recall data and customer usage; the logistics companies get greater visibility and can eliminate mis-routing; the retailers will know true on-shelf availability and have a level of theft protection, on all items, that is currently reserved for only high-value security tagged items. So, if everyone benefits, we would expect everyone to contribute to the costs. The order of half a billion tags from Gillette to Alien Systems was regarded by some manufacturers as having set an unfortunate precedent of 'manufacturer pays'. In reality, that early order did stimulate the RFID market and has benefited manufacturers and retailers alike as a result. Currently, across the retail industry, there is a 'lively debate' over the most equitable apportionment of costs and benefits.

4.3   What About the Consumer?

Given that the ultimate vision is to tag all products at item level when the costs have reduced, arguably the largest group affected will be end consumers. To its credit, the Auto-ID Center recognised this at an early stage and established a Public Policy Forum, led by respected consumer and privacy advocates such as Elliott Maxwell (a former White House advisor). Their remit was to help shape an informed debate on public policy issues and promote an ethical framework within which the technology

---

[5] The Electronic Product Code (EPC) is the naming standard for the unique identifier for tagged items. In structure it is similar to a bar code but allows for the unique serial number that allows individual items to be recognised rather than generic product types.

[6] While the USA presses ahead, there is a danger that delays in agreeing and implementing common European standards may delay non-US implementations. Final amendments to the standards are due to be agreed by the end of 2005.

could be implemented. A number of consumer advocacy groups (most noticeably Consumers Against Privacy Invasion And Numbering — CASPIAN) were also vocal in the debate. Their concerns centre on the potential for abuse of an 'invasive' technology. Arguably, loaded terms such as 'invasive' are justified on the basis that unlike bar codes, RFID tags do not require a conscious scan action, and so the consumer is often oblivious to the fact that a read has taken place.

Some of the scenarios advanced by the privacy groups include:

- the capability of third parties (e.g. retailers) to track consumer purchases as they walk from one store to another without knowledge or consent;

- as RFID tags do not require manual scanning, consumers will, unless items are clearly labelled, not even be aware that they are buying tagged goods in the first place;

- retailers (either by design or accident) may not properly deactivate tags;

- the potential misuse of data collected.[7]

Many of these arguments are not new and can be applied to existing loyalty card schemes as well as RFID tags. The privacy advocates would argue that the fundamental difference here is that RFID provides an environment where all this can take place without the consumer knowing or giving consent. Indeed, this argument has been so well received in some US state legislatures that they have been moved to regulate, although progress has been patchy. Legislation passed in the Utah House of Representatives then failed in the Senate in March 2004 and Californian proposals have been diluted. In general, legislation now under consideration in several states would require that any product including an RFID tag be clearly labelled as such and that consumers consent to any data collection. The original Californian proposal also required the deactivation or destruction of tags after the point of purchase but this was subsequently dropped.[8]

Ironically, as they often seemed on opposite sides of the debate, the legislation sought by the privacy advocates is largely in line with the 'ethical framework' that was advanced by the Auto-ID Center. The Center was clear that, above all, consumers should retain control and choice through clear labelling,[9] opt-in schemes and, ideally, the right to choose tag deactivation at the point of purchase. Moreover, many of the safeguards over data collection and use that are being debated in the USA are already enshrined in UK and EU regulation.

The ability to kill[10] the tag at the point of purchase is the cornerstone of much of the thinking on consumer privacy. However, against a legislative backdrop in Europe that is emphasising reuse or recycling at the end of a product's life, there is an argument that some form of 'partial tag deactivation' would be better for some products. For example, items containing noxious or recyclable substances covered

---

[7] There was a story often told to illustrate this of a man who fell in a US grocery store and tried to sue the store. The store then used his loyalty shopping data to show that he made frequent alcohol purchases and had a history of drinking.

[8] California Senate Bill 1834 — amended 1 April 2004.

[9] The term 'EPC Inside' was coined as a standard for a label to mirror 'Intel Inside' on PCs.

[10] In the Auto-ID architecture, the tags are deactivated by writing back to them using a specific 'kill code' that is authorised to deactivate that tag. In practice, this will probably result in a complex key management problem (which has not yet been fully thought through in the industry). However, the complexity is required to stop unauthorised deactivation, for example, as part of a theft. Physical destruction of the tags would likely not be an option as it would damage the original item.

under the Reduction of Hazardous Substances (RoHS) or Waste Electrical and Electronic Equipment (WEEE) EU directives could retain an active 'hazard flag' while losing unique product identity. This would help with sorting and processing at the end of the product's life.

During an often ill-informed debate ('spy chips the size of a grain of sand') several protest Web sites appeared (see, for example, Fig. 4.3) targeting companies who were either running or thinking about trials (e.g. Gillette — 'I would rather grow a beard... than use a tagged razor' and Benetton — 'I'd rather go naked... than wear tagged clothing'). The announcements from Gillette that they would not tag universally at item level before at least 2013 was claimed by CASPIAN as a victory although Gillette maintain that there was no direct link from the protest activities.

Fig. 4.3   Protest Web site.

The Auto-ID Center did some research into consumer reactions to RFID tagging.[11] The results varied from country to country but the overall reactions ranged from neutral to negative. It also raised a perceived health concern in some parts of Europe following recent publicity surrounding mobile handsets and masts.[12] While there were some concerns over crime (e.g. muggers reading valuables from a distance or stalkers tracking an individual), the negativity was largely rooted in a mistrust of public and private institutions. Crucially, the pervasive nature of this technology was seen as an enabler that could help facilitate malfeasance on the part of government or business, and that is why consumers reacted negatively.

Apart from the research, there was also evidence of this lack of trust, for example, in the debate over patient safety and pharmaceuticals. As a potential consumer benefit, one drug company offered the perfectly reasonable concept of a 'smart medicine cabinet' where tagged prescription bottles could be linked to particular drug batches and location would be known (by registering the bottle to your cabinet) should there be a need to recall a batch of drugs. This was immediately countered with the spectre of '... a snooper from the life insurance company on the other side of

---

[11] Executive Briefing: 'Public Policy — Understanding Public Opinion' — paper published by Auto-ID Center February 2003 (ref CAM-AUTOID-EB-002).

[12] RFID health concerns were most marked in Germany where they felt the technology would contiribute to what they termed 'electrosmog'.

the wall wondering why I have HIV medication in my house but it's not declared on my policy'. Leaving aside the science (i.e. one can build authentication into the read process, and one should also be securing the data which would show that a particular EPC relates to HIV medication, and read ranges make the scenario unlikely anyway), this illustrates that emotion, rather than fact, often rules the privacy debate.

4.4 Summary

Proponents of RFID often point out that if tracking and surveillance are of concern to people, then many already carry a device with such capabilities at the moment — a mobile telephone. Perhaps therein lies the main factor that will determine the success or failure of any ubiquitous technology with privacy implications. Although many people do not know the tracking capabilities of their mobile telephones, even those who do still carry them because there are considerable benefits (convenience, safety, etc) and these outweigh the potential negatives. The problem is that the Auto-ID Center research showed that consumers felt there would be little or no benefit for them, although many of the retail sponsors are on record as saying that they would pass any cost savings on to the consumer.

In closing, RFID in retail is an evolving story. For the next 5 to 10 years, cost and other implementation barriers mean that widespread tagging at item level will be unlikely except on higher-value products. One major exception will be where a single 'item' is also one 'case' (e.g. a television set). This will ease the privacy debate as the RFID tagging will largely be seen as an internal supply chain solution. In the long term, however, should the technology become truly ubiquitous, benefits to consumers and/or society will need to be clearly communicated, such as food or drug safety, lower prices, better recycling, crime reduction, etc. Otherwise it remains to be seen the extent to which the general public will accept a universal technology they fear could be abused.

References

1. Uniform Code Council — http://www.uc-council.org/

2. EPC Global — http://www.epcglobalinc.org/

5

Care in the Community

S Brown, N Hine, A Sixsmith, and P Garner

5.1   Introduction

The UK population is ageing. At the time of the 2001 census there were 8.1 million people aged over 65 living in the UK, 3.1 million of them living alone. By 2011 the number of over 65s is projected to reach just under 12 million, and by 2026 over 13 million [1]. The extra workload this will place on health and care services will be compounded by political ambitions aimed at meeting the challenges of rising patient expectations [2]. In addition to this, the Department of Health aims to promote the independence of older people by providing enhanced services from the National Health Service (NHS) and councils to prevent unnecessary hospital admission [3]. As a result we can expect to see a continuing rise in the number of elderly people living at home and requiring good-quality health and social care services.

The Department of Health hopes for a substantial change in the uptake of telecare[1] and other electronic assistive technologies to increase independence for older people [4]. Existing telecare solutions currently provide elderly and vulnerable individuals (clients) with the means of raising an alert should assistance be required. Trials have also been conducted with 'smart sensors' that incorporate a degree of intelligence. These second-generation systems[2] automatically call a designated carer in the event that the client is incapacitated and unable to raise an alert.

The Care in the Community Centre [5] is researching the possibility of developing and deploying third-generation telecare systems capable of monitoring long-term activity trends that may indicate a general decline in the 'well-being' of the client. The information provided by a third-generation system could be useful to both formal and informal carers and possibly the clients themselves in helping to prevent injuries and improving the client's quality of life.

BT is leading the DTI[3] funded Care in the Community Centre in collaboration with several UK universities. The programme consists of four projects, each working towards the common aim of developing and deploying a demonstrator. This chapter discusses the concept of well-being and how we might detect changes to it

---

[1] Telecare — the application of electronic information and communication technologies to support elderly people who live alone.

[2] Telecare solutions can be grouped into three generations — first- and second-generation systems allow clients to alert carers if they require immediate assistance. Second-generation systems incorporate a degree of intelligence that allows the system to alert the carer if the client is incapacitated. Third-generation systems monitor long-term changes in activity trends to assess the well-being of the client and put in place care solutions to prevent incidents from occurring.

[3] DTI — Department of Trade and Industry, the government body that promotes the development of trade and industry within the UK.

through monitoring common activities within the home. Design, deployment, and service issues are also discussed, resulting in the identification of a number of key challenges that face the project.

5.2   The Concept of 'Well-Being'

5.2.1   The Difficulty with Defining Well-Being

While terms such as quality of life (QoL) and well-being are commonly used within academic literature and the health and social care professions, they are concepts that are not easily defined. The following represent just a few attempts: '... the individual's achievement of a satisfactory social situation within the limits of perceived physical capacity' [6], '... possession of resources necessary to the satisfaction of individual needs, wants and desires, participation in activities enabling personal development and self-actualisation and satisfactory comparison between oneself and others' [7], '... in general terms, quality can be defined as a grade of *goodness*. Quality of life in relation to health is a broader concept than personal health status and also takes social well-being ... into account' [8].

There is an underlying idea that well-being is in some way about the 'goodness' in someone's life, but beyond this it is apparent that there is no straightforward or agreed definition. The lack of a specific or agreed definition means that the term presents us with an immediate problem. If we are going to develop a system that monitors well-being among frail older people, then some kind of working definition, framework, or model is required.

5.2.2   A Conceptual Model of Well-being

The aim has been to map out the various domains of well-being, and this is provided in Fig. 5.1, which represents a model of well-being drawing on the various literature sources [9–11], as well as results from three focus groups, a workshop with two healthcare professionals and two face-to-face interviews with older people in receipt of social care services. The focus groups were divided into three sessions — the first two sessions were with professional care providers and managers, each consisting of around 10 participants, the third session being attended by four informal carers. The sessions were semi-structured discussions based on an agenda of issues, including:

- definitions of well-being;

- problems people encounter;

- positive aspects of life;

- the potential role of monitoring technologies.

This semi-structured approach allowed these issues to be explored in depth, emphasising the perspective of the participants. The interviews and focus groups were tape-recorded. The moderator took notes and a post-session summary was

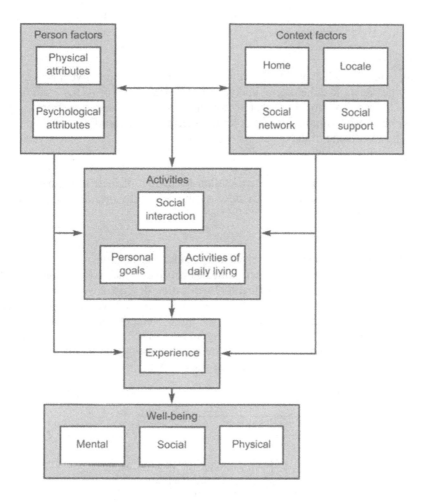

Fig. 5.1   Conceptual model of personal well-being.

written up. A thematic analysis was carried out through listening to the recordings in conjunction with field notes.

While the conceptual model shown in Fig. 5.1 is simple, it provides a robust basis for the project and emphasises a holistic perspective, where people's abilities, circumstances, and experiences contribute to their sense of well-being. The model is described as follows.

- Person factors

  These refer to people's attributes that have a direct bearing on their well-being. Key factors include physical attributes such as their general level of health and fitness, as well as psychological attributes that help them to adapt to changes that may occur in later life.

- Context factors

  The context within which a person lives has an important bearing on well-being by either facilitating or constraining the person's goals and actions. These factors include the person's home environment, the social network and social support, neighbourhood, services provided, and information.

- Activities

  This refers to what people actually do within their home. We believe most activities relate to either social interaction, personal goals, or ADLs (activities of daily living). It is important that at least a sample set of activities from each of these categories is monitored in order to determine if a significant change in the general well-being of the client has occurred.

- Experience

  This refers to the subjective interpretation by people of their life situation. It is through this process that life activities become personally meaningful, subjective, and idiosyncratic.

- Well-being outcome

  This refers to the person's perceived well-being, e.g. positive or negative effect, life satisfaction. These are internal mental processes that are not amenable to direct monitoring. The World Health Organisation describes well-being in terms of three discrete elements — physical well-being, mental well-being, and social well-being [12]. It is important that all three elements are considered when attempting to identify a change in the general well-being of an individual. We believe that the activity categories we intend monitoring can be mapped directly to these three elements of well-being, as shown in Table 5.1.

Table 5.1.   Mapping elements of well-being to activity categories.

Well-being element	Activity category
Physical	ADLs
Mental	Personal goals
Social	Social interaction

5.3   How to Measure Changes in Well-Being

5.3.1   Identifying Target Groups

The well-being monitoring system we are developing will not be able to directly monitor changes in person and context factors, as a human carer might. Instead the system will rely on monitoring changes in the activities the client performs, which means it is important that we choose activities that are affected by changes in person and context factors.

Our first attempts at identifying these activities proved difficult mainly because of the large number of activities involved. Developing sensor and data analysis solutions for all of these would have proved extremely time-consuming and beyond the resources available within the projects. The decision was taken to reduce the number of these activities by focusing on a specific client target group (see Table 5.2).

Table 5.2   National Service Framework for Older People [13] — priorities and standards.

General group	Specific group	NSF Standards
Old age general	Physically frail older people and those with specific physical impairments, who require some level of long-term help and support from health and social care services	Standard 1. Rooting out age discrimination:
		Standard 2. Person-centred care
		Standard 8. The promotion of health and active life in old age
Mental health	Dementia	Standard 7. Mental health in older people
	Depression	
	Other (e.g. anxiety disorders)	
Other NSF priority groups	Stroke	Standard 5. To reduce the incidence of stroke
	Falls	Standard 6. To reduce the number of falls

A number of target groups were identified based on the standards published in the Department of Health National Service Framework[4] for Older People [13]. Adopting this strategy has ensured that the solution we develop will be directly relevant to UK Government policy. Table 5.2 provides an outline of what the UK Government sees as the key priorities.

The first column in Table 5.2 describes three general groups given priority under the NSF for Older People. The second column lists sub-groups of these that have been adopted within the project as target groups.

The decision was taken to focus on physically frail[5] older people, and to identify an initial set of activities that could be monitored to identify a change in well-being for this group. The rationale for focusing on the physically frail target group was based on the fact that physical frailty is the most common problem suffered by older people (see Fig. 5.2).

In addition to this, the activities carried out by physically frail people are likely to be more predictive than those carried out by people who suffer from depression or dementia. If we are successful in demonstrating well-being monitoring for this target group, we could then focus our attention on what we consider to be the more challenging groups.

---

[4] National Service Framework (NSF). The NSF for Older People is a document published in 2001 by the Department of Health. It sets new national standards and service models of care across health and social services for all older people, whether they live at home, live in residential care, or are being looked after in hospital — http://www.dh.gov.uk/

[5] Physically frail — it should be emphasised here that the greatest benefits from well-being monitoring are likely to be gained if the system is deployed before the individual becomes too frail. The time at which this occurs is of course open to interpretation but should ideally rely on the judgment of professionals and formal/informal carers, as well as the individuals themselves.

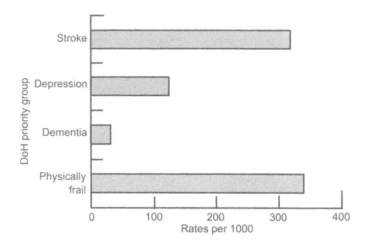

Fig. 5.2   Comparison of priority groups.
[Sources: DoH Health Survey for England 2000, and Alzheimer's Association]

5.3.2   Identifying Activities for Monitoring Physically Frail People

Two activities from each of the three activity categories identified in Fig. 5.1 were identified for monitoring. This initial set of six activities includes:

- leaving and returning home (category: social interaction);
- visitors (category: social interaction);
- preparing food and eating (category: ADL);
- sleeping patterns (category: ADL);
- personal appearance (category: personal goal);
- leisure activities (category: personal goal).

A method for identifying the appropriate sensor hardware and algorithms required to monitor changes in these activities was developed. The first step in this method was to consider some of the 'high-level' questions that might be asked by formal carers about the mental, social, and physical elements of a client's general well-being. An example of this is given in the mindmap shown in Fig. 5.3, which illustrates how the high-level questions relating to just the social element of well-being help to identify the associated high-level algorithm requirements and, if considered further, the types and locations of sensors required. The expectation is that the information generated from these high-level questions can be used to answer several 'low-level' questions, the answers to which may hold some interest to the carers depending on the level of detail they require. As an example, Q1 asks: 'Tell me about the person's social life outside the home.' The system is not designed to monitor the number and quality of social interactions that may occur outside the home, but it can provide us with detailed information about the client leaving and returning home, which to some degree reflects the social interaction that may be occurring. The motion sensor data can be used to determine three time durations:

- [Duration-A] the time duration of high levels of activity indicating that the home is occupied;

- [Duration-B] the time duration of low levels of activity, but the home is known to be occupied;

- [Duration-C] the duration of time when there is no activity and it is known that the home is unoccupied.

Other sensors can be used to detect when the front door is opened and closed in order to improve the accuracy of the recorded occupancy state of the home. Using the recorded durations A and C it is a simple calculation to determine the maximum amount of time that social activity might be occurring outside the home. As shown in Fig. 5.3, it is also possible to begin asking other low-level questions of the data in order to determine if there might be a change in behaviour relating to social interaction outside the home.

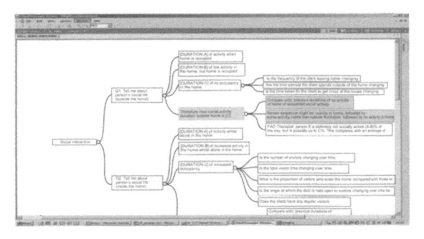

Fig. 5.3   High-level questions mindmap.

5.3.3   A Functional Architecture for Monitoring Activities

A wide variety of systems and equipment already within the home may be possible sources for capturing data. Some of these sensors may be built into existing equipment that can give a better impression of 'what' people are doing compared to the 'where they are' information that comes from conventional location activity sensors.

The functional overview illustrated in Fig. 5.4 shows a comprehensive view of the primary candidate technical functions of a well-being monitoring system. The functions utilised in any specific instance may be a sub-set of the functions shown, particularly the activity monitors being deployed. The selection of functions may depend on a number of factors, including vulnerability of the specific user, care service package, and technology available.

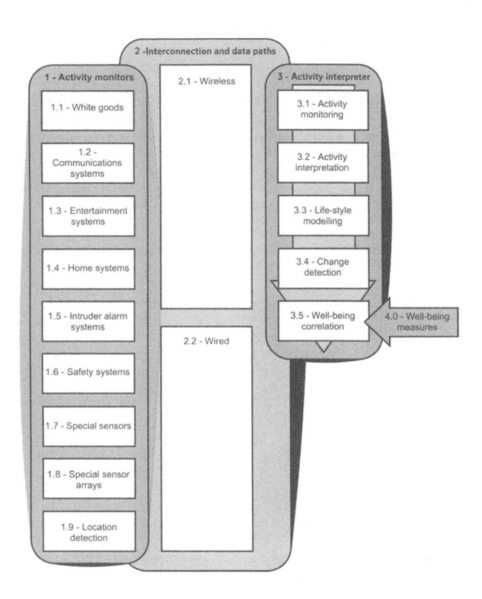

Fig. 5.4   Functional architecture of a well-being monitoring system.

The 'activity monitors' function shown in Fig. 5.4 detects user activity by monitoring the state of sensors or sensor arrays. The sensors may have data processing functionality associated within the monitoring function. The 'interconnection and data paths' function provides the data channel from the activity monitors to the activity interpretation functions — wired and wireless options are indicated. The 'activity interpretation' function provides the interpretation of activity events in order to determine which activities are being performed, the patterns governing those activities, and the deviations from those patterns that could be an indicator of a change in the well-being of the client.

5.4 System Design, Deployment, and Service Issues

5.4.1 Design Requirements

The design of the well-being monitoring system will partly depend on how it is to be used within the care domain. Consideration should also be given to contentious issues such as cost, performance, data security, and ease of installation. Equally important is ensuring the design takes into account ethical issues such as the privacy of the client.

Obtaining consent from the client to install a well-being monitoring system might be a major issue, particularly if the person is suffering early symptoms of dementia. Dementia welfare organisations are increasingly emphasising the involvement of end users, rather than decisions being made for them. With this in mind, an informal carer could be involved to provide reassurance or support to clients while the system is being explained to them. Designing a system that meets these requirements is important despite the complexity it introduces, or we risk developing a well-being monitoring solution that is potentially impossible to implement.

5.4.2 Formal and Informal Care Markets

Formal care is provided by paid care workers who work for either a local authority or a private care agency. In both cases a 'contract' is assumed to exist between the community care provider and client, with the care provider expected to adhere to an agreed level of care provision. The largest formal community care providers in the UK are local authorities, each of which provides personal care to older people through referrals into a social services department. During 2000/2001 the budget for local authority personal social services expenditure for older people was £5899 million. Of this amount £498 million was spent on assessment and care management, and £1810 million on non-residential provision [14].

Our research has involved developing an understanding of the referral procedure in conjunction with an occupational therapist and senior managers of several social services departments. A focus group discussion was also conducted with social workers from one unitary authority[8] to gain a grass-roots understanding of the procedure.

Figure 5.5 is a model of the referral procedure common to most social services departments throughout England. The diagram shows how a referral first needs to pass through tough eligibility criteria before the client is assessed in order to receive the appropriate care package. It also shows the care being delivered by a private care agency rather than care workers employed directly by the local authority. This outsourcing approach is becoming more common as local authorities seek to reduce care costs.

---

[8] Unitary authority — a term used in the UK for local government bodies that form a single tier of administration. The more common alternative to this is a local authority that has a two-tier arrangement where each county has a council and contains multiple districts with councils of their own.

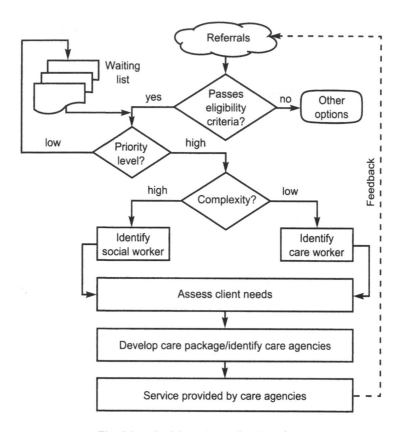

Fig. 5.5   Social services referral process.

Our discussions with social workers revealed a number of issues that exist with the current referral process. These included long waiting lists (sometimes in excess of nine months) and having to spend more time organising the provision of care rather than assessing the client's needs. The main reasons given for this were increasing workloads and a general shortage of in-house and agency care workers.

Social services do keep client records and aim to check up on the effectiveness of a care package at least every six months. In practice, these follow-up checks are often missed out due to workload pressures, and clients often have to re-enter the referral process at the start when a change to the care package is required.

Excessive work loads often prevent the social worker from monitoring the progress of the client and providing more proactive care provision. When viewed together with the process shown in Fig. 5.5, it is not easy to see how well-being monitoring could reduce this workload. In fact, it is more likely to have the opposite effect by identifying clients with unmet needs that social services may then be obliged to meet.

In addition to the formal care market (i.e. social services and private care agencies), there also exists an informal care market made up of volunteer carers such as family members, friends, and charity workers. The 2001 Census for England and Wales identified approximately 5.2 million informal carers defined as people who

'... provide unpaid care to individuals suffering from either long-term physical or mental ill-health or disability, or problems related to old age' [15].

More recent studies indicate that the number of informal carers has now risen to 5.7 million, and that one half of these carers look after someone who is aged over 75 years [16].

High levels of working hours are creating issues within informal care that are similar to those being experienced within formal care. UK Government statistics show that 1.7 million informal carers provide more than 20 hours of care per week, and that almost 1 million provide more than 50 hours' care per week [16]. In addition to this, it is not uncommon for informal carers to also have a part- or full-time job.

The implications of well-being monitoring for the formal and informal care markets are considerable. We believe well-being monitoring would result in an overall cost reduction in caring for older people, while maintaining or improving the quality of care provided. However, it is also true to say that if such a system became generally available, then the work of looking after older people would shift more towards the community and the informal care market. This may require governments to look at increasing funding towards community-based care while expecting to see savings in other areas of health, such as hospitals. Perhaps the greatest challenge will be to convince most local authorities to take on a more proactive role regarding care in the community when their resources are already overstretched.

5.4.3 Configuring and Installing a Well-Being Monitoring System

As discussed previously, our sense of well-being is based on person factors, context factors, personal experiences, and activities, with changes in well-being affecting the way in which we perform certain activities. This suggests that the pattern of things that change our level of well-being, and the way in which we exhibit that change, is quite unique.

Our aim is to build a system that can learn to understand this 'uniqueness', but it might be possible to give the system a helping hand at the start by instructing it to look for a particular pattern or change in pattern of specific activities. These instructions could be based on information gathered from the client, carers, friends, and family. The information could also significantly affect the type and quantity of sensors that are installed. In many cases it may be possible to put the client into one of three broad categories — low risk, at risk, or specified risk. Figure 5.6 describes these categories in more detail and illustrates the different deployment configurations that apply.

The monitoring of a specific individual will involve a selection from within the possible set of sensors depending on their perceived or demonstrated vulnerabilities and risks. Individuals who are causing concern may agree to a simple monitoring package, whereas individuals that have experienced serious episodes such as falling or wandering from their homes may agree to a more comprehensive package of sensors. At all stages of the negotiation, deployment, and use of these systems, the users' preferences in the selection of appropriate sensors and algorithms should be taken into account, and a secure and ethical framework for the handling of the sensor data should be devised.

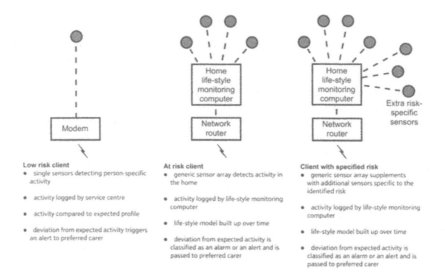

Fig. 5.6   Technology deployment model.

The process used for installing a well-being monitoring system will also have a major effect on its design. For example, installation by a trained technician would mean the sensors could be relatively dumb, requiring the technician to manually register them on the network. This may result in lower design and hardware costs but higher installation costs. However, if the system is to be installed by an untrained person such as the carer, or perhaps even the client, then we may need to make it self-configurable, which would have the opposite effect. It is impossible at this stage to estimate what the true hardware and installation costs would be, but the view taken within the project is that in most cases practical issues such as attaching the sensors to walls will require a trained technician. In view of this we believe the simpler low-cost hardware design is the most sensible option.

5.4.4   Monitoring Clients and Responding to Changes in Their Well-Being

Assuming a well-being monitoring system were installed within a client's home as described in Section 5.4.3, we would need to put in place protocols for monitoring and responding to changes in the well-being of that client.

The information provided by the well-being monitoring system may provide the carer with an overall indication of positive or negative changes in well-being, or it may provide an indication of changes in specific activities that affect the well-being of the client. Formal care organisations, such as social services and private care agencies, could access this information through a PC connected to the server. Other, more intuitive interfaces such as the 'digital family portrait'[9] developed by researchers at the Georgia Institute of Technology may be more appropriate for some

---

[9] Digital family portrait — a simple display set into the frame of a photograph that changes in some way to reflect the health or well-being of the person within the photograph. This concept was first developed at the Georgia Institute of Technology.

informal carers. Whatever interface is used, it is important that the system provides information that is acceptable to the client and useful to the carer. Therefore, both clients and carers should be involved in helping to design the monitoring interface and response protocols.

In the event that the system should indicate the possibility of a significant change in the well-being of the client, the carer could use this information to make a more timely and effective response. Depending on the amount of information given, the carer may be able to initiate a discussion on a specific issue that may be worrying the client. Figure 5.7 shows a snapshot of a proposed well-being GUI for use by formal carers who might wish to monitor changes in the well-being of their clients. The top half of the GUI provides individual summaries of several activities. Each activity is described in terms of its historical state, change in state over a three-month period, and current state. Different colours are used by the GUI (shown as tints in Fig 5.7) to represent the four distinct states:

- red — experiencing significant difficulties with this activity, which is having a negative effect on the person's general well-being;

- orange — the client may be experiencing some difficulties with this activity;

- yellow — no cause for concern;

- green — this activity represents no problems and is having a positive effect on the person's general well-being.

Clearly there is some blurring between these states, and the GUI represents this by mixing the colours between these boundaries to represent the transitions. The bottom half of the GUI shows how the client's overall level of well-being is changing. The same colour coding is adopted as before except that it is banded horizontally. The black line illustrates the level of general well-being based upon a number of significant activities.

In the event that the system should indicate the possibility of a significant change in the well-being of the client, the carer could use this information to make a more timely and effective response. Depending on the amount of information the carers are given, they may be able to initiate a discussion on a specific issue that may be worrying the client. The proposed well-being GUI (illustrated in Fig. 5.7) is for use by formal carers who might wish to monitor changes in the well-being of their clients. The feedback from formal carers, such as social workers and occupational therapists, is that generally they would not have the time to study detailed graphs that may indicate changes in well-being. However, they would find a GUI such as that shown in Fig. 5.7 useful to glance at occasionally, and which also provides access to the underlying data in case they wish to look at a particular activity in more detail.

The well-being data collected may also be useful to other stakeholders such as general practitioners (GPs) and hospitals in the event that the client requires treatment for a medical condition. Provided the necessary security and privacy systems are put in place, the well-being data could be appended to the client's own electronic patient record within the NCRS (National Care Record System) currently being developed by the NHS. Combining health and social care data in this way would fit in with the Department of Health's long-term plan of making the NCRS a health and social record.

A final point to bear in mind is that well-being monitoring is not designed to alert the carer to emergency situations, but to highlight changes in activity that may

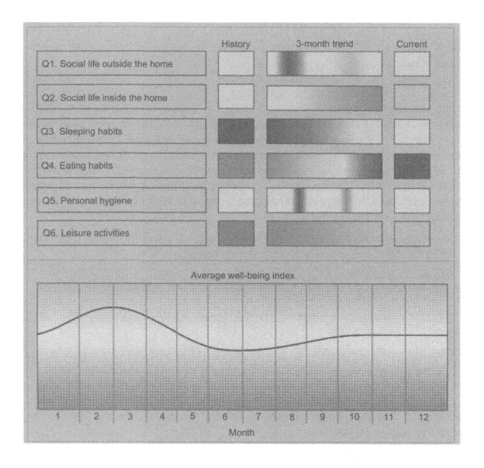

Fig. 5.7   Well-being GUI.

indicate a change in the well-being of the client. Given this fact, it is reasonable to assume that the system would be used in conjunction with a first- or second-generation community alarm system operated in the usual way.

5.5   Summary and Key Technical Challenges

We have described how this work is leading the development of a third-generation telecare system capable of monitoring changes in the well-being of elderly clients at home. The aim of the system is to help carers deal with increasing workloads while maintaining or improving the level of care received by the client. We have discussed how the system will be designed to work on a network of non-intrusive sensors monitoring specific activities. The process of instrumenting these activities takes into account cost, ethics, performance, ease of installation, and technical feasibility. Where possible, use will be made of existing sensors such as smoke alarms and security alarms. The system will not only be intelligent enough to learn about clients and their activities, but will also be matched to them through an assessment procedure. It is expected that a trained technician will install the system.

The strategy adopted for monitoring well-being has led to a number of key requirements. Firstly, it is important we understand the care domain in order that we develop a system that can be implemented successfully. The system design must be flexible to allow the building of bespoke systems based on different client needs and environments. Powerful software algorithms will be required if we are to identify patterns in the huge volume of data likely to be generated. Sensors will generally need to be low-cost, powered by batteries that can last for several months, and fit into many different environments. Secure data storage and transmission protocols will be required. It may also be necessary to develop an assessment tool for use by the carer in order that bespoke well-being monitoring systems can be designed.

The technical challenges faced by the teams designing the sensors, networks, and intelligent software systems are considerable. In some cases what is being asked of the technology may not be practical or feasible, which could mean the need to identify alternative activities for monitoring, or accept higher costs or lower performance. The key technical challenges facing us focus mainly on developing low-cost, low-power sensors, and software that is intelligent enough to spot slight changes in activity trends represented by thousands of individual sensor firings.

References

1. UK Population Projections by Age Group. Population Trends 32 — Spring. National Statistics, 2003.

2. Milburn A. The NHS Plan: Introduction by the Secretary of State. July 2000 — http://www.nhs.uk/nationalplan/intro.htm

3. The Department of Health. National Service Framework for Older People: Standard Three — Intermediate care. March 2001:47 — http://www.dh.gov.uk/assetRoot/04/07/12/83/04071283.pdf

4. Ladyman S. Homing In. Integration of Community Equipment Service (ICES) Conference. March 2004:1 — http://www.dh.gov.uk/NewsHome/Speeches/SpeechesList/SpeechesArticle/fs/en?CONTENT_ID=4075877&chk=k9YRoU

5. Care in the Community Centre — http://www.nextwave.org.uk/centres/care.htm

6. Mendola W F and Pelligrini R V. Quality of Life and Coronary Artery Bypass Surgery Patients. Social Science and Medicine, 1979:13A:457–492.

7. Shin D C and Johnson R V. Avowed Happiness as an Overall Assessment of the Quality of Life. Social Indicators Research, 1978:5:475–492.

8. Bowling A. Measuring Health. Open University Press, Buckingham, 1997.

9. Veenhoven R. The Four Qualities of Life: Ordering Concepts and Measures of the Good Life. Journal of Happiness Studies, 2000:1:1–39.

10. Lawton M P. Environment and Aging. 2nd edition, Brooks/Cole Publishing Co, Los Angeles, USA, 1986.

11. Bowling A. Measuring Health: A Review of Quality of Life Measurement Scales. 2nd edition, Open University Press, October 2004.

12. Active Ageing — A Policy Framework. 2002:12 — http://www.who.int/hpr/ageing/ActiveAgeingPolicyFrame.pdf

13. Department of Heath. National Service Framework for Older People. March 2001 — http://www.dh.gov.uk/assetRoot/04/07/12/83/04071283.pdf

14. Department of Health. Health and Personal Social Services Statisitics — http://www.performance.doh.gov.uk/HPSSS/TBL_E5.HTM

15. 2001 Census — http://www.statistics.gov.uk/cci/nugget.asp?id= 347

16. Carers — http://www.carers.gov.uk/pdfs/Care.pdf

6

Pervasive Home Environments

P Bull, R Limb, and R Payne

6.1   Introduction

An increasing number of computers and other equipment, such as games consoles and multimedia appliances for the home, have networking capability. The rapid growth of broadband in the home is also fuelling the demand for people to network their homes. In the near future we will see a number of market sectors trying to 'own' the home by providing gateways either from the traditional ISP or from games and other service providers. The consumer is bombarded with attractive advertising to acquire the latest technological advances, but is left with a plethora of different appliances, which have a bewildering range of requirements and features in terms of networking, user interface, and higher-level communications protocols. In many cases, these are proprietary, preventing interworking. Such technical and usability anarchy confuses the consumer and could ultimately suppress market adoption.

An obvious solution is for a consumer to buy all the appliances and services from one supplier. This is a dream solution for the supplier as they now 'own' the home and can sell more value-add services as they know and understand the existing equipment. It is more likely that most consumers will prefer to buy equipment and services from a number of suppliers, as is currently the norm. In any case, it is unlikely that a single supplier could cover the full breadth of appliances and services. The user needs to be assisted in managing this complex network of devices with a solution that works for both the consumer and the suppliers.

In this chapter we discuss an approach that supports the user by creating a smart environment that removes much of the confusing configuration difficulties and management issues, allowing users to focus on what they want to do, rather than how to make the equipment work. This is not an easy task, reflected in its increasing popularity as a field of research. This research is based on the common belief that in the near future there will be a large number of 'smart devices' in the home. However, it is not just the number of devices that is important; it is also the belief that these devices will be networked, small, and low power. These trends will allow them to become part of the home infrastructure, in other words, 'pervasive'.

The issue is not just about connecting devices, which is in some ways the least problematical. It is important to address security, user interfaces, personalisation, and configuration.

This chapter will introduce ideas on these topics that are current areas of research for the authors. We will also discuss the concept of an 'information space' that deals with how users create, access, store, and retrieve information that is relevant to them coupled with the data communicated between devices.

Before discussing technology, the chapter first presents a vision of what the pervasive home environment will be like, setting the scene by describing the environment, the typical range of devices, who will be a typical user, and the motivation for the research. Finally, we will present some commercial opportunities, in particular those for the service provider, such as provision of value-add services and management of the home.

6.2   Vision

Our vision for the pervasive home environment is one in which the overt technology of today will 'disappear' into everyday artefacts in the home. The devices will communicate via a range of wired and wireless technologies appropriate to the device and context. The communication mechanisms will be bridged to form a 'data ring' as unobtrusive to the user as the mains power ring and water supply are today. Many current visions for the networked home are predicated on the continuing existence of devices that we see in our homes today, such as the television and the PC. Entertainment is widely seen to be a strong driver for networking the home, and consequently the set-top box (STB) is frequently presented as the 'gateway' to the home, running uncounted applications and controlled by the service provider. But imagine the scenario where the television decomposes into separate functional devices — we no longer have a 'set' on which to stand the STB! This trend has already started with the emergence of flat panel displays and separate tuner boxes. Consumers tend to buy affordable devices from a variety of suppliers that provide a single or limited range of functions, as opposed to a major investment in fixed infrastructure or single supplier and we anticipate that this will continue to be the case. Now imagine that, in addition to communicating with each other, these devices can share capabilities so that the total functionality is greater than the sum of the parts. This opens up the prospect of a huge range of applications and services that can detect and combine these capabilities together as required. For this environment to become usable, it must be:

- heterogeneous — non-proprietary, supporting many types of device and connectivity using open standard interfaces and protocols;
- distributed — devices contribute resources to the environment, and these resources can be combined to form 'virtual' devices — control should also be distributed to minimise dependency on a central point of failure, a key area of concern for consumers;
- autoconfiguring — it must be easy for the user to add and remove facilities (actually, total autoconfiguration is probably unachievable, but minimising user involvement should be the goal);
- self-healing — a reliable infrastructure is a key requirement — if resources disappear, either through failure or just because a user removes them, the environment should recover or at least degrade gracefully;
- secure — provide appropriate levels of privacy and security, which encompasses resource access control and security of information — there may also be safety considerations here, e.g. in a telemedical context.

We envisage that the environment will possess an 'information layer' that supports a reasoning ability —sometimes referred to as ambient intelligence. Our experience with home environments as they currently exist shows that the hierarchical file systems and monolithic applications that come from the IT space do not transfer well into the pervasive home; we are therefore investigating alternative approaches to the information space that will better support this new requirement. The role of intelligence is to understand the capabilities of the environment and the needs of the occupants, and react accordingly. How to provide this intelligence is the subject of ongoing research, covering areas such as explicitly programmed behaviour versus learned behaviour and how much autonomy can be delegated to computationally small devices.

Why anyone would want this pervasive environment is initially difficult to imagine, because we do not see a single, or even a few 'killer applications' that would individually drive adoption. However, when consumers start buying 'pervasive ready' appliances, for particular purposes, the environment will grow naturally. The flexibility of such an environment would enable different bundles from a wide range of applications and services to be used and we confidently predict that new services will emerge as consumers begin to experience the possibilities. A brief list of possible services includes:

- security;
- well-being;
- care (cost benefit to local councils and NHS);
- education;
- continuous learning;
- entertainment;
- energy management.

The authors, through use of their own home installations, have experienced first hand the way family members adopt and adapt the environment. We see its role in entertainment, education and in supporting social interaction, for example. We have experienced how quickly it becomes a core part of family life as well as the frustrations resulting from the limitations of current technology. 'If only I could ...' and 'why can't I ...?' are frequently heard.

In the introduction we stated that this is a popular area for research so it is appropriate to give some background on related work. AutoHAN [1] from Cambridge University has a number of similarities with our approach. They used universal plug and play (UPnP) [2], which the team extended to include semantic descriptions of the application that has been built into the devices. This description may be coded in a language developed for the purpose, called AutoHAN Language. The AutoHan team has also worked on user interfaces, concentrating on a remote control style of architecture based on some novel devices using infra-red. This is one of the key differences with our work, where we want to provide a more 'invisible' architecture using novel user interface techniques and develop emergent behaviour using embedded agents. This work is described in more detail in Chapter 24. It does not appear that work on AutoHAN is continuing at present.

MIT and others (including HP, Philips, and Nokia) have been working on Project Oxygen [3] for some time. The user interface aspects are more in line with our work;

their proposal is to move away from the need for users to have to use specific devices for user interaction (the mouse, keyboard, etc) and move to more natural methods of interaction including speech and gesture.

HP also has its own research project called CoolTown [4]. The focus is on extending the now common experience of using the Web to a more ubiquitous computing model using hand-held devices, using, for example, infra-red communication. It appears that HP is reducing effort on CoolTown specifically and taking its research in different but related directions.

The University of Washington has a project called one.world [5] that aims to develop a framework for pervasive computing, which specifically supports application development. This is just one (albeit very important) aspect of a pervasive computing environment.

6.3   Technical Challenges

Producing a pervasive home environment introduces a number of technical challenges. In this section we describe these, with reasons why they are important and discuss our approach to addressing the issues involved.

6.3.1   Configuration

Almost any device beyond the complexity of a simple switch requires configuration or some form of user set-up. Today, it is common for suppliers to assume that a (peripheral) device will be connected to a PC and so each device is shipped with a CD-ROM containing documentation, device drivers, and installation and configuration software. In the future pervasive home environment, devices will be more autonomous, and access to a PC should not be assumed. There will be more reliance on self-configuration, and device and service discovery, for when things go wrong.

Self-Configuration
There are already some limited solutions to self-configuration, particularly in configuration of network connectivity. Devices that are to be used on a home network generally assume there will be a method to automatically obtain and assign an Internet (IP) address. This is typically done using a DHCP server [6], or more recently, especially in relation to UPnP devices, AutoIP [2]. Beyond that, devices may have some 'hard-coded' default settings, which can then be modified and updated by the user.

In a pervasive environment, with many small devices, there is a need to develop more sophisticated methods for self-configuration. There are a number of issues here.

- Network settings

   A decision has to be made about what types of setting could be self-configured, apart from the obvious one of network addressing described above. The kinds of information that may need setting include locality, peer or server addresses, date and time, and more advanced network settings, e.g. security. These examples range from quite easy (date and time can be communicated over a network) to difficult, such as advanced network and security settings.

- Communication of settings

  We need to consider if the self-configured settings need to be communicated to the user in some way and, if so, what the most appropriate way to do this should be. In most cases the user will not need or wish to see the settings. However, this is quite easily solved through device discovery and networked user interfaces.

- Autonic setting modification

  Finally, there is the issue of whether modification and updating of settings can also be an automatic and autonomous process. Although we argue that the user should not have to be involved, access should be available if desired. This is related to the second issue above, although we expect that devices that can self-configure should be also self-updating.

Investigation of all these issues is in progress.

Device and Service Discovery

An automated pervasive environment is dependent on devices that can announce their capabilities and services, as well as discover other devices with which they may need to interact. There are a number of maturing methods readily available such as Jini [7], UPnP [2], Salutation [8], SLP (service location protocol) [9], IrDA [10], Bluetooth [11], and HAVi (home audio video interoperability) [12]. There are also many new protocol proposals in the research arena, often developed for specific solutions or to work alongside new network topologies, such as peer-to-peer and *ad hoc* networks [13, 14]. Each of these has their strengths and weaknesses and a number of papers have been published that report on comparisons between some subset of them, notably by California Software Labs (CSWL) [15].

As noted in Section 6.3.1, one of the key aspects of a device or service will be location. This is not, in general, supported by the protocols cited above and is something that needs to be addressed. It is important because how a device operates or interacts with other devices or the user can be dependent on its location. For example, a user may want to indicate that if it is evening and the television is on in the lounge, then the lounge lights are dimmed, or side lights turned on and the main light turned off.

We have decided that for our current research in this area, we will use UPnP in the majority of cases for our device co-ordination. The main reasons are that it is an emerging standard, real devices are beginning to support it, and it is fairly easy to add support in software, either for virtual devices or for real devices by proxy. UPnP is also gaining support from both the IT and consumer electronics industries. We have an example of such a proxy where we have produced a software component that does two things — it communicates with a networked printer via an SNMP [16] interface that collects information about the printer, and the component also exposes this information and some limited services as a UPnP interface on to the network. We are aware that it is not credible that only one discovery mechanism will be deployed in the future home environment. Our architecture is therefore being designed to be flexible in allowing other protocols to co-exist, again by the use of proxies and plug-in components.

6.3.2   Device Decomposition

Our research is following a model of a pervasive home environment where the steady increase in networked devices, with device and service discovery capabilities, leads to the point where functional decomposition occurs. This means that what we now think of as a 'device' such as a video recorder is presented on the network as a number of functional components that can be combined with other components to deliver an application or service. In this example the components would typically include a tuner, a timer, and a storage device. These could be combined locally to operate as the original, stand-alone video recorder. Alternatively, the tuner could be combined with a remote interface and display to form what we would currently call a TV, or even deliver the tuned programme to several displays. If we introduce a layer of intelligence coupled with advanced user interfaces, then we have an environment where users can focus on tasks rather than technology. For example, a user will initiate a task such as 'record my favourite TV programme tonight and make it available for viewing in my bedroom by 10 pm', rather than:

• Oh, it's Thursday, I must set the video for 8 pm, digital channel 3;

• I need a spare tape;

• I must make sure the set-top box is powered on.

How the programme is recorded, which combination of tuner, timer, and storage and playback facilities are used are now of no concern to the user. It may be that there is a problem with the timing service usually associated with the video recorder, and so an alternative will be discovered and assigned to the task. So we see the beginnings of the vision of a truly pervasive environment where the technology becomes part of the house, and the user is not really aware of it. Another potential advantage of this approach is that it alleviates the trade-off between cost and complexity of small devices. Traditionally, devices can be small, simple, and cheap (the light switch) or complex and relatively expensive (a portable DVD player). By building up functionality from a distributed network of devices and services, we can achieve complexity in a much more flexible and cost-effective way. If the environment has a suitable tablet-style display device, a media source, and a high-speed network, the portable DVD player can be dynamically created for the duration of the required task.

6.3.3   Resource Reservation

Because resources in the pervasive environment are shared, there will be instances where contention for use of a resource will arise. Continuing the entertainment example, imagine that there are a number of locations in the home where a media stream can be viewed. Then imagine that the occupants of the home have subscribed to a media-streaming service where two streams can be assigned to any of a larger number of available channels. Bob can request to watch channel A and stream 1 is allocated to channel A. Mary wants to watch channel B and stream 2 is allocated to channel B. Susan can ask to watch channel A or B and be connected to the appropriate stream, but if she requests another channel, she is told that there are no available channels until a stream is released. Thus, we now need a mechanism for users to request use of a resource for a certain length of time, after which it is released for reallocation. This may mean that Mary says, 'I want to watch programme A,' which now defines both the channel to be assigned and the duration of that assignment. It may also use QoS (quality of service) mechanisms to temporarily change traffic priorities. There will also have to be some notion of priority for access to a resource, perhaps related to importance (e.g. safety overriding comfort) or to individual user profiles. As reservation is not supported by current versions of protocols such as UPnP, we are having to develop this extended capability.

6.3.4   User Identity

To enable really personalised services to be offered, the identity and, preferably, the location of the individual are required. This can be approached in two ways:

- the environment is all-knowing, in a big brother manner;
- the individual knows who they are and where they are and provides sufficient information to allow the service/facility required.

In public spaces most people would prefer the latter, but this would require the carrying of some intelligent device that could communicate with the surroundings. In a home environment, where the information can be secured to the confines of the house, then the former can be more acceptably considered.

Identifying and tracking can go hand in hand and many approaches have been tried. In practice, each service could place a unique demand on the resolution of location, from who is in the house, to which room, and even where their hand may be. The ideal solution will probably be a multi-modal approach where individual systems communicate to give the accuracy required for a given person and situation. Flexibility should always be built in to allow personal choice.

Linking together infra-red movement sensors, RFID tag readers, facial recognition cameras, and high-resolution ultra-sound systems could offer the full spectrum and would allow the introduction of new systems as they become available. We need to consider the practical constraints of the home environment, but it is this ability to link and add sensors to an existing system that will allow a truly powerful holistic approach.

As discussed later, open standards for protocols and interfaces are required to allow this flexible scheme. Imagine buying a new widget that seamlessly integrates into your security sensor service and at the same time enables monitoring of your well-being by noting your movements around the home. Lack of reliance on individual stove-pipe solutions would also allow a slow degradation of services, rather than a sudden collapse in the event of component failure.

6.3.5   User Interfaces

In previous sections a number of references have been made to user interfaces. It could be argued that in creating the truly pervasive computing vision, this becomes a non-issue because there will be no user interface [17]. This is a little disingenuous because the user will need to interact somehow so that tasks and actions happen. This means that we need to completely rethink what the term 'user interface' means. The mouse, keyboard, and monitor are frequently inappropriate and they tie the user to a particular location. Even if wireless, the user cannot be too far away, and the mouse will need a flat surface to operate reliably.

The smart home vision of previous decades often depicted people talking to the walls or to an invisible electronic being. The problems of realising this are now well understood, both technically (speech recognition, user identification) and socially (are people comfortable talking to something that 'isn't there'?), but there are obvious advantages to taking this approach.

Other techniques worth pursuing include electronic tags that 'announce' the presence of someone, gestures detected using cameras or motion detectors, touch-sensitive areas on walls, tables, etc. For output interfaces, a combination of multimedia displays, computer monitors, wall displays, Web pads, and PDA screens could be used. In some circumstances, simply attracting attention using the room lighting may be the most appropriate mechanism. There may also be a place for computer-generated speech technology, but again, this has to be done in an appropriate manner, sensitive to user needs and not be intrusive.

6.3.6   Information Spaces

People are creators as well as consumers of information. We write letters, make notes and shopping lists, take and leave messages for other members of the family. Some information is less explicit — we personalise the settings on the computer (the information resides in the PC), we have individual, personal preferences and routines (the information resides in our, and possibly others', memory). Our experience from use in our own homes is that the current 'IT' paradigms do not meet the needs of our pervasive home. So a key aspect of our research is focused on the 'information layer'.

We believe there is a need to include in the infrastructure the means to enable users to create, store, retrieve, and manage information, including information created by devices. Here, we must point out our distinction between information and data. Data will come in many forms, usually from devices and sensors, examples being:

- environmental — temperature and humidity;

- temporal — date, time, timer events, location events triggered by motion detectors, etc.

Once data is augmented with context, we have information. This in itself is not a new idea; context and information concepts have their roots in information retrieval research spanning decades. In the pervasive home environment we introduce context in a number of ways — rich meta-data in device and service descriptions, location data, personal preferences, and other meta-data that may, for example, be associated with multimedia.

A related distinction is that data is often in raw machine-readable form, whereas information is generally presented in a form meaningful to a human, such as text, sound, video, or alarm. A pervasive environment must provide suitable mechanisms for transforming and presenting this information to the user in the most appropriate, consistent, and meaningful way.

6.3.7   Storage

In a distributed environment we need somewhere to store information. The pragmatic approach we are taking in the short term is to have some information stored centrally and some distributed, located within devices. This has the advantage of giving us a solution that is immediately realisable, while giving time to develop more advanced solutions. We are developing our thinking along the lines of a fully distributed architecture that includes research on novel methods for defining data structures and methods of storage. The advantage of this approach is that we avoid central points of failure.

6.3.8   Security, Privacy, and Trust

In any networked environment, security is an issue that occurs at many levels — network and application protocols, data access, user rights and administration, 'guest' access, intrusion detection, remote administration, etc. This is a complex research activity in its own right and so in developing a pervasive network architecture we have taken the decision to acknowledge this and implement as much security as is practical, without making this the main focus of our research.

UPnP currently is not secure, in that there is no built-in security at the UPnP protocol level, though steps are being taken to address this [18]. Devices announce their services that in turn announce actions that can be taken. There is no built-in mechanism for denying or granting access to the services and actions. At the transport level, UPnP, being TCP/IP-based, will use whatever is available, e.g. Wireless Equivalent Privacy (WEP). The UPnP organisation has a committee specifically addressing security issues, who will make recommendations for additions to the protocol as well as device and service description templates. In the meantime, it is our intention to add security mechanisms at the application level, integrated with UPnP in a way that does not undermine the underlying protocol.

The security of data and provision on access control is fairly well understood. There are added complications when dealing with the distributed, *ad hoc* nature of a pervasive environment, but again, our architecture is pragmatic in taking a flexible approach that will allow us to start with some fairly basic access control and then add more complex enhancements as components at a later stage. If user data is of a particularly private nature (financial records, for example), then one would have to consider including encryption. It is possible this could be added as a service to the environment. This idea could be extended to a secure off-site managed data repository (see Section 6.4).

6.4   Commercial Opportunities

Current trends in broadband, multimedia, gaming and associated services indicate that equipment service providers want to 'own the home', i.e. provide their proprietary solution such as a gateway device, set-top box, games console, or media server (or some combination of these).

This provision often assumes a PC in the house for use as a software repository and to provide access for configuration. This centralised approach is a long way from the pervasive environment discussed in this paper. Such a proprietary 'lock-in' approach is a familiar feature of an immature market, but is likely to limit growth. Eventually the competing players are forced to co-operate to their mutual benefit and that of the consumer. Our vision is one where the consumer is not tied to one provider, and will want to make technology purchases from diverse suppliers, based more on functionality and price than compatibility issues. They will expect to be able to connect them to their existing environment with little or no detailed configuration required. To facilitate this it is imperative that products are built using open standards and with a commitment to interoperability.

Given this scenario, it is expected that competition will be high to gain a foothold in the home. This lends itself to companies being innovative with value-add products and services that can be delivered to the user, probably over high-speed networks (initially broadband), although some services such as simple remote monitoring would only require narrowband speeds. There are also opportunities for companies to offer management services, which could provide for example remote diagnostics, application updates, and alerts when something requires attention (e.g. by e-mail or SMS).

6.5   Summary

The vision of a pervasive computing environment is an exciting one, giving users the freedom to focus on what they want to do rather than wrestling with technology. It also provides opportunities for a wide range of new products and services, brought about from the liberated nature of a network of devices and sensors that can self-configure, work autonomously, and self-heal. Some people may view this as a threatening vision of technological dominance from which no one can escape and where people become reliant on ever-increasing levels of technical complexity that is beyond their comprehension and become fearful of catastrophic system failure.

We believe that people will value freedom without subservience to technology if we can provide a future environment that is supportive, useful, and unobtrusive. We have focused on the technical challenges in taking the next steps towards our vision and we have considered some of the commercial opportunities that will arise. There is no single grand plan that will provide 'the solution'. We are on an evolutionary and revolutionary road, but one that the authors believe is going to lead to a fundamentally new way in which we interact with technology, information, and each other.

References

1.   Blackwell A F and Hague R. AutoHAN: An Architecture for Programming the Home. Proceedings of the IEEE Symposia on Human-Centric Computing Languages and Environments, 2001:150–157.

2. UPnP — http://www.upnp.org/

3. MIT Project Oxygen — http://oxygen.lcs.mit.edu/

4. Debaty P, Goddi P and Vorbau A. CoolTown: Integrating the Physical World with the Web to Enable Context-Enhanced Services. HP Technical report: HPL-2003-192, December 2003 — http://www.hpl.hp.com/techreports/2003/HPL-2003-192.pdf

5. one.world — Programming for Pervasive Computing Environments. A poster presented at the 18th ACM Symposium on Operating Systems Principles, Chateau Lake Louise, Banff, Canada, October 2001 — http://cs.nyu.edu/rgrimm/one.world/papers/sosp01-poster.pdf

6. DHCP — http://www.dhcp.org/

7. Jini — http://www.sun.com/jini

8. Salutation — http://www.salutation.org/

9. Service location protocol — http://www.ietf.org/html.charters/svrloc-charter.html

10. IrDA — http://www.irda.org/

11. Bluetooth — http://www.bluetooth.com/ — https://www.bluetooth.org

12. HAVi — http://www.havi.org/

13. Preuss S. Efficient Service Discovery in *ad hoc* Networks. Second International IFIP-TC6 Networking Conference: Networking, Pisa, Italy, 2002 — http://wwwtec.informatik.uni-rostock.de/~spr/SpoNet/articles/jsdp.pdf

14. Balazinska M, Balakrishnan H, and Karger D. INS/Twine: A Scalable Peer-to-Peer Architecture for Intentional Resource Discovery. Pervasive 2002, International Conference on Pervasive Computing, Zurich, Switzerland, August 2002.

15. UPnP, Jini and Salutation — A Look at Some Popular Coordination Frameworks for Future Networked Devices. California Software Lab — http://www.cswl.com/whiteppr/tech/upnp.html

16. SNMP — http://www.ietf.org/rfc/rfc1157.txt

17. Weiser M. The Computer of the 21st Century. Scientific American, September 1991:94–100.

18. UPnP Device Security Service Template Specification — http://www.upnp.org/download/devicesecurity093.pdf

7

Traffimatics — Intelligent Co-operative Vehicle Highway Systems

G Bilchev, D Marston, N Hristov, E Peytchev, and N Wall

7.1   Introduction

The increasing demand for transport creates a huge challenge to local and central governments. As it is clear that simply building new roads will not be the answer, optimal transport strategies will be needed. In particular, optimal traffic control will require a lot of supporting infrastructure including road sensors (inductive loops). What if the traffic information were gathered seamlessly by the participating vehicles and sent to the other road participants and to the traffic control centres? This is one of the goals of the Traffimatics project,[1] which aims at investigating the feasibility of such a large-scale vehicle network based on an open telematics architecture.

The term 'telematics' is most commonly used to refer to information and communications technologies related to transport; it includes both the vehicles and the road infrastructure. Transport telematics is not a new area and has been around for many years. The recent hype around telematics is fuelled by the increasing availability of low-cost hardware and software systems (following the '.com' boom) and ubiquitous low-cost communications technologies. The cars have also been evolving, although at a slower pace. Modern cars have a multitude of sensors (traction, light, temperature, and surface sensors, to name a few) and intelligent electronic modules that communicate securely within the in-vehicle network. Currently all that sensor information stays in the car and is not communicated externally. But what if this information could be harnessed, communicated, and interpreted to allow numerous value-added applications that will enhance the driver experience? The idea is not so far-fetched, and several research projects (e.g. BMW Connected Drive) have been set up to investigate its feasibility. Traffimatics is one such project [1], partially funded by the UK Department of Trade and Industry (DTI), that differentiates from similar projects in the area such as CarTalk [2], FleetNet [3], Drive [4], Adase [5], and Chauffeur [6], in that it looks at the problem end-to-end. Traffimatics harnesses the sensor data within the in-vehicle network, analyses the data via the in-vehicle telematics platform, and communicates useful information to the traffic control centre or to a dynamically formed mobile *ad hoc* network of nearby vehicles. In this respect the project is well aligned with the EC funded 6th Framework project GST [7].

[1] A collaboration between BT, Influx Technology, Nottingham Trent University, and Shadow Creek Consulting Ltd, supported by the UK DTI Next Wave Technologies and Markets programme.

This chapter describes the vision of the Traffimatics project and discusses some implementation and business issues. It is organised as follows. Firstly, it describes the vision of the connected car, which is central to Traffimatics. It then focuses on the possible realisations of that vision from looking at the current state-of-the-art of in-vehicle networks, communications technologies, and systems in the traffic control infrastructure, and finally exploring the market issues of such a system.

This chapter is intended as an overview of intelligent co-operative transport solutions based on the connected-car vision. The connected car has two strands of communication, namely car-to-car and car-to-infrastructure. Applications might use either or both modes and might require some sort of continuity of service from one to the other. For example, when a slippery surface is detected, the immediate course of action would be to signal to vehicles nearby, but at the same time the message should also be sent via the road infrastructure to the traffic control centre to take remedial action (as in the case of spillage on the road).

7.2 Vision of Intelligent Co-operative Vehicle Highway Systems

Drivers are isolated from the world around them by the confinements of their vehicle. This kind of isolation is both physical and informational. The latter could perhaps explain the popularity of radio in cars. Radio broadcasts, however, are only one way, with information quite often not pertinent to the particular driver. This information isolation has been reduced to a degree by the popularity of the mobile telephone. However, the use of a hand-held mobile telephone while driving is strongly discouraged. The connected-car vision (Fig. 7.1) aims at improving the driver experience by creating a dynamic information flow that is personalised to the car and the driver. The dynamic information flow could be used to pass sensor information from the vehicles to control centres, thus contributing to optimal traffic control. It can also be used to pass information from one vehicle to another, for example, the scenario where a 'slippery road' warning could be communicated to vehicles behind. The connected-car vision is based on a number of possible scenarios as described below. It should be noted that the vision once established could promote the development of more value-added applications and services not initially envisaged.

The scenarios enabled by the connected-car vision are numerous and beyond the scope of this chapter. The last count of use cases from the Automotive Multimedia Interface Collaboration group (AMI-C [8]) shows no less that 150 instances. Below are only a handful of scenarios that give a flavour of the connected-car vision.

In the context of ambient intelligence and pervasive computing there are a number of vehicle-to-vehicle enabled applications that could improve drivers' and passengers' experience and safety. They can be loosely grouped into the following categories:

- Safety

    When a potentially dangerous traffic event occurs, it could be appropriately communicated to the vehicles nearby. Examples include slippery surface, obstacle ahead, and faulty vehicle. This kind of application would require the

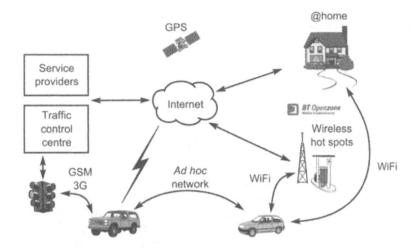

Fig. 7.1   The connected car.

means for reliable communications. This is especially crucial where the car should take an automated decision such as braking. Concept demonstrators of this kind of application exist.

- Traffic control

    These kinds of co-operative vehicle application include automated maintenance of optimal distance between cars as well as local traffic control. Having optimal vehicle distance and speed is critical for the traffic flow as most of the congestions due to sheer volume of traffic occur from 'stop and go' vehicle behaviour. This will also require a reliable means of communication. The local traffic control applications occur when, for example, at non-regulated crossroads, the vehicles communicate locally and take the decision as to who has priority or should give way without having to communicate the data to a central traffic control centre.

- Information related

    The vehicles can be viewed as mobile sensors to gather potentially useful data such as real-time weather conditions, road/surface condition, light conditions, etc.

- Back-seat applications

    These are mainly entertainment applications for passengers such as chat and interactive games.

Apart from applications involving vehicle-to-vehicle interactions, there are a number of useful telematics applications that could be enabled by the Traffimatics platform. Some of these are described here.

A significant percentage of the traffic in a city centre is driving around looking for a parking space. A system that will help drivers to optimally find a parking space will not only reduce their stress levels, but will also save fuel (e.g. cost savings) and will lower pollution levels. This application could be implemented by enabling the cars to communicate with the parking system. Another implementation would be, when a car leaves a parking space, to announce the vacant position to nearby vehicles.

Another feature that will reduce stress levels is the integration of an automated payment system within the car for congestion charging. The introduction of congestion charging will happen independently of whether or not cars have such automated payment systems (e.g. London congestion charging, where tickets are bought over the Internet, by telephone, or at ticket machines).

The availability of an intelligent telematics platform in the car might fuel the development of new applications that could not only help drivers, but also reduce the running costs of maintaining a vehicle. An example would be the possible introduction of 'pay drive' insurance, where premiums are dependent on actual mileage and/or area and time of the day. Another example would be the possibility of remote diagnostics for vehicle trouble codes, where the diagnostics could be run from a remote central car manufacturer site (via a communications channel).

Vehicle manufacturers experience the problem of not having a direct relationship with the customer (once the car leaves the factory, little is known about its history). This could affect customer retention. With the possibility of having a direct channel to the end customers (e.g. drivers), a car manufacturer could experience the benefits of customer relationship management (CRM).

To start with, the connected-car vision will most probably be deployed within high-end vehicles as a market differentiation tool [9]. Such an early deployment could also be as a response to end-user needs to remotely connect to their vehicles (to download MP3 files and latest navigation maps, etc). Connecting other end-user devices such as mobile telephones and PDAs could also create an early need for in-vehicle wireless connection.

Once the connected car becomes a reality, it will take a life of its own by generating a new market for intra-vehicle and inter-vehicle applications. One application that has often been talked about is the so-called 'platoon driving' as mentioned above. It involves an automated distributed co-ordination between cars to form 'vehicle trains' on the road, thus optimising the distance between vehicles and traffic flow. Although such an application might seem a bit futuristic, the state-of-the-art technologies that could enable it exist right now.

7.3   Vision Implementation

This section deals with the state-of-the-art technologies that could enable the Traffimatics vision. It starts with an overview of the in-vehicle intelligence and in-vehicle networks. It shows that a lot of effort and work has already been done in this space and identifies the lack of industry-wide agreed common (single) standards as the major barrier for the take-up of telematics services, and overviews recent progress in standardisation activities. The section continues with an indication of available and upcoming wireless communications technologies and open in-vehicle telematics platforms. Finally, technologies in the infrastructure are briefly outlined.

7.3.1   In-Vehicle Intelligence

Modern vehicles are equipped with various sensors and electronic control units (ECUs) that control and monitor the engine, the transmission, the multimedia and almost all the major controls in the vehicle. These sensors and management systems are interlinked by a series of in-vehicle buses:

- one challenge for Traffimatics is to identify the nature of the information that is circulating within the vehicle for traditional purposes, and to mine this for information that can be used for other purposes, e.g. what can an intelligent vehicle infer from the fact that the turn right indicator has been operated, or that the windscreen wipers are operating;

- a second challenge is to recognise trends, in order to identify possible new sources of information that will produce valuable information in the future.

An example of a module is the global navigation satellite system (GNSS) receiver. If this is integrated as a module, rather than a component buried within a stand-alone system, it will deliver significant benefits, particularly if it can be linked to an internal map-matching system. Such a system would introduce the capability to establish a geographical context for the information that is being passed over in-vehicle buses. For example, if the vehicle stabilisation logic operates while driving at a sensible speed round a roundabout, then this could raise an alert that a diesel spillage was suspected. Similarly an alert could be produced by a car that is stationary behind a blind corner, in order to warn any cars approaching the corner. These services are dependent upon knowledge of geographical context.

There are several motivations for the introduction of GNSS modules within vehicles:

- the likelihood of the introduction of road user charging, based on actual routes taken and time of travel will require the use of GNSS;

- the introduction of the European Galileo GNSS planned for 2008 will overcome many of the limitations of the current GPS service [10], giving a much more reliable service.

The vision of a modular telematics platform depends upon the adoption of an appropriate open architecture. One of the underlying parts of the architecture is the ability to establish interconnection of the various modules.

7.3.2   In-Vehicle Communications

In recent years there has been a trend in the automotive industry of continuous growth in the variety and complexity of the electronic components used in the vehicle. The development time nowadays is much shorter with the introduction of rapid prototyping. At the same time the requirement for emission control is increasing every year, which creates many problems for the calibration and diagnostic engineers. To resolve some of these problems, the engineers are adding more processing power — electronic control units and intelligent sensors. This introduced the problem of making all the modules in the vehicle act as one system. To resolve this problem, in-vehicle networks were developed.

Currently the in-vehicle networks are classified by speed — mainly specified by the Society of the Automotive Engineers (SAE) [11]. SAE specifies class A, B, and C in-vehicle networks. Class A specifies the low-speed networks that are used for communication between the vehicle assembly units such as doors, seats, climate control, etc. Class B is used for general-purpose information communication and class

C for real-time control. An example of a class C network is CAN (controller area network) [12], the most commonly used network in the industry at present. CAN is a network that supports speeds up to 1 Mbit/s, but is mainly used at 500 kbit/s. In many cases CAN is used as a class A network as well as class B on lower speeds (125 kbit/s or 250 kbit/s). This classification currently is not exactly accurate, because the introduction of more and more electronic control units was followed by increases of speed of the in-vehicle networks.

With the introduction of X-by-wire (drive by wire, steer-by-wire, brake-by-wire, etc), the requirements for error tolerance and time-determinism of message transmission have increased. This led to the huge interest of the automotive industry in the time-triggered architecture (TTA). The TTA is a distributed, composable architecture for the implementation of fault-tolerant, real-time systems. Its main advantage is the common knowledge in each bus node of every other node's transmission time. TTA will mainly be used in safety-critical applications.

TTA protocols currently developed or are under development are:

- TTP/C — a proven time-triggered bus protocol for fault-tolerant automotive applications that meets the SAE requirements for a class C automotive protocol (TTP/C is driven by the TTA Group);

- FlexRay [13] — a relatively young bus protocol driven and specified by the FlexRay Consortium, research work for which is ongoing;

- TTCAN (time triggered controller area network) — a time-triggered protocol based on CAN physical layer and driven by Bosch and the CiA (CAN in Automation), providing mechanisms for time-triggered as well as event-triggered CAN messages.

A separate class of networks that is being integrated in modern vehicles is the multimedia network. The standard bus — USB, IDB-1394 [14], Ethernet, and the automotive-specific MOST (media oriented systems transport) [15] — networks are used as vehicle multimedia bus solutions. Optimised for automotive applications, MOST is a multimedia fibre optic network. The applications for MOST networks can be devices such as radios, video displays, navigation systems, amplifiers, and others. Some of the key features of MOST networks are ease of use, speeds up to 24.8 Mbit/s, support of synchronous and asynchronous data transfer, multiple masters, and support of up to 64 devices.

All these networks make the task of acquiring data from the vehicle much simpler using telematics systems or by connecting directly to the specific network. The sensors in the vehicle supply information about the engine management system, anti-lock braking system (ABS), transmission system — this information can be useful in traffic control centres, or vehicles nearby. Self-diagnostics is something that can increase the safety significantly by supplying diagnostic information to the service centres.

Another major task of the Co-operative Vehicle Highway System (CVHS) is developing and adopting standards. The authorities in the USA and Europe together with some international organisations have been working on the definition of standards in the areas of diagnostics, calibration, measuring equipment, telematics, and multimedia. In the automotive world, ASAM (Association of Standardisation of Automation and Measuring Systems) has specified many standards adopted by the majority of the car manufacturers and their suppliers. Currently there are many different standards in this area, but ASAM was able to come up with solutions in many areas that are adopted by more and more automotive companies around the world.

Another organisation that is developing standards for the automotive industry is AMI-C [8], which has developed a vehicle interface API (application programming interface) for use in telematics systems. Currently the Traffimatics project is developing a system that will use the AMI-C vehicle interface API for communication with vehicle networks. Part of the role of such a vehicle interface API is to also act as a firewall between the mission-critical in-vehicle network and the telematics system. Without such a firewall, security could be compromised. In a recent demonstration within the Traffimatics project, a denial-of-service attack was shown on an in-vehicle CAN network, where the lack of a firewall made it possible to flood the CAN network with messages, effectively shutting down the engine management system.

Once accessed, the in-vehicle sensor data needs to be communicated outside the vehicle. The next section looks at the technologies that could be used to achieve that.

7.3.3   Communicating Vehicles

The concept of a communicating vehicle is central to the vision of the Traffimatics project. A communicating vehicle is a vehicle capable of collecting data about the condition of itself and of the road, and of communicating this data both to other vehicles travelling on the road network, and to the infrastructure of the traffic control systems. These inter-vehicle and vehicle-to-infrastructure communications have a variety of applications

In order for this to happen, open communications networks are needed and the Traffimatics project aims to investigate the requirements for communicating vehicles, and to propose solutions meeting those requirements, considering the available communications technologies. The project also aims to develop scenarios in which communicating vehicles may add value both to individual vehicle drivers, and to management of traffic as a whole.

A number of communications technologies are under consideration for the vehicle environment, ranging from standard, widely available communications solutions (IEEE802.11b, GPRS, Bluetooth) to specifically designed vehicle communications systems (Mesh-Networks [16], etc). A comparison of the features of these communications technologies is given in Table 7.1.

It is important also to note that the suitability of a given communications technology depends not only on the pure technological characteristics of that technology, but also on the business implications of the technology. The cost of a given technology is vitally important when considering a system designed for widespread deployment in both vehicles, and in the roadside infrastructure.

The level of coverage also plays a major factor in the choice of technology for a ubiquitous telematics network; if a communications system can be designed that makes use of networks already widely deployed, or in the process of being deployed, a significant proportion of the up-front cost of the network can be removed. This particularly points towards the suitability of GPRS as a network with very wide coverage, and increasingly to 802.11 (WiFi) as the deployment of wireless hotspots increases.

Table 7.1   Wireless technologies.

Technology	Max data rate	Range	Data cost	Ubiquity
WiFi (802.11a/b/g)	54 Mbit/s	400 m	Low	Widespread
WiMax (802.16)	10 to 100 Mbit/s	1 to 50 km		Not yet available
MobileFi (802.20)	16 Mbit/s	Tens of km		Not yet available
SMS	28 bit/s^2	Tens of km	Very high	Widespread
GPRS	50 kbit/s	Tens of km	High	Widespread
3G	~128 kbit/s^3	Tens of km	High	Becoming widespread
RDS	~730 bit/s	Tens of km	Low	Widespread
DAB	32 kbit/s	Tens of km	Low	Becoming widespread

The requirements for inter-vehicle communications and vehicle-to-infrastructure communications are largely similar, but do have some subtle differences. The inter-vehicle communications pose some unique problems as the vehicles to which the communications will be directed will only be chosen based on their physical location (in proximity to a given point), rather than through any knowledge of the vehicle's identity. This differs from the vehicle-to-infrastructure communications, which will largely be used to send messages from a vehicle to a fixed network address, or from the infrastructure to an identified vehicle. These differences are summarised in Table 7.2.

Table 7.2   Differences between inter-vehicle and vehicle-to-infrastructure communications requirements.

Inter-vehicle	Vehicle to infrastructure
Dynamic routing	Fixed routing
Ad hoc network	Fixed network
Short to medium range	Medium to long range

The communications technologies chosen for inclusion in a vehicle networking system also depend on the requirements of the applications to be deployed across the network. These applications will present a number of different requirements on the cost, speed, and availability of the communications. An urgent safety message for example is likely to require a high availability communications channel, with the cost of the message being of lesser importance.

An interesting question is what level of mobility support will be required by such a telematics system. Mobile IP [17] could be used if the level of mobility required is high. This could involve seamless handover between multiple networks. If the required mobility support is low, then reliable sockets [18] could be sufficient. Using

---

[2] An SMS has 140 bytes and it usually takes 4–5 sec for delivery.

[3] Theoretical data rate is 2 Mbit/s but in practice, for a moving client, this will be less.

reliable sockets, IP connections could be suspended and then resumed. This could be very useful with WiFi technologies as currently hotspots could be miles apart. WiFi is also a good candidate for the short range and *ad hoc* applications.

One possible use of this capability is at traffic lights (assuming the traffic light is WiFi enabled) where a queue of Traffimatics-equipped vehicles will be able to notify the traffic control centre of the number of vehicles waiting, removing the need for expensive embedded loops in the road. The information gained from the vehicles can also include details such as turn indicator activation, giving the traffic management system more information than it could have gained previously using only the road sensors. The next section looks at state-of-the art technologies for traffic control.

7.3.4   Programming Paradigms and Platforms

The lack of agreed standards regarding the in-vehicle software and hardware platforms has been one of the major factors delaying the widespread implementation of telematics solutions. This gap has been recognised by most car manufacturers and several consortia have been formed aiming at defining standard interfaces (APIs) and architectures.

Of particular significance is the AMI-C [8] group, which has recently published release 2 of its specification. The specification has selected OSGi (Open Services Gateway Initiative) [19] as the software platform, which is based on Java and thus is OS independent. One of the major APIs AMI-C has developed is the vehicle gateway API, which defines a standard way of interfacing into the vehicle management system. The idea of the vehicle gateway is to act as a firewall between the telematics platform and the vehicle management system, separating the proprietary in-vehicle systems from the telematics platform. In such a way third parties could develop OSGi bundles communicating with the vehicle in a vehicle-independent manner.

Regarding operating systems for in-vehicle telematics platforms, there are several competing solutions. Microsoft's automotive solution [20] is based on their .NET platform. Linux embedded has also been used in vehicle environments and references could be found on the Linux Devices Web site [21]. Some of the disadvantages of the above operating systems stem from the fact that they have not been designed as real-time operating systems, which might be desirable in some in-vehicle applications. In such situations, QNX [22] is a popular OS in the automotive sector.

The Traffimatics concept relies on the creation of a common architecture that will deliver a multi-application telematics platform. The common architecture requires standards to be developed to enable all components to be multi-sourced. It also requires the adoption of a system firmware that enables new applications to be downloaded on to the platform.

International standards are being established in Europe by CEN 278, and in ISO TC204. These two organisations are now collaborating closely and have a wide range of working groups in order that each has clear terms of reference. Even so, there are standardisation activities outside this structure, for example, urban traffic management and control (UTMC) is being standardised in isolation. Without an overall architecture, system integration will be far from plug and play.

7.3.5   Intelligence in the Infrastructure

It is widely recognised that the demand-responsive control gives best results as far as the traffic management and control is concerned. In this respect the UK started to develop and introduce demand-responsive urban traffic control (UTC) systems such as MOVA and SCOOT 20 years ago. These systems are now being upgraded to the UTMC (urban traffic management and control) standard, which uses IP-based communications and protocols. SCOOT remains central to the operation of traffic control. SCOOT derives its name from the description of its functionality — split, cycle-time, and offset optimisation technique, where:

- split is the ratio of time allocated to each direction of travel — the ratio can be varied where there is heavy traffic in one direction, perhaps after a football match;

- cycle-time is the time to go round the complete sequence — in heavy traffic it is more efficient to allow fairly long green periods, whereas in light traffic conditions a short cycle time will enable all the cars in a queue to pass through the lights, and will ensure that vehicles encountering a red light have to wait the minimum time before it changes to green;

- an offset from an adjacent junction can be set so that 'green waves' can be established, with traffic leaving the first set of lights, travelling within the speed limit, arriving at the next set of lights as they change to green, allowing a very efficient flow in that direction.

It has been widely accepted that traffic control should centre on systems like SCOOT and the development of a unified way of coping with the traffic congestion problems. This has initiated the development of a set of standards, protocols and concept demonstrators known as UTMC. UTMC is a set of effective traffic management tools which supports a wider range of policies than are served by existing UTC systems, thus encouraging competition, innovation and growth in the international intelligent transport systems market-place.

The aim of this initiative is not only to open up the communications framework in which the traffic information can be exchanged freely and seamlessly, but also to provide the overall architecture of the system. In such an architecture there will be many different applications, each providing different services and ultimately providing this traffic information to other users and applications.

The UTMC approach specifically accommodates the exchange of information between systems and supports centralising intelligence or distributing the intelligence around a system. The UTMC architecture enables maximum design flexibility and an overview is presented in Fig. 7.2.

In this overall view the place of the Traffimatics project is within the 'in-vehicle comms' block, 'Internet services' block, and 'other systems and services' block. Traffic control centres around the country are deploying increasingly sophisticated traffic management systems based on advanced information technology. In parallel the amount of electronics within vehicles is increasing rapidly. Bridging these two strands of development will be beneficial for traffic control. Linking the intelligence in the vehicle with that controlling the roadside devices is the function of co-operative vehicle highway systems (CVHSs). Such a bridge could be formed by using mobile communications technology to allow individual vehicles to communicate with the roadside infrastructure and other vehicles. Simple versions of

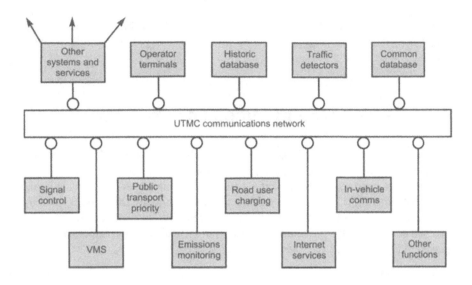

Fig. 7.2   UTMC — overall view.

a CVHS are already with us, where 'probe vehicles' send data on traffic conditions back to a central processing point to give drivers information to make their journeys safer and more efficient. Another example is where information on any traffic hold-ups is digitally transmitted to a vehicle via the radio data service traffic message channel (RDS-TMC) and automatically interpreted by a navigation system within the vehicle. This can advise the driver of potential delays or even offer an alternative route. In parallel with this vision, the exchange of traffic information in the Traffimatics project is no longer a feature only of the infrastructure. The communication is entrusted to the in-car devices and these devices communicate with each other to decide the type and amount of information that needs to be sent to the traffic control centre. In this task the in-car devices can choose between communicating over an *ad hoc* network, UTMS (3G) or GPRS (2.5G), thus making use of all available communications technologies, as previously discussed.

The Traffimatics vision for the future of the traffic control is summarised in Fig. 7.3, where several *ad hoc* networks exchange data and take part actively in the traffic control.

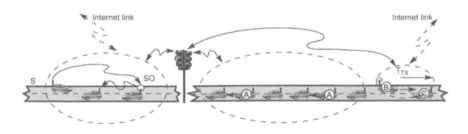

Fig. 7.3   New generation traffic control systems will use a telematics framework for delivering traffic information and control — floating vehicle networks control.

The Traffimatics project aims to lay the foundation for future investigations of *ad hoc* networks formed by urban traffic becoming one global vehicle network, and to consider the routing of such information in the urban global vehicle network (UGVN).

7.4   Market Opportunities and Barriers

The promise of an emerging mass market for the diverse range of intelligent transport system (ITS) services has existed for more than 10 years. While a number of ITS products and services have been developed, the market is far from achieving its expected potential. We need to understand the nature of the market, and the barriers to achieving its potential, if the benefits from the Traffimatics project are to be realised commercially. Our analysis shows four critical success factors, which are discussed in the following sections:

- establishment of market demand;

- proven real benefits;

- delivery of cost-effective systems;

- creation of an open architecture/platform to allow new services to be added at very low incremental cost.

7.4.1   Market Demand

There is a lack of confidence in the consumer demand for many of the ITS services. This is largely because the many benefits are not appreciated, and some early systems have, perhaps, fallen short of consumer expectation. However, there is strong demand where systems meet specific government objectives. This has resulted in the fragmentation of the market, with clear focus on the specific, but isolated, opportunities with the strongest market drivers. The main drivers are described below.

- Government legislation

  Government may mandate the adoption of ITSs, or establish a framework to enable its introduction. Relevant legislation might include:

  — the introduction of the new customs and excise lorry road use charge;

  — the inevitable introduction of wide area road user charging;

  — eCall capability;

  — eTachographs;

  — eDriving licences and electronic vehicle identification (EVI).

  Additionally, government may legislate to allow new services, for example, the enabling legislation for the Trafficmaster traffic information service.

- Cost reduction

  Motor manufacturers have replaced traditional wiring looms with local controllers at light clusters, doors, etc, which are interconnected by a CAN bus and power. This change has been made to reduce the costs of development, production, fault location, fault rates, and repairs.

- Support of government policy

  Policy, such as encouraging modal shift to the use of public transport, is often supported by grants for specific actions such as increasing the usefulness of public transport information.

  In the UK, local authorities are responsible for the introduction of UTMC and real-time passenger information. They submit a five yearly local transport plan (LTP), based on guidance from the Department for Transport (DfT). Funds are released according to the approved LTP.

- Maximise value from current assets

  Road capacity needs to be designed to handle the peak traffic demand. Any technique that reduces the peak demand, e.g. by peak spreading, reduces the need to construct more capacity. Peak congestion should be reduced with benefit to all road users. Dynamic road user charging (RUC) will create a powerful motivator for behaviour changes. Current techniques include the use of variable message signs to advise drivers to use specific routes. More advanced techniques are needed to give advance notice of problems to allow drivers to make sensible route choices.

- Product differentiation

  Car manufacturers need to build in product differentiation from other makes and within their own ranges. To date, manufacturers have introduced ITS functionality in a way that enables them to test the market. ITSs will become an increasingly important differentiator. While this also introduces a barrier to those ITS applications that rely upon universal availability, it is an essential stage in developing best practice and proving the business cases.

- Customer demand

  There is little evidence of customer demand for travel information services. Focus group members like the ideas in the ITS vision, but do not perceive the true value, and therefore do not expect to pay very much for ITS services.

7.4.2   Proven Real Benefits

It is essential that ITSs demonstrate real benefits. In practice, the benefits from ITS services do not always flow back to the investor, because of the complex set of interactions between stakeholders and users of these systems. For example, analysis of the benefits from installing centrally controlled traffic signals shows that payback can be within three months. However, the benefits are widely distributed, and no additional revenues flow back to the local authority that has paid for the system. This is a recurring problem — the value to society needs to be measured, and given as a grant from central government, but this is unacceptable when cost has to be seen to be kept under control, resulting in roll-out being slower than it might be.

7.4.3   Cost Effectiveness of Systems

A major barrier to the roll-out of ITS services is the high capital and revenue cost of operating the systems. The cost of telecommunications is one of the most significant expenses in current systems. In fixed networks we see a (long overdue) move from the use of analogue private circuits to IP networks. The final 100 metres to the roadside equipment still remains a problem, with underground cabling to be installed. Wireless LAN technology offers a potential solution here. Wireless LANs, operated in an *ad hoc* mode, also offer the potential to substitute the bulk of the data that would otherwise be carried over the GSM mobile network. In practice, the cost may reduce to a few percent of the cost of using GPRS. The use of *ad hoc* networks has the potential to transform previously impossible business cases into attractive mass-market propositions.

7.4.4   Creation of an Open Platform

We have established that there is a limited number of specific ITS services where there is a strong demand, with many more ideas where the business case is unproved. Given this situation, the most effective way to launch these new services is to ensure that those systems with a firm requirement and business case are designed and implemented in such a way that the systems implementations are also able to support those services where the demand is limited. This leads to the creation of an open platform that will provide core capability once, for all the applications. There should be:

- one global navigation satellite service (GNSS) position determining system;
- one human/machine interface (resolving the conflict when several applications need to communicate with the driver);
- a single configuration management system that allows new applications to be downloaded without any hardware changes;
- one set of communications systems (note that the introduction of an ultra-low-cost *ad hoc* networking capability will not satisfy all the communications needs) — there also needs to be a GSM or 3G capability, which will offer a much higher level of availability for applications that need an immediate assured connection.

The Traffimatics project has adopted an approach that should deliver these critical success factors.

Research, such as simulations from the FleetNet project, suggests that data from only a low percentage of cars (e.g. ~5%) is sufficient to provide the data for a Traffimatics system to achieve the full benefits of real-time dynamic traffic information. While technically it is possible today to develop such a system, the barriers against its wide-scale deployment stem from the multi-faceted telematics-stakeholders profile. As a result, no clear business model could be agreed, with no one seeming to be prepared to take the risk. Therefore, the initial deployment of such a system might come as a result of EU or national government legislation that will introduce intelligent 'black boxes' in the vehicles. A potential candidate is the tolling black box, which is already being introduced in parts of Europe for commercial vehicles. The black boxes could be capable of running value-added services and evolve towards the vision of the Traffimatics system. However, these may be implemented in a closed way, unless there is a motivation to adopt an open architecture. Another possible deployment scenario is driven by car manufacturers and customer demand for safety, entertainment, and navigation services. This is already happening in the USA [23] and Japan [24]. The biggest barrier to this deployment scenario is the lack of an overall architecture and agreed standards. Current initiatives, most notably the AMI-C [8], are addressing some of these issues. The problem, however, lies in the fact that car manufacturers are somewhat slow at implementing these interfaces, partly due to the different life cycles of vehicle and computer system development.

7.5   Summary

Traffimatics is taking an end-to-end view of CVHS applications. The project has established that the Traffimatics concept is capable of providing novel CVHS applications that make use of existing in-vehicle sensors and communications systems that were provided for other purposes via the in-vehicle CAN networks.

Work to establish whether *ad hoc* wireless LAN technology has the potential to be used as a viable alternative to 2G and 3G mobile services continues. It is too early to draw conclusions from the experiments performed to date. There are, however, applications that required local short-range communications, where *ad hoc* networks are the most promising technology.

Traffimatics is intended to operate as a proof-of-concept activity. Further work is needed to develop and exploit the principles established. We believe that work started in Traffimatics should be carried forward to establish a top-level architecture that will provide a linkage between the diverse standardisation activities.

If an open modular platform architecture similar to that proposed by Traffimatics is not adopted, then it is likely that early 'killer applications' like road usage charging will be implemented using closed designs. In that case the systems will not be able to support the wide range of novel applications that could be envisaged. An open platform is needed to support unproven ITS and CVHS applications, allowing them to be implemented economically.

References

1. Traffimatics — http://traffimatics.org/

2. CarTalk — http://www.cartalk2000.net/

3. FleetNet —http://www.informatik.uni-mannheim.de/informatik/pi4/projects/FleetNet/

4. Drive — http://www.ist-drive.org/index2.html

5. Adase — http://www.adase2.net/

6. Chauffeur — http://www.chauffeur2.net/

7. GST — http://www.ertico.com/activiti/projects/gst/home.htm

8. Automotive Multimedia Interface Collaboration (AMI-C) — http://www.ami-c.org/

9. BMW ConnectedDrive — http://www.bmw.com/generic/com/en/fascination/technology/connecteddrive/

10. ITS-UK — http://www.its-focus.org.uk/

11. Society of the Automotive Engineers (SAE) — http://www.sae.org/servlets/index/

12. Controller Area Network (CAN) — http://www.canopen.org/

13. FlexRay — http://www.flexray-group.com/index.php

14. IDB-1394 — http://www.firewire-1394.com/what_is_idb-1394.htm

15. MOST — http://www.mostcooperation.com/

16. MeshNetworks — http://www.meshnetworks.com/

17. MobileIP — http://www.ietf.org/html.charters/mobileip-charter.html

18. Reliable sockets (rocks) — http://www.cs.wisc.edu/~zandy/rocks/

19. OSGi — http://www.osgi.org/

20. Microsoft Automotive — http://www.microsoft.com/automotive/

21. Linux Devices — http://linuxdevices.com/

22. QNX — http://www.qnx.com/

23. OnStar — http://www.onstar.com/

24. G-Book — http://g-book.com/pc/

8

Mixed-Reality Applications in Urban Environments

J Bulman, B Crabtree, A Gower, A Oldroyd, and J Sutton

8.1   Introduction

Pervasive computing covers the management of many distributed sensor and information networks. If these need to interact with the user at the point of information collection, then there will be a need for some kind of interface between the information and the user of that information. We have been exploring the use of virtual and augmented reality techniques in a number of applications to enhance the real world with additional, contextually relevant information. In this respect we have been looking more at the issues concerned with representing information in this mixed-reality world, rather than the particular source of the content. In this way we are neutral with respect to pervasive computing where the information producers are distributed in the world and therefore local to their point of use. In our applications we gather all the information centrally to be processed. This allows the information to be analysed and relevant material shown at the point of use. In most cases this will be locally relevant, but there may be more general information presented. Figure 8.1 shows the kind of information filtering that might occur to reduce the amount of information that is presented in a mixed-reality environment.

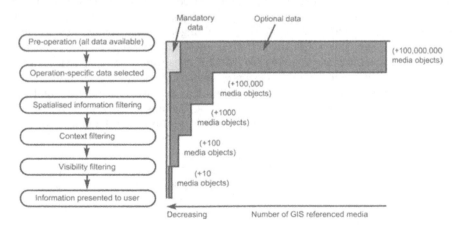

Fig. 8.1   Information filtering.

The effect is a funnel — all the information is 'poured' in at the top, and only the relevant information is left at the end. We could take as an example giving information about London buses — pre-operational would give us all information about every London bus. Operation-specific filtering might restrict this to buses that are routed to the particular destination. Spatial filtering would then limit the buses to those in the vicinity. Context filtering would further limit the selection to those buses going directly to the destination. So from starting off with information about all the London buses, we would only display information about the nearest bus that is heading in the correct direction. Typically in this kind of environment it is important to reduce the amount of information displayed to that needed just for the task in hand, as the information is likely to be displayed on a low-resolution device, or possibly by audio or touch, depending on the application.

8.2   3D Virtual-Reality and Mixed-Reality Scene Rendering

Unlike virtual reality (VR), which provides the user with a completely computer-generated environment, mixed-reality systems (sometimes referred to as augmented reality) enhance a user's perception of the real world by seamlessly merging computer generated text, 2D images, 3D models, and audio with the user's real-world view. The motivation behind developing a mixed-reality system is that existing visual and spatial skills can be utilised, thereby enhancing interaction with, and comprehension of, spatialised information.

The rest of this chapter describes three very different applications that use virtual- and mixed-reality views of information, and discusses some of the issues involved with presenting that material. The first, and most mature, application[1] is a mixed-reality location-based game involving co-operative game play in urban environments. Typically there is a mix between mobile players with hand-held devices and desk or home-based players who have access to a much richer environment. The second application covers an industrial workforce management application where we are exploring provision of contextually relevant material to network repair engineers who need to visit customer premises for their job. We provide information about the job, routing of cabling and nearby faults to assist them in their work. The final application is based on a current project for the defence sector. The project is focused on the provision of enhanced situational awareness to ground forces and command and control personnel using multiple-fused information and data sources. A key issue within this work is the use of a 3D geographical information system (GIS) that enables a common spatialised reference model to be used by mobile users and command-and-control operatives for the generation and provision of information.

All of these applications have been developed using an enhanced version of BT's real-time rendering architecture, TARA (total abstract rendering architecture), to underpin all the 3D visualisations in this work. TARA requires the following pieces of information to generate mixed-reality visualisations:

- a live camera feed of the real-world scene;

- the position, orientation, and field of view of the real-world camera;

---

[1] This application underwent trials in BT during December 2003.

- a 3D model of the real-world scene;
- a 3D model of the virtual-world scene.

Given these pieces of information, the mixed-reality visualisation is created using the following steps:

- an image is captured from the live camera feed and used to fill the colour buffer;
- the 3D model of the real-world scene is rendered into the depth buffer using the position, orientation, and field of view of the real-world camera — this provides occlusion information to items subsequently rendered but has no visual impact on the final image;
- the 3D model of the virtual-world scene is rendered into the frame buffer using the position, orientation, and field of view of the real-world camera.

8.3　Pervasive Gaming — Gaming in Urban Environments

In pervasive gaming,[2] the majority of current games enables players to interact with each other and game content using hand-held and fixed devices, in different locations and in unusual social contexts.

The games differ greatly in terms of format and use of the physical environment. Its Alive!'s 'Bot Fighters' [1] is a location-based 'shoot-em-up' game using cellular location to identify players in the same zone, and text messaging as the primary interface for fighting. Newt Games's 'Mogi' [2] provides map interfaces available on both mobile telephones and fixed PCs to enable players to find, collect, and trade virtual creatures at specific locations. These two games are developed to enable casual game-play over a long period of time.

Other games rely on more co-operative play and draw the local environment into the game as a mental or physical challenge. In Blast Theory's 'Can You See Me Now' [3], players on the streets of a city hunt virtual players who navigate a 3D replica of the game space. The street players are equipped with a map interface on a PDA that displays the virtual location of the on-line players. GPS tracks the location of the street players and sends that location information to the virtual player's PC interface. This kind of game format requires players to have a mutual understanding of each other's situation, which means sharing information about location and context, and players being able to communicate with each other at appropriate times. At the same time, to make the game more challenging, information needs to be managed and sometimes deliberately contain uncertainty to keep players engaged [4].

Systems also need to be able to adapt to unpredictable situations, which can include network failure, unusual player behaviour or missed cues in the game environment. In Blast Theory's 'Uncle Roy All Around You' developed in collaboration with the Nottingham University's Mixed Reality Lab, BT, and UCL, the pervasive game is mixed with theatre and involves actors interacting with players

---

[2] Cross-platform gaming on fixed and mobile networks with multiple real-time players. Games may be embedded into the physical environment and contain added TV, movie, and music hooks.

at specific staged locations (see Fig. 8.2). These critical interactions depend on players and actors being in the right place, and on schedule [5].

Fig. 8.2   Uncle Roy All Around You — a street player, in an office, and meeting an actor.

In order to support a range of game formats in pervasive gaming, we have developed an infrastructure that can support multiple game modules over fixed and mobile networks, including broadband, GPRS, and WiFi. To add more functionality to the server, a game management system has been added, which enables the management of complex media streams and real-time communications not only between fixed and mobile players, but also between game managers and players. These two systems have undergone trials in a team-building event, which we call 'Encounter 1.0'.

8.3.1   Encounter 1.0

Encounter 1.0 was held in November 2003 in and around BT Centre, St Paul's, London (see Fig. 8.3). Within the event four teams of three were invited to compete in an hour-long challenge. The challenge was for each team to collect intelligence about the area, identify and locate key targets, and recreate photographs received from 'control'. Finally, they were required to return to base with the correct data from the correct location. The winning team had the most accurate information, and more intelligence collected.

Fig. 8.3   Encounter 1.0 — the game area mapped into a 3D environment.

To enable players to have a specific role targeted to each device, location, and network connection, the infrastructure has been designed to marshal information between four classes of client — spectator, administration, street, and virtual.

The spectator client is limited in functionality. Conceived as a secondary overview interface, this can be used to track the progress of each team in the game by anyone with access to the viewer. Typically displaying a rich 3D environment with avatars, the scene is updated with the current location of all the players in the streets. Cameras can be attached to the avatars and to key areas, and spectators can navigate through the space themselves. Spectators are able to replay games as logged by the server. In the future it is planned for spectators to take on a role in the game, adding obstacles or bonus challenges.

The virtual client is a media-rich broadband client the team leader uses to track player location, uncover location-specific media on a map, and receive streaming video, audio, and images. The client enables asynchronous communication with the street players using text messaging and can also sustain real-time audio connections. This player commands the team and gives them the background to achieve the goals (see Fig. 8.4). Messages are also received from 'control' and non-player character (NPC) game characters.

Fig. 8.4   Encounter 1.0 — team leaders guiding their teams through the challenges.

The street client is a very thin client that to date runs on a PDA, with GPRS/WiFi and GPS. Varying amounts of information are available on the PDA, including maps, video, and images. The more limited this information, the more communication is required between the team members in the game to achieve the goals. Communication can happen in two ways — text input (which is difficult on the move) or audio (using upload of segments via GPRS or streaming via WiFi) (Fig. 8.5).

Fig. 8.5   Encounter 1.0 — teams on the streets competing to get to target locations.

The most complex group of clients belongs to the administration class. These clients consist of a media mark-up interface, a player administration interface, and an agent interface. The mark-up interface enables a game manager to create location targets on a map and associate media clips with them before and during the game. As street players reach locations the associated media clips are triggered. The player administration interface is used by the managers during the game to communicate with all players, to change target locations on the fly, and change the game status. The agent interface clones street player functionality creating a series of NPCs in the game.

The following methods were used to gather user data from Encounter 1.0:

• audio and data logs;

• an observer dedicated to each team on the street;

• an observer for the team leader game zone;

• a group feedback session at the end of the game.

8.3.2   Playing the Game

To run the event, only a sub-set of the system features was employed. A breakdown of GPRS on the event day required us to adapt the system within a few hours. Street players were given a PDA with all the data for the game held locally rather than remotely — these consisted of maps with target locations and images of the target. They were also equipped with a mobile telephone that connected them to their team leader via audio conference, and a digital camera to capture data. GPS data was downloaded locally to the PDA.

Each street team observer tracked the teams in the field and reported location directly to the management team. Position data was updated on the server using the administration tools. In this way street player positions were updated on the control player's interface continually throughout the game. Neither team leaders nor street players were aware the process was manual.

Team leaders received instructions via text messages on their game interface. On a map they were given a target location, could see their team's current location and images of the target photograph they needed the team to recreate. A pin number would be sent to them to relay to their team colleagues. Entering the pin into the PDA released another media clue for the street players. Team leaders would guide their teams to the location, where the team recreated the photograph clue. Observers would verify the goal was achieved and the next clue sent to the team leader.

There were over 15 locations to achieve within the hour-long game. As street players went from location to location, their movements triggered media clips on the team-leader's interface — classed as intelligence. Points were awarded for each clip released. The more of the game zone covered, the more intelligence is gathered. Teams able to find locations quickly were handicapped on the fly by the management team, who could change the order of targets to those farthest apart. Weaker teams could be led to more media-rich areas to enhance their score.

8.3.3   Feedback from Game Participants and Administrators

The results of the game were very positive from an experience point of view. The teams were highly competitive and the nature of the game gave the players different levels of competition. On return to base, all images were downloaded and numerical targets compared — accuracy of image reproduction could be rewarded.

Players responded very well to the always-on audio contact within the team. As well as the competitive nature of the game leading to sense of speed and urgency, the audio allowed constant feedback between team members. In contrast to 'Uncle Roy All Around You', in which communication is asynchronous and somewhat ambiguous, the audio conference allowed for clear direction and spontaneous chat.

Street players were frustrated by too much information on the PDA. Having a map removed some of the challenge in finding the target locations and removed some of the dependency on the team leader, who also had a map. For these players the more ambiguous the data, the more exciting the game became.

Team leaders were not immediately aware of the significance of the media clips being released and were less interested in where the players had been than where they were going to. They requested that clips appear near target locations as additional clues for guiding their players to the location. In a sense the concept that this could be media being streamed from the street players was lost in this particular game format.

Verification of achieving a target or mission was another issue. Team leaders requested that they could verify that the image had been taken and thus have the next clue automatically. Having the observers relay the information to the management team was an overhead and caused some time delays. Team leaders also requested that they could see the image taken by their team and judge its accuracy in real time, and perhaps directing them more closely.

Game administrators had many of the tools they needed, except for the ability to set up a sequence of targets in advance for the system to work through automatically. All game decisions were made in real time, which required constant communication between observers and administrators. This is not a scalable model, GPRS issues aside, and results have been fed back into the tool-set.

8.3.4   Discussion and Further Work

One of the main results from our trial is how we deal with unpredictability in the network. Our aim is to move over completely to WiFi, in which users can play stand-alone elements (capture data, look up local data on the client machine) and then move to interactive hotspots. The hotspots would allow reliable streaming and communication at specific points. Users could drop data in these locations for others to pick up without the need to deploy extended mesh networks.

Secondly, more research is needed to define the feature sets for managing content on each client interface. Content is specific to the kind of experience you wish each user to have, and is not necessarily the same data, repacked for each player or device. It is possible to imagine that street players receive information about an area that is vastly different from that which the team leaders have.

In contrast, the administration class have common features across game formats. It is possible to conceive that the features in them could be used as a decentralised game control interface, allowing users or groups of users to define their own media-rich experiences.

New features required will include adapting elements for the military project discussed in Section 8.5, and to accommodate large-scale media events beyond the current context of pervasive gaming. Mark-up features are in development for Encounter 2.0, which will enable non-geographic-specific games, allowing players to collaborate and compete across cities and towns rather than in one specific game zone.

8.4   Workforce Management Application

The primary aim of the workforce management application is to develop a 3D visualisation of a geographic area overlaid with information on BT's network and selected faults. The 3D visualisations have been built up from a combination of aerial photography, OS mapping, building outlines, BT's network, and current fault information. This type of visualisation is beneficial to a number of end-user groups. Call centre operators are an obvious user group, as they are likely to have little knowledge of the area where a fault is reported. So being able to see the local geography will provide background information that may prompt appropriate questions to better estimate the time taken to get to the premises or arrange for any access issues to be resolved. Another group is a fault analyst who will use the 3D model to look for fault patterns based on the physical geography.

The area we will focus on in this chapter is using this visualisation to provide an overlay on the real world from an engineer's viewpoint. In our application the repair engineers can look at fault and network information overlaid on the road network (see Fig. 8.6). The benefits of this are to allow the engineers a view of the routing of the network leading up to a fault location, which may aid in diagnosing network-based faults due to road works, flooding, and other localised problems. The system will:

- give an overview of the routing of cabling to a customer's premises;
- overlay fault and network information on a view from the engineer's van;
- provide a 'helicopter view' to aid the discovery of related faults and connectivity;
- let the engineers preview the locality in case there are access issues.

Fig. 8.6   Artist's impression of 3D visualisation tool used by fault repair engineers.

The image in Fig. 8.6 shows an artist's impression of how a 3D visualisation tool might be seen by a repair engineer. The display shows the street overlaid with additional information that would aid the engineer. Specifically underground cabling is shown along with locations of faults with summary information showing their relative importance. It is also envisaged that this would be a collaborative tool used in conjunction with a central controller who can look at other virtual views of the same scene. The compass on the lower right of the display links the view of the controller with the view of the engineer, which can be used to align the two views if necessary.

The conceptualisation might be the ideal scenario, but in reality there are many issues that need to be addressed to make this a reality. One of the issues that we have been exploring is the problem of registration[3] of the real and virtual worlds using readily available equipment. To recreate a virtual overlay in exactly the correct place for it to be useful there are a number of things that need to be aligned — the exact position of the viewpoint, the focal length of the lens, and the orientation of the camera. Of these we have been looking at how we can achieve accurate enough orientation and position without the need for very expensive components. GPS can be used to give an approximate position in outdoor environments to the order of a few metres, while differential GPS can improve this to the order of a metre. In addition, GPS can also give direction information while the receiver is moving. An electronic compass can be used to provide orientation with some small lag, which is accurate to a few degrees.

The images in Fig. 8.7 show how the 3D models are used to aid overlaying information on the live scene. Figure 8.7(a) shows a perspective view of part of a residential area. The road network is shown and house models taken from the Ordnance Survey MasterMap datasets [6]. The routing between the exchanges and local distribution points is shown overlaid. The image in Fig. 8.7(b) shows a different area from a lower viewpoint with a fault flag over a building giving a rough indication of the severity of the fault. The lower viewpoint shows that height information is used to place the buildings at the correct heights on the ground. With the information in the 3D model we can then choose to show as much or as little data overlaid as we wish.

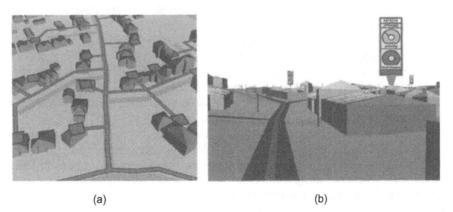

(a)   (b)

Fig. 8.7   Perspective views of a residential area.

---

[3] Aligning information to overlay on to the correct place in the real world.

The image in Fig. 8.6 shows the conceptualisation of how a view might look for a field engineer. The view in Fig. 8.8 shows more of the reality. Here we have overlaid on a view of a residential area the routing of cabling and positions of distribution points. The cabling is clearly shown as an overlay on the road,[4] and the distribution point positions are shown as columns. The view does not do any occlusion based on the positions of buildings in the real world, although this would be possible as the building data is available. The heights of the DPs give an indication of their relative proximity and 3D position.

Fig. 8.8   Mixed-reality view of residential area.

The approach we have taken is to move away from a hand-held unit due to the inherent movement involved in holding the unit and instead have chosen to base the location and orientation data for the overlays on a vehicle-based unit. The main driver for this is to be able to use additional data to aid with positioning and orientation. The Ordnance Survey provides accurate positions of the roads and road network, and we also use ground height data to place virtual roads in a 3D space.

As we have made the assumption that the display unit will be vehicle based, we can make a number of assumptions on the position of the vehicle. Firstly, we make the assumption that the vehicle is on the road, and in the UK to the left-hand side of the road. We can also assume that the viewpoint is a fixed height above the road. With these assumptions we can use a relatively approximate location from a GPS sensor together with road network information to more accurately position the location of the observer on the road. Figure 8.9 shows the improvements.

As we also have ground height information we can use this to give the camera an accurate orientation not only in the X-Z plane but also the inclination of the camera.

In summary, we have been keen to explore the use of mixed-reality environments for network fault-engineer-based applications. We have addressed some of the issues of registering the real world to overlay the information accurately in position over the real-world objects by using a combination of GPS and road network information to get more accurate position and orientation. We could always improve registration using differential GPS and an electronic compass to get a better overlay, but there is

---

[4] The cabling is shown to take up much of the road so the engineer can clearly see that there is a cable on the road. The exact position of the cable can be determined by the engineer.

the question of the necessity of doing this. We are interested in comparing the use of overlays such as we have generated in Fig. 8.8 with a virtual-reality view from Fig 8.7(b). The virtual-reality view does not suffer from the need to have very accurate position and direction — a standard GPS device would suffice for this. The engineer can make the link between the object in the virtual world with its real-world equivalent.

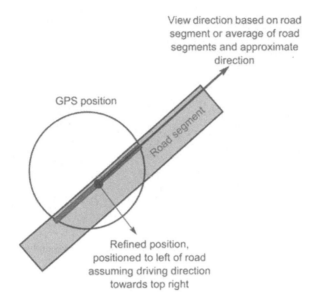

View direction based on road segment or average of road segments and approximate direction

GPS position

Road segment

Refined position, positioned to left of road assuming driving direction towards top right

Fig. 8.9   Refined vehicle positioning using GPS and road data.

8.5   Military Operations in Urban Environments

Increasingly the success of military operations in urban environments is dependent on possessing an enhanced awareness of the current situation. Ground forces in unfamiliar urban terrains require an enhanced appreciation of their local situation, where pertinent information and knowledge effortlessly augments their perception of the environment. Command and control require a complete understanding of the remote situation in order to help manage uncertainty, ignorance, and surprise across the battle space.

To provide these capabilities, a system is required that supports mutual understanding through the sharing and provision of information and knowledge directly related to the physical space.

8.5.1   Benefits and Scenarios

Such a system will enable ground forces to be aware of others in their proximity, thereby helping to prevent friendly-fire incidents. It will also facilitate the creation of spatialised information and knowledge by ground forces, and the further dissemination and presentation to others. When operations are held in a previously visited location, pertinent information such as a secured entrance to a building or a hotspot of recurring social unrest could be highlighted to ground forces unfamiliar with the environment (see Fig. 8.10).

Fig. 8.10   Enhanced perception of the real world for ground forces.

Similarly, in rehearsed tactical manoeuvres, probable sniper locations and hazards previously identified by reconnaissance could all be highlighted. Furthermore, generic information such as street names and buildings could be provided and important military resources such as telecommunications and power lines, broadcast aerials, etc, could be made apparent.

The use of a virtual replica of the battle space (see Fig. 8.11) will enable command and control to better understand the intricacies of the terrain and the location and status of friendly and enemy monitored ground forces and resources. Location-specific commands such as anticipatory orders and requests for intelligence can be easily created and delivered to ground forces in an organised and managed way. In operational planning and review, the virtual battle space could also be used to rehearse and replay operation tactics.

8.5.2   Supporting Technologies

The key technologies required to support the development of the mixed-reality system for this defence application are outlined below.

3D GIS Generation

The 3D GIS tool-kit enables an accurate virtual duplicate of a real-world space to be quickly created by fusing data and information from a variety of diverse sources, including existing vector and raster maps, LIDAR (light detection and ranging) data, satellite imagery, and aerial photography.

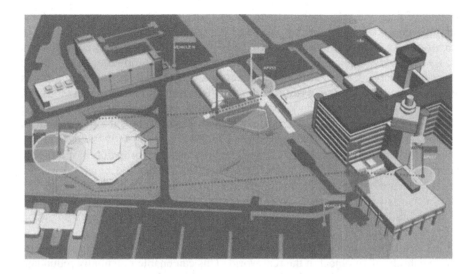

Fig. 8.11   Virtual replica of the real-world environment for command and control.

The use of a 3D GIS enables a common spatialised reference model to be used by ground forces and command and control for the generation and provision of GIS-referenced information.

GIS-Referenced Media

Both the command and control and ground forces have the capability to create GIS-referenced media. In order for a media to be GIS referenced, it must be attributable to a point location, defined area, or an addressable 3D object within the virtual scene or real-world environment. Meta-data associated with all GIS-referenced media enables information filtering to be used effectively. At a minimum meta-data should include a description of what it is, who created it, where it was created, and when it was created.

Virtual- and Real-World Tracking and Registration Software

Mixed-reality systems require computer media (2D and 3D graphics, audio and haptic/tactile representations) to be accurately registered to the user's viewpoint in real time so that the virtual media is convincingly placed with the real-world scene. Past research [7] has demonstrated that this can be achieved using hybrid systems that combine magnetic tracking (digital compass, inertia sensors, and differential GPS) with computer-vision-based tracking techniques.

GPS and magnetic tracking systems are used to provide an initial estimate of position and orientation of the viewer. Computer vision real-time object tracking algorithms are then used to register the real-world video image with the virtual-world image. This is achieved using real-world static objects as markers that have a virtual equivalent within an accurate virtual representation of real-world scene.

Information Provisioning System

Urban environments are extremely complicated. They are populated by large numbers of people, areas, buildings, and vehicles, all of which can have vast amounts of data and information stored about them. It is therefore very easy for a user to become overwhelmed by the sheer volume of information available. To overcome the problem of information overload, an information provisioning system (IPS) will be developed that is able to filter superfluous information and provide only useful, relevant, and pertinent information to the user. Recent research in this area has demonstrated positive results using hybrid information filtering methods [8].

The IPS provides a framework for utilising spatial and visible filtering combined with an understanding of the user's context to refine relevant GIS-referenced information that is presented to the user (see Fig. 8.1).

Spatial filtering can be used to manage the display of information based on the proximity of the user to a GIS-referenced point. A user-centred bounding sphere delineates an area of space within which a GIS-referenced point can be detected. If a point intersects within the user's bounding sphere, the user can see and interact with the media associated with that point. Expanding or contracting the user's bounding sphere provides farther or nearer distance-related information.

Visible filtering can be used to manage the display of information based on the user's visibility of an object in the real world. This can enable potentially redundant information associated with a physical object to be filtered.

Context filtering utilises any available information about a user and interprets that information (which may include complex analysis, through feature extraction and modelling, to inferring a context) to refine relevant GIS information that is presented to the user.

Information Displays and Interfaces

The multimodal interface system enables the user to interact with complex media via a conventional chest-mounted LCD display. Information is also displayed using alternative body-worn displays that do not fully dominate the user's attention. These include a peripheral vision display mounted in goggles, spatialised audio via a stereo headset, and a body-worn tactile display. Figure 8.12 shows all the types of display and other hardware carried by potential users.

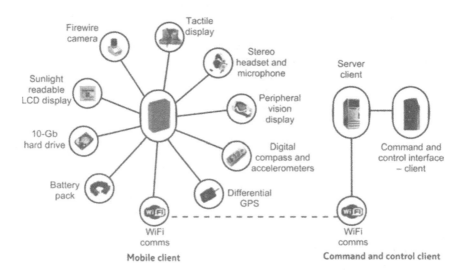

Fig. 8.12   Various 'displays' used by mobile users.

8.6   Future

Between now and the end of 2006, the DTC DIF Mixed Reality System for Urban Environments Project will develop a proof of concept mixed-reality system demonstrator, which can be evaluated in a number of simulated military and civilian situations. The results of the evaluation will then be used to inform the development of future situational awareness systems for field operatives and for command-and-control personnel within the military domain.

Although the exploitation of this research work is predominantly focused within the military domain, many opportunities exist for commercial exploitation within the wider civilian arena. Generated IP and selected technologies are likely to be transferable to the emergency services, mobile engineering work forces, civil engineering, and business and consumer mobile broadband markets.

8.7   Summary

This chapter has discussed three applications involving virtual-/mixed-reality environments as a means of presenting information related to the local environment. In the gaming application area it will be interesting to see how the more collaborative aspects being developed as part of Encounter 1.1 can be introduced into future mixed-reality systems. Unfortunately, in the workforce management and military applications it is still too early to measure the effectiveness of using mixed-reality techniques such as content filtering and real-world/virtual registration as an aid to providing information to a user. It is clear that a move to pervasive computing environments will help with information filtering where the information might be held locally to its point of use, but in turn this may introduce problems of content access if the receiver is not in the immediate vicinity of the information.

What will be fundamental to future spatialised information provisioning systems is the relevant use and appropriate display of media to users regardless of its origin. This chapter has gone some way to showing what types of information can be used, and how they can be presented to the end user.

References

1. It's Alive! — http://www.itsalive.com/

2. Newt Games — http://www.newtgames.com/

3. Blast Theory — http://www.blasttheory.co.uk/

4. Benford S et al. Coping with Uncertainty in a Location-Based Game. IEEE Pervasive Computing, September 2003.

5. Flintham M et al. Uncle Roy All Around You: Mixing Games and Theatre on the City Streets. Proceedings of Level Up: The First International Conference of the Digital Games Research Association (DIGRA), Utrecht, The Netherlands, November 2003.

6.   Ordnance Survey — http://www.ordnancesurvey.co.uk/oswebsite/products/osmastermap/

7.   You S, Neumann U and Azuma R. Orientation Tracking for Outdoor Augmented Reality Registration. IEEE Virtual Reality, 1999:36–42.

8.   Julier S, Bailot Y and Brown D. Information Filtering for Mobile Augmented Reality. IEEE Computer Graphics and Applications, September/October 2002:12–15.

9

A Sensor Network for Glaciers

K Martinez, A Riddoch, J Hart, and R Ong

9.1   Introduction

The continuous advancements in wireless networks and miniaturisation have made the deployment of sensor networks to monitor the environment increasingly feasible. The potential advances to environmental sciences could be as great as the revolution produced by the development of remote sensing during the 1970s. Sensor network technology can provide basic scientific data as well as hazard warnings. This is particularly important in remote or hazardous environments where many fundamental processes have never been studied due to inaccessibility. In addition, more accessible environments could be monitored on an unprecedented scale.

Chong and Kumar [1] illustrate that sensor networks combine state-of-the-art technologies from the fields of sensors, communications, and computer science. We have suggested [2] that in an environmental sensor network, a holistic design is required, including specialist user-domain knowledge. A sensor network comprises sensor nodes that gather data autonomously and usually pass it to one or more base stations, which forward the data to a sensor network server (SNS).

Due to the innovative nature of the technology, there are currently very few environmental sensor networks in operation. Those that are, which monitor a variety of environments, include NASA/JPL's project in Antarctica [3], Huntington Botanical Gardens Sensor Web [4], Berkeley's habitat modelling at Great Duck Island [5], the CORIE project, which studies the Columbia River estuary [6], deserts [7], and volcanoes [8], as well as the GlacsWeb project discussed in this chapter.[1] These projects have demonstrated the value of using environmental sensor networks for environmental studies — primarily as they are cheap, are reasonably easily configured and installed, are inherently redundant, and have the potential to produce data of high spatial resolution. It is foreseeable that this technology could become pervasive and expand to the point where information from numerous networks (e.g. glacier, river, rainfall, avalanche, and oceanic networks) are aggregated at higher levels to form a picture of a system at resolutions that are unfeasible or unattainable with current technology.

We are considering a future where there will be large-scale repeated deployments of different types of environmental sensor networks around the world and they will become truly pervasive. To move towards this, fundamental issues relating to power, communications, deployment, cost, maintenance, and security need to be resolved. Separate sensor networks monitoring different aspects of the environment will

[1] The GlacsWeb project is financially supported by the Royal Society, Paul Instrument Fund, the Department of Trade and Industry, and the EPSRC, UK.

require a simple way of automatically interchanging data. We envisage using Web Services and Semantic Web technology to expose the data to other sensor networks and to the software, which derives information from sensor networks. This would enable a more complete view of an environment. In the case of an ice cap, data could be gathered from very different systems — fixed weather stations, fixed river flow stations, mobile sensors in snow, ice, or sediment, and so on. This should be manageable even though the sub-networks are from different vendors. It should also be possible to retrieve summary data rather than process raw temperature data, e.g. max/min could be all that is required.

A relatively small number of nodes might produce a summary of one data stream such as average ice melt per day. While researchers may need in-depth data access, tourists, for example, may be interested in accessing more general information about the area they are visiting.

In order to maximise data efficiency from nodes (where a vast amount of data may be potentially supplied), domain knowledge of the environment combined with the generation of specific algorithms will need to be generated. The production of this type of sensor network is thus an interdisciplinary project.

The GlacsWeb project described in this chapter has deliberately focused on producing a robust platform for one particular environmental area. The lessons we have learnt in two deployments have led us to adapt our architecture and philosophy. The main advances have been in hardware design, which will be described in more detail. We have maintained a general approach throughout with the objective of generating useful designs for a wider range of applications.

9.2   The GlacsWeb Project

The aim of the GlacsWeb project is to build an environmental sensor network to understand glacier dynamics in response to climate change. Glacier behaviour is moderated by local conditions, in particular the nature of the bed. Currently 90% of the discharge from Antarctica is from the ice streams, whose behaviour is controlled by sub-glacial processes and not climate. Briksdalsbreen, a glacier in Norway, was chosen as an excellent analogue for Antarctica, as it has similar bed conditions, but is far more accessible, and so allows the development and testing of the first glacial environmental sensor network (see Fig. 9.1). The intention of the environmental sensor network was to collect data from sensor nodes (probes) within the ice and the till (subglacial sediment) without the use of wires, which might disturb the environment. The system was also designed to collect data from the surface of the glacier (position, weather).

Finally, all the data would be combined in a database on the sensor network server together with large-scale data from maps and satellites. In this way, specific data from the sensor nodes (which reflect point data) is combined with larger-scale data to understand the glacier as a whole. The data was collected from within the ice by radio communications (which has never been achieved before). These requirements led to the following research objectives:

- miniaturisation;
- low-power design;

Fig. 9.1   Briksdalsbreen with field site location indicated with arrow.

- *ad hoc* networking;
- autonomous and adaptive behaviour.

The GlacsWeb system is composed of probes embedded in the ice and till, a base station on the ice surface, a reference station (2.5 km from the glacier with mains electricity), and the sensor network server (SNS) based in Southampton (Fig. 9.2).

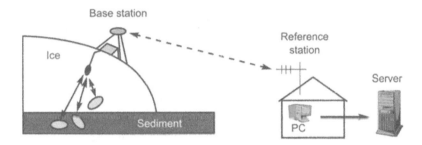

Fig. 9.2   Simplified system overview.

Design of the prototype system began in late 2002, and a prototype was installed in the glacier during the summer of 2003. The probes were embedded via holes drilled into the glacier with a hot water drill.

In 2003 nine probes were inserted. These probes communicated with the base station at 868 MHz, a licence-free channel that was chosen with consideration for theoretical losses within pure ice and the size of the probe. However, the amount of water within a temperate glacier such as Briksdalsbreen meant that radio losses were significantly more than anticipated; hence only one probe transmitted data for 10 days [2, 9]. Nevertheless, this showed that the system was feasible with more powerful communication modules.

During 2004 the probes and base station were redesigned based on the experience of the previous year. Eight probes were embedded in the summer of 2004 which immediately transmitted their data. The details of the new system (version 2) and the results are discussed in Section 9.3.

9.3   System Architecture Version 2

9.3.1   Probes

The electronics and sensors are enclosed in a polyester egg-shape capsule measuring 148×68 mm (see Fig. 9.3). Its two halves are permanently bonded with cyanoacrylate and epoxy resin. The probes were made as small as possible to behave like rounded natural stones, which also simplified insertion in the ice. Each probe is equipped with one pressure, temperature, and resistivity sensor, two accelerometers (orientation in three dimensions), and a strain gauge. These sensors were glued and potted into the probe to prevent water intrusion. The probe's electronics were mounted on three octagonal PCBs — one each for the digital, analogue, and radio sub-systems — which efficiently utilises the available volume and modularises the design, as shown in Fig. 9.4.

Fig. 9.3   Probe housing shown open.

Fig. 9.4   Analogue, digital, and radio PCBs.

At the heart of each probe is a PIC microcontroller (PIC16LF876A), which is used to configure, read, and store the attached sensors at user-specified times, handles power management, and communicates with the base station, as shown in Fig. 9.5. The probe's orientation is measured using two dual-axis 180° micro-electro-mechanical accelerometers (from Analog Devices) capable of sensing static G. The microcontroller reads the analogue sensors (pressure, resistivity, strain) with its in-built analogue-to-digital converter (ADC). The temperature sensor, real-time clock (RTC), and a 64-kB FlashROM are accessed via the inter-integrated circuit (I^2C) bus. 3.6 V lithium thionyl chloride cells were used due to their high energy density

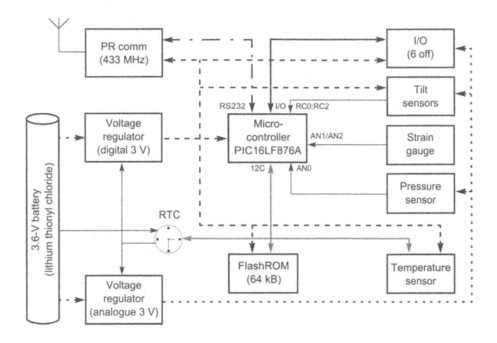

Fig. 9.5   Diagram of the probe (version 2).

and good low-temperature characteristics. The radio transceiver uses conventional ¼ wave-length 'stubby' helical antennas that, although quite large, were more efficient than the dielectric antennas used in the first prototype.

The probes 'awaken' six times daily from sleep mode to collect data, but only enable the transceiver once each day to conserve power. This acquisition rate is acceptable as the data is not expected to change rapidly. The recorded data (96 bytes/day) is time-stamped and stored in the FlashROM, which is organised as a ring buffer. This set-up allows the probe to store up to 682 days' worth of data in the event that it loses communication with the base station.

In sleep mode all the electronics, except the RTC and voltage regulators (outputs disabled), are unpowered — consuming only 9 µA (32 µW). The microcontroller sets the RTC's alarm to the next 'wake-up' time before commanding it to disable the voltage regulator outputs (powering off the system). Although this is a risky manoeuvre — corruption of the RTC's alarm registers could result in unpredictable operation — write access to these registers is always verified by the firmware. When powered, the probe consumes only 4.1 mA (~15 mW) with the transceiver disabled, 24 mA (86.4 mW) when enabled, and approximately 130 mA (~470 mW) when transmitting. An estimated consumption of 100 mW over the 180 sec the probe's transceiver is active is reasonable considering the fact that transmissions occur infrequently. Hence, the daily power consumption is approximately 5.8 mWH (15 mW × 10 sec for five wake-up times + 100 mW × 180 sec when transceiver is active + 32 µW × 86 210 sec for sleep time), which means its 3.6 V 6 AH (21.6 WH) battery could last for more than 10 years! The probe's battery voltage is measured once a day as an indication of its energy status.

Based on the outcome of the previous season, the frequency of the link between the probe and base station was lowered from 868 MHz to 433 MHz, and the radiated RF power substantially increased, to improve ice penetration. Xemics DP1201A-E433 transceiver modules were used in place of the Adlink 868-MHz modules. The new modules allowed us to incorporate a programmable RF power amplifier to boost RF transmission power to over 100 mW. Although this is outside the legal power level, the massive attenuation of the ice and water meant that the RF power is well within the 10-mW limit for this licence-exempt band on the surface of the ice. To further improve communication, the base-station transceivers were buried 30 to 40 m under the ice.

The probe's firmware, stored in the microcontroller's program memory, is divided into two segments — the program space (5k words) and the user space (3k words). The program space contains the initialisation and control routines that configure the microcontroller's built-in modules (e.g. I^2C, ADC) upon starting. It also streams the bytes transmitted to and received from the on-board UART (universal asynchronous receiver transmitter), interprets received packets, and executes commands issued by the base station (via the packets) and user space. The program space is unalterable.

The user space, which holds the program that is autonomously executed whenever the probe 'awakens', comprises the upper 3k words of the microcontroller's program memory. This program is written as a C function and calls the same set of commands that could have been sent via the transceiver. Multiple programs could be stored in the user space (memory permitting), and the desired program is selected by issuing a specific command. Programs could also be loaded and removed from the user space as the microcontroller has the ability to reprogram its memory while running. This feature greatly increases the flexibility of the probes since their automated sequence could be remotely altered from Southampton even when they are buried in a Norwegian glacier. Finally, a mechanism is in place to ensure that rogue programs will be terminated if they exceed some preset time-out, and they will not automatically execute the next time the probe 'awakens'.

9.3.2   Base Station

The base station controls the probes, gathers surface data from the weather station and GPS, and links to the reference station in the valley. This system is powered from lead-acid gel batteries with a total capacity of 96 AH in parallel with two solar panels (15 W in total). A permanent weather- and movement-tolerant pyramid structure holds sensors, antennas, and tethers the equipment, as shown in Fig. 9.6. The weight of the batteries inside the box stabilises the base station by creating an even surface as the ice beneath melts. A differential GPS unit is read on a daily basis to measure its location in conjunction with data from the reference station's GPS. This is carried out by taking 10-min recordings at both the base and reference stations. A 500-mW radio modem provides a 9600-baud link 2.5 km down the valley to the reference station PC.

The base station uses a commercially available StrongARM-based (PXA255) embedded computer (BitsyX) with 64 Mbytes of RAM, running Linux. It has a custom board comprising a microcontroller (PIC16F876A) for power management

Fig. 9.6   Base station on the glacier with pyramid support.

and sensor interfaces. It also uses a compact flash card as a permanent data store. The controller, temperature and tilt sensors, signal and power isolators, RS232 level converter, RS232 splitter/combiners, and switch-mode power supply (DC-DC 3 V and 5 V) regulators, as shown in Fig. 9.7, are part of a separate PCB. The GPS, GSM, weather, and LR communications modules are external devices connected to the BitsyX's case. The host and debug ports are connected to the BitsyX's second and third serial port — these are just to aid development. A third 'breakout' PCB — mounted above the BitsyX's case — was used to connect other external devices to the BitsyX via the ADSmartIO, PR1 comm, PR2 comm, camera, and port modules.

The controller and the temperature sensor are accessed by the BitsyX via the I^2C bus. This microcontroller controls the isolators (solid-state relays and analogue switches), which physically disconnects the power and signals to all modules. Such a design meant large power savings were achievable. Only the BitsyX, power and signal isolators, RS232 splitter/combiners, and RS232 level converter are always on, which consumes very little power (when the BitsyX is in sleep mode). The controller also acts as an I^2C bridge for the tilt sensor. This sensor was found to be useful in determining the stability of the base station.

BitsyX is powered directly from the 12-V batteries, and 5 V are generated for the devices that are continuously powered, as shown in Fig. 9.8. The remaining modules

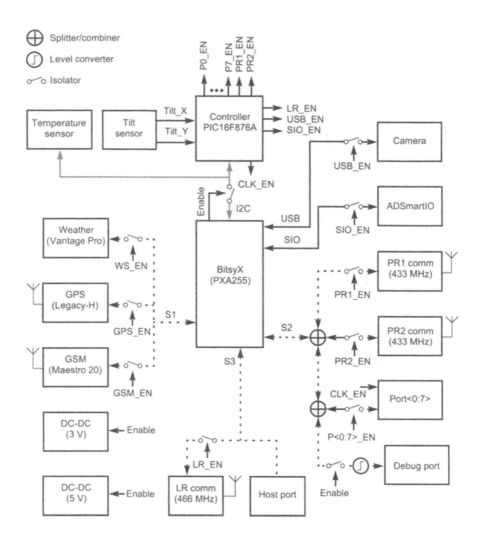

Fig. 9.7   Diagram of the base station (communication).

are either powered from the 12-V batteries or the 5-V/3-V DC-DC converters (on the PCB), depending on their voltage rating, via the power isolators. Both 5-V and 3-V sources are DC-DC converted from 12 V for efficiency, and there are two of each module for redundancy. The DC-DC converted outputs also pass through linear voltage regulators to minimise power rail noise. The outputs of these modules can be disabled by the BitsyX since they may become unstable when no load is present (i.e. in sleep mode).

The USB port connects to a Webcam mounted on the pyramid support for observing the general condition of the site. In practice, the Video for Linux drivers were found to be too unstable for this to be used regularly. The ADSmartIO module consists of eight I/O lines — four of which have ADCs — and power (3 V, 5 V, 12 V) lines. The I/O lines are controllable by BitsyX and were connected to a plough meter (measuring strain) and tilt cells (measuring glacier advancements relative to

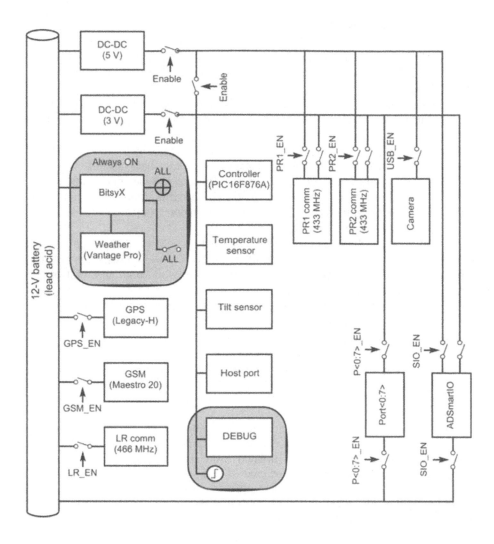

Fig. 9.8   Diagram of the base station's power control.

its bed). These more traditional instruments will be used to compare the probe performance with conventional wired sensors.

Communication between BitsyX and the other modules is via its three serial ports, S1, S2, and S3. A four-way RS232 splitter/combiner was designed to split/combine the RS232 signals from/to serial port S2 of BitsyX. This allowed four different modules to share a single serial port — which is possible in this design — as these modules interpret packetised data and are slaves with respect to BitsyX (i.e. the modules only transmit packets when commanded). Although the weather station (Weather in Fig 9.7), GPS and GSM modules are connected to the same serial port, these modules are never used together. Their respective isolators guarantee that only one device is connected to BitsyX at any time. On the other hand, the host port and LR comm could be enabled concurrently (for debugging), and it is the user's responsibility to only connect one device at a time.

PR1 comm and PR2 comm modules connect to the transceivers, which communicate with the probes. Two independent channels were designed for this vital link as one of the serial cables in the ice could be damaged in the course of a year. The debug port is primarily used for monitoring the packets during development.

A GSM modem was implemented in the prototype base station (in 2003), which allowed data to be sent directly to the UK via text messages (SMS), if the long-range link fails.

This was an important piece of equipment in that system (which had less efficient antennas) and was also included in the current design as a back-up link. Only the probe and base-station data is transmitted in ASCII coded hexadecimal characters — daily GPS data is too large (typically > 10 kB) for SMS transfers. Apart from sending SMS, the GSM modem could be used for data communications in the future (i.e. a back-up dial-up into the base station).

The differential GPS module is used in conjunction with an identical unit in the reference station to measure the exact position of the base station, which is moving at roughly 15 cm/day in summer. For this technique to work, both GPS units must record at the same time.

The two files are processed off-line using Topcon's software, and an accuracy of 1 cm is typical (it depends on satellite coverage).

The weather station is a commercial unit that measures precipitation, pressure, temperature, humidity, wind speed and direction, solar radiation, and ultra-violet radiation. This module is powered continuously (45 mW idle, ~80 mW reading) and uses a 'tipping-bucket' method to measure precipitation. The sensors are read periodically (varies according to sensor) and the data is stored on a console, which is accessed by BitsyX once a day.

Long-range communication is handled by a pair of 500-mW radio modems operating at 466 MHz. One of these is connected to port S2 of BitsyX (LR comm module). The LR modem can be isolated from BitsyX, but the host port is permanently connected and always powered — this provides a means of logging on to BitsyX via a point-to-point connection. This has been used on the glacier with a laptop to monitor system activity and reconfigure the system. The prototype used a custom protocol, but the use of TCP/IP has greatly enhanced the usability of the link for administration.

As a whole, BitsyX itself consumes about 120 mA (~1.45 W) when operating, and 10 mA (120 mW) in sleep mode. When the second PCB is enabled, power consumption rises to approximately 165 mA (~2 W — excluding GPS, GSM, and LR comm modules). The estimated power consumption when the base station executes its job is approximately 4 W over 15 minutes (1 WH per day). Combined with a consumption of 170 mW (120 mW BitsyX + 50 mW weather station average) in sleep mode, the total estimated daily consumption is 5 WH. This means the 96 AH (1152 WH) batteries should last approximately 230 days. The extra power is derived from the solar panel, which is estimated to produce about 15 WH per day during summer (approximately 100 days); hence the base station should have enough power to run for a year. The overall battery voltage is recorded daily to record the power status. Experience from 2003 shows that the base station is subjected to temperatures down to −9 °C in the winter and that the batteries remain in a reasonable condition.

9.3.3   Reference Station

The reference station is a mains-powered 500-MHz EPIA-PC running Linux (RedHat 9) located in a café in the valley. This low-power PC format was chosen as it can be supported for longer on a UPS, as well as being small (micro-ATX form factor) and near silent. It is connected to the base station via the radio modem, and periodically to the Internet via an ISDN router. Data is sent daily (as a compressed tape archive file) to the data server in Southampton. As its name implies, it also acts as the reference point for the DGPS system. The distance between the base and reference station is 2.5 km without a clear line-of-sight. Hence, high-powered, low-frequency radio modems are employed. In addition, a short directional Yaggi-type antenna increases the sensitivity to the signal and the low (9600) baud rate reduces bit errors.

9.3.4   Communications Protocol

Data transmission is the most power-consuming task for the probes — hence it is important to minimise not only their time awake, but also their transmission time. As it is unfeasible to continuously power the entire system or to stagger the communication window of each probe, the entire system thus relied on a unified time schedule. This decision means that there has to be a communications protocol between base station and probes. In addition, this communications link must be suitably robust to maintain data integrity. Clearly, benefits would be achieved by using an *ad hoc* protocol, such as probe data hopping back through other probes, in order to get to the base station and possibly power-saving from inter-probe communications being over smaller distances. However, the PIC processor used in the probes would constrain the amount of memory available and, in the time available, implementing an *ad hoc* network would have been risky. So a star network topology was chosen and furthermore the probes would be polled from the base station rather than autonomously send data. This would have required either precise timing or a MAC protocol to avoid power-consuming collisions. Similarly security protocols were not used as these would add complexity; however, base-station links used Linux security.

A packet-based communications protocol with identifiers (ID) and error detection (checksum CS) was devised for probe communications. Although many packet-based protocols such as UDP and TCP are widely available, they are deemed unsuitable for the PIC microcontroller with limited resources. Hence, a simple protocol, shown in Fig. 9.9, was developed.

0	1	2	3 18	19
HD/SZ	ID	CMD	Data	CS

Fig. 9.9   Communication packet format (maximum size).

Each packet varies between 5 and 20 bytes and has 6 fields. Although variable packet sizes increase the complexity of the packet interpreter, this approach substantially reduces power consumption since most command and information packets are significantly shorter than 16 bytes. Each byte is transmitted least-significant-bit first, and the packet is transmitted least-significant-byte first. The gap between each transmitted byte has to be less than 3 ms — this feature ensures that spurious data will not greatly inhibit valid communication. A communication error occurs if this condition is not met and the base has the option of retrying.

The first byte contains the packet header (HD — upper nibble) and the size (SZ — lower nibble) of the data field. The header determines if the packet is a command or an information packet. When a command packet is sent by a source (the base station in this case), it expects an information packet to be transmitted by the sink (typically a probe) within a preset duration. If a packet is not received in time, it is classified as a communication error. Unlike command packets, information packets could be sent by any device at any moment, and they do not expect a reply. These were used successfully for debug information.

The ID field is that of the target device in command packets; or a device's own ID in the case of an information packet. The addressed probe responds with an information packet with the ID set as its own. If the base station receives an information packet from another source, it is classified as a communication error. No devices will respond to a command packet if the ID is set to the broadcast value. This exception allows the base station (or any controlling device) to 'broadcast' commands (e.g. set RTC time and sleep) to all devices simultaneously.

The command (CMD) field allows up to 256 different enumerated commands to be defined. The data field varies between 1 and 16 bytes and the checksum (CS) is used to check the packet's integrity. When any communication or packet errors occur, the sender can resend the command packet. The maximum number of retries is a compromise between reliability and power consumption, and we currently use three.

9.3.5   Sequence of Events

A traditional way to run such a sensor network is to power up all the systems and let the nodes send data autonomously. This approach was not taken as it was felt that reducing the power-waste of collisions would be critical in a large-scale deployment and that simpler software could be designed. This led to a design where the nodes only respond to commands and (at the moment) do not inter-communicate. The entire system works on a unified daily schedule relying on synchronised clocks. The probes wake up six times daily — five for data log periods (1 sec each) and once for up to 180 sec during the communications (comm) period. The base station also wakes up for the comm period and controls everything rather than acting as a router. The reference station, which is permanently powered, transfers its data to Southampton during the transfer period.

Upon 'waking up' during a data log period, the probe reads and stores its sensors, sets its RTC alarm for the next period, then goes to sleep. This procedure is repeated during the comm period (1200 UTC) apart from its staying awake for up to 180 sec after setting its RTC alarm. It is this window that the base station uses to communicate with the probes as shown in Fig. 9.10.

The base station's comm period starts shortly before the probes 'awaken' when it reads and stores its own sensors. It then goes into a polling sequence broadcasting

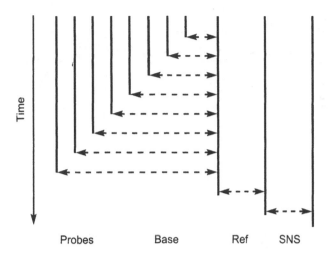

Fig. 9.10   Sequence of events at communications time showing probes waking simultaneously, talking to the base station, and then sleeping.

the GPS system date/time and interrogating each probe in turn. Tests have shown that the RTCs do drift up to ± 2 sec per day relative to the GPS time; hence time broadcasting is vital to keep the system synchronised. If a probe replies, the base station reads all its unread data before commanding it to sleep (hence the staggered sleep times of the probes as shown in Fig. 9.10). The base station could also perform other tasks such as extracting old data or changing the probe's user-space programs, if necessary, by modifying the base station's job file (a shell script) or by commands issued from Southampton via the Internet and reference station.

After the probe's comm period, the base station starts a 15-min GPS recording. A separate GPS period was used in 2003 that could be shifted manually because satellite visibility varies considerably over a year. For simplicity and to make use of the base station's 'idle' time when GPS recording takes place, GPS recording is fixed for 2004. The base station now sends the previous day's GPS file to the reference station while GPS recording takes place. The day's data is transferred to a server in Southampton during the transfer period, which occurs in the late evening to avoid hogging the dial-up ISDN line that is shared with the Internet café.

9.4   Example Results

Eight probes were installed in August 2004 and immediately relayed their data. By the final day of the fieldwork we obtained results from six of the eight probes using only one wired transceiver. The results can be summarised as shown in Fig. 9.11. The temperature was a relatively constant 0.18–0.31 °C. The probes, which remained in air, as indicated by the external resistance, have a constant low pressure and stress as well as stable position (vertical). One probe under 6–8 m of water showed fluctuations in pressure and stress (see Fig. 9.11). The tilt data shows the probe

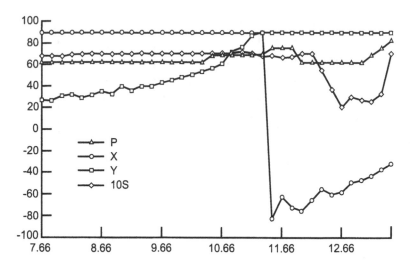

Fig. 9.11   Sample probe data. P is pressure in kPa; X and Y are tilt in degrees;
10S is 10 × strain gauge reading. The X-axis shows days in August 2004.

settling until day 11 when water pressure rose and the probe rolls on its axis. The strain gauge shows it is subject to a mild pressure around day 12.

The results show that the radio communication, base station, and probes are functioning as they should and the probes have entrained their sensors to provide consistent and reliable data. A log file is created showing useful system status, such as how many retries occurred, which probes communicated, and a trace of packet data. This will allow a more detailed system analysis as more data is received.

9.5   Summary and Future Work

Our pragmatic choices of hardware and protocols allowed us to install the first prototype in less than one year as well as understand the challenges ahead. Understanding the properties of the system and any malfunctions has been greatly enhanced by our hand-crafted approach. Future research is needed in the area of the probe location system, miniaturisation, *ad hoc* networks, Web Service development for the data, and a simpler system administration. Although an *ad hoc* network was not used, we intend to implement our own in the next version within the constraints of power-saving and the base-driven architecture. Scalability was also an aim because networks in the future will cover large areas and involve hundreds of nodes. In practice these would involve many base stations with relatively few nodes, and therefore our 256-node limit per base station is not seen as restrictive. The capability to add new nodes and manage decaying old nodes relies on maintenance of the protocol or backwards-compatibility efforts. Clearly using a standardised protocol would greatly help in this area; however, using a simple, efficient protocol and having full control over its source code are beneficial to the research. For multi-vendor systems of the future, a standard will, however, be needed. An issue that will be present in such systems for a while is simplicity of use so that sensor networks can be installed and maintained by end users in the future. Similarly, the availability of data from environmental sensor networks will require standards such as data ontologies so that researchers can gather data globally in the future.

Environmental sensor networks represent a new step forward in understanding and monitoring the environment. This system has produced useful data never seen before by glaciologists and has generated considerable interest in environmental sensor networks. Developing such a system requires the latest technology in sensors and communications. This study is one of the first in a glacial environment, and the research has demonstrated that the system is robust and is beginning to transmit results that will be vital for environmental science applications. We have found that an interdisciplinary approach is essential and GlacsWeb has involved people with expertise in radio communications, embedded systems, electronics, Linux, mechanical engineering, GPS, system administration, physics, and glaciology. One contribution this research has made is to build a complete system for a specific purpose, and it will become a platform for studying real-world implementations of theoretical concepts in sensor networks research.

References

1. Chong C-Y and Kumar S P. Sensor Networks: Evolution, Opportunities and Challenges. Proc IEEE, 2003:91:8:1247–1256.

2. Martinez K, Hart J K, and Ong R. Environmental Sensor Networks. Computer, 2004:37:8:50–56.

3. Delin K A et al. Sensor Web in Antarctica: Developing an Intelligent, Autonomous Platform for Locating Biological Flourishes in Cryogenic Environments. 34th Lunar and Planetary Science Conference, 2003.

4. Huntington Botanical Gardens — http://sensorwebs.jpl.nasa.gov/resources/huntington_sw31.shtml

5. Szewczyk R et al. Lessons from a Sensor Network Expedition. Proc 1st European Workshop on Wireless Sensor Networks (EWSN '04), Berlin, Germany, January 2004:307–322.

6. Steere D C. Research Challenges in Environmental Observations and Forecasting Systems. Proc ACM/IEEE Int Conf Mobile Computing and Networking (MOBICOMM), 2000:292–299.

7. Delin K A et al. Sensor Web for Spatio-Temporal Monitoring of a Hydrological Environmental. 35th Lunar and Planetary Science Conference, League City, Texas, 2004.

8. Lorincz K et al. Sensor Networks for Emergency Response: Challenges and Opportunities. IEEE Pervasive Computing, Special Issue on Pervasive Computing for First Response, October-December 2004.

9. Martinez K, Ong R, and Hart J K. GlacsWeb: A Sensor Network for Hostile Environments. Proc First Annual IEEE Communications Society Conference on Sensor and *Ad Hoc* Communications and Networks, 2004:81–87.

10

Co-operation in the Digital Age — Engendering Trust in Electronic Environments

A Seleznyov, M O Ahmed, and S Hailes

10.1   Introduction

Mark Weiser had a vision of ubiquitous computing that was motivated by his belief that profound technologies disappear into the physical environment that surrounds us [1]. This vision has become a reality. Fewer than 2% of all microprocessors sold go into conventional PCs, the vast majority of the remainder becoming part of embedded systems, although few of these are currently networked. It is not, however, difficult to foresee that the efforts aimed at overcoming the inherent complexities in producing truly ubiquitous networked systems are most likely to bear fruit in the short to medium term.

Emerging ubiquitous infrastructures are characterised by huge numbers of autonomous, heterogeneous entities, interacting across diffuse organisational boundaries. Precisely the same lack of clarity in organisational structures that has led to the failure of public key infrastructure (PKI) outside highly homogeneous and carefully managed domains means that it is impossible to rely on specific or centralised security mechanisms that holistically administer trust in ubiquitous systems.

The increase in opportunity and capability for interaction naturally leads to an increase in the number of bilateral trust relationships between the entities that populate ubiquitous infrastructures, forming PGP-like webs-of-trust on a scale never before seen. Since this model reflects the type of organisational culture that results when economies are free, it will remain difficult to predict and define trust relationships between components with the degree of certainty purportedly on offer in neatly hierarchical PKI systems.

The trust management problem has been extensively studied and discussed, and many definitions have been proposed, but it has not been properly addressed by contemporary solutions [2]. The increased complexity of defining, managing, and enforcing the policies of interaction for ubiquitous systems means that many of the current technologies used to protect and provide assurance in traditional networked systems are inapplicable. The way they make their trust decisions is *ad hoc* and application-specific, rendering them inflexible, un-scalable, and un-portable [3]. Centralised control, relying solely on the *a priori* definition of the role, authority, and relationships between components, is undesirable because of the restrictions that must be imposed on the dynamism of systems to make behaviour easier to predict.

Moreover, it is also unsustainable because of the imperfect and incomplete information inherent in such environments that results in uncertainties in the knowledge bases of components. In short, it is necessary to abandon the over-simplistic search for certainty and instead treat uncertainty in trust as a first-class concept, in precisely the same way as we do in everyday life.

Typically, the concept of trust is used in human society to deal with high-risk situations, in which little or no information about each other is available to the parties involved in the interaction [4]. While this concept has been widely addressed in distributed societies of agents [5–7], the appropriateness of the solutions presented to provide flexibility and assurance in electronic environments is still questionable. While the capacity of virtual communities to model and reflect the organisation of groups of real individuals and their interactions provides motivation to develop digital trust mechanisms, the human notion of trust is still too nebulous and complex for digital environments.

A further problem that rarely merits consideration in the academic literature is the problem of sustainability. There is a grave danger of academic conceit in proposing single solutions to the problem of trust management that are supposedly optimal on some criteria. The reality is that it is impossible to predict the future usage of such systems. Thus, for example, many existing solutions to the trust management problem do not take into account the idea of concept drift, assuming that trust relations and the semantics of the terms used to describe them are fixed for all time. However, local trust decisions are based on shared trust resources and they, in turn, are constantly changing. Having no control over these changes, a trust management system is forced to adapt over a range of time-scales, some of them relatively long term, and failure to do this can only increase error probability and decrease users' trust in the system as a whole. Thus, by hard coding trust decisions into trust management systems, contemporary developers make systems inflexible, denying them the ability to learn from past behaviour in order to adapt to changes and modify their behaviour.

The remainder of the chapter is organised as follows — Section 10.2 provides a background to the ubiquitous environment, discussing the premises of this work and highlighting the characteristics of ubiquitous environments that raise the level of uncertainty. Section 10.3 discusses the notion of distributed trust management. Section 10.4 outlines the conceptual architecture of an Autonomic Distributed Authorisation Middleware and its implementation. Finally, Section 10.5 concludes this chapter.

10.2   Security Issues in Ubicomp

New flexibility and interconnectivity increase opportunities for interactions unbounded by physical distance or organisational structure. However, realising this level of functionality significantly decreases the level of control one has over the environment, and, in particular, the electronic transactions that take place within it. We therefore face a dilemma — on the one hand, a global electronic environment provides more flexibility and functionality, making it easier to co-operate and interact between both people and devices, while on the other hand, this flexibility leads to the uncertainty due to a lack of control over the environment, which is gradually transformed into a lack of trust in the environment, resulting in a reluctance to use it.

There are two key notions implicit in the discussion above — co-operation and trust. Although these are two different concepts, they cannot easily be separated. Without some degree of mutual trust there can be no co-operation, while people do not need to trust anyone if they do not intend to co-operate. To encourage co-operation, it is necessary to provide users with the means for making their own trust decisions. In the context of the digital environment, this means that users should have automatic tools that recognise and assess trust-warranting properties of other entities locally, without reliance upon omniscient and omnipresent services. These tools should be lightweight, so as to work in resource-constrained environments (such as *ad hoc* or sensor networks), and transparent enough to make sure that the burden introduced does not exceed the potential benefits. In this work, we propose ADAM (Autonomic Distributed Authorisation Middleware), a middleware system to provide users with such tools [8].

Before we discuss how trust management addresses the problem of situating decision-making and the features of ADAM that support the requirements discussed so far, we discuss how characteristics of the ubiquitous environment create the uncertainties that lead to the opportunities and problems discussed.

10.2.1   Physical Heterogeneity

Within the ubiquitous electronic environment, physical variance is found within the capacity, structure, and space of devices and systems. The capacity of components refers to there being a variety of devices, with different capabilities. The variance in the structure of devices is expressed through the composition of systems. Typically, a loose coupling of traditional centralised networks providing the back-bone infrastructure to support numerous small, lightweight, and often mobile components that provide sensory input and actuation, which may interact in an *ad hoc* manner.

Within many systems, components are embedded in their operational environment and remain fixed in space, while others are mobile. Policies cannot therefore presume that components remain fixed in their location, have the same range of capacities, nor adhere to the same structure; instead, different policies may be appropriate for different (classes of) location, capacity, and structure.

The reader is referred to the work of Estrin et al [9] for a further discussion of physical heterogeneity.

10.2.2   Behavioural Heterogeneity

Behavioural heterogeneity refers to the variety of operational characteristics displayed by components. These include differences in their task, scope, autonomy, policies of interaction, and the utilities gained from interaction. Variance within the task and scope of components means that we cannot optimise them for a particular mode of operation.

Within global electronic environments, variance in scope is often expressed through the context of interaction within the operational environment. Devices are beginning to exploit information about their physical location, resources available, and the activity of the user to enhance the user experience. The CoolTown project, which extends the Taligent framework [10], is an example of this. Designed for use by mobile users, CoolTown expresses components in terms of how their role affects places, people, and things. However, this is a static method, which does not provide mechanisms for dynamically configuring or changing these properties.

The variance in policy is obvious — components belonging to different principals are governed by the differing policies expressing the concerns of their owners. However, it is not feasible to predefine the sets of all possible interactions, nor to rely fully on trusted third parties to regulate interactions [11], complicating the process of negotiation to achieve faithful interaction.

Variance in utility arises because principals have incomplete information about the beliefs, desires, and intentions of prospective trustees. This complicates the assessment of threats posed by prospective trustees. While differing levels of autonomy affect the complexity of the computational models used to create components, the predictability and control of the components mean that highly autonomous components must be autonomic in their constitution and behaviour.

Because components are capable of interacting beyond their system boundaries, their behavioural constraints affect the emergence of global ubiquity. To facilitate transient association of components, while maintaining a high level of assurance, it is necessary to provide for the identification and management of the relevant behavioural constraints possessed by the components.

10.2.3   Scale

The immense number of the devices that must interact to provide the required ubiquity[1] raises two issues:

- Invisibility

  To realise the vision of invisibility, devices must necessarily become smaller and more tightly embedded in their environments. While current trends continue to forecast ever-increasing capacity in ever-shrinking devices, we can still safely assume that size will limit capacity [9, 12].

  Capacities such as battery, computation power, memory, and sensing capabilities limit the amount of useful work that a device is able to perform locally, thereby severely affecting the scope of security solutions [13]. With respect to this, Estrin et al remark: 'Fidelity and availability will come from the quantity of partially redundant measurements and their correlation, not the individual component's quality and precision' [9].

- Management

  The increase in the number and heterogeneity of components in the environment leads to a dramatic increase in the complexity of managing the environment. Centralised methods do not scale well and hinder the dynamism of systems, making them unsuitable [3]. This problem is particularly acute within the management of the authentication and authorisation process.

---

[1] It is estimated that by the year 2009 there will be more than 3 billion active-network-capable devices using the Internet to operate.

10.2.4   Embodiment

The embodiment of components in their environment is among the main requirements to achieve ubiquity. Embodiment means that components are embedded in their operational environment, therefore physical access is limited. Issues such as the update of functionality or management policies cannot be performed easily, further highlighting the need for a degree of autonomic and self-regulating capabilities.

The pressure towards critical mass has many drivers, but problems in usability act as a brake. Dynamism in the ubiquitous environment means flexibility and convenience of usage, and this should attract users. However, dynamism and heterogeneity of environment also mean complexity and lack of predictability, which creates uncertainty and, consequently, a pressure against embracing the technology for fear of the consequences of doing so. Empowering the user and restoring at least a perception of control, while ensuring that the system can actually function on a second-by-second basis, is the key to acceptability. One of the ways to approach this social challenge is to increase the awareness of potential users. Every person deals with uncertainty in everyday life; each real-life situation or event involves uncertainty up to some point and people learn to live with this. In view of the real uncertainties inherent in the ubiquitous computing environment, it would be a mistake to attempt to misrepresent the nature of the system as one in which certainty obtains. Once some degree of uncertainty (and hence the possibility of error) is deemed to be acceptable to end users, it is possible to unconstrain the system, and to make use of incomplete and possibly incorrect information in making decisions about everything from service discovery through to the establishment of trust.

The ubiquitous environment, with its heterogeneity of devices and networks, will inevitably lead to a non-negligible set of interactions that are relatively complex and not foreseeable *a priori*. This is analogous to real-life interactions between people, in which many interactions are among those we know well, but a significant number are with those about whom we have little information. In both cases it is not possible to predict all future situations and, therefore, uncertainty is inherent in them. Before ubiquitous systems can become a reality, it is absolutely necessary for users to accept and even embrace uncertainty as a part of the decision-making process. Note that this definition includes the situation in which people trust the technology largely because they are unaware of its existence (intentionally so in invisible computing environments) — there is an implicit agnosticism about its effects: 'don't know, don't care, will not ask too carefully'. Nevertheless, this all validates the need for autonomic management of systems, to provide solutions that are more flexible, robust, and distributed [8].

10.3   Decentralised Trust Management

Trust management mechanisms address the above issues by situating the decision-making process in the local context of the interaction. Trust management is aimed at addressing the notion of digital trust holistically, while moving away from looking at the security needs of specific programs and processes.

The term 'decentralised trust management' was coined by Blaze [14] to address the relationships between security policies, security credentials and trust relationships. This work led to the development of PolicyMaker, the basis of which is a compliance checking algorithm that uses a request, a policy, and a set of credentials to try to find a proof that the given credentials and request comply with the policy. A bit-wise response (0 or 1) is returned depending on whether the proof has been found or not. The main problem with this approach is that it is very difficult to devise a fast algorithm for finding proofs, as the underlying process is NP-hard.

Other policy-management-oriented approaches include Centaurus [15] and Vigil [16] developed by Kagal et al. The aim of the above-mentioned systems is to provide service-independent policy management in heterogeneous environments. Centaurus is based around a system of service managers, communications managers, clients, and services. Service managers provide service discovery capabilities and act as proxies between clients and services, enabling remote execution of code for resourcing poor clients. Communications managers implement various communications protocols, enabling services for heterogeneous devices. At the heart of this architecture are the security agents, responsible for authorising access to services within the group. Security agents carry all policy information regarding the groups they represent and reason about the credentials of prospective trustees. Centaurus ties all clients and services to service managers that handle all security information for them. Vigil extends the Centaurus architecture by introducing certificate controllers and role assignment managers.

The trust mechanism for Centaurus systems is based around a Prolog compliance checker that attempts to find a proof that a given assertion (a right for a prospective trustee) is valid. The focus of this framework is to realise a trust management system that reasons about policy by allowing and regulating capabilities such as delegation. However, it is unsuitable for the target environment of this work for a number of reasons:

- the use of goal-oriented planners means that the assessment of rights is computationally demanding and complex;

- the number of components means that it is large, and the reliance upon trusted security agents means that the attack resistance of the trust mechanism is reduced to a single point of failure, i.e. the compromise of the security agent compromises the whole group;

- the system is moderately static and does not allow for the negotiation, or the dynamic change, of rights and roles.

The Simple Universal Logic-oriented Trust Analysis Notation (SULTAN), developed by Grandison [2], is intended to be a simple, comprehensive framework to analyse and manage trust relationships and is designed to underpin trust management. SULTAN uses a goal-oriented planner to refine rules, which often requires a network of policies (both authorisation and obligatory). This computational complexity renders the approach unscalable in complex situations, because the refinement process can become extremely difficult, if not intractable. Although a generic specification is proposed for SULTAN, there is no efficient algorithm to automatically perform trust management operations, and additionally, although the notions were defined, there is no direct (or indirect) built-in mechanism supporting trust recommendation (referring) rules. SULTAN, however, presents a more holistic approach to trust management by introducing risk management as part of the trust assessment process.

Distributed trust management systems face a number of obstacles.

- Perception of the environment

  Sensor-derived information is error-prone and imperfect. Translating it to knowledge and truth is plagued with the problems of identifying the context from which information is obtained, important signalling features of the environment, and false-positive reactions.

- Flow control

  As the boundaries between systems become blurred, individual components cannot easily be segregated. Capacities such as mobile and distributed code further complicate this problem; therefore, information flow models, rather than traditional control flow models, are more applicable.

- System addressing

  We are no longer able to address systems through their component units but must address them in terms of sub-systems that may be unbounded in large open environments.

- Policy constraints

  If these components span organisational as well as physical boundaries (as is likely), a range of policy constraints will govern their behaviour, introducing further uncertainties and complicating the design of the control mechanism. Therefore, a compromise must be reached between the autonomy and manageability of suitable architectures.

10.4   ADAM

We have developed the ADAM (Autonomic Distributed Authorisation Middleware) architecture, aimed at the automation of the trust establishment and maintenance process. ADAM is based on forms of distributed knowledge acquisition and management to deal with the uncertainties introduced by the requirements of information access in ubiquitous environments. It uses self-organisation techniques to make the information that principals receive more relevant to their dispositions and to segregate malicious principals. Moreover, the explicit declaration of context means that decision taking can be situated close to interactions.

To date, many definitions of trust have been proposed, and we will not present a new definition in this work, but instead adapt an existing definition and concentrate on the management of trust relationships. The focus of this work is on building an efficient system that controls the full life cycle of a trusting relationship — starting from its establishment through to its revocation. The proposed system incorporates reactive elements that monitor the manipulation of network resources and respond when malicious activity is detected. However, these elements are beyond the scope of this chapter.

For our work, we adapt the definition of trust in a way that treats it as '... a measure of willingness of a responder to satisfy an inquiry of a requestor for an action that may place all involved parties at risk of harm, and is based on an assessment of the risks and reputations associated with the parties involved in a given transaction'. As this definition states, all parties involved in interaction may be harmed by its consequences. By providing access to its resources, a principal may be explicitly harmed by the malicious actions of trustees. Third parties involved with the principal in existing trust relationships may implicitly be compromised by the relationship. Trustees are at risk, since obtaining incorrect or contradictory information compromises the integrity of their knowledge base and those of their trusting parties. These situations may arise as the result of intentional malicious activity or through legitimate error such as software bugs, network failures, and user errors. Within ADAM, the potential risk of undesirable outcomes are assessed by checking the credentials of participants and the history of their behaviour with respect to the value of the resource that potential users request; only then is a decision made about whether the risks likely to be posed through interaction are acceptable.

In establishing trust relationships, the following attributes are important — the participants, the scope (spatial and temporal restrictions applied to a current trust relationship) of the relation, the risk (as a degree of potential damage) associated with the relation, and security to describe the characteristics of trust. Each access control relation expresses sets of principals that use and provide resources in the environment, actions that may be applied to the resources, and policies governing the use of the resources.

ADAM is a multi-agent system that relies on autonomous agents to carry out users' requests on one side, while protecting resources/services on the other. Agents are policy-aware entities that use distributed knowledge management to collect evidence on the trustworthiness of prospective users and make decisions regarding whether to co-operate. Trusting decisions within ADAM are not binary (only to co-operate or to defect); for example, users may be offered more limited access than requested if the amount of or strength of the collected evidence about their trustworthiness is insufficient for the requested action (according to the local policy of the resource or service being requested). If the importance of the transaction is high, users may continue negotiating, providing additional information about themselves until either the resource manager is satisfied or the user deems the cost to be too high. All decisions regarding interaction are made by the ADAM's trust engine and are based on collected evidence about the trustworthiness of prospective participants and the local policy of a resource or service.

Within ADAM, interaction starts with a request for a service; requests are tuples, consisting of a resource, the set of actions to be performed, and the identity of the user. In order to facilitate this, there must be a service/resource discovery mechanism that allows prospective trustees to look for services, view the actions available and the credential requirements of the services, and choose between them. ADAM does not itself perform authentication, it only authorises. When a user submits their request, an authorisation agent is launched by the resource to collect evidence about the behavioural disposition of the identity presented. There are three main sources of information from which entities' trustworthiness can be derived [17]. The first source is from direct observations that are formed by recording outcomes of previous interactions with an entity. The second is the recommendations of trusted entities that allow the propagation of trust. The third source is in the reputation of an entity. Reputations are knowledge about an entity's behaviour derived from their history of interactions. They may be derived from the common knowledge of an organisation or a community, or based on specific predefined knowledge [18]. For our system, we use knowledge that is accumulated over time in communities of practice to assess reputations of network entities.

The process of interaction starts with the authorisation procedure, during which resource agents perform risk assessment and check whether the potential risk posed by the interaction is acceptable in terms of the local policy of the resource. The potential damage to the user's reputation and the potential for identity loss or loss of associated values are assessed, i.e. money may be charged if a credit card number is provided.

Resource agents analyse the evidence presented with respect to the potential damage the resource may incur if the requested actions are granted. It may therefore be the case that users will be declined access when using one of their electronic identities and granted access when using another.

10.4.1   System Architecture

In the previous section, we described the principles on which our system is founded. Next, we discuss ADAM's conceptual architecture in more detail, giving practical considerations about its implementation.

Authorisation decisions in ADAM are produced as the result of negotiations between two agents — user agents and authorisation agents. The former are implemented as mobile agents. They are aware of local policy on the user side and represent user interests in the negotiations. The user agent contains information about its legal user (and secret keys), and the certificates required for the user authentication (it may include some other information, such as credit card numbers, user names and passwords for different resources, etc). All information is encrypted and, to be activated, a user agent requires a correct PIN or password to be entered. A PIN constitutes part of a decryption key for user agents and can only be activated by authorised people. It also denies access to user agents when they are inactive or travelling. The mobility of agents allows them to move across networks or between devices. For, example, for the user's convenience, an agent may be resident in the user's PDA.

The user agents not only simplify users' lives, but they make network management easier since they automate certain tasks, such as password and certificate management. For example, to reissue a user password, the user agent is notified. After this, it moves to the network server responsible for managing users' profiles, where the password is changed in a secure environment, making it unnecessary to transmit sensitive information over the network. This method also has other benefits. Since the user does not need to remember their password, it is possible to choose strong passwords automatically without requiring any extra activity from users.

Some information is stored in user agents for users' comfort. It is necessary to remember only one PIN or password. Once the user agent is activated, it can submit some user information on request, e.g. user names and passwords for other resources, certificates. However, clearly, some information, such as private keys, should never leave user agents. There is still a small probability that a malicious person manages to obtain information from an agent. We consider this to be rather smaller than the risk of finding out some or all of the PINs used to activate an agent.

In Veijelainen et al [19], it is argued that, when correctly implemented, this kind of user information storage does not bring new security risks to those already present in computer networks.

Authorisation agents are meant to protect network resources by ensuring that only valid users obtain access to them. Agents are aware of local policy on the resource side and enforce policy rules and procedures. Also, after the authorisation procedure, agents enforce access control restrictions and monitor usage of resources in support of reactive security.

Consider the negotiation process in detail. Figure 10.1 shows the main phases through which ADAM must go in order to process each request. Initially, there are two interested parties that are potentially willing to co-operate — client and service. The former is looking for a service or resource to use for their needs. The latter is willing to provide this service. Firstly, the client needs to locate an appropriate server. Secondly, in order to co-operate, they must convince each other that they are sufficiently trustworthy to perform this transaction. These actions take place in a number of steps as numbered in Fig. 10.1 and described below.

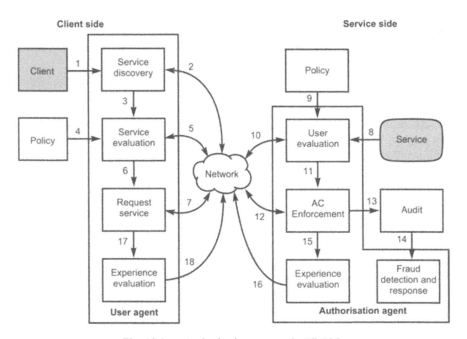

Fig. 10.1   Authorisation process in ADAM.

Each user has to activate their user agent by giving the correct PIN/password (1), as discussed above. A secure channel is established between the user terminal and the agent. If no agent with this user's information is found, a new agent is created and assigned the task of carrying out user requests. After this, in order to find an appropriate service, the client needs to perform service discovery. During this procedure, information about different services advertised in the network is gathered (2). This information includes types and descriptions of services and information that the client has to provide in order to be able to use them. Depending on local policies, different resources may have different requirements. Thus, the user agent must select the most suitable service that requires information the user is happy to provide.

The client may need to evaluate the chosen service (3) before using it. The evaluation is performed with the help of local policy (4). Additionally, the client may wish to check the quality of the service by collecting opinions of other clients (5). When this is done, the client may wish to continue, and makes a request (6, 7).

When the request is received on the service side, an authorisation agent is created to handle it. This performs risk assessment and checks whether the potential risk is acceptable in terms of the local policy of the resource (9). In doing this, it assesses the potential damage to the user in terms of the harm it is possible to do to the reputation associated with this identity, including identity loss, or loss of associated values (money may be charged if a credit card number is provided). It then compares this to the potential damage that could be sustained by the resource. It is therefore possible that users will be declined access when using one of their electronic identities and granted access when using another.

Depending on the circumstances, the authorisation agent may request additional information to be provided by the user (7). However, this may contradict user policy. For example, the user policy may not allow the release of some information from its local network.

When the client provides the information required by the service, the authorisation agent must collect evidence that the information provided is correct and that the user who requests the service is indeed the declared person (8).

At this point, the authorisation agent that processes the request has obtained the information on which it will base its authorisation decision. However, it does not yet know whether this information is trustworthy nor whether it has been sent by a legitimate source. The agent does not perform authentication itself. Instead, the authorisation agent delegates this task to third parties that have had previous experience of interactions with this user or different authorities (10). This runs an automatic credentials discovery (ACD) protocol. However, its basis is that there are different sources available that can be used to verify the user identity, provide information about a user's reputation, and verify information provided by a user. In pervasive systems, these sources could be distributed over numerous networks and, as a result, might not be capable of working co-operatively. Consequently, the authentication agent must collect their recommendations and combine them to have a reasonable basis for the access control decision it will take. For example, the local profile management server may verify a password's hash sent along with the request; or a request signed by a user's private key may be verified if one of the parties provides the corresponding public key; or there are authorities who can verify credit card numbers. We would like to note that local policies and the availability of information dictate the number of steps in this process and proof of identity required to obtain access.

After a request for user credentials is made, the authorisation agent must collect pieces of knowledge about the user in a secure and private manner. This information must be transformed from heterogeneous opinions into homogeneous data that can be automatically combined and thus allow a decision about user reputation to be made (11). It is worth noting that the result of negotiations between agents is not binary. The negotiations themselves are regulated by a set of fuzzy rules that are dynamically created and reflect local policies. Thus, the authorisation agent may decide that a user's credentials are inadequate to authorise the requested action, e.g. 'read/write', but are adequate to allow another, say 'read'. The client may accept or decline the offer, or be willing to give some extra information to obtain the desired service (for example, some companies require a deposit or a card number if a client does not have a credit history). After a user's credentials have been collected and evaluated, the authorisation agent decides whether or not to perform the action. If 'yes', the agent creates an association that is given to the client (12). The agent enforces access restrictions by controlling this association. Over the lifespan of an association, authorisation agents perform continuous auditing as a basis for the later (re)assessment of the user's reputation. Audit trails are also used for reactive fraud detection and response (14). Agents perform both misuse and anomaly detection and notify interested parties about any problems. When the action has been completed, the authorisation agent classifies its experience as positive or negative (15) and disseminates updates to user credentials (16). After this, the agent is destroyed, invalidating the client's association. At the client, the user agent evaluates user experience (17) and disseminates service credentials when appropriate (18).

While we have no space here to explore this further, it is unreasonable to assume that recommenders always provide accurate testimonies; the system can be subverted both maliciously and as a result of the use of different knowledge management methods or policies. Thus, evaluations of testimonies (fraud detection) and agents' ratings are used to maintain overall system integrity by favouring better recommenders.

10.4.2　Implementation

It is a requirement of any implementation of this architecture that it be sufficiently flexible to support heterogeneity of resources and transactions in the environments in which it is going to operate. Consequently, ADAM is being implemented as distributed lightweight component-based middleware. Figure 10.2 outlines its structure.

The system consists of independent components that can easily be re-implemented and replaced. Multiple instances of some components allow the system's behaviour to reflect underlying physical heterogeneity (in Fig. 10.2 there are five components marked that are most likely to have multiple instances). Although the detailed interfaces for each component are outside the scope of this paper, the components themselves can be described at a high level.

- Component manager

  The component manager is the system core and enables the remaining component instantiations to communicate. Since it provides the essential integration between all other components, it must necessarily be lightweight and small. It is primarily intended as a mechanism to allow components to communicate, but it is also responsible for the management of those components — for loading and unloading components. At present, for ease of design, XML is used for internal message description. It is expected that components will sometimes be unavailable due to failures, breaks for updating, connection loses, etc. Thus, we explicitly allow for the possibility of asynchronous communications between components and we further allow components to be distributed for cases in which a single node does not have the required power to support the entire architecture, but where a small collection of neighbouring nodes might.

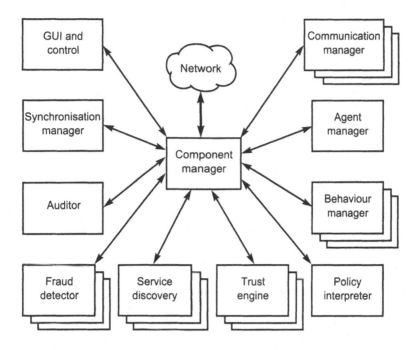

Fig. 10.2   ADAM component organisation.

- Communication manager

  The communication manager is a component responsible for support of method invocation and messaging with outside parties, including responsibility for interaction with name services and for message routing, particularly in *ad hoc* networking environments.

- Synchronisation manager

  The synchronisation manager is responsible for maintaining locally reliable time and date information to ensure freshness of messages and for audit purposes. It is not necessary to have the absolute time; indeed, Lamport's logical clocks might provide sufficient information to allow for the ordering of messages within sessions.

- Audit

  The audit component is used for collection and storage of information about transactions for debugging, for non-repudiation, and for fraud detection purposes. This can log information using different levels of verbosity, as determined by the fraud detector or GUI and control components. The audit component allocates and maintains the space required to store the audit log file, including the garbage collection of data as it is no longer needed.

- GUI and control

  The GUI and control component is needed to control the system, to permit the explicit change of components and the system configuration, and for debugging purposes. The GUI element allows for visualisation of the operation of different components.

- Service discovery

  The service discovery component is responsible for discovery and evaluation of networked services. Users provide criteria for service evaluations and searches. Multiple instances of this component may implement different service discovery mechanisms.

- Agent manager

  The agent manager maintains the agents created to perform different tasks for ADAM. It is responsible for space allocation, creation, deletion, and migrations of agents. It maintains current system state by continuously polling agents to check whether they are alive. It is responsible for maintenance of links to external agents in case existing agents (not controlled by the system) need to be connected to the system.

- Policy interpreter

  The policy interpreter takes organisational/environmental and user-specified policy and translates it into a universal underlying format. During this procedure it must resolve conflicts between policies and filter unnecessary policy rules. The result of conversion is used by the behaviour manager. The policy interpreter may interact with GUI and control components to facilitate user-defined policy specification.

- Trust engine

  The trust engine provides the core mechanism for trust-based decision making, along the lines described in detail above.

- Behaviour manager

  The behaviour manager uses encoded policy provided by the policy interpreter and abstract code from the trust engine to refine agents' behaviour. There might be more then one component providing abstract code. This code specifies behaviour of created agents. Thus, by registering more than one instance of the component it is possible to implement a variety of behaviours for agents (e.g. data collection agents, intrusion detection agents).

- Fraud detector

  The fraud detector provides misuse (and possibly anomaly) detection mechanism to detect abuse of given privileges. Its multiple instances may implement different fraud detection techniques.

10.5   Summary

This chapter has presented a conceptual description of the distributed access control system (ADAM), which is aimed at automation of a trust establishment process by performing distributed knowledge acquisition and management. The architecture is based upon two groups of agents — mobile user agents protecting user interests and authorisation agents protecting network resources. The access control decisions are results of negotiations between them. Local policies are translated into sets of fuzzy rules and the negotiations aimed at finding consensus between these sets.

The system allows automated trust establishment by gathering information about network entities and, later, maintenance of trust by constantly controlling information flow and manipulations with network resources. Several foundational aspects of ADAM make it different from the other trust management systems:

- it is designed to work in a range of networks, allowing automatic trust establishment and maintenance between entities situated in different network and administrative domains — this provides additional flexibility and allows ADAM to function in an ambient computing environment;

- it allows each user to have multiple electronic identities — it only authorises, it does not authenticate, the authentication task being delegated to separate parties;

- ADAM authorises transactions (actions), based on the history of the identity presented, with respect to the risk these actions pose to the resource if sanctioned, rather than the users.

Overall, the ADAM system facilitates automatic trust establishment and maintenance independently of the type and topology of underlying networks. This provides considerable flexibility and allows ADAM to function in pervasive environments.

References

1. Weiser M.   The Computer for the Twenty-first Century. Scientific American, 1991:256:94–104.

2. Grandison T. Trust Specification and Analysis for Internet Applications. PhD Transfer Report, Imperial College of Science, Technology and Medicine, Department of Computing, 2001.

3. Grandison T. Trust Management for Internet Applications. PhD thesis, Imperial College of Science, Technology and Medicine, Department of Computing, 2003.

4. McKnight D H and Chervany N L. The Meanings of Trust. University of Minnesota, 1996.

5. Abdul-Rahman A and Hailes S. Supporting Trust in Virtual Communities. 33rd Hawaii International Conference on System Sciences, 2000.

6. Chopra K and Wallace W. Trust in Electronic Environments. 36th Hawaii International Conference on System Sciences, 2003:331–340.

7. Marsh S. Formalising Trust as a Computational Concept. PhD thesis, Department of Computer Science and Mathematics, University of Stirling, 1994.

8. Seleznyov A and Hailes S. A Conceptual Access Control Model Based on Distributed Knowledge Management. IEEE, 18th International Conference on Advanced Information Networking and Applications, 2004.

9. Estrin D et al. Connecting the Physical World with Pervasive Networks. IEEE Pervasive Computing, 2002:1:1:59–69.

10. Kindberg T et al. People, Places, Things: Web Presence for the Real World. Proc WMCSA2000, 2001.

11. Eustice K et al. Enabling Secure Ubiquitous Interactions. 1st International Workshop on Middleware for Pervasive *Ad Hoc* Computing, 2003.

12. Stajano F. Security for Whom? The Shifting Security Assumptions of Pervasive Computing. Proceedings of International Security Symposium, Springer-Verlag, 2002.

13. Stajano F and Crowcroft J. The Butt of the Iceberg: Hidden Security Problems of Ubiquitous Systems. In: Basten T, Geilen M, and deGroot H (editors). Ambient Intelligence: Impact on Embedded System Design. Kluwer Academic Publishers, 2003.

14. Blaze M, Feigenbaum J, and Lacy J. Decentralized Trust Management. IEEE Symposium on Security and Privacy, 1996.

15. Kagal L et al. Centaurus: A Framework for Intelligent Services in a Mobile Environment. The 21st International Conference on Distributed Computing Systems Workshops (ICDCSW '01), 2001.

16. Kagal L et al. A Security Architecture Based on Trust Management for Pervasive Computing Systems. Grace Hopper Celebration of Women in Computing, 2002.

17. English C et al. Trusting Collaboration in Global Computing. The First International Conference on Trust Management, Springer-Verlag, 2003:2692:136–149.

18. Mui L, Mohtashemi M, and Halberstadt A. A Computational Model of Trust and Reputation. 35th Hawaii International Conference on System Sciences, 2004.

19. Veijalainen J, Seleznyov A, and Mazhelis O. Security and Privacy of the PTP. In: Makki K et al (editors). Mobile and Wireless Internet: Protocols, Algorithms, and Systems. Kluwer Academic Publishers, 2003:165–190.

11

Maintaining Privacy in Pervasive Computing — Enabling Acceptance of Sensor-based Services

A Soppera and T Burbridge

11.1   Introduction

During the 1980s, Mark Weiser [1] predicted a world in which computing was so pervasive that devices embedded in the environment could sense their relationship to us and to each other. These tiny ubiquitous devices would continually feed information from the physical world into the information world. Twenty years ago, this vision was the exclusive territory of academic computer scientists and science fiction writers. Today this subject has become of interest to business, government, and society. Governmental authorities exercise their power through the networked environment. Credit card databases maintain our credit history and decide whether we are allowed to rent a house or obtain a loan. Mobile telephones can locate us in real time so that we do not miss calls. Within another 10 years, all sorts of devices will be connected through the network. Our fridge, our food, together with our health information, may all be networked for the purpose of maintaining diet and well-being. The Internet will move from being an infrastructure to connect computers, to being an infrastructure to connect everything [2, 3].

The development of pervasive computing will expose personal information to a host of applications. How will people maintain control of their personal information and enforce their privacy in this brave new world? This chapter presents the privacy and pervasive computing communities' efforts to develop technology, guidelines, and models that can be used to manage privacy in the new world of pervasive computing.

This pervasive computing revolution has already started. A group of researchers at the University of California, Berkeley, have designed tiny sensor motes, using low-cost commercial components, which can automatically organise themselves into an *ad hoc* radio communications networks when dispersed into the environment. Each device contains an open source operating system known as TinyOS [4] that can fit in less than 8 kilobytes of memory and can be configured or reprogrammed remotely. They can be used for an enormous range of applications including surveying natural environments and wildlife, monitoring buildings and structures, and tracking objects.

Similar devices have already been deployed in the automotive sector. Sensors, black boxes, and telemetry tools have been built into vehicles to improve their security, to notify when the engine needs to be serviced, and to warn the driver of imminent danger. In the future this information may also be used by insurance companies to create personal driving profiles and insurance quotes, or by highway authorities and law enforcement agencies.

Technology developers need to anticipate when the deployment of privacy-invading technology may generate resentment in end users and block the huge potential for the growth of beneficial applications. In such cases they need to be aware of the tools available to give control of personal data back to the users. Over the last quarter-century, principles for the treatment of personal data have been developed around the globe for IT systems and communications networks. Such principles can extend in scope to cover data collected from pervasive devices and sensors, but as we see in this chapter, pervasive computing has its own challenges to develop solutions to support these principles.

In the following section we describe the opportunities and threats for pervasive computing, by introducing some of the emerging uses and the concerns for privacy that they are generating. We then discuss the social aspects of privacy, illustrating a model that can be used to analyse how people perceive privacy, and the factors that can be used to control and manage privacy. Following this we look at the development of fair information practices, concentrating on the OECD guidelines for privacy, and how these relate to pervasive computing. Finally, we survey technology that can contribute to enhancing privacy and discuss these solutions in two parts. We first mention methods to control or minimise the release of sensitive information, before talking about how the flow and use of personal data can be managed. We focus our technology discussion towards techniques that can enhance the participation of the data subject, since we consider this to be the major hurdle in pervasive computing.

11.2   Emerging Pervasive Computing — Opportunities and Threats

Take a look into the future of a world in which minimal computing power devices are so cheap that they are embedded in the fabric of everyday life. Devices that do not look like 'real' computers will be able to disappear so effectively that end users will lose awareness of the devices' presence or purpose. The Internet will extend its presence to the physical world, and across it will flow large volumes of data that are analysed and correlated by powerful servers (Fig. 11.1). We must discuss the consequences that this scenario introduces into everyday life before it becomes reality. Today, we can barely perceive the benefits that might be ultimately delivered, or the ingenious uses that it might be put to by malicious or indiscriminate parties. Nevertheless, worrying scenarios have already been described in books, journals, and research articles.

Disappearing sensors are welcome because they hide complexity, but this also introduces some serious usability issues. If you cannot interact with the computer, how can you tell what data is collected, where the data is flowing to, and, more importantly, what the consequences of your actions are? The lack of a clear user interface introduces a tension between technology and human factors. Can we do something to maintain control or will we finally lose the ability to control our privacy?

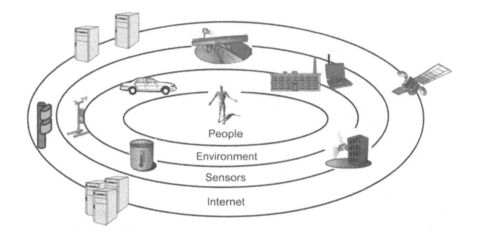

Fig. 11.1   Connecting the physical world with the pervasive network.

Already private companies such as Wal-Mart and Gillette have deployed the first generation of systems to automatically monitor their supply chains and increase the security of their assets. These systems are based on radio frequency identification (RFID) tags [5]. These are small and commonly passive devices that transmit an identifier when scanned by a reader. Part of the appeal of this technology lies in the fact that these chips do not require line of sight to be read (i.e. they can be read with radio technology), can be scanned simultaneously, and can contain a global unique identifier for the item. The objective is to make them a powerful replacement for optical bar codes. This technology enables objects to be clearly identified, and thereby linked to an associated data record held on the Internet or in a remote database. While many companies are running trials for their supply chains and retail operations, users could also benefit from the tags by obtaining ingredient origins, dietary information, expiry dates, cooking instructions, or example recipes — and that is just for foodstuffs.

Since RFID tags can be scanned unobtrusively from a distance, it is easy to realise the potential for privacy violations (Fig. 11.2). Both consumer and manufacturer communities have already shown their concerns about this technology. For instance, Benetton made the headlines when a proposal to use RFID tags in their shops was misreported. Benetton proposed a solution to track clothes from the time they were produced until the time they were sold. The impression was that these tags would remain active even after the point of retail sale, so that they could be used to track returns or identify customers entering the shop wearing clothes previously bought from the same retailer. To protect the privacy of customers, checkout clerks can just 'kill' the tags, or alternatively the use of tags can be confined to disposable packing.

Security and privacy worries are not restricted to consumers or retail environments. Two further areas that are related to the use of RFID inside organisations and do not receive as much press are described below.

- End-user tracking

   Individuals, or the employers they work for, could decide to have permanently active tags for use by authorised readers. However, other parties and applications than intended by the holder may exploit these tags. For example, remote access cards to enter premises may be used for security, and for building fire evacuation. They might also be used to clock working activities and hours, or read by third parties to identify someone who works for that company.

- Corporate espionage

The ease of monitoring competitor activities can lead to industrial espionage. For example, competitors can easily track the movement of pallets or trucks. Firms consider it unacceptable that the private information of their supply chain is visible to the outside world and can be exploited by competitors or other parties (such as thieves).

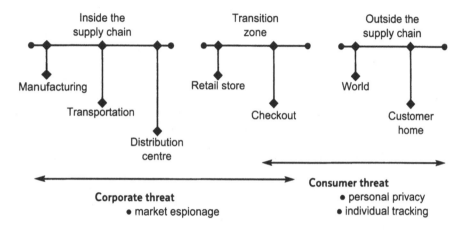

Fig. 11.2   RFID tags — an ocean of privacy issues from the manufacturer to the consumer.

RFID represents the first real effort to extend the Internet to global physical activity, where other sensor networks have generally been limited to closed physical environments (such as an area of forest or tidal flow). The privacy issues that a highly digitised world will face are far more complex than the consequences of simply associating an identity to each object with an RFID tag. With such tags, we can identify them and control access (through killing/activating the tag, encryption, pseudonyms, or blocking technology). Other technologies may be far less noticeable, or be beyond our physical reach. Devices such as cameras or microphones read the physical world directly, rather than an associated electronic tag. We cannot encrypt or otherwise police access to the physical world. Technologists and system designers that implement and deploy pervasive computing or intrusive technologies should be concerned by the nature of networked environments and the vulnerabilities from increased connectivity of information systems.

The collection of digital information about the activities of individuals and assets, through sensor networks and aggregation with intentionally revealed information in the Internet such as purchasing or registration activities, could create detailed profile information. While from a point of view of privacy this trend of increased interaction can be seen as a great threat, some companies can foresee great business opportunities to reduce costs, and increase services. A large amount of embedded devices will ease the process of collecting personal information and enable our environment to adapt to our presence. A better collection and aggregation of personal data will allow different businesses to have a deeper view of consumers' behaviour and provide a better service.

Several questions arise about the value of this data. If personal data is valuable, why should not individuals benefit from this value? Can the market set a correct price for personal information by returning value to the consumer? Can we guarantee that information is acquired and disclosed only for legitimate purposes? These questions will soon require an answer.

11.3 Understanding Privacy in Pervasive Computing

If privacy in pervasive computing is such a hot topic, why has the impact on technology been rather minimal? One reason is surely the fact that only a few research groups around the world have developed comprehensive pervasive or sensor systems.

To date, such systems have only been deployed in restricted environments. For example, measuring humidity in a forest is unlikely to cause any great privacy uproar.

Another reason is the ambiguity of people's perception of privacy. The definition of private is normally found in the field of legal studies, and technologists have a hard time to define a model that considers not only technical, but also social and economic implications. Only recently the research community has studied conceptual models of privacy to assist system designers and service providers in the deployment of (pervasive) computing.

Definitions and discussions about privacy have a long history with the expectations of individuals continually evolving in different cultures. As early as 1890 the paper 'The Right to Privacy' [6] defined privacy as 'the right to be let alone'. Today, privacy is more often about selecting what information we would like to disclose.

Over the course of the 20th century, the privacy focus has shifted with technological developments and social threats. The exploitation of detailed public records during the World War II, by Nazi Germany, allowed them to identify the Jewish population in many cities. Many European countries have developed laws to prevent such misuse of centrally stored information within their own country. During the 1960s, and particularly the 1970s, the introduction of information technology, and the use of mainframe computers and databases, prompted the demand for new national laws on the collection of personal data. Westin at this time defined information privacy as '... the claims of individuals, groups or institutions to determine for themselves when, how and to what extent information about them is communicated to the others' [7].

This section first takes a look at work to model users' perception of privacy, along with the factors that can be controlled in order to make the release of information to be acceptable. Sections 11.3.2 and 11.3.3 follows discussing the development of international guidelines for privacy, and how they fit with the emerging world of pervasive computing.

11.3.1   Privacy Models

Privacy has always been a very broad term, encompassing both fundamental human rights [8] and less definable personal factors. Definitions of privacy can vary widely according to the context and environment in which they are used. In the last quarter-century, definitions have often related to data protection, and these focus on the privacy of data items that contain personal secrets. It is often easier to define privacy as a border between the society (government and private sector) and one's personal affairs. Marx [9] refines the concept of borders by introducing natural, social, spatial or temporal, and ephemeral borders. Natural borders are those governed by the natural senses, and physical boundaries such as clothes, walls, sealed envelopes, and direct telephone calls. Social borders govern the expectation that information is shared within a social group, such as friends, family, work, or healthcare. Spatial or temporal borders separate aspects on one's life, such as moving to university or starting employment. Finally, ephemeral borders are based on the assumption that information is transitory and not captured or preserved longer than expected.

With the development and availability of personal information technology, privacy models have considered the interactions between the users and the digitised world. With the Internet, users can be exposed to systems that provide different degrees of privacy and security. Users should be able to verify what privacy protection is implemented and how their data will be used. In multimedia communications environments, Adams [10] has identified four key factors that affect the user perception of privacy — information sensitivity, information receiver/ manipulator, information usage, and the context of disclosure.

Perceived infringements of privacy can lead to users rejecting the technology and thereby decreasing its commercial value. A new challenging tussle is emerging between the subjects that share information and the manipulators that exploit it for their own value. This conflict arises because the intent of the manipulator cannot be clearly identified. Sensitive information disclosed to a trusted party may not affect our privacy, while low-sensitivity information can create resentment if disclosed to the wrong people. The user's control and feedback from the computing environments are important variables that affect the perception of privacy.

The introduction of pervasive computing raises the level of the challenge to protect privacy. Computing devices embedded in the fabric of everyday life will require systems that are able to evolve with the needs of the society and able to interact with the users to meet their requirements for privacy. Lederer [11] has proposed a cohesive model of privacy in pervasive computing by synthesising Adam's user perceptual model with Lessig's societal model [12]. Lederer extends this model by introducing the metaphor of faces. In the real world people choose which face to present in different situations, and this concept can be extended to pervasive computing services. A face, in this case, is a meaningful representation of a user's privacy preferences in that context. Lessig's model illustrates privacy as a balance of four different forces — law, market, norms, and technology. The discussion in Sections 11.3.2 and 11.3.3 about information practices covers some aspects of law and norms. Section 11.4 goes on to discuss how technology can play a role in the protection of privacy. The market can be also used to control privacy. Companies must protect their brand through reputable dealings, including the treatment of private data. Also, the data subject can be returned value through the release of the personal data. This can be through better services, or simply as monetary rewards. For example, it is common practice in the USA to offer rebates on goods when personal information is disclosed.

Allesandro Acquisti [13] is one of a new wave of economists examining the value of privacy. He suggests that there is a current imbalance between the value of information to business, and the costs perceived by individuals when releasing private information. Users find it hard to assess the long-term risks against the immediate gratification of obtaining a service. With little margin to be made from the bulk of customers for the integration or privacy into services, Acquisti argues that there is a privacy-concerned minority market that is unaddressed. Since the mass has not driven the development of technology, the costs of providing service to this privacy-aware market are significant. As the market for ubiquitous devices and services develops, we may see a growth in this unaddressed area. There is hope that the technology market may be pushed by continued regulation, and that standardisation will lower the costs of implementing a privacy-sensitive service.

Although there is hope that the economic barrier to privacy may be broken down, there is perhaps a far greater hurdle to overcome, before privacy-enhancing technology becomes as commonplace as the ubiquitous services that we have foreseen. While it may become more economically feasible to offer privacy, in the world of pervasive computing there is a significant danger than privacy will become unmanageable. We want pervasive computing to disappear into the fabric of the physical world — not to intrude continuously to ask whether information should be released to other parties and services. Anyone managing a firewall has had the barest glimpse of the complexity that may exist in managing our privacy through rules and policies. The greatest challenge facing us will be to provide mechanisms to control privacy that are natural and lightweight, yet comprehensive in achieving the expected levels of privacy.

Protecting privacy in this 'brave' new world depends on the same factors identified by Lessig and Adams. We must receive value for releasing our information, have trust in practices, have protection and control through technology, and have legal recourse should our rights be infringed. We need to control our personal data, and to receive feedback on how such data is communicated and used in order to build trust.

11.3.2 Fair Information Practices

One of the influential pieces of early privacy legislation was the US Privacy Act of 1974 [14], which set down a number of fair information practices. Even earlier than this, many European countries had begun to implement laws to protect information privacy. Within the Organisation for Economic Co-operation and Development (OECD), there was concern that the development of disparate legislative approaches to privacy in member countries (including Europe and the USA) would hinder trans-border flow of information, and thus '... cause serious disruption in important sectors of the economy, such as banking or insurance' [15]. Hence, in 1980, the OECD encapsulated eight principles among its privacy guidelines to member states. These OECD guidelines have formed the basis for much discussion and development of guidelines and legislation around the world over the past quarter-century. Even today the formation of an Asia-Pacific privacy standard across the APEC economies is starting from a set of principles very close to the original OECD guidelines [16].

The eight OECD principles are reproduced below. Whereas they appear as guidelines 7 to 14 in the OECD document, we have renumbered them here as Principles 1 to 8.

1. Collection limitation principle

There should be limits to the collection of personal data and any such data should be obtained by lawful and fair means and, where appropriate, with the knowledge or consent of the data subject.

2. Data quality principle

Personal data should be relevant to the purposes for which they are to be used, and, to the extent necessary for those purposes, should be accurate, complete and kept up-to-date.

3. Purpose specification principle

The purposes for which personal data are collected should be specified not later than at the time of data collection and the subsequent use limited to the fulfilment of those purposes or such others as are not incompatible with those purposes and as are specified on each occasion of change of purpose.

4. Use limitation principle

Personal data should not be disclosed, made available or otherwise used for purposes other than those specified in accordance with Principle 3 (Paragraph 9) except:

    a) with the consent of the data subject; or

    b) by the authority of law.

5. Security safeguards principle

Personal data should be protected by reasonable security safeguards against such risks as loss or unauthorised access, destruction, use, modification or disclosure of data.

6. Openness principle

There should be a general policy of openness about developments, practices and policies with respect to personal data. Means should be readily available of establishing the existence and nature of personal data, and the main purposes of their use, as well as the identity and usual residence of the data controller.

7. Individual participation principle

An individual should have the right:

    a) to obtain from a data controller, or otherwise, confirmation of whether or not the data controller has data relating to him;

    b) to have communicated to him, data relating to him within a reasonable time; at a charge, if any, that is not excessive; in a reasonable manner; and in a form that is readily intelligible to him;

c) to be given reasons if a request made under subparagraphs (a) and (b) is denied, and to be able to challenge such denial; and

d) to challenge data relating to him and, if the challenge is successful to have the data erased, rectified, completed or amended.

8. Accountability principle

A data controller should be accountable for complying with measures which give effect to the principles stated above.

Reproduced from 'Guidelines on the Protection of Privacy and Transborder Flows of Personal Data' OECD 1980 [15]

In 1998, the OECD reviewed the continued relevance of the 1980 OECD guidelines in consideration of the 'development and diffusion of digital computer and network technologies'. Their declaration [17] stated that they reaffirmed their commitment to the 1980 OECD privacy guidelines. Despite this, the OECD guidelines are not without their critics. Some criticise the goal of the OECD principles as furthering economic trade instead of preserving the rights of individuals [18], while others question the relevance of the OECD guidelines to the modern technological world [19]. Much of the discussion around the OECD guidelines concerns the number of discretionary clauses and lack of requirements for legal enforcement. Instead, in this chapter we are primarily concerned with the principles themselves, and how well they fit with a pervasive computing world.

Clarke [18] points out that the OECD guidelines may be contradictory in that they state that the principles are '... valid for the processing of data in general, irrespective of the technology employed', while they are also limited to data on which 'automatic processing' is performed. This leaves some room for debate about what constitutes automatic processing. However, by the former statement, we can consider the OECD principles to apply to personal data gathered by pervasive sensors and other devices. In the following section we consider how well the OECD principles fit into the world of pervasive computing, in terms of both the wording of the principles themselves, and the problems of implementation.

11.3.3 The OECD Principles and Pervasive Computing

In this section we consider some of the problems with the application of the OECD principles to the world of pervasive computing technology. We find that there remain areas of privacy concern that are not covered by the wording of the OECD principles, alongside outstanding technical problems with their implementation in this new world.

Personal Data and Identity

Perhaps the main question is: 'What is personal data?' The OECD guidelines define personal data to mean '... any information relating to an identified or identifiable individual (data subject)'. This means that much information, where a person's identity may not be immediately discerned, may fall outside the scope of the OECD principles. This is of great concern where pervasive devices are collecting huge volumes of data, which may only be collated to ascertain personal information at a later stage. Furthermore, the OECD principles can be interpreted to mean that data collected anonymously would be free from restrictions on use. This raises concerns, not only about the later identification, but also about tracking or behaviour analysis, along with invasions of privacy through directed marketing and customised services. For example, we do not require identity to track the path of a person leaving school at the end of lessons. For others, the offering of services based upon the identification of physical characteristics (height, weight), the clothes we wear, and the objects we carry may be seen as intrusive — for example, the offer of a new dietary product.

There is also a problem with the use of 'identity'. The OECD appears to only consider the identity of a physical individual. However, in an information world we may present ourselves through the use of multiple identities. For example, in our use of the Internet, a single individual might typically use multiple log-in names, e-mail and IP addresses. Many of these cannot immediately be linked to an individual's physical identity, but this is possible through aggregation with other data. Perhaps more fundamentally, users may regard such aliases as part of their identity, or to hold value that cannot be simply thrown away continuously to protect their privacy. For example, an alias might have been used to build a transaction history (e.g. on eBay), or to establish a presence in an Internet chat community. The use of identity to mean the physical individual also then opens the possibility of surveillance of assets and physical goods, whether owned by a company or an individual. Although a burglar surveying one's house for various goods electronically must be considered a security risk, should it be considered an invasion of privacy? Similarly, corporate espionage might not relate to an individual and falls outside the scope of the OECD considerations. Of course, there is also a grey area between individual identity and assets. For example, the identification of an asset such as a car can lead easily to the identification of the potential drivers.

We have seen that the OECD principles have not clearly considered the full extent of the privacy issues that arise in the new age of information technology, networks, and particularly pervasive computing. In the remaining part of this section we consider the problems of implementing the principles in a pervasive computing world. We first look at the problems surrounding the interface of the physical and information world, and the involvement of the data subject. We then look at the management of how the data is stored and used for the remainder of its life cycle.

Data Collection

The collection of data is mainly governed by OECD Principles 1 to 3. To summarise, the collection of data should be limited, obtained with the knowledge or consent of the subject, and relevant for a purpose that has been disclosed to the subject.

In the age in which the OECD principles were developed, and indeed in many uses in today's information world, subjects are present when such data is recorded. In this manner, such notices, fine print, and on-line privacy statements may be read before, or during the process of giving up their personal data.

Perhaps the most fundamental change in the world of pervasive computing is this lack of a two-way interface between the subject and the information world. A camera may record your movements, but how do we notify the subject and obtain consent for use? The current conventions of 'CCTV cameras in operation' and roadside speed camera signs are not scalable with the spread of pervasive devices and their uses — or will become meaningless to the extent of displaying 'pervasive computing devices in this area' signs. The OECD guidelines already only specify obtaining consent 'where appropriate'. With the spread of pervasive computing, the number of uses will grow for which it may seem impractical to ask consent. More and more of our privacy will fall beyond our ability to control.

Section 11.4 looks at some techniques for controlling our privacy. Broadly, these technologies take two approaches. The first seeks to minimise the collection of personal data through anonymity techniques. The second, and more immature area, looks for ways whereby subjects can provide consent and retain control without their immediate presence.

Data Usage, Storage, and Access

In this section we concern ourselves with the OECD Principles 2, 4, 6, 7, and 8. Broadly, the principles listed deal with the processes to control the legitimate usage of the data, the maintenance of correct data, and the access by the subjects of the data to their own personal data.

The OECD model relies on the 'data controller' being accountable for their adherence to the other privacy principles (as stated in Principle 8). The OECD guidelines specify that 'adequate sanctions and remedies' must be in place to ensure the good behaviour of the data controller. In Europe [20] and other implementations of the OECD principles, this means the existence of supervisory bodies and supporting laws to enforce compliance. Each data controller must register the categories of data collected, and the purposes to which they are put, with such supervisory bodies. These bodies then have powers to audit the compliance of the data controllers with their specified intentions.

The data subject is given powers to request, from a data controller, what personal data is maintained, and to challenge the purpose for which it is held. However, in the OECD principles, and the EU implementation, such communications may be charged at a reasonable cost (to protect the data controller involved). This process relies on the fact that notice has previously been given to the data subjects that their personal data is being collected. Without such notice, it is hard for the data subjects to identify which data controllers may hold their personal data. As has already been stated, such notice will become harder to give in a pervasive computing world, and additionally it will become impossible without assistance for the data subjects to maintain knowledge of all data controllers that have some of their data.

Section 11.4.2 examines some techniques that allow the data subjects to maintain a role in the maintenance and usage of their personal data after it has been released. Proposed technologies seek to maintain the data subjects' control remotely through the use of cryptography and policies, while giving data tracking and auditing capabilities back to the data subjects.

11.4   Technical Approaches to Privacy

Before diving into specific techniques to enhance and protect privacy, it helps to have a technical overview on the security characteristics of sensor networks. These networks may consist of hundreds or thousands of low-power, low-cost wireless nodes, each with limited hardware capabilities. From a security point of view, one of the main risks is the reliance on wireless network communications, so that adversaries, even if they are physically distant, can easily eavesdrop on the radio transmission. Unfortunately, traditional cryptographic solutions can only partially solve the problem. The fact that the devices are extremely limited in computation and communication resources means that they will require very lightweight security protocols. Another problem is the fact that every node represents a potential point of attack. An adversary in control of a few nodes inside the network can then launch attacks against the whole sensor network. Technologists can build tamper-resistant devices, but this raises the cost of such devices. In this chapter we acknowledge this problem space, but concentrate on the overall privacy of the data subject. Low-cost transmission security techniques are evolving, but perhaps as important for privacy is the control of the information flow, as opposed to protecting that flow from eavesdroppers. The first OECD principle states that '... there should be limits to the collection of personal data'. If personal data is not collected, then it cannot be misused, and expensive solutions to control such usage become unnecessary. Given the difficulties with establishing explicit consent (due to lack of two-way communication, or limited device computational power), techniques to restrict the release of information, such as anonymity and pseudonymity, are often considered a better approach.

11.4.1   Anonymity, Accountability, and Pseudonyms

Anonymity techniques ensure that users may use a resource or a service without disclosing their identity (see Fig. 11.3). In the communication domain we can define anonymity as the inability to link a communication to any particular sender or receiver [21]. The assumption is that if data cannot be related to the individual, it poses no threats in terms of privacy, and therefore there is no need to restrict its collection. However, it must be realised that associated information about an identified individual may be used to attack the anonymity of other data. Also, while anonymity might protect some definitions of privacy, as described in Section 11.3, anonymous data may still be used for malicious purposes.

Accountability may be considered to be an opposing objective to anonymity. In order to have accountability, we need to identify who has taken various actions. For some sensor networks and applications, accountability is important. For example, we may wish to know which doctors have accessed the drugs storage in a hospital. Pseudonyms can be used to preserve anonymity in normal usage but allow identification and accountability in certain cases. A pseudonym normally means an ID that can be used to uniquely link an action to an identity and authenticate the party (or asset) involved. The strength of anonymity decreases, as more is known about a particular pseudonym — for example, as it is used for more and more transactions.

The ultimate strength in terms of anonymity is achieved by changing the pseudonym for every transaction. In this manner, correlation of different transactions (and other data) cannot be used to infer identity. Another property of continually changing the pseudonym is that the item or person cannot be traced though the repeated use of the same pseudonym, which may or may not be desirable. For example, we do not wish a mugger to be able to tell that an anonymous person

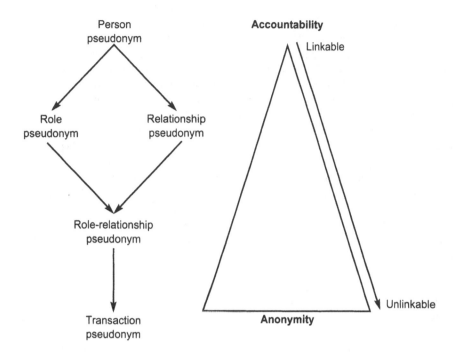

Fig. 11.3   Protecting privacy through pseudonyms — decreasing correlation leads to
increasing anonymity (reproduced from Pfitzmann and Köhntopp [21]).

regularly takes a certain route between shop and bank at the end of the day, but we
do wish to analyse road traffic flows of anonymous cars.

Pseudonym techniques are currently being proposed for use in RFID tags [22].
Each time a tag is queried by a scanner, the output must be indistinguishable from
truly random values, and unable to be linked by unauthorised parties to the actual ID
of the tag. This kind of technique is simple and cheap to implement on the tag, but
authorised readers must have access to the list or chain of pseudonyms that will be
used and be able to map backwards from the pseudonym to the actual ID.

While pseudonym techniques are useful for anonymity, they do not offer perfect
protection for personal information for two reasons. Firstly, as has been explained,
anonymous information may be correlated with other sources of information, and
even anonymous information may hold some value against the interests of the data
subject. Secondly, ubiquitous computing environments include sensors that sense
our real identity or other physical properties. For example, it is much harder to
continually change our physical appearance to fool a digital camera than it is to
change an electronic ID in an RFID tag. This is compounded by observations
performed by people — such as knowing when a person leaves a house in the
morning. Although pseudonyms might have uses such as to hide number plates on
cars from parties other than the police or highways authorities, we must realise that
our current social interactions and presence in the real world cannot be completely
hidden behind pseudonyms. Unless we decide to live in a completely digitised world
and interact only through computers and networks, some information about our real
identity will always be disclosed.

The final problem with anonymity is that we risk removing valuable services. For example, we can share pseudonym information about car registration numbers with the police, but for every additional party we wish to be able to offer services, we must explicitly arrange for them to be able to break our anonymity. A common approach to this problem is to use trusted intermediary (or group of intermediaries) to protect our information, but still allow provision of multiple services. Past approaches have taken the approach of mixing information from different subjects, or aggregating subject information. A few examples of such systems for use over the Internet are Mix-nets [23] for anonymous e-mail and Crowds [24] for Web browsing.

Interest has been awakened in solutions to protect privacy during the provision of location-based services. This is particularly important in the light of European directive 2002/58/EC [25]. This directive brings the European privacy directive 1995/46/EC [20] and its telecommunications counterpart 1997/66/EC [26] up to date for 'new advanced digital technologies' and the 'introduction of new electronic communication services'.

Along with new guidelines for the use of e-mail, services, directories, anonymous communication, and transport data (such as routing records), the directive in Principle 3 (Paragraph 9) also specifically focuses on location-based services. It states that: 'Where location data ... relating to users ... can be processed, such data may only be processed when they are made anonymous, or with the consent of the users'. It goes on to state that, prior to consent, the users must be informed of the 'type of location data' that is being used, along with the 'purposes and duration of the processing', and any third parties involved in the delivery of value-added service. Furthermore, users must have the means to temporarily withdraw their consent per communication of location information. Given the arduous tasks of implementing such notification and consent procedures, it is likely that location-based services will instead choose to process anonymous data.

Two interesting approaches to providing anonymity for location-based services are Mix Zones [27] and k-anonymity [28]. In Mix Zones, the user's location data is transmitted to a trusted intermediary. Users have the ability to specify location regions or zones, within which they are willing to share their location information. Critically, while within one of these zones, instead of presenting the users' ID to the location-based service, a pseudonym is generated and used instead. A new pseudonym is created every time users change zone. Although potentially the tracing of individuals is possible, given high enough populations and errors in location accuracy, the application's confidence in tracking a single individual is quickly diminished. In the approach of Gruteser and Grunwald [28], the user identification is also removed, but, in addition, the user location information is blended together such that a user's location is indistinguishable from the location of $k-1$ other data subjects.

We can see that anonymity solutions are key technologies to delivering services in the world of pervasive computing. They rely on the principle of minimal release of information, such as through the mixing or aggregation of data. If data is not released, then it is impossible to abuse. Pseudonyms can also be used for selective release of information through the careful release of data that allows the pseudonym to be matched to an identity. Similarly encryption techniques can be used to distribute information in a controlled manner. In Section 11.4.2 we look at techniques for controlling access to information (OECD principles on collection limitation and purpose specification), and methods for tracing and auditing its use (OECD principle on openness, participation, and accountability).

11.4.2 Privacy Management

In his controversial book 'The Transparent Society' [29], Brin introduces a world in which privacy is non-existent. The Internet allows people to gather information across great distances and to correlate information at unimaginable speed. Brin warns that governments and major businesses are exploiting technology for ubiquitous spying and suggests that the only possible remedy is to have a world where information is free and everybody has the capability to spy on everybody else. In this manner we can at least see who is spying on us. While this approach might work in anarchist socialism [30], where the people have the power to back up the information and to enforce correct behaviour, it is hard to imagine it working in today's society. Even if we do not share the same pessimistic vision of Brin, we can agree that a total protection of our privacy will hardly be achievable, or desirable. What we can expect is the introduction of more technology to enhance our privacy.

Many Web sites and Internet applications now carry associated privacy policies. Similarly there are privacy notices in the real world (e.g. CCTV) and small print on subscription forms. Aside from the odd tick-box, how many people actually manage to read such notices and assert control over their privacy? In a Federal Trade Commission Workshop on Consumer Data [31], the Excite@Home privacy officer stated that only 100 out of 20 million visitors accessed the privacy policy the day after they featured in an Internet privacy segment of a popular TV show [32]. To address this problem, work has started within the W3C on the Platform for Privacy Preferences or P3P [33]. This project enables Web sites to express their privacy policies in machine-readable XML formats. Before a page is accessed from the user's browser, an agent first checks the privacy policy for that page, and alerts the user to any discrepancies between the page and the user policy. Along with the criticism of the legal foundation for P3P, the technical criticism of P3P has been curiously bipolar. On one hand, there are concerns that the policy expression is not complicated enough to accurately capture a company's (or user's) privacy policy [34], and that it does not allow negotiation over privacy settings or operate over more than just HTTP [35]. On the other hand, there are suggestions that user policies across multiple applications or Web clients is unmanageable, and that users will be unable to understand and express their own complex policies and have to fall back to default settings [36]. Most critics are agreed that P3P is a step in the right direction — just that it has some way to go before maturity.

So is P3P a solution for pervasive computing? The answer is likely to be 'no' for a number of reasons. If the complexity of policies is hindering the development of a privacy solution for Web access, then these problems will be massively compounded in the pervasive computing domain. Following the privacy model of Adams (see Section 11.3.1), we might wish ultimately to express policies in terms of data, destination, purpose, and contextual information. For example, I might wish to allow Tesco to use my location information only when I am in the Ipswich-based stores, and only for the purpose of notifying special offers. We can only imagine how complicated it might become to express such policies for every possible interaction in a highly pervasive computing world of the future. Although our ability to express computer-understandable policies will grow, we cannot get rid of the requirement for users to understand what is happening with their data. However, policies are likely to form another key component in the support for personal privacy — but perhaps in limited domains where they can be easily understood and codified.

The greater restriction of P3P that limits its applicability to pervasive computing is the requirement for the user (or at least a user agent) to be present in the information transfer. In pervasive computing, the information may flow from a user-controlled device, but might equally flow from another sensory device in the environment. In this latter case, there is no clear binding to an identified subject. For example, although cameras and microphones might pick up privacy-sensitive information, there is no easy way at that point either to identify the person involved, or to examine that person's privacy preferences. Langheinrich has proposed one solution to this problem in his Privacy Awareness System [37]. In his system, sensors beacon their identity to the environment, so that users can then contact a privacy proxy for that device and negotiate their privacy settings. An alternative solution that does not require standardisation of local wireless communication protocols would be for a user device to employ a positioning service, and to examine sensors near that location for their privacy policies. Apart from removing the requirement for a standard announcement protocol and wireless communications medium, this solution also has the advantage that other locations (perhaps in advance of our travels) can be examined. Both approaches have applicability for general pervasive device control beyond just privacy settings — for example, the detection and setting of a central heating system.

A similar binding between the data subject's preferences and the data read by the sensing device is achieved with RFID tags by using 'soft blocking' [38]. When the RFID reader scans tags within range, one or more of these tags may be a soft blocker tag. In the simplest scenario, the presence of a soft blocker tag indicates that information about other tags (that are flagged as private) may not be transmitted. In a more complicated scenario, different soft blocker IDs may indicate different treatments of other tags, and the privacy policy associated with that soft blocker tag is found by a database look-up. Although the soft-blocking proposal relies on trust between the tag owner and the reader, we can imagine a scheme where the information on the RFID tag is encrypted or pseudonymised. The soft-blocking tag might then provide a link to the authorising party in a similar manner to the Casassa-Mont et al [39] solution described ahead.

Another problem with the approach of P3P is that the information is delivered to a single application, and therefore controlled by a single policy. In a highly pervasive computer world, information from one sensor may be delivered simultaneously, along with other sensor information, to numerous applications. For this reason Casassa-Mont et al [39] suggest attaching a 'sticky' policy to the information. Information fields can be encoded using identifier-based encryption (a technique to allow the string-based encryption of data, and the subsequent generation of the decryption key [40]) and delivered to multiple applications. The application then refers to a trust authority and attests to fulfilling the conditions of the use policy before gaining the keys for access to the information. The trust authority, in this manner, also is able to perform tracing and auditing of the data flow and usage. One advantage of this end-to-end approach is that the information can be communicated freely over any untrusted communications medium from the users to the applications. The use of sticky policies suffers from the problem of how to attach such sticky policies to the data in the first instance. Although the techniques discussed above, such as from Langheinrich [37], might allow the user to interact with the sensing device, the construction of a suitable policy might be extremely complex. This problem is exacerbated since the policy is constructed knowing only the data and any user context information. At the point of policy construction no information is available on the destination of the data, or indeed on the purpose for which it will be used. Thus, the sticky policy approach might at first appear a poor match for the implementation of either Adams' privacy model, or the OECD principles. However, it is easy to imagine that such a solution might be extended to include negotiation over destination and usage at the point that the application contacts the trust authority. In fact, Casassa-Mont et al suggest that the policy might specify that the trust authority must obtain explicit user authorisation before releasing the data. A similar mechanism could be added to initiate further policy negotiation with the user or a user policy agent.

The solution of Casassa-Mont et al shows how the tracing and auditing of privacy-sensitive data may be achieved. Such a solution can be used to realise Tygar's suggestion that strong audit mechanisms are available to 'watch the watchers' [41]. Everyone using personal data should be subject to auditing, and alternatives to the current European (and OECD) model, where data collection and purpose are registered with a central authority, should be examined. Such distributed alternatives aim to maintain the link between the data subject and their personal data, and to allow the data subject to participate in the auditing function.

Opponents of such strong auditing can make the case that the complexity and expense of achieving a secure solution will be prohibitive and will cripple the deployment of new services. Another advocate of sticky policies is the work by Karjoth et al on a 'Platform for Enterprise Privacy Practices' (E-P3P) [42]. In contrast to the work by Casassa-Mont et al, the E-P3P approach uses sticky policies to consistently manage a data subject's privacy within an enterprise. The policy is constructed within the enterprise in accordance with the external policy to which the data subject has agreed concerning release of the information. Access to the data is then restricted to specific users or roles within the enterprise, and for specific purposes. Such work allows the organisation to have clear visibility and control over personal data and to easily demonstrate its accountability to auditors or data subjects.

11.5 Research Challenges

In the absence of direct interaction on the part of the data subject, the use of policies is essential to protecting privacy in pervasive computing environments. Although it can be seen such work is starting to develop, more needs to be done to make such solutions realistically achievable across a range of applications.

Along with further work on binding policies to data (beginning with binding data subjects and sensors), we can imagine further complexities that have not, to the authors' knowledge, been solved. One example is the multiple 'ownership' of data. For example, a camera will inevitably include multiple data subjects in a single frame and may also claim ownership of some of the information such as the background or timestamp. Allowing these multiple parties to each control their privacy will be a huge problem. Simply going for the highest common privacy protection may not be an adequate solution since this will block some users from obtaining legitimate services.

In any scenario where multiple parties may claim ownership of sensory data, any solution must rely on trust. We must trust the infrastructure not to release sensitive information to illegitimate users, and in addition we must also trust the co-owners of the data not to act against our interests. Thus, a more valid solution in this area may be based primarily on awareness rather than total control. For example, a trusted sensory platform [43] in the office environment might only allow users who were present at a location to recall and share their information with services. A legitimate user would not only be able to see the information that had been recorded, but also see who else is granted access to the data. In this manner, a user can evaluate the risk that these additional information flows pose to their privacy, and also confirm that the additional parties were indeed conforming to the contextual requirements (such as location) that are required for access.

Systems such as Lederer's faces [11] work using contextual information within the same domain as the data orgination to control information flow, in conjunction with the identity of the destination. For example, I may share my location to specific people when I am within certain geographic zones, or performing certain activities. Trusted platforms such as described above may control information release based upon more external parameters than just identity. If such platforms become popular, we will need new authentication services for such additional information. Role-based access control [44] extends the concept of identity to include some concept of usage. We will see the emergence of certification authorities for other types of personal data [45] and platforms to attest to contextual information such as location.

As the complexity and capabilities of ubiquitous environments grow, we may also see a trend away from control systems based upon complicated contextual policies and towards systems that capture notions of trust or exploit existing interactions (such as geographic locality or previous communications). Reputation systems may evolve outside the famous example of eBay, and form the basis for privacy decisions [46].

Another potential problem occurs during the decomposition or aggregation of data. The splitting, or aggregation of privacy policies in such cases, will be hard since it is not clear how much information is lost in such operations and whether the previous policies are still valid.

11.6   Summary

A comprehensive review covering all angles of the privacy problem and potential solutions for pervasive computing has not been possible in this chapter. Although privacy is not a new problem, the examination of privacy in the area of pervasive computing is immature, and we have tried to provide the reader with a flavour of how current legislation and technology fit with this emerging field, along with some of the new research being conducted. What emerges is that many of the components that we require to protect privacy in this new age are either in place or beginning to develop. However, a comprehensive approach that sets forth a set of privacy principles for pervasive computing, and a technical framework to aid those principles, is missing. Perhaps, at least in the case of technology, the absence of an overall framework is correct. For example, it is hard to imagine the development of a policy-based control mechanism or auditing function that might be universally applied.

The cost and complexity of a universal policy-based system, along with the problems of standardisation, may mean that such a system is never implemented. Instead, perhaps, the problem of privacy is better addressed in pieces. Through restricting the range of applications, and hence the data, purposes, and other contextual information, we can begin to make policy-based systems manageable. For example, it is easy to imagine that policies might be expressed to control location data to a range of services operating over a common privacy-enabled middleware platform.

References

1. Weiser M. The Computer for the 21st Century. Scientific American, 1991:256:3: 94–104.

2. Krikorian R. The Net Comes Home. New Scientist, February 2003.

3. Overby C S. The X Internet and Consumer Privacy. Forrester Report, December 2003.

4. Culler D et al. TinyOS: An Operating System for Sensor Networks. In: Rabaey J (editor). Ambient Intelligence. Springer, 2004.

5. Sarma S E et al. Radio-Frequency Identification: Security Risks and Challenges. RSA CryptoBytes, 2003:6.

6. Warren S and Brandeis L. The Right to Privacy. Harvard Law Review, December 1890:IV:5.

7. Westin A. Privacy and Freedom. Atheneum, New York, 1967.

8. Laurant C. Privacy and Human Rights: An International Survey of Privacy Laws and Developments. Electronic Privacy Information Center, Washington, DC, 2003.

9. Marx G. Murky Conceptual Waters: The Private and the Public. Ethics and Information Technology, July 2001.

10. Adams A. Multimedia Information Changes the Whole Privacy Ballgame. Proceedings of Computers, Freedom, and Privacy, 2000.

11. Lederer S. Everyday Privacy in Ubiquitous Computing Environments. Workshop on Socially-informed Design of Privacy-enhancing Solutions in Ubiquitous Computing, UbiComp, 2002.

12. Lessig L. The Architecture of Privacy. Taiwan Net Conference, 1998.

13. Acquisti A. Privacy and Security of Personal Information: Economic Incentives and Technological Solutions. In: Camp J and Lewis R (editors). The Economics of Information Security. Kluwer Academic Publishers, 2004.

14. US Privacy Act of 1974 — http://www.usdoj.gov/foia/privstat.htm

15. OECD — Recommendation Concerning Guidelines Governing the Protection of Privacy and Transborder Flows of Personal Data. September 1980.

16. Greenleaf G. Australia's APEC Privacy Initiative: The Pros and Cons of OECD Lite. Privacy Law and Policy Reporter, 2003.

17. OECD — Ministerial Declaration on the Protection of Privacy on Global Networks. October 1998.

18. Clarke R. Beyond the OECD Guidelines: Privacy Protection for the 21st Century. January 2000 — http://www.anu.edu.au/people/Roger.Clarke/DV/PP21C.html

19. Justice M K. Privacy Protection, A New Beginning: OECD Principles 20 Years on. Privacy Law and Policy Reporter, 1999.

20. EU Directive 1995/46/EC of the European Parliament and of the Council on the Protection of Individuals with Regard to the Processing of Personal Data and on the Free Movement of Such Data. October 1995.

21. Pfitzmann A and Köhntopp M. Anonymity, Unobservability, and Pseudonymity — A Proposal for Terminology. Workshop on Design Issues in Anonymity and Unobservability, Berkeley, California, 2002.

22. Juels A. Privacy and Authentication in Low-Cost RFID Tags. RSA Laboratories, 2003.

23. Chaum D. Untraceable Electronic Mail: Return Addresses and Digital Pseudonyms. Communications of the ACM, 1981:24:2:84–90.

24. Reiter M K and Rubin A D. Crowds: Anonymity for Web Transactions. ACM Transactions on Information and System Security, 1998.

25. EU Directive 2002/58/EC of the European Parliament and of the Council Concerning the Processing of Personal Data and the Protection of Privacy in the Electronic Communications Sector. July 2002.

26. EU Directive 1997/66/EC of the European Parliament and of the Council Concerning the Processing of Personal Data and the Protection of Privacy in the Telecommunications Sector. December 1997.

27. Beresford A and Stajano F. Mix Zones: User Privacy in Location-aware Services. IEEE International Workshop on Pervasive Computing and Communication Security (PerSec) 2004.

28. Gruteser M and Grunwald D. Anonymous Usage of Location-based Services Through Spatial and Temporal Cloaking. ACM/USENIX International Conference on Mobile Systems, Applications and Services (MobiSys) 2003.

29. Brin D. The Transparent Society. Addison-Wesley, 1998.

30. Guerin D. Anarchism: From Theory to Practice. Monthly Review Press, 1970.

31. Federal Trade Commission. Workshop on the Information Marketplace: Merging and Exchanging Consumer Data. Washington DC, March 2001.

32. Fred H C. Principles for Protecting Privacy. The Cato Journal, March 2002.

33. Cranor L et al. The Platform for Privacy Preferences 1.0 (P3P 1.0) specification. W3C Recommendation, April 2002 — http://www.w3.org/TR/2002/REC-P3P-20020416

34. Pedersen A. P3P — Problems, Progress, Potential. Privacy Laws & Business International Newsletter, February 2003.

35. Thidadeau R. A Critique of P3P: Privacy on the Web. August 2000 — http://dollar.ecom.cmu.edu/p3pcritique/

36. Birchman J A. Is P3P 'The Devil'? Law and the Internet Seminars, University of Miami School of Law, May 1998 — http://www.law.miami.edu/~froomkin/sem97/birchman.html

37. Langheinrich M. A Privacy Awareness System for Ubiquitous Computing Environments. 4th International Conference on Ubiquitous Computing (UbiComp) 2002.

38. Juels A and Brainard J. Soft Blocking: Flexible Blocker Tags on the Cheap. Manuscript 2003 — http://www.rsasecurity.com/rsalabs/staff/bios/ajuels/publications/softblocker/softblocker.pdf

39. Casassa-Mont M, Pearson S, and Bramhill P. Towards Accountable Management of Identity and Privacy: Sticky Policies and Enforceable Tracing Services. IEEE 14th International Workshop on Database and Expert Systems Applications (DEXA'03) September 2003.

40. Boneh D and Franklin M. Identity-based Encryption from the Weil Pairing. Crypto, 2001.

41. Tygar D. Security with Privacy. ISAT 2002 study, December 2002.

42. Karjoth G, Schunter M, and Waidner M. Platform for Enterprise Privacy Practices: Privacy-enabled Management of Customer Data. 2nd Workshop on Privacy Enhancing Technologies, April 2002.

43. Cui W, Duan Y, and Wei K. Toward Trustworthy Ubiquitous Computing Environments. CS261 Class Project Report, Department of Electrical Engineering and Computer Sciences, University of California, Berkeley, Fall 2002.

44. Ferraiolo D and Kuhn R. Role-based Access Control. 15th NIST-NCSC National Computer Security Conference, 1992.

45. Altenschmidt C, Biskup J, Flegel U, and Karabulut Y. Secure Mediation: Requirements, Design and Architecture. Journal of Computer Security, 2003:11:3.

46. Goecks J and Mynatt E: Enabling Privacy Management in Ubiquitous Computing Environments through Trust and Reputation Systems. Computer Supported Cooperative Work (CSCS 2002 Workshop in Privacy in Digital Environments: Empowering Users), 2002.

12

RFID Security and Privacy — Issues, Standards, and Solutions

A Soppera, T Burbridge, and D Molnar

12.1   Introduction

Radio frequency identification (RFID) is a high potential enabling technology that can radically change the way that information is gathered about the physical world. RFID tags are typically used to perform the identification of multiple objects without requiring line-of-sight or manual intervention.

With RFID, a pallet of goods within the supply chain can be inventoried without unloading or unpacking the pallet. Embedded into consumer products, RFID could provide the customer with a new shopping experience by permitting queue-free checkout and suppressing counterfeiting.

After the initial point of sale, the RFID tag may be used by the consumer to enable services within their home, or used for product returns, recycling and second-hand sales. Automated identification devices have already been successful in libraries and media rental companies to improve the efficiency of rotating inventory systems. In the future, we may see many more items being tagged, and many new applications being enabled.

RFID technology has been around for many years in manufacturing processes, in asset and people monitoring, and in physical access control systems. Various applications have exploited this technology to solve very specific needs. The current boom is mainly due to a successful match between business and technology. Tag manufacturers have been able to produce tiny tags that cost less than 15p (the cost is expected to drop as low as 5p in the next few years). These tiny chips can be easily and economically applied to many commercial items and can be read *en masse*. Wal-Mart has already stated the requirement that suppliers tag every box and pallet with RFID tags.

Jump Start, the pharmaceutical industry's first trial in RFID deployment, will use tags to track pharmaceutical products from the factory to the pharmacy. The combination of RF connectivity with a standard unique addressing scheme has represented a significant step forward compared to the physical limitation of current barcode technology. Tags provide the promise of reading products at very high speed and at low cost.

RFID is not just about providing benefits to supply chain players whose inventory systems can be further improved with the use of RFID.

RFID deployment will most likely have an impact on consumer purchasing habits. Consumers can obtain better product information through referencing the tag ID on the Internet. RFID promises to allow receipt-free returns and to reduce post-sale theft. However, as many new communication technologies have already experienced, RFID technology has raised concerns in term of privacy.

Surveys from activist groups have repeatedly raised a variety of privacy concerns. At the same time retailers such as Tesco and Benetton have been largely criticised for their RFID trials involving tagging individual items [1, 2]. Governments have started to consider whether this technology needs regulations. In November 2004, Germany's Federal Office for Information Security (BSI) highlighted the need for an up-to-date Data Protection Law and for anonymising techniques to protect personal data in RFID systems [3].

On the same lines, the US Food and Drug Administration (FDA) has produced guidelines to encourage companies to begin exploring the use of RFID in the pharmaceutical supply chain and to develop this technology in harmony with consumer interests [4]. A set of privacy directives supports the notion that tags must not contain information beyond a simple ID. A proposed California state law plans to go even further by requiring consent from the user before associating personal information with information collected via an RFID system [5].

This chapter concentrates on the privacy implications of using RFID in the consumer domain, although similar privacy concerns may be held by businesses that operate tags in open shared physical spaces instead of secure warehouses. Blanket legislation to restrict the possibility of RFID technology would be premature, given the infancy of RFID and the unexplored benefits to businesses and consumers. Instead, prompt development of technical privacy solutions is required to enable compliance with privacy regulations and practices in different applications. Unfortunately, many privacy solutions that have been proposed for RFID assume features that are hard or expensive to implement due to their requirement for additional computation, storage, and communication capabilities on the tag. The deployment of privacy-supporting RFID systems will require collaboration between business and consumers, and between technologists and regulation makers.

Recently, RFID privacy has been studied widely. Researchers have concluded that in order to prevent information leakage and tracking, the tag output has to be used only once and adversaries should not be able to distinguish a tag output from a random value.

However, solely changing the tag output at each reading cannot be considered a total solution. Most of the current schemes assume that anyone given access to the tag has that access for the lifetime of the tag. Tags, by their nature, do not stay within a single ownership domain. We will first examine different privacy issues and then introduce solutions under the assumption that tags must be transferable, preserving the privacy of each owner in turn.

In the next section, RFID technology is described, along with some existing applications. Section 12.3 explores the privacy threats from the collection of tag information and the correlation of this data with personal information. From these threats we start to build the requirements for a secure RFID system. The privacy problem is then expanded to examine threats from the communication and application layers of RFID systems, before exploring how privacy needs can be met by innovative RFID solutions, developed at BT, that support the notions of ownership transfer and access delegation.

12.2 RFID Tags Technology — An Overview

12.2.1 A Bit of History

During the last few decades, consumer product descriptions have been considered one of the main enablers to improve the way that customers find products and purchase them. The Universal Product Code (UPC) and the European Article Number (EAN) were introduced in the 1970s by a consumer goods industry consortium [6] and formed the first widely adopted barcode scheme. This initiative was motivated by the need to develop product-code-keyed catalogues to facilitate the exchange of information between retailers and suppliers.

The UPC allows manufacturers, retailers, and others to automatically identify objects along the supply chain and in particular at the retail checkout. The code is divided into two parts — a part that defines the code owner (assigned by some root authority) and a part that identifies the product (assigned by the code owner).

It is instructive to compare RFID tags with the barcode labels previously used for item identification. In Table 12.1 we present a list of important differences between the two technologies. We can see from the list that while RFID tags have limitations preventing their use in some applications, the capacity for long-distance reading and reading large numbers of tags at once makes them attractive for many applications, including the supply chain.

Table 12.1   Major differences between the barcode and RFID technologies.

	Barcode labels		RFID tags
✓	Inexpensive (but can deteriorate)	✗	Costly (but can have long life)
✗	Not reusable	✓	Can be reused or recorded multiple times
✓	Work with almost all the products	✗	Problems with products containing liquids and metals
✗	Readers require line-of-sight and can read one bar code at a time	✓	Current readers can read hundreds of tags per second
✗	Have a limited read range	✓	Can be read from longer distance

A few years ago, another industry consortium, EPCglobal, under the banner of the Auto-ID Center, developed the electronic product code (EPC) [8, 9]. The EPC differs from the UPC in the fact that it allows the code owner to uniquely identify every single item instead of just the product type. In Fig. 12.1, we depict the structure of the EPC, including a manufacturer ID number that is assigned by EPCglobal. As we describe ahead, the rest of the EPC is reserved for assignment by the manufacturer itself. It should be noted that in the RFID world 'EPC' can refer to both the EPC naming scheme or to a particular kind of RFID tag technology specified by the EPCglobal consortium.

The property of having uniquely identified items allows them to be referenced by the object name server (ONS) and by the EPC discovery service (EPC-DS). ONS is an Internet-based information service that allows supply chain players to map the item EPC to on-line product information such as manufacturer details. Specifically, the ONS maps the manufacturer ID of the EPC to a URL provided by the manufacturer. The URL points to a database that can provide more information, given the rest of the EPC.

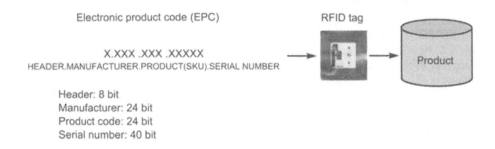

Fig. 12.1   The 96-bit structure of the EPC.

The vision is that in an EPC-enabled network, each manufacture will run an EPC Information Service (EPC-IS) that can deal with product queries referred to it through the ONS. EPC-DS is a dynamic service that holds all the sightings of a tag by different readers registered with the EPC-DS. A client with access to the EPC-DS can track a specific EPC label (i.e. a product) throughout the world. Because these services are just emerging, we do not yet know their scope or who exactly will have access. Based on our experience with UCC codes, however, we can expect that the mapping from IDs to manufacturers will be available to all for little or no cost. Therefore, EPCs will have a privacy 'leak' of at least the manufacturer of a given item.

12.2.2   RFID Technology

RFID systems in their most basic form consist of RFID tags integrated with RFID readers and data processing systems.

- RFID tags

  These are equipped with a small chip and an antenna. Passive tags induce the energy required to transmit their code from the field generated by an external reader.

- RFID reader

  This consists of a control unit and a coupling element to interrogate tags by radio frequency communications. The permissible frequency ranges are determined by the radio regulations of the country. The performance of the reading will vary according to the frequency used and the reader power output, along with other factors such as tag density, orientation, and the surrounding environment.

- Data processing system

  This stores and processes the information received from the readers. It comprises a company's own databases and applications, along with external services such as EPC-IS or EPC-DS.

Very cheap and small RFID tags are characterised by the following properties.

- Low computational power

  The chip has very limited computational capabilities due to the cost restrictions required by supply chain application and reinforced by the lack of a proper energy source. A tag is equipped with a few thousand logic gates, which makes it difficult to integrate security functions [10].

- Limited storage capabilities

  RFID tags also have limited storage capabilities. The cheapest tag can just carry the tag ID or EPC. In retail and supply chain applications, EPC has emerged as the standard identifier for RFID tags requiring 96 bits of memory (see Fig. 12.1). A few Kb of memory is available on some writable tags.

RFID tags operate at different frequencies that allow different communications properties, including range. Supply chain tags operate in the range of 860–960 MHz. This radio frequency enables read ranges of up to 10 m. It is interesting to notice that information sent by readers can be received over distances of hundreds of metres, but the information sent by the tag is limited by the properties of the tag antenna. Tags that operate at different frequencies such as 13.56 MHz (commonly used by library tags) and standardised by ISO 18000-3 have significantly different reading characteristics [11, 12]. This frequency enables read range up to a metre. In terms of privacy implications, it is clear that tags with longer range are more susceptible to leakage of information than shorter-range ones.

For completeness, we discuss three different deployments of RFID in terms of the technology used for each. These deployments show off the diversity of technologies that fall under the RFID banner. Privacy protection measures appropriate for one deployment and technology may fail for another — this is one of the challenges we face when defining the problem of RFID privacy and security.

- Supply chain deployments (for example, Wal-Mart)

  These deployments use 915-MHz tags with an intended read range of roughly 5–10 m. We have already discussed the limited capability of this class of tag. We discuss the standards in this class and a specific pharmaceutical application of deployments in the next section.

- Library deployments

  Libraries such as the University of Nevada, Las Vegas, and the National University of Singapore have begun using RFID for security and asset tracking. These deployments use 13.56-MHz tags with an intended read range of less than 1 m. These tags are also more expensive than supply chain tags, costing as much as 50p per tag, but they may hold up to 2K of data. Tags in this type of deployment may follow the ISO 15693 [13] or ISO 18000-3 standards. Some tag manufacturers market tags in this frequency range that include cryptographic primitives, but none of these tags is deployed in libraries [14].

- Electronic passports

  The International Civil Aviation Organisation (ICAO) has created a standard for next-generation passports that includes an RFID tag [15]. The tag contains a photograph of the bearer, name, and passport number. These tags use the ISO 14443 standard, with an intended range of 10 cm. Additionally, the ICAO standard includes optional features that require the use of cryptography, such as RSA signatures and 3DES encryption. The United States plans to deploy passports with these tags by the end of 2005.

12.2.3   RFID Standards

The recent developments of RFID technologies have created a need for a common standard. The market offers two distinct versions for supply chain applications — the new EPC Generation 2.0 (backwards compatible with version 1.0) [16] and the emerging ISO 18000-6 standard [17].

Recently, the International Organisation for Standardisation has developed the ISO/IEC 18000-6 that defines the air interface for RFID devices operating in the 860-MHz to 960-MHz industrial, scientific, and medical (ISM) band used in supply chain management. The ISO standard only addresses the air interface and specifies the details of reader–tag communication.

The EPC Generation 2.0 is compatible with the ISO 18000-6 and is a more comprehensive standard. It proposes a more advanced collision avoidance protocol that can read up to 1500 tags/sec. It also introduces special privacy functionality such as the kill command.

12.2.4   RFID Applications

Various scenarios have outlined the potential value of RFID tag technology. Identification through radio frequency represents a major step forwards compared with classic optical bar code identification. In this section the value of RFID technology within the healthcare industry is presented before exploring the associated privacy threats in the next section.

Pharmacy industries can see great opportunities from being able to track bottles and pill boxes. Governments are also pushing for trials to apply RFID technology to drug items. Their aim is to defeat counterfeiters by giving a unique identifier to each product so that its point of origin can be verified. This will provide great advantages in terms of safety to end users and allow companies to protect their markets against the influx of cheap, dangerous drugs. CVS/Pharmacy Corp [18] has led the use of RFID, introducing item-level tracking. Pharmacy and wholesale distributors' shelves will be equipped with readers that will be able to track each item until the moment when the consumer purchases the drug and leaves the store.

This trial will open the door to innovative management of stock. Stores will be able to automatically detect when a product is going to expire and optimise the delivery of new drugs to pharmacies that have urgent need. Inventory systems will prevent expensive items from being lost or misfiled. If the technology is going to be integrated with the personal health records, we could even expect the system to help with drug compliance. In the future, if readers are deployed in the house, the system could even remind the user when to take a pill.

While it is clear that this technology could provide great advantages to pharmaceutical manufacturers and healthcare systems, as well as increasing the safety and well-being of the user, we have to make sure that we develop it in a way that takes into account user privacy and security requirements. We have clear ideas about the benefits, but we struggle to identify the dangers. Consumers have particular concerns about their medical records and the way that information is treated. We require basic safeguards to be embedded within the technology to prevent easy disclosure of information.

12.3 Understanding Privacy in Pervasive Computing

Consumers, and in particular consumer associations, have strong expectations of privacy. Currently, individuals can purchase items with cash and maintain their anonymity. They can pay with credit cards or use loyalty cards disclosing some personal information. Although personal information is disclosed during these transactions, privacy regulation, such as the data protection act in the UK, ensures that the information collected is kept private. Everyone who collects personal information has an obligation to notify the user when the information is collected, maintain confidentiality, and allow the user to have access to the collected information. Privacy laws protect consumers against unwanted intrusion and give to the consumer the control on how to disclose personal information.

In an RFID-enabled world, these privacy regulations will be disrupted. RFID technology operates through the radio spectrum and anyone with an appropriate RFID reader can potentially get access to the information. For example, we might consider a consumer carrying tags on his jeans, shirt, and bag. A reader would be able to read all these tags. Tag information could then be easily correlated with time and location, and the individual identified by the presence of the three tags. If the reader is working in tandem with a credit card reader or, even better, with a camera, the real identity of the subject can be disclosed.

12.3.1 RFID Privacy Risks and Desirable Properties

The fact that RFID tags can be read without requiring line-of-sight, and can be invisibly embedded in consumer products, makes it hard to control the privacy of their information. If we consider then that tags have to be cheap (making it impossible to afford strong security) and read at high speeds simultaneously (making it impossible to mandate complex notifications and authorisations), the issue becomes complex. We can show that privacy risks lead to two fundamental requirements — preventing information leakage and preventing tracking. In addition, we desire a third property from RFID tags. Tags, by their nature, do not stay within a single ownership domain. Thus, tags must be transferable, preserving the privacy of each current (and past) owner in turn. In applications where multiple parties must read the same tag without the transfer of ownership, we also require the ability to delegate access to the tag to secondary parties.

- Preventing information leakage

  RFID tag technology operates through the radio spectrum, which makes communication vulnerable to eavesdropping. Access to the tag is hard to restrict by physical means, and read operations on the tag are not visible to the human eye. Since tags do not currently implement any sort of security protection, it is not possible to prevent a reader from accessing the tag information. An RFID tag contains data that is intrinsically associated with a product or object. In a supply chain, including pharmaceutical information, details about the drug type or prescription can threaten the privacy of the consumer. This is because specific medical conditions can be inferred by the nature of the medication. Even if the content stored on the tag is restricted to a simple identifier such as the EPC, the problem is not resolved. The EPC is a static standard identifier, and even if the association with the product is not initially public, this information can be easily inferred over time. For example, adversaries can discover information about the meaning of EPCs by examining the physical product.

- Preventing traceability

   An unchanging code presented to multiple readers allows tracking. The tag can be tracked even if the code itself is encrypted in order to prevent the association of the code to product information. If a tag cannot be tracked, this implies that there is no understanding of the tag code. Thus, prevention of tracking can be viewed as a stronger security mechanism to the protection of information. The prevention of tracking can be achieved through continuously changing codes, or through access control to the tag.

- Transfer and delegation

   If the same EPC is used throughout the product lifetime, or even if the ID is encrypted with a secret key that remains unchanged, then the product can be tracked along the supply chain. Any party who can access a tag has the ability to do so for the lifetime of the tag, with no regard to the privacy of the current owner. This problem becomes more pronounced if the same password or secret is used for large numbers of tags. We can expect scenarios of industrial espionage, such as retailers sending agents to check on competitor's inventory information. In an Orwellian world, governments could collect information about people's life and behaviour.

In an ideal world, we would expect that tag information would be confidential to the parties or users that have physical control of the product associated with the tag, and perhaps to other parties that the owner allows access. There is a need for solutions that limit the amount of information available from tags to different parties at different times of the tag's life.

12.4   Privacy as a Multilayer Problem

Although privacy is recognised as a dominant concern for the deployment of RFID technology, the ability to provide efficient privacy solutions is limited. The lack of a conceptual model makes it difficult to define where the different privacy issues can affect both the technology and the end users. Building on the multilayer communication model presented by Avoine and Oechsline [19] and shown in Fig. 12.2, we are going to outline the security issues and weaknesses of an RFID tag device. Privacy is a complex issue that needs to be analysed by examining the different communication layers of an RFID tag device. The rationale is that privacy cannot be guaranteed by just securing a given layer, but that we need a deep analysis

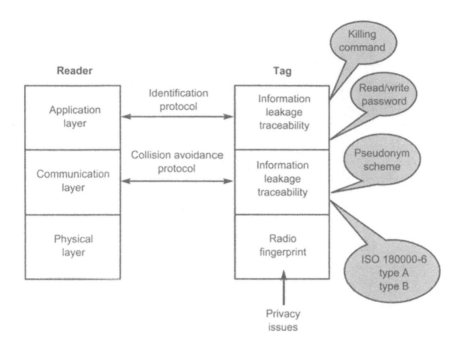

Fig. 12.2   RFID tag communication model and privacy risks [19].

of the inter-layer security to prevent the subversion of mechanisms at other layers. An analysis conducted by Molnar and Wagner [20] on the ISO 15963 standard for 13.56-MHz tags, as used in library applications, demonstrated that a tag can be uniquely identified during the collision avoidance protocol. This shows that even if tag information were protected, a leakage at the communication layer can compromise privacy.

The RFID tag can be represented as a three-layer communication device: the application layer, the communication layer, and the physical layer. In order to make our analysis more comprehensive, we need as well to consider interactions between the tag and the data processing system. We show these interactions in Fig. 12.3; the 'layers' of the conceptual model for the reader side are on the left, while vulnerabilities and countermeasures are shown on the right for the tag. The arrows in the middle represent points of interaction between reader and tag that may lead to privacy problems if not carefully designed.

- Application layer

    This layer manages the digital content of the tag. It includes the secure functions to produce encrypted output and to protect the link between the identifying code and the physical object. Here we must prevent information leakage and traceability, as previously discussed, through the use of an appropriate control scheme.

- Communication layer

    The purpose of this layer is to perform a collision arbitration mechanism that enables the reader to receive information from multiple tags. As we have

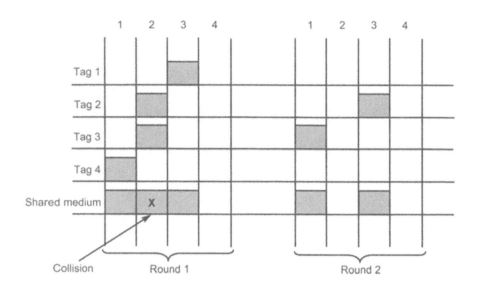

Fig. 12.3   ISO 18000-6 Type A collision avoidance protocol.

discussed, the collision avoidance mechanism may lead to information leakage or traceability if not properly designed.

- Physical layer

    This layer defines the operational frequency for RFID tags, the carrier modulation, the power control, and the data rate and coding. Here, radio fingerprinting of tags is a special threat that may lead to traceability if not taken into account.

In the following section we perform an analysis of the communication layer and application layer as applied to the ISO/IEC 18000-6 and EPC Generation 2.0 standard, proposed for supply chain management applications. Although analysis of the physical layer is not found in this chapter, attacks on security and privacy are possible at this level. In addition, decisions made at the physical layer also affect how easy it is to eavesdrop or perform man-in-the-middle attacks at higher layers.

12.4.1   Communication Layer

The purpose of the communication layer is to perform a singulation mechanism to enable collision-free communication between the reader and multiple tags. When multiple tags are willing to communicate on the same channel, a set of rules, known as a collision avoidance protocol, has to be applied to determine which tag can get the use of the channel.

When the collision situation is resolved, the reader gets a tag identifier through which it can interrogate the tag. In order to prevent surreptitious tracking, this identifier should be different from the one used at the application level and should change during each reading operation. Unfortunately, this is not always the case. For instance, the ISO 15963 standard for 13.56-MHz tags used in library applications defines the use of a 64-bit unique ID, and the collision avoidance mechanism reveals this ID. In this case the privacy of the tag is compromised even if the reader does not access the data maintained in the tag.

Below we describe two classes of collision avoidance protocol used in the ISO 18000-6 standard — type A uses an Aloha-based mechanism and type B a binary tree mechanism. The new EPC Generation 2.0 standard uses a proprietary method of type B.

It is worth noting that collision avoidance mechanisms are often proprietary algorithms. Consequently, our goal is not to say if a standard is secure or not, but to raise awareness of potential privacy problems so that organisations can choose tags that do not identify themselves through the collision avoidance method.

- ISO 18000-6 Type A

  This is a slotted Aloha-type singulation protocol as depicted earlier in Fig. 12.3. Probabilistic protocols allocate tag transmissions into slots and rounds. They rely on the fact that a tag selects a specific slot in a round and the reader determines which slot is active.

  The reader initiates a round and determines the number of slots in a round. The number of slots in a round depends on the number of collisions expected. On receiving the 'initiate_round' command, tags select a slot in which to respond and initiate a slot counter to 1. Tags that have selected slot 1 will transmit immediately. Tags that have selected a slot greater than 1 will wait for the selected slot. For each reading slot there are three possible outcomes — no transmission, collision, or successful reading. The reader will then interrogate the next slot until all slots have been explored. If a collision has been detected in a round, the reader will send another initiate_round command and restart the process. This process will be repeated until all the tags have been identified. During the collision avoidance process, the tag transmits its signature (4 random bits) along with its data or ID. The reader will then use the signature in its communication with the tag to make sure that only one tag will respond to the reader command.

- ISO 18000-6 Type B

  This is a binary tree singulation protocol. It relies on the fact that the tag identifier does not change during the collision arbitration phase. It is assumed that the identifier used in this phase is the same identifier used at the application layer. At the end of the collision avoidance phase the reader will automatically know the ID of the tag.

  The collision arbitration protocol assumes that the tags support two pieces of hardware on the tag — an 8-bit counter 'COUNT' and a random number generator with two possible outputs (0 or 1). When the tags are queried, all the tags with COUNT at 0 should transmit their ID. If there is a collision, the reader sends a FAIL message. All the tags that receive a FAIL message with the counter set at other than 0 should increment their counter. The tags that receive a FAIL with COUNT of 0 should generate the random number. If the random number is 1, COUNT is set to 1; otherwise the tag can try to send the ID again. When the reader receives an ID without collision, the tag is detected and a success command is generated.

It is clear that the security of the collision avoidance protocol relies on the nature of the identifier. If the tag uses a static identifier, an adversary can easily track the tag and the tag may not be private. We call an identifier static if its value does not change during multiple reading operations. ISO 18000-6 does not specify the nature of the identifier, but we could implicitly assume that it is static. Under the assumption that the tag ID changes for each collision avoidance round, the ISO 18000-6 scheme may be considered secure. An adversary would only be able to track the tag for the duration of the collision avoidance session.

12.4.2   Application Layer

In order to maximise privacy and security in RFID applications, a good practice is to minimise the amount of information written on the tag. Product information should be encoded in a way that enables supply chain practices but limits the disclosure of information to unwanted parties.

Encrypting RFID information, before writing this information in the tag, is not sufficient to prevent privacy risks. Adversaries can still perform point-to-point tracking through the static information released by the tags. Moreover, products can be identified after associating the unique encrypted data to the physical object.

This shows the need for security tools made available in the design process and the fact that policies alone cannot provide a strong protection if they are not supported by the technology. EPC tags have started to support privacy protection commands incorporating a password-protected 'Kill' command and a 48-bit read password to provide access control capabilities.

Killing the tag aims to protect the individual privacy and at the same time allow retailers to exploit the RFID technology benefits. The rationale is very simple — at the point of sale the tag is disabled so that the tag cannot be further tracked. Even though this solution is an inexpensive way to address consumers' privacy risks, it suffers from the major problem of preventing all post-sale applications. For instance, some retailers may wish the tag to remain active so that they can operate returns procedures, or provide after-sales service to enhance the value of the product to their consumers. Moreover, if we consider RFID used for libraries or video rental business, we can say that the tag cannot be killed, as the RFID information needs to be used when the item is returned. Consequently, we must keep the tag 'alive' and should control the disclosure of the information during the tag–reader interaction.

Recently ISO 18000-3 and EPC Generation 2.0 have been discussing the possible use of a 48-bit read password solution. The reader, in order to access the tag, needs to provide the read password. Unfortunately, this approach also suffers some major drawbacks. First, the password has to be sent in plain text and can be easily overheard by adversaries. Once the read password is public, the security of the tag is compromised. This may limit the validity of this solution to short-range tag applications. The second issue is a complexity issue that exists if each tag has a different password. In this case a reader is not able to decide which password to pass to which tag, and the only solution is to try all the passwords available. If we consider that a reader should be able to access (read) several hundreds of tags per second, we can conclude that this solution has limited applicability. The alternative of sharing the same password across multiple tags significantly weakens the security, as parties will inevitably end up knowing the passwords for tags to which they should have no access. Furthermore, multiple parties sharing the same password increases the risk of the password's being leaked. For these reasons, read passwords were removed from the most recent version of the EPC Generation 2.0 specification [16].

We can see that the latest RFID standards fall far short of providing RFID privacy. The two schemes outlined above perform a crude segregation of the world into those who can read the tag and those who cannot. A password can be granted to add a new reader, and the kill command used to permanently revoke all reading rights of all parties. This solution is only suitable if we never desire protection from previous owners, or if we have a cataclysmic event in the lifetime of the item, such that we need never read the RFID tag again. Although currently, reaching the checkout of a retail store might constitute such an event, in future years we may well want a more general solution that allows the granting and removal of access rights so long as the tag and item exist together.

A different approach that allows the tag to 'live' in post-sale applications and aid consumer privacy is to modify the identifier of the tag each time the tag is queried by a reader. The association between the product identifier and the product information is maintained in a secure database. This is the pseudonym scheme proposed by Ohkubo, Suzuki, and Kinoshita [21]. The rationale behind this solution is that a tag should not respond predictably to the reader queries. The tag refreshes autonomously its identifier through the use of two hash (H and G) functions as depicted in Fig. 12.4. Cryptographic details of the scheme's operation are given later, in Section 12.5.2; for now it suffices to say that the tag outputs a different pseudonym on each read. The secure database can map the tag output with the product information, because it has access to the secret value used to generate the sequence of tag outputs.

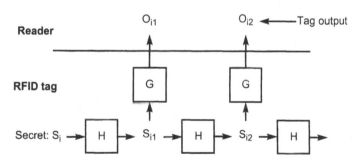

Fig. 12.4   Pseudonym scheme [21].

This solution is robust in terms of information leakage and tracking and requires tags to implement secure hash functions, which we consider to be a realistic assumption in the close future. However, this solution suffers from scalability problems that limit its applicability to environments where the number of known tags is limited. A secure database requires in the order of $m \times n$ operations to decode a tag, where n is the number of tags the database can access and m is the number of times a tag has already been read.

A pseudonym scheme can be implemented by enhancing the ONS, with a system capable of decoding the pseudonym produced as the tag output. This object pseudonym system (OPS) could decode tag IDs depending upon the credentials provided by the reader, effectively being able to grant or remove access to new readers and owners of RFID tags. The problem with this approach is that every single tag-read operation must be referred to the OPS and cannot be understood locally by the legitimate owner of the tag.

We can conclude that, in order to prevent information leakage and tracking, the tag output has to be used only once and an adversary should not be able to distinguish a tag output from a random value. Although privacy at the application level has been widely studied [20–26], the problems of transference and delegation remain an open research area.

12.5   Transfer of Ownership at the Application Level

In the previous sections we have concluded that privacy can be maintained if the tag output is indistinguishable from a random value. However, solely changing the tag output at each reading is not a total solution, since any party who can access the tag has the ability to do so for the lifetime of the tag. When a tagged product is sold, the retailer can still track the user with no regard for the current owner of the tag. At the same time, distributors could be able to collect inventory information from retailers without their permission. For a general solution we require the ability to be able to grant and revoke access rights to RFID tags.

The problem, while often worded as privacy, can now be considered a problem of control. When a reader accesses the tag information, it is hard to know:

• where the information is flowing to;

• who is controlling the reader;

• how the information is going to be used.

The problem is even harder if we consider consumer goods that stay with the users for years and 'leak' private information over a long period of time.

An obvious approach to RFID privacy is to use writable tags and to perform a recoding operation when the product changes hands [27], e.g. when the product is passed from the distributor to the retailer, at the point of sale or during a second-hand sale. In this case a reader would rewrite the tag with a new set of information and hold the mapping between the original EPC and the new code. Previous or future owners of the product will not be able to access tag information without having the access to the mapping. Access to the mapping can be controlled by a privacy policy enforced by the database that holds the mapping — therefore, we shift the problem of enforcing privacy off the resource-limited tag on to the database. We can expect that the consumer could use recoding as a tool to produce private catalogues about their personal libraries of books, CDs, and DVDs, and to browse information on the Internet without identifying themselves.

This approach can be extended to the point where every privacy domain uses private codes. In addition to the physical tags, the previous ID-EPC mapping, or a temporary one used for the transition, must be passed across to the new owner. This requires costly systems integration, or the use of a secure information exchange hub. Molnar, Stapleton-Gray, and Wagner call such a hub an infomediary and show how recoding could be used to implement an infomediary in the context of the EPCglobal structure [28]. Specifically, the infomediary acquires a special 'manufacturer ID' and registers with the ONS. When a party wishes to learn the identity of an object, the ONS redirects to the infomediary, which can then check the user's privacy policy before deciding how much information to return.

We can see that there are problems with the recoding approach. Due to deployment costs, it is unlikely, in the near term, that every retailer or other transition point in the supply chain will have readers in place to perform recoding, and it is even less likely that the user will have a reader with write capabilities available in their house. As RFID becomes more commonplace, and as the consumer starts to make use of their own tags, then we expect home readers to become available.

Another obvious problem with using writable RFID tags is that we require some form of write control to avoid malicious overwriting of tags. This write-control password itself may be considered sensitive and should not be common to multiple parties. Ideally we desire a solution that does not require the rewriting of a tag during the transfer of ownership.

Unfortunately, as we have shown, the recoding solution is not ideal since the readers must be connected to an on-line infrastructure at the point of transfer. The new owner needs to identify the previous owner and communicate with their systems (or via a third party) to obtain the mapping information. This requires significant systems integration to work with all potential sources of RFID tags, or alternatively, global standards for this communication. Even with such standards, unless the private ID presented by the tag is globally unique, then we have the problem of transferring the identity of the previous owner. We now briefly introduce two new solutions, developed by BT, that work under the assumption that the owner of the tag should be in control of tag information, while at the same time removing some of the requirements for an on-line network infrastructure at the immediate instance of the transfer.

12.5.1   The Acceptor Tag

An alternative to using an on-line authority to release secret information to readers is to delegate this function (for limited tags and readers) to a device, such as a more capable active RFID tag. This device can travel physically along the supply chain, automatically taking the secret information to where it is required by readers. In this manner the owner of the tag can load the access profiles of future readers on to a device that we call an acceptor tag.

The passive RFID tags are protected from adversaries (e.g. by using passwords or pseudonyms), but access secrets can be released to authorised readers through an authentication process performed by the acceptor tag. We can consider this solution as one of the first efforts to provide an 'opt-in' approach for RFID privacy, since without the presence of an acceptor tag with the correct information stored on it, the RFID tags cannot be read.

Thus, for example, a consumer transferring items between the private domains of the retail store and the house could use such an acceptor tag. On selling the item, the retail store might rewrite the tag with a random value and place the mapping of this new ID to the EPC on the customer's acceptor tag. On arriving home, a reader would automatically retrieve the data from the acceptor tag after presenting its credentials, and rewrite the tag to a private code used within the house.

In a more complex environment, an acceptor tag accompanying a pallet of goods can be programmed by the owner of the goods to release tag information to other parties. For example, a certificate can be loaded to allow the reading of tags by customs authorities, but not the ability to write to the tags. We can imagine that other parties may be able to create, and load on to the acceptor tag, certificates with subsets of their own access rights.

It is also easy to imagine that the acceptor tag may be given more complex functionality. For example, with an on-board GPS, more complicated access policies can be written to incorporate geographic location along with the purported identity of the reader. Such functionality would obviously vastly increase the cost of a purpose-built acceptor tag, but other devices may become suitable for the role in future, such as mobile phones or PDAs that implement a trusted computing platform. In these cases, the reader of the tags may be the owner of the acceptor tag device.

When using an acceptor tag, we must consider who owns the device, and how it will be transported between the privacy domains for the purpose of transferring the secret tag information. For example, if the acceptor tag is owned by the recipient of the tagged goods, then the owner must transport the device into the previous privacy domain (in order to collect the secret tag information). This approach appears suitable for consumers visiting retail outlets. Freight and courier companies may also use the acceptor tag in this fashion, as they physically visit the shipping and receiving company premises. At the end of the transaction, the acceptor tag is retained by the owner and can be reused. If the acceptor tag is used along the supply chain, we may imagine the acceptor tag to be integrated with reusable product containers. The sender may assert ownership of the acceptor tag, and use it for its own purposes, in much the same manner as consumers reuse protective padded envelopes.

Two things are important to note about acceptor tags. Firstly, because one acceptor tag may serve dozens or hundreds of regular tags, they need not meet the stringent cost constraints of commodity RFID tags (although they may still be inexpensive in quantity). In fact, RFID maker Alien Technologies is already shipping special battery-powered backscatter tags with sensors and 4K of memory intended for use at the pallet level; these tags or something like them might act as a platform for implementing future acceptor tags. Secondly, we can add special connectors such as a USB port to an acceptor tag, ensuring that they can talk with a PC and perform authentication even if no RFID reader is present. This alleviates the issue in consumer applications that a consumer may not have a dedicated RFID reader.

Although the acceptor tag may be a useful device to replace or supplement the need for an on-line authority, it inherits the problems of the security scheme used by the RFID tags that it is protecting. For example, once a password is released, the reader is free to read that RFID tag from then on. Revoking the access would require the rewriting of the acceptor tag information, along with the RFID tags for which access needs to be revoked. The acceptor tag overcomes some of the problems involved in transferring private tag information, but is limited in its ability to provide privacy protection from previous owners of tags. Thus it is most suitable where it is used only for the transfer of tags between two parties, after which recoding takes place. The next solution provides a more general solution where access to RFID tags may be granted temporarily without the requirement for recoding.

12.5.2   Secure Tree Protocol

We introduce a different approach that does not use additional devices but instead seeks to overcome some of the problems associated with pseudonym schemes. If we recall, a pseudonym scheme, based upon a hash-chain of outputs, has inherent scalability problems. In addition, the secrets are either delegated to the local reader (preventing access revocation) or held centrally by a pseudonym service (requiring all reads to be referred to this authority).

Ohkubo, Suzuki, and Kinoshita [21], as described in Section 12.4.2 and Fig. 12.4, suggested a pseudonym scheme. At set-up time, each tag is given a unique secret S_{ID} and an identity ID. A secure database will store the list of pairs (ID, S_{ID}). The tag computes the output with two one-way hash functions (H and G), so that the output does not reveal any information about the inputs. When queried, the tag hashes the elements generated from the secret S_{ID} and obtains elements: S_{ID1}, $S_{ID2}...S_{IDn-1}$, S_{IDn}. For each value S_{IDi}, an output $O_i = G(H(S_{IDi}))$ will be generated and sent to the reader. Even if this scheme is secure against surreptitious tracking, it does not provide a private 'transfer of ownership'. Any party that has access to the tag can do so for the lifetime of the tag and it is impossible to revoke without 'killing the tag'.

We require a similar scheme, but one in which access can be delegated to readers for periods of time, and removed thereafter. This is not possible in the pseudonym scheme above since a single secret is used to understand all pseudonyms.

Firstly we describe the tree structure presented in Fig. 12.5. We require two one-way hash functions to build a binary one-way tree that generates independent pseudonyms.

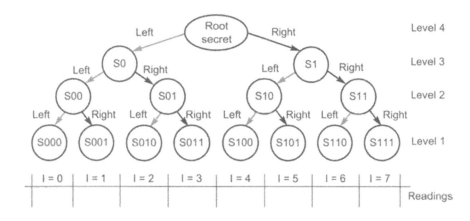

Fig. 12.5   Binary one-way tree to generate independent pseudonyms.

We call them the 'left' and the 'right' functions. The tree is constructed in the following manner. An initial root seed 'secret root' is associated with the tree and a parameter of depth d expresses the number of the leaves of the tree, $n = 2^{d-1}$.

At set-up time, each tag is given a unique 'secret root' and an identity (ID). When queried, the tag hashes the secret root and obtains a new leaf of the tree. A new leaf is generated at each reading operation. For instance, from Fig. 12.5 the first reading generates leaf $S_{i=0=left(left(left(SecretRoot)))}$, the second leaf $S_{i=1=right(left(left(SecretRoot)))}$, the third leaf $S_{i=2=left(right(left(SecretRoot)))}$, and so on. For each leaf an output $O_n = S_i$ is generated. We say that the tree generates independent pseudonyms because an adversary that obtains a leaf output does not learn any information about previous or future tag outputs.

The reader is assumed to know the intermediates node of the tree. When a reader wishes to identify a tag, it computes the possible leaves of the tree; if any result matches the tag output, then the tag has been identified. In order to provide a secure and private transfer of ownership, we could expect to reveal to the reader an intermediate value of the tree. In this way the reader can authenticate the tag for a limited amount of reading operations. For example, a reader that has access to S_0 (S_0 *is secret at level three*) can read for four outputs from the tag S_i with $i = \{1,2,3,4\}$. After these four reading operations, the access to the tag is automatically revoked. When the product changes hands, in order to verify that the tag is private, we need to ensure that the tag output is generated from a part of the tree that is not known to the previous owner. This is achievable by performing multiple reading operations of the same tag.

We propose that an object pseudonym system (OPS), as presented in Fig. 12.6, knows the root secret of the tag. Subordinate access keys can then be delegated to readers after checking their credentials and any access policies associated with the RFID tag. In order to grant the access, the OPS will communicate to the reader an intermediate node of the binary one-way tree. The use of OPS could make possible private and secure transfer of ownership while increasing the scalability of the system since the access can be delegated to readers for periods of time. In addition, information from the intermediate nodes of the tree can be used to improve the efficiency of the pseudonym space search.

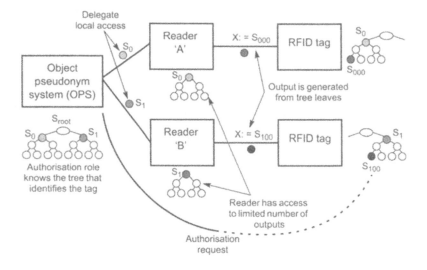

Fig. 12.6   An object pseudonym to provide secure transfer of ownership.

The tree-based pseudonym approach presented above provides an innovative scheme that allows the secure transfer of ownership, while allowing the preservation of privacy by preventing information leakage and tracking. Importantly, the scheme does not require readers to refer to an on-line authority to decode every read operation.

12.6   Summary

If we limit our vision of the application of RFID to supply chains, it is easy to dismiss work in RFID privacy as unnecessary. Such advocates argue that the tags are used exclusively in physically secure supply chains between trusted parties. The tag is removed or killed before the goods are allowed to pass into domains in which privacy becomes a more sensitive issue. In implementing RFID systems, cost is king, not privacy.

Although these arguments are undoubtedly true today for those companies operating supply chains, we must start to look now at solutions that enable the application of RFID tags in a much wider context. In environments where many readers have sufficient physical access to be able to read our tags, privacy becomes crucial. RFID has a huge future potential beyond supply chains — in our homes and everyday lives. Through technology we can ensure that neither heavy-handed legislation, nor public outcry, limits us from exploring the use of RFID to its fullest potential in years to come.

Tags capable of preserving privacy will always be more expensive than those that do not. Perhaps we will always see the use of very dumb tags that disclose their EPC to anyone who asks. The important argument is that we must develop privacy-supporting tags as credible technical alternatives, so that the market can decide which tag, at which cost, best meets the needs of the application.

References

1. Stop RFID — http://www.stoprfid.org/

2. EPIC RFID Privacy Page — http://www.epic.org/privacy/rfid/

3. Risks and Chances of the Use of RFID Systems (Article in German) — http://www.bsi.bund.de/veranst/rfid/

4. Combat Counterfeit Drugs. A Report of the Food and Drug Administration, February 2004 — http://www.fda.gov/

5. Bowen Seeks Balance in RFID Law. RFID Journal, March 2004 — http://www.rfidjournal.com/

6. European Article Numbering — EAN International — http://www.ean-int.org/

7. Shutzberg L. Radio Frequency Identification (RFID) in the Consumer Goods Supply Chain: Mandated Compliance or Remarkable Innovation? An Industry Whitepaper, Rock-Teen Company, October 2004.

8. Auto ID Center — http://www.autoidlabs.org/

9. EPCglobal Inc — http://www.epcglobalinc.org/

10. Feldhofer M, Dominikus S, and Wolkerstorfer J. Strong Authentication for RFID Systems Using the AES Algorithm. CHES 2004, LNCS, Springer, 2004.

11. ISO/IEC 18000. Automatic Identification — Radio Frequency Identification for Item Management — Communications and Interfaces. 2004.

12. ISO/IEC 18000-3. Information Technology AIDC Techniques — RFID for Item Management — Air Interface — Part 3: Parameters for Air Interface Communications at 13.56 MHz. 2004.

13. ISO/IEC 15693-2:2000 Identification Cards. Contactless Integrated Circuit(s) Cards, Vicinity Cards, Part 2: Air Interface and Initialization. 2000.

14. American Library Association RFID Resources — http://www.ala.org/ala/oif/ifissues/rfid.htm

15. ICAO Page on Machine Readable Travel Documents — http://www.icao.int/mrtd/biometrics

16. EPCglobal UHF Generation 2 Standard, 2004 — http://www.epcglobalinc.org/

17. ISO/IEC 18000-6:2004 Information Technology. Radio Frequency Identification for Item Management, Part 6: Parameters for Air Interface Communications at 860–960 MHz. 2004.

18. Garfinkel S. Retailer's Perpective: CVS Pharmacy. MIT, to be published in 2005.

19. Avoine G and Oechslin P H. RFID Traceability: A Multilayer Problem. Financial Cryptography, FC'05, LNCS, Springer, March 2005.

20. Molnar D and Wagner D. Privacy and Security in Library RFID: Issues, Practices, and Architectures. Conference on Computer and Communications Security (CCS), ACM Press, 2004.

21. Ohkubo M, Suzuki K, and Kinoshita S. Cryptographic Approach to Privacy-Friendly Tags. RFID Privacy Workshop, MIT, USA, 2003.

22. Sarma S, Weis S, and Engels D. RFID Systems and Security and Privacy Implications. CHES 2002, LNCS, Springer, 2002.

23. Juels A, Rivest R, and Szydlo M. The Blocker Tag: Selective Blocking of RFID Tags for Consumer Privacy. Conference on Computer and Communications Security (CCS), ACM Press, 2003.

24. Avoine G. Privacy Issues in RFID Banknote Protection Schemes. CARDIS'04, Kluwer Academic Publishers, 2004.

25. Juels A. Minimalist Cryptography for Low-Cost RFID Tags. The Fourth International Conference on Security in Communication Networks (SCN 2004), LNCS, Springer, 2004.

26. Juels A and Pappu R. Squealing Euros: Privacy Protection in RFID-Enabled Banknotes. Financial Cryptography, FC'03, LNCS, Springer, January 2003.

27. Stapleton-Gray R. Would Macy's Scan Gimbels? Competitive Intelligence and RFID. scip.online, December 2003.

28. Molnar D, Stapleton-Gray R, and Wagner D. Killing, Recoding, and Beyond. In: Garfinkel S and Rosenberg B (editors). RFID Applications, Security and Privacy. Addison-Wesley, March 2005.

13

Ambient Technology — Now You See It, Now You Don't

R Payne and B MacDonald

13.1   Introduction

There were 152 million PCs shipped in 2003 with 170 million expected by the end of 2004. The total number of PCs delivered worldwide over the last 10 years or so is now over one billion — but the processors in these PCs account for just 1–2% of all processors sold annually, the vast majority of the other 98% being embedded in equipment such as mobile phones, TVs, washing machines, game consoles, and cars. On the basis of these figures, an installed embedded processor base of something like 50+ billion is not an unreasonable estimate, and the average person in the UK can expect to come into contact with 100+ embedded processors a day without realising or thinking about it. This is especially true if you are driving a modern car, such as the latest Mercedes C-Class, which has 153 processors controlling things like fuel supply, braking efficiency, and navigational and safety features.

Pervasive computing (which we will use as being synonymous with ubiquitous and ambient computing) has its roots back in Xerox PARC's computing research department, where Mark Weiser's first thoughts on ubiquitous computing in 1988 were both futuristic and profound — especially since the necessary hardware at the time he wrote his paper was either very expensive or physically large. Weiser's own words from his seminal paper on ubiquitous computing put his vision into context:

> The most profound technologies are those that disappear. They weave themselves into the fabric of our everyday lives until they are indistinguishable from it.

and:

> Such a disappearance is a fundamental consequence not of technology but of human psychology. Whenever people learn something sufficiently well, they cease to be aware of it ... in this way are we freed to use technology without thinking.

and:

> I believe that what we call ubiquitous computing will gradually emerge as the dominant mode of computer access over the next twenty years. Like the personal computer, ubiquitous computing will enable nothing fundamentally

new, but by making everything faster and easier to do, with less strain and mental gymnastics, it will transform what is apparently possible. [1]

The development of the disappearing hardware technology itself is just an enabler for intelligent spaces and pervasive computing, which then opens up interesting questions about the new uses and business opportunities it enables. We are not discussing the business opportunities arising from the creation of the 'intelligent spaces' themselves, but they will certainly include the home, care, entertainment, car, workspace, classroom, and airport environments, some of which are discussed in depth elsewhere in this book. Pervasive ICT needs to follow other 'disappearing' technologies from the past — the electric motor, electricity, and the telephone, where, when they are functioning, nobody gives them a second thought. This means that we need to attach intelligence to lower- and lower-denominator pervasive devices. To achieve this, technology developments need to be progressed in the following key areas:

- low-power processing;
- memory storage;
- ubiquitous displays (fixed, mobile, large, and small);
- wireless connectivity;
- user/device interface;
- proximity and location-sensing technologies;
- powering techniques.

The pervasive computing environment is very dynamic and sometimes hostile, with devices, people, and objects consistently moving around in a sea of different input/output interfaces. Together they create 'intelligent spaces' that can assist users in carrying out the tasks required. These intelligent spaces (iSpaces) will allow individuals to create, manipulate, and access information while carrying little, or no, technology. Coupling with such things as public displays and other embedded technologies will allow tasks to be carried out simply and easily. The supporting software for these dynamic spaces will need to be distributed across the ubiquitous hidden hardware, coming together as connections are constantly made and broken. The scaling issues involved are complex and are the subject of ongoing research not discussed here.

Interacting with shared/public resources and displays, for example, introduces major difficulties that need to be addressed before they can become a practical reality. How would a user know which interfaces and devices to trust and what are the privacy issues? By what authority can you use them? If they are not free, how do you pay for the service?

The interfaces will need to become more intuitive and user-friendly, especially if distributed or shared use is envisaged. A multi-modal approach, i.e. not relying on a single magical interface that will solve all problems — remember the predictions for speech recognition not so many years ago — will aid in solving this dilemma. The interface should reflect the environment and be contextually aware, e.g. a speech-driven interface may be perfectly valid in a quiet secluded space but a pen may be more realistic on a crowded train. MIT's 'Project Oxygen' [2] is looking at speech and gesture as a combined interaction rather than the clumsy keyboard and mouse.

13.2   Living in a Moore's Law World

Before we look at some individual technologies, let us look at some past predictions and forecasts that have led us to believe the pervasive vision is technically feasible.

In 1965, Gordon Moore of Fairchild Semiconductor (now Intel) had built an integrated circuit with 30 transistors and was finishing a component with 60 transistors. It was then that he made his famous prediction that the number of transistors on a chip could double each year for the next decade. Since then he amended that to a doubling every 24 months, before settling on a time-scale of 18 months, a figure that has more or less held steady over 19 iterations of semiconductor device development to date, even in the face of dramatic economic cycles. This prediction of exponential growth became known as Moore's law [3].

It has been the driver behind many of the impressive hardware developments in the pervasive computing space, but it is still just one of the factors influencing the rapid growth of miniaturised low-cost electronics.

We have gone from 30 transistors on a single wafer to 55 million in under 30 years, and it is expected to reach 1 billion by 2007. It is not only the number of transistors that has been influenced but also cost, size, energy efficiency, and reliability have all drastically improved. An interesting interpretation of Moore's law is that every 18 months for a given size chip, the cost halves. In 1965 for example, the cost of a single transistor was about $5; today $5 will buy you 5 million transistors on an integrated chip. This adds up to increased-capability ICT at decreasing costs; extrapolated, this points to a future where it is economically, if not environmentally, viable for disposable electronics.

A Moore's law interpretation is also being abstracted to factors beyond just the number of transistors and has been applied to both computational capability and storage capacity. Data storage density, for example, is doubling faster than Moore's law, at every 12 months.

Kurzweil [4], one of the leading authorities on artificial intelligence, states in his book, *The Singularity is Near*, that Moore's law is just part of an uninterrupted exponential technology curve that extends smoothly back in time for over 100 years, long before the invention of the semiconductor. Through five paradigm shifts — such as electromechanical calculators and vacuum tube computers — the computational power that $1000 buys has doubled every two years, but for the past 30 years it has been doubling every year. However, as can be seen in Fig. 13.1, not only does each paradigm lie on an exponential curve, but the total curve is also exponential. This means that the next 20 years of technological progress will be equivalent to that occurring in the entire 20th century. Each individual technology follows an elongated S-shaped curve of slow progress during initial development, upward progress during a rapid adoption phase, and then slower growth from market saturation over time. A more generalised capability, such as computation, storage, or bandwidth, tends to follow a pure exponential — bridging across a variety of technologies and their cascade of S-curves. If history is any guide, Moore's law will continue on and will jump to a different material system than CMOS silicon. It has done so five times in the past and will need to again in the future.

There have been many predictions for the end of Moore's law, but continuing sustained innovation in the semiconductor industry is expected to extend its lifetime certainly beyond the next 10 years, by which time the technology of building devices from the bottom up using techniques such as nanotechnology will be starting to approach the full manufacturing stage.

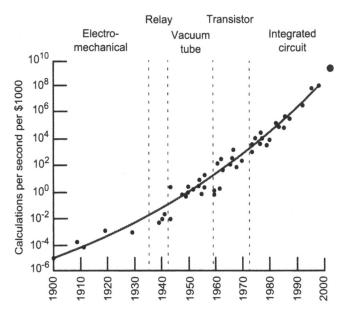

Fig. 13.1   Law of accelerating returns.

13.3   Hardware Technology Influencers and Issues

It is relatively easy to demonstrate prototype hardware technology in the laboratory, but it is another thing to transfer that technology into a high-volume, high-yield manufacturing process without which a technology cannot become pervasive. As new technologies are developed, the infrastructure and setting up costs for manufacture can be very high, and return on investment can govern which technologies will succeed.

13.3.1   The Learning/Experience Curves for 'High-Tech' Manufacture

The learning curve effect states that the more often a task is performed, the less time will be required on each iteration. The experience curve is broader in scope than the learning curve and encompasses factors beyond labour time such as marketing, distribution, administration, and manufacturing. The curves in Fig. 13.2(a), show that each time the cumulative volume for a product doubles, costs fall by a constant and predictable percentage. Learning and experience curves apply across a whole range of industries and products, and the semiconductor industry in particular provides a very good example with a cost-falling constant of 0.8. The experience curve allows for the orderly decline of chip prices while still maintaining profitability because costs have genuinely declined. It is not too difficult to appreciate that to get costs for ubiquitous computing down to levels that will drive market penetration, volumes need to increase significantly over existing manufacturing levels.

Figure 13.2(a) shows smooth curves, which will eventually flatten. The diminishing returns are due to scaling and mean that innovation actually has to speed up just to stay on the expected performance line. In actual practice, continuous innovation in a product enables you to jump on to a new cost/volume curve as shown in Fig. 13.2(b). In the case of the semiconductor industry, these jumps, such as moving the fabrication technology to a smaller device feature size, can be costly to implement.

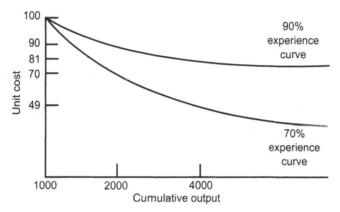

Fig. 13.2(a)   The experience curve.

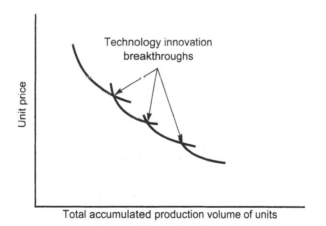

Fig 13.2(b)   Innovation and the experience curve.

The cost of a new wafer fabrication plant follows an observation called Rock's law, which suggests that chip plant construction costs double every four years. For a semiconductor facility being built using 130-nm design rules, the cost is between $1 and $2 billion. Extrapolating out to 45-nm design rules in 2010, this will bring the facility cost into the region of $10 billion. It is economic factors such as these that could hold back the pace of technology progress. There is also the real possibility that increased costs will mean fewer manufacturers, which leads to less competition, causing a possible monopoly situation. An example that is already happening can be seen with Samsung and IBM agreeing to combine their efforts for future manufacturing lines using 65-nm and 45-nm silicon design rules.

13.4   The Key Hardware Technologies for Enabling iSpaces

13.4.1   The Future of Silicon Scaling and Where Next

The semiconductor industries continue to break down the barriers that hinder the following of Moore's law, but it is getting increasingly difficult and expensive to do so. However, innovation occurring in companies such as Intel, IBM, and NEC, is maintaining the expected increase in speed and reduction in cost. In 2004, semiconductor design rules resulted in the commercial manufacture of devices with feature sizes such as the interconnect width, averaging 90 nm. Future iterations scale down every three years by 70%, as shown in Table 13.1 [5]. Although these are average design figures, parts of the chips can be much smaller, and so the table also shows the physical size of a CMOS transistor gate. It is the attainment of these features sizes that requires much of the innovation.

Table 13.1   Scaling of future iterations of feature size.

	2004	2007	2010	2013	2016
Average feature size (nm)	90	65	45	32	22
Physical gate length (nm)	37	25	18	13	9

What manufacturing issues need to be addressed? The first is about producing devices on a mature manufacturing line with high yield across a silicon wafer that is 300-mm diameter now. Increasing to 450-mm diameter in the near future will allow for higher overall throughput and less wastage of an extremely expensive bit of what is, after all, just processed sand.

When you approach gate lengths of around 10 nm, the oxide layers beneath them are just 0.8 nm thick, equivalent to 4 silicon atoms. At these sizes and thickness, quantum physics starts to take over and specifications, like leakage currents across the oxide layer, become a major issue. These small feature sizes introduce the possibility of electrons crossing interconnects or being on both at the same time. Despite these difficulties, NEC has recently revealed a working prototype device with 11-nm design rules and a gate length of just 5 nm, albeit with initially poor characteristics. Below 5 nm, tunnelling occurs, i.e. electrons pass without an applied voltage, hence transistors become unreliable because the probability of spontaneous transmission is around 50%. This minimum gate length will be reached in about 2018 to 2020. And even if this can be overcome when/if a 3-nm gate length is reached, the heat generation would cause thermal meltdown. Some of the above problems can be alleviated by a move to transistors with metallic gates. A metal gate can make a thicker gate act like one that measures only 0.4–0.5 nm thick, which would be extremely difficult to achieve physically with current materials. But this will only delay the inevitable, to, say 2025, and changing to vertically structured 1.5-nm gate length design. We have now hit the limit of the minimum well size from which an electron can be extracted.

History tells us that the semiconductor industry will overcome the manufacturing bottle-necks for silicon scaling for a few years yet, but at some point before 2025 there will need to be a paradigm shift to a new material [5]. The best bet at the moment is carbon, or to be more precise, carbon nanotubes and graphene (a graphite sheet only one atom thick) all based around the Carbon-60 molecule. The electronic properties of carbon nanotubes, about 1–2 nm in diameter, depends on their chirality, which is dependent on the direction in which the graphene sheet is rolled up. They can exist as semiconductors or as metals — two thirds naturally become the former.

So by stretching them lengthways between source and drain of a traditional transistor, the first carbon nanotube hybrid transistor was produced. This improves the performance and reduces power consumption, but there is no gain in size reduction terms. More esoteric is Nantero's [6] use of van der Waals forces to effect a non-volatile faster switching transistor. Ribbons of nanotubes are suspended above a carbon substrate. In this state no current can flow, but by applying a charge to the ribbon it is attracted to the substrate below and current can flow. Even if the charge is removed, the van der Waals force holds them in place. Altering the charge repels the nanotubes and turns it to the 'off' state. Nantero's design-based chips are fairly large at present and rely on expensive semiconductor manufacturing processes, but we are at the stage of development Moore was when he made his prediction all those years ago.

In October 2004 a metallic-channel field-effect transistor was demonstrated, fabricated from sheets of graphene [7]. These sheets of carbon boast some remarkable properties; they are highly flexible, stable, and strong, but, most importantly in this case, they show remarkable conductivity. Electrons will travel across the material without scattering over submicron distances. This makes them ideal for very fast switching transistors. It is early days yet, but we have 15–20 years to commercialise the technology before Moore's law will have to jump to a new S-curve. The future's black, the future's carbon.

These innovations will continue well into the future and, from a ubiquitous computing point of view, it is important to remember that, as each design iteration arrives, the cost of chips using the previous one drops steeply, certainly enough to start thinking of embedding them into lower- and lower-value pervasive products.

13.4.2 Mass Compact Storage

In this section we will show how progress in memory technologies will mean that portable high-density storage is not a major issue now, and will be even less so in the future. The problems that are arising now, and will increase in the future, are not: 'Can I store this data?' but 'How do I synchronise it, back it up, or how do I search its contents?' — which may comprise text, images, and video.

What can a user do, now that this increased storage capacity is available to them? As an example, Microsoft describes the latest variation on the idea of capturing your life as you move through it — SenseCam [8] is worn as a piece of jewellery and captures images, triggered by motion, light, or temperature changes. If you add time, position, and even biometric measurements, the amount of data collected in a single day would be immense.

The drive for large data storage capacities at the lowest prices has ensured that semiconductor memory, such as flash, DRAM, and static RAM, has benefited from the progress in semiconductor scaling just mentioned. There is one technology area, however, that is running ahead of the semiconductor industry in the Moore's law exponential race — magnetic hard disk storage capacity, with a doubling of data density being achieved every 12 months since 1997. Accompanying this has been a massive reduction in the cost of magnetic storage over the last 5 years, from $1 a megabyte to below $1 a gigabyte. Improvements in the areal density (the number of bits stored per square inch of magnetic medium) has been the significant technology driving force behind these historic improvements, and, from a ubiquitous computing viewpoint, storage is becoming so inexpensive and plentiful that, for many devices, internal storage capacity is not a limiting factor.

Disk drive manufacturers have shown great innovation to overcome the 40 Gbit/in^2 areal density barrier caused by an effect called the superparamagnetic limit. When magnetic regions on the disk become too small, they cannot retain their magnetic orientations and data decay occurs due to thermal effects. There are a number of ways being developed to overcome it.

- Ruthenium layer

  IBM first developed an improved magnetic coating consisting of a three-atom thick layer of ruthenium sandwiched between two magnetic layers. An areal density beyond 100 Gbit/in^2 can be achieved with this extra ruthenium layer that has the magical name of 'Pixie Dust' [9]. This technology is now used in the Toshiba drives in the larger Apple iPod music players.

- Perpendicular recording

  Normally magnetic disks are magnetised in a longitudinal direction, but developments are now appearing with perpendicular recording from companies like IBM/Hitachi, Toshiba, and Seagate. Perpendicular recording arranges the magnetic bits vertically, enabling the head to both record and read much more information per unit area. This should at least double the areal storage density to way beyond 200 Gbit/in^2.

- Thermally assisted recording

  The use of higher-coercivity materials that are more resistant to thermal instability at normal operating temperatures will help to push back the superparamagnetic limit, but the problem is that these materials are harder to magnetise. This can be overcome by thermally assisted recording using a local laser to provide a precise spot of heat at the disk during the writing of data, reducing the required magnetic field to a level accessible by the recording head. Areal densities beyond 1 Tbit/in^2 will be possible with this technology.

- Magnetic media patterning

  Patterning the magnetic media into isolated islands allows a single magnetic domain to represent a bit, in contrast to the hundred or so magnetic grains, or domains that make up each bit on normal magnetic thin-film media. In principle, it is possible to use lithography to make 12.5-nm islands, which would give a disk density of 1 Tbit/in^2.

There seems little doubt that drives with 1 Tbit/in^2 magnetic data densities will be in production by the end of this decade, and following closely behind are even more exotic storage products such as holographic memory. These increasing densities, shrinking sizes, and declining prices have already allowed the hard drive to become firmly ensconced along with the embedded processor in consumer electronics and communications products, such as the personal video recorder and data storage in portable music and video players, digital cameras, and mobile telephones. Storage will soon be embedded and available everywhere in the ubiquitous computing environment.

Figures 13.3(a) and 13.3(b) show state-of-the-art miniaturised hard drives from Toshiba and Cornice [10]. The 1-in 2-GB Cornice storage element costs only $70 for 100,000 off and is appearing in a number of products from companies such as Samsung, Thomson, and Texas Instruments. It will shortly be increased to 4 GB — so anyone for an iPod in your wristwatch?

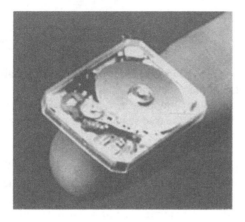

Fig. 13.3(a)   Toshiba 0.85-in hard drive.

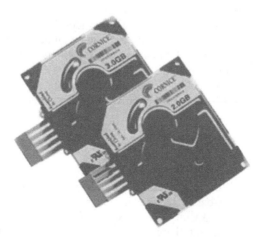

Fig. 13.3(b)   Cornice 2- and 3-GB storage elements, soon to be 4 GB.

Figure 13.3(c) shows a potentially very low cost 1-GB plastic holographic storage element from NTT, which could grow to 10 GB soon. The only drawback at the moment is that they are not rewritable. Another area in its infancy is molecular

Fig. 13.3(c)   NTT 100 layer stamp-sized 1-GB holographic memory [12].

memory, which has been proved in the laboratory but will probably take 10 years to reach practical mainstream manufacturing.

The advent of short-range, low-power wireless connectivity added to small memory devices could result in the true scattering of memory everywhere.

For a Few Bits Less
Although you can store vast quantities of data on such things as hard disk drives and they are relatively small, they are still not 'invisible'. In some cases, only small amounts of data are required to be stored — the last few temperature readings or a page of text. In this case solid-state memory of a few bytes, or kilobytes, may be all that is required. The advantages of this type of memory are that it is very low-cost and requires very little power. Examples of small data-carrying devices are the iButton [11] from Dallas Semiconductors and even car keys with embedded security codes in them. With the predicted falling costs in silicon fabrication of devices, it is not difficult to envisage small data capsules that can be embedded into anything and everything, for little or no cost. Addressing the information can be achieved by physical contact (e.g. iButtons), induced electromagnetic field (see RFID in Section 13.4.4), or short-range radio. Section 13.4.6 describes how it will be possible to print memory and even power it from the paper on which it is printed.

13.4.3   Ubiquitous Displays

Flat-panel displays are becoming prolific, from LCDs on desktops to large plasma screens in public areas. With prices falling they are now infiltrating the home and will probably outsell CRT-based screens in the UK domestic market by 2008, triggered by the soccer World Cup or the next Olympics. Although the above two technologies dominate at present, there are some current and up and coming threats to their position. With plasma screen size likely to be limited to 100-in diagonal, due to glass substrate size and the inherent handling difficulties without massive investment, the large-screen market may be dominated by rear-projection based on DLP (digital light processor — micro mirrors) and LCOS (liquid crystal on silicon). And although LCD prices have plummeted due to manufacturing moving to China and Taiwan and the latest plants able to handle substrates sizes of 1.87 m × 1.22 m, further pressure will come from the development of alternative technologies that have the potential for lower cost and reduced power requirements.

One possibility is from field emission display (FED) [13] technology, which, even after many years, had failed to get into manufacture, but has had a boost from Samsung [14], which has created a carbon nanotube display version. FED is based on a flat cathode ray tube (CRT) but with millions of electron guns instead of the traditional three. Samsung's method of using nanotubes for the guns overcomes the earlier problems associated with creating such small electron emitters. The nanotubes act as mini-accelerators giving the electrons sufficient energy to activate the phosphor, but in very low-voltage fields. FEDs can turn on and off quicker than LCDs, thus reducing smearing of images, and are not vulnerable to screen burn, as are plasma screens, due to the reduced power.

Another pressure comes in the form of a variation on the standard LCD that has been discovered by Hewlett-Packard, which it calls 'post-aligned bistable nematic' (PABN) LCD [15]. When liquid crystals are put in contact with a polymer 'post' less than a micron across, the rod-like crystals naturally align around the post in one of two directions, horizontally or tilted upward in a spiral around the post. Both states are stable and applying an electric field can switch between the two, the horizontal creating a dark pixel and the tilted a lit pixel. This results in a screen that requires no power to hold a displayed image. Presently the speed of response of the pixels is very slow, of the order of a second, but this is expected to improve. With manufacturing costs about one fifth of that for LCD, they are likely to find niche markets at first until performance allows them to go mainstream. The ideal use being promoted at the moment is for e-magazines with simulated page turning.

With the potential for very low-cost screens, it is not a case of displays being ever-present but of how do we interact with the ones we do not own. Maybe it is time for the mobile phone to become the remote control for life.

The above technologies only result in 'hard', flat screens. Alternatives are being developed with flexibility in mind. These 'plastic' displays are based on technologies such as OLED (organic light emitting diode) or the electronic ink process from the E-Ink Corporation [16] that is being licensed by companies such as Philips (PolymerVision [17] — see Fig. 13.4), Sony, and Fujitsu. This 'ink' consists

Fig. 13.4   Philips' PolymerVision.

of thousands of capsules containing positively charged white particles and negatively charged black ones. Applying an electric field through the organic circuit to a particular area of the display attracts either the black or white particles, causing that part of the screen to turn either white or black.

Plastic displays have the potential for improved weight, power, viewing angle, and brightness specifications, but progress towards commercial availability has been slow, with few products on the market. However, Philips says its pilot line will be ready in 2005 to make one million displays a year. Examples of where flexible screens might be found in the future are shown on the manufacturers' Web sites. They all espouse the view that roll-up screens will turn up in such things as pens, and even clothing will have display capabilities in the next few years.

So in the future it is not difficult to imagine a journal, manual, or book, downloaded to an electronic device, as user-friendly as a paperback. But if you are still a die-hard paper fan, how about an intelligent version with embedded chips contained within the sheets. Japanese Company Oji Paper [18] has developed a technology that allows wireless enabled chips to be built into paper. The chip is 0.5×0.5 mm and has a built-in antenna, which can operate at frequencies between 13.56 MHz to 2.45 GHz. While the paper is thicker than regular paper, it can be used for printing with applications suggested by the manufacturer such as cheques, money, and other security-enabled services.

13.4.4   Sensors and Actuators

There are still many challenges and opportunities in wirelessly interfacing the physical world with a hidden pervasive network of embedded sensors and actuators that measure and control elements such as position, gesture, temperature, vibration, and moisture. These ubiquitous distributed networks require that not only are the individual nodes kept as small as possible but their cost is very low as well. Just as important is the ability to be able to power these nodes without, in many cases, a suitable mains power supply being available — so clever use of battery power management or energy-scavenging techniques will be needed. Moore's law is providing us with the opportunity to drive the miniaturisation of electronics, but to be able to integrate a processor and a sensor/actuator with a radio or optical transceiver in the same module, and then to power it, requires some clever engineering. Key to this development work is the use of MEMS (micro-electromechanical systems) [19]. Most people come into contact with MEMS technology every day without realising it, since it is at the heart of the silicon accelerometer used in the airbag sensor of a modern car.

Much of the early work of MEMS in a pervasive sensor environment has its roots at the University of California in Berkeley, which sought to develop 'smart dust' [20] technology. Smart dust is essentially an autonomous computer called a mote, smaller than a match head but capable of sensing conditions and events in its environment, and to communicate wireless information and raise alerts. The mote shown in Figs. 13.5(a) and (b) is about 1 mm square with a connectivity range of a few tens of metres and encompasses a complete sensor network node including processor, sensor, power supply, and communications mechanism. It communicates with other motes in a low-power *ad hoc* network routing arrangement. Honeywell is testing an early version of smart dust in grocery stores, where a dozen sensors monitor refrigeration units to anticipate breakdowns.

Fig. 13.5(a)　　Smart dust mote compared to US cent.
[Photo courtesy of IEEE Sensors Council]

Fig. 13.5(b)　　Micrograph of mote.
[Photo courtesy of IEEE Sensors Council]

The cost of motes is falling as commercial manufacture starts to ramp up. They are still about $50 each today but are anticipated to fall to $1 within five years. Dust networks [21], the spin out from Berkeley to exploit smart dust, is focusing on three key areas:

- building automation — low-cost power monitoring of compressors, condensers, lighting, etc, to optimise energy expenses (this is prohibitively expensive with traditional sensor systems);

- industrial process monitoring, especially temperature — the drop-and-play system significantly reducing costs while delivering more comprehensive data;

- defence — self-configuring, self-organising wireless sensor networks for hostile environments that can be 'crop dusted' into action.

Actuators are altogether more difficult at this scale, and the promise of micro-robots crawling around as a result of MEMS technology is yet to materialise, despite eye-catching SEM images of miniature gear wheels and motors fabricated in laboratories. Even small ant-like creatures have been created that could swim through our blood stream removing fatty deposits like miniature health workers. The reality of this is still some way off, and the most prolific use of MEMS actuators is in projectors using Texas Instruments' DLP micro-mirrors [22] — so for the moment we are safe from nanotechnologies, self-replicating 'grey goo', etc.

Another important link from the physical into the virtual world is through the use of RFID technology. RFID is a generic term for technologies that use electromagnetic coupling in the RF portion of the electromagnetic spectrum to transmit signals for automatic identification of individual items, and can be a non-line-of-sight replacement in many circumstances for the ubiquitous bar code. The system consists of a tag, made up of a microchip with an antenna (see Fig. 13.6(a)) and a reader with an antenna (see Fig. 13.6(b)). The reader sends out electromagnetic waves that form a magnetic field that couples with the antenna on the RFID tag. A passive RFID tag draws power from this electromagnetic field and uses it to drive the micro-chip's circuits. The chip then modulates the waves that the tag sends back to the reader, and the reader converts the new waves into digital data. The tags are specified over one of three frequency rages: high (from 850–950 MHz to 2.4–5 GHz), intermediate (from 10 to 15 MHz) and low (from 100 to 500 kHz). Low-frequency tags are used for applications such as security access and asset management, which require shorter-distance read ranges. High-frequency systems are used for applications such as car toll collection and storage container tracking, which require longer read ranges. While high-frequency tags transmit data faster and can be read from farther away, they also need to be actively powered, or respond to a high-energy density field, and are more expensive than low-frequency tags.

Fig. 13.6(a)   Miniature RFID reader 'SkyeRead^{TM} M1-mini' from SkyeTek.

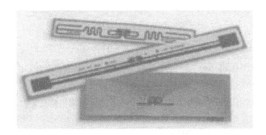

Fig. 13.6(b)   RFID passive tags.

Although there are issues with the implementation of RFID technology including user privacy, and the ability to obtain reliable operation near water and metal objects, companies like Wal-Mart in the USA and the US Department of Defense Authority are instructing their top suppliers to start implementing the technology at the box/ pallet level of their supply chain management over the next couple of years. This will begin to increase volumes and lead to significantly reduced implementation costs.

The cost of RFID tags has been the stumbling block to their mass roll-out. They are too expensive to put on every product, and the demand is not high enough to reduce the cost to acceptable levels (chicken and egg). The 5-cent tag cost is seen as a threshold for mass adoption to begin. This 5-cent cost is for a complete RFID inlet structure shown in Fig 13.6(a) — substrate, chip, and antenna.

A typical tag inlet today costs about 30 cents. The RFID silicon chip itself needs to be no more than one cent; if you apply manufacturing experience curve predictions to today's cost, then you are talking about quantities of 30 billion chips being needed.

Fortunately, a great deal of innovation is occurring in the industry, including a technique called fluidic self-assembly from Alien Technologies [23] that enables chips to be attached to the antennas in bulk, and Motorola's BiStatix technology uses printed carbon ink for the antennas. Hitachi has now started taking orders for its mu tag inlets and a compact reader [24]. The inlets, a combination of a mu chip and an external antenna, are priced at 5–10 pence, approximately one third to less than one tenth the price of products already on the market.

You know when a technology is becoming ubiquitous when a mobile phone manufacturer announces a product with a built in RFID reader. Nokia's 3220 RFID phone is able to read tags at very close proximity. Their tie-up with VeriSign [25] allows users to obtain information by simply 'touching' an advert or product containing a tag. The information is simply downloaded to the phone over the network; the tag is merely a trigger ID. But this information could lead to a whole new generation of services based on knowing where you are and what you are looking at, be it for good or ill (see also Chapters 4 and 12).

13.4.5   Wireless Connectivity

Wireless connectivity is the key to the realisation of pervasive devices communicating with each other. This connectivity needs to be very low-power and offer anything from a few bits to full high-definition video.

Standards are probably the solution to true pervasiveness, as can be seen by the large take-up of WiFi-based systems (IEEE802.11) [26]. The evolution of the species to include Zigbee [27] (IEEE802.15.4) and ultra-wideband [28] (UWB-IEEE802.15.3) will allow everything from low power to high bandwidth to be addressed.

The Zigbee Alliance, led by Philips, Invensys, Mitsubishi, Honeywell, and Motorola plus about 20 other companies, has set the objective of creating a very low-cost, very low-power, two-way wireless communications standard with a high density of nodes per network, e.g. 254 client nodes, plus one full functional device (master) and a bandwidth of up to 250 kbit/s. The intention is to embed this wireless communications solution into consumer electronics, home and building automation, industrial controls, PC peripherals, medical sensor applications, toys and games.

2005 will probably be the start of the roll-out of Zigbee, but it will take a few years to become truly pervasive.

UWB is in a similar position to Zigbee with regards to adoption and exploitation but addresses a different market need. It is short-range, 10 metres or less, but offers throughput of 110 Mbit/s now, and moving to 500 Mbit/s in the future, allowing it to distribute very high-quality video or multiple lower-resolution video channels. This could lead to a truly wireless home but could also allow the use of large public screens from handheld devices.

Freescale [29], a Motorola subsidiary, and Universal Scientific Industries have launched products using the IEEE1394 [30] (Firewire) standard as the transport medium, thus giving immediate compatibility with computers and consumer electronics being sold today. They are using direct sequence ultra-wideband (DS-UWB), which is the leading contender for the IEEE802.15.3 standard, and offers 110 Mbit/s data rates with minimum power consumption. First embedded products are expected to be available during 2005.

With the proliferation of WLAN, Bluetooth, and other radio devices, there is serious concern that this could lead to radio congestion and denial of service because you live next to someone with a 'better' base station. Hostile blocking of base stations is already beginning to happen, and, with devices like TV home 're-transmitters' occupying the same radio space as WLAN, is the UK heading in a similar direction to that of the USA, where certain frequencies are a no-go in some geographical locations?

13.4.6   Low-Cost Polymer Electronics/Printable Electronics

Although silicon transistors have made great strides under Moore's law in terms of cost and size, there is a growing effort to develop organic electronics so that ambient intelligence can be universally applicable everywhere at the right cost point. Polymer electronics can take the cost advantage of an in-line, roll-to-roll manufacturing process based around techniques like ink-jet printing and device stamping processes.

Polymers can behave as semiconductors if they have the correct chemical structure. Materials such as pentacene have produced working transistors, albeit with an inferior speed specification compared to silicon, due to electron and hole mobility through the material being up to 100 times worse. They are, however, good enough for applications such as a transistor drive backplane for flexible displays and for RFID tags. In fact, the 3M Corporation demonstrated in 2003 the first 'plastic' RFID tag capable of handling frequencies above 1 MHz [31]. The 5-in diagonal plastic display from PolymerVision shown in Fig. 13.4 is built from a 200-µm electronic ink front plane over 25-µm thick polymer driving electronics. The shift registers in the display drivers are the largest organic electronics reported to date. The display has a resolution of 85 dpi and a bending radius of 2 cm.

One of the main companies developing the manufacturing processes is Plastic Logic [32], a spin-off from Cambridge University, which uses specialised dot-matrix printers for direct writing of organic circuits on to a polyester backing. Other companies in the race to integrate flexible circuitry displays and tags include DuPont, Siemens, Xerox, and Philips.

There are still many challenges ahead, however, before polymer electronics begins to penetrate the ubiquitous computing market, particularly extending the lifetime and improving the speed performance. An EU-funded project started in November 2004 called PolyApply [33], and led by ST Microelectronics, has the aim '... to lay the foundations of a scalable and ubiquitously applicable communication technology that will make ambient intelligence commercially viable through the use of low-cost, polymer-based electronic circuits'. This four-year project should overcome many of the manufacturing problems, and so we can expect devices to start to become commercially available before the end of the decade.

By combining printable electronics with RFID and novel battery techniques, you can achieve remarkable things, as can be seen with PowerPaper's PowerID™ [34]. PowerID's smart active RFID labels are data-carrying devices that are thin and flexible and contain a micro-power source, integrated circuit, and antenna. PowerPaper has developed a technology that enables the mass production of low-cost, thin, and flexible energy cells. Its core technology is an innovative process that enables the printing of caseless, thin, flexible energy cells on a polymer film substrate, by means of a simple mass-printing technology and proprietary inks. The cells are composed of zinc and manganese dioxide. The cathode and anode layers are fabricated from proprietary ink-like materials that can be printed on to virtually any substrate, including speciality papers. The cathode and anode are produced as different mixes of ink, so that the combination of the two creates a 1.5-V battery that is thin and flexible.

13.5   Summary

The continuing progression of Moore's law has enabled the miniaturisation and dramatic cost reduction in electronics over the last few decades and has made a start in the challenges of hiding key hardware technologies from the user. But there is still considerable progress to be made before Mark Weiser's original predictions for ubiquitous computing progress beyond the early adopter stage into widespread use. The major hardware challenge is still its seamless integration into the pervasive environment, but significant progress is being made in making the devices cheap and small enough to begin the construction of the vision. The list below captures the essence of what needs to be done to drive forward the vision of a pervasive communications environment:

* increase penetration by continuing to reduce manufacturing costs;
* miniaturise key hardware components, controlling size, weight, and power;
* address the continuing need for new powering techniques;
* enable a natural transparent human–machine interface;
* understand and answer the user technology perception and resistance issues.

Users have already shown their worry of hidden technology, e.g. RFID tags. There needs to be mutual trust between the infrastructure and the devices in a minimally intrusive manner.

Many of the core technologies mentioned above — computing processing power, data storage density, wireless connectivity, and advanced displays — are being driven by Moore's law. Although marketing hype can sometimes be way ahead of actual delivery, we are at least beginning to get there. We are still in the early years of a truly digital decade, and it will take beyond the end of it before we can really start to sense and live in this pervasive environment. Bill Gates said in March 2004 [35]: 'Ten years out, in terms of actual hardware costs you can almost think of hardware as being free — I'm not saying it will be absolutely free — but in terms of the power of the servers, the power of the network will not be a limiting factor, wireless technologies will have come in and created, whether it's in the consumer space or in the enterprise space, ways that you're connected all the time.'

What he omitted to say was that some technologies will have shrunk and morphed themselves into the very fabric of everyday life.

References

1.   Weiser M. The Computer for the 21st Century. Scientific American, 1995:256:3:94–104.

2.   Project Oxygen — http://www.oxygen.lcs.mit.edu/

3.   Moore's Law, Intel — http://www.intel.com/research/silicon/mooreslaw.htm and ftp://download.intel.com/research/silicon/moorespaper.pdf

4.   Kurzweil R — http://www.kurzweilai.net/

5.   International Technology Roadmap for Semiconductors 2003 — http://public.itrs.net/Files/2003ITRS/Home2003.htm

6.   Nantero — http://www.nantero.com/

7.   Field-effect Transistor — http://www.sciencemag.org/cgi/content/short/306/5696/666/

8.   SenseCam — http://research.microsoft.com/users/lyn/

9.   Pixie Dust — http://www.research.ibm.com/resources/news/20010518_pixie_dust.shtml

10. Cornice — http://www.corniceco.com/

11. iButton — http://www.ibutton.com/

12. NTT Holographic Memory — http://www.info-mica.com/en/index.html

13. FED — http://www.meko.co.uk/fed.shtml

14. Samsung Nanotube display — http://www.technologyreview.com/view/article.asp?p=12168

15. HP PABN LCD — http://www.hpl.hp.com/news/2004/oct_dec/bistable_display.html

16. E-Ink Corporation — http://www.eink.com/

17. PolymerVision — http://www.polymervision.nl/

18. Oji Paper — http://www.fecinc.com.my/downloads/ PressRelease_20041109-01_E.pdf

19. MEMS — http://www.mems-exchange.org/

20. Smart Dust — http://robotics.eecs.berkeley.edu/~pister/SmartDust/

21. Dust networks — http://www.dust-inc.com/

22. Texas Instruments DLP — http://www.ti.com/corp/docs/company/history/digitaldisplay.shtml

23. Alien Technologies — http://www.alientechnology.com/

24. Hitachi mu tags — http://www.hitachi-eu.com/mu/

25. VeriSign — http://www.verisign.com/verisign-inc/news-and-events/news-archive/us-news-2004/page_016547.html

26. Wireless Standards 802.X — http://grouper.ieee.org/groups/802/

27. Zigbee — http://www.ieee802.org/15/pub/TG4.html

28. UWB — http://www.uwb.org/

29. Freescale — http://www.freescale.com/

30. IEEE1394 — http://www.1394ta.org/

31. 3M Organic transponder — http://www.eetimes.com/at/c/news/showArticle.jhtml?articleId=18310357&kc=6385

32. Plastic Logic — http://www.plasticlogic.com/

33. PolyApply — http://www.polyapply.org/

34. PowerPaper — http://www.powerpaper.com/

35. Bill Gates quote — http://www.microsoft.com/billgates/speeches/2004/03-29Gartner.asp

14

Integrated Sensor Networks for Monitoring the Health and Well-Being of Vulnerable Individuals

D J T Heatley, R S Kalawsky, I Neild, and P A Bowman

14.1   Introduction

The inescapable fact that people are living longer today than ever before means that the number of elderly people needing care or medical treatment has never been higher. In response to this there is a growing trend to place the elderly and infirm in residential homes or in sheltered accommodation, where they live in a protective environment while retaining some independence. Current healthcare systems in residential, sheltered, and community settings generally operate on a reactive basis rather than a pre-emptive basis [1]. This means that the people being cared for (the 'clients') are often already clinically ill and in need of medical attention, sometimes urgently, by the time the healthcare system engages, whereupon the treatment and recovery regime can be protracted and costly [2]. Unfortunately, a significant majority of our ageing population do not have the benefit of this level of healthcare [3], despite the evidence that our ageing population are regarded to be at an increased risk of falls [4], malnutrition [5], and failure to take prescribed medication [6]. It is this self-neglect that is of great concern. A far better scheme for all parties is one that continuously monitors clients who, although in fine health at that time, are considered to be at risk and likely to need attention at a time in the future, particularly if they are elderly and live alone. By continually monitoring certain behavioural characteristics of an individual, it is feasible to ascertain their well-being or detect when things deviate from the norm.

Fortunately, many indicators exist, which when correctly interpreted, are reliable predictors that medical attention is needed. Provided these indicators can be spotted at a very early stage, remedial action can be administered promptly and intensive follow-up treatment perhaps avoided [7]. Systems such as this could fundamentally reduce the UK's healthcare bill and ease the burden on carers and support organisations.

Monitoring the well-being of people is a complex undertaking, if this is to be done with minimal intrusion on the life-style of the individual, and also without compromising social and ethical considerations. A particular challenge is to provide healthcare monitoring in a multiple occupancy environment. BT and Loughborough University have been undertaking collaborative research, part-funded by the DTI, towards developing an experimental healthcare system that allows a longitudinal trend analysis of well-being to be undertaken over a period of time. The underlying system, although relatively complex in its totality, incorporates a lightweight sensor network comprising an array of distributed sensor nodes designed to be deployed in the client's setting. This chapter provides an overview of the design and operation of the sensor network.

14.2   Importance of Well-Being Care Provision

The underlying principle of continuous well-being monitoring is that human behaviour is habitual and any deviation can be readily detected or inferred from an analysis of longitudinal trends.

By examining the deviation from the norm for an individual, a decision can then be made by a healthcare provider about whether or not it signals a deterioration in well-being. However, people are intrinsically complex and unpredictable, and so at first it would seem inappropriate to adopt continuous well-being monitoring that relies so strongly on habit or trend-forming behavioural patterns. Fortunately, people do exhibit an unerring predictability in areas that are fundamental to their general well-being, for example, eating regularly, sleeping regularly, using toilet facilities, having a shower or bath, and many more. Furthermore, it is known that peoples' tendency towards habitual behaviour increases with age [8], all of which mean that the elderly social groupings of interest to this study are particularly well disposed to continuous well-being monitoring, as are the residential, sheltered, and community settings that they occupy.

14.3   Activities of Daily Living

Activities of daily living (ADL) is a term in common use within the health-care profession [9, 10] and is used extensively throughout this chapter. Generally it is defined as '... the tasks that we all perform in order to lead a normal life'. Typical examples are:

Washing/grooming	Bath/shower	Managing medication	Walking
Cooking	Eating/drinking	Using stairs	Reading/writing
Toilet use	Bed use	Handling money	Using the telephone
Chair use	Dressing	Opening front door	Household cleaning

Many of these ADLs have a unique signature that is quantified by the task performed and the actions taken by the individual. In many instances it is possible to detect the activity and its completion by monitoring other secondary events. By determining that a number of these ADLs are being performed by the individual and are occurring at appropriate times, a measure of the individual's well-being can be deduced.

14.4 Ethical Considerations

Deploying suites of sensors around the home could deeply affect many aspects of the way we live because of their perceived intrusive nature. Closely monitoring personal behaviour on a continuous basis has tremendous social implications. By consolidating data from a cluster of sensors around a home it is possible to infer a level of meaning from the behaviour patterns of the person/people being monitored that far exceeds what is justifiable purely for the purpose of well-being monitoring. This is particularly so if television cameras were deployed as sensors since they would be capable of giving a second-by-second account of almost every activity in the home, when they occurred, how long they took, how many times they were undertaken, and so on. Such a situation would have an unprecedented impact on personal privacy, and the true sociological impact is unknown at this stage.

A variety of alternative monitoring techniques for determining well-being can be deployed which are far less intrusive. For example, simply monitoring when a cooker is used and when water is being used could provide a fairly basic indication that activity is occurring within the home. In an environment that comprises many invisible sensing methodologies, the concern then becomes protecting the personal information embedded in the data, and care must be taken to minimise privacy threats. The threats take various forms and could include eavesdropping on the wireless signal from the sensors, data sniffing on the data network leaving the home, or even at the remote site where data is being processed. Arguably the weakest link is the possibility of eavesdropping on the data transmitted by the individual sensors since they will tend to be relatively unsophisticated and will adopt minimal on-board processing to keep the power budget and cost low. However, this presupposes that an eavesdropper has knowledge of how individual sensors are configured and what their data state changes mean. At a simplistic level no detectable activity could mean that the home is unoccupied, and this knowledge could be useful to people with malicious intent. There are ways to remedy this such as periodically transmitting dupe sensor data which the system knows to ignore but would give an external eavesdropper a signal that suggests someone is at home, and therefore deters any malicious intent.

All of these issues and others can be resolved with the right technology. Perhaps the greatest challenge to be overcome is that of convincing occupants that their personal privacy is not being compromised. One possible way to achieve this is to give users more control over how their personal information is used. For example, they might wish to choose which parts of their data are made available to an outside healthcare organisation, or to family and friends who wish to be kept aware of the well-being of their loved one. Generally speaking most people would want minimal information being transmitted from their homes, in which case at least some processing of the sensor data must be undertaken in the home and an aggregated data stream sent from the home with high levels of data encryption.

People seem generally less concerned about the use of very simple sensing and monitoring devices that merely record things such as power being consumed in the home, opening and closing the fridge door, general movement detection, etc. Therefore, by deploying a wide range of discrete/simple sensing devices in the home, it seems feasible to monitor certain activities of daily living without being intrusive.

Questions about ethics and privacy inevitably arise with any technology that continuously monitors the daily activities of people so intimately, and then shares that data with other people and organisations. Interestingly, the prevalence of surveillance cameras in public places raises similar questions, yet society has grown accustomed to their presence and generally accepts that they are necessary. However, our extensive work with healthcare professionals and their clients has shown that this kind of image-based monitoring within the privacy of the client's setting is highly contentious and widely regarded as unacceptable except in the most extreme of circumstances.

A less contentious approach is to deploy sensors that create images but do not convey them in a recognisable form. Instead these images are processed within the sensor and only 'activity' data is transmitted. Examples of this include general movement that has been detected within the room, or a localised hot spot has come on/off within the room which might signify that the fire has been turned on/off, and so on. These kinds of sensor are attractive because of the broad range of sensing tasks for which they can be configured; however, the need for a digital camera front-end, and relatively complex on-board processing, means that their cost and power requirements are currently prohibitive for our purposes. Consequently, our research has focused on strictly non-imaging sensing methodologies that are simple and non-invasive.

Electronically tagging individuals is another controversial proposition for healthcare monitoring, particularly since that approach is tending nowadays to be associated with the tracking of criminals [11]. There is considerable debate about the human rights issues raised by tagging as part of a criminal justice system. It is inevitable that these issues will arise if electronic tagging is considered for elderly people or those who are vulnerable or at risk. Interestingly, the precedence has already been established by the Royal College of Nursing (RCN), which has published guidelines on the issue of electronic tagging [12]. The guidelines emphasise that electronic surveillance is not a substitute for good nursing care and that such methods must never be used to disguise inadequate staffing levels. In promoting best practice and identifying the issues involved in the use of electronic surveillance the RCN has adopted a similar approach to other organisations.

Ethical and privacy issues can also arise in connection with the data that sensors accumulate on client well-being, how that data is conveyed to the healthcare professionals, and what they in turn do with that data.

Encrypting the sensor data will mask the particular client activity to which they relate, hence nothing can be inferred about the client's well-being should the data be intercepted during transit to the healthcare professionals. Furthermore, by ensuring that sensor data can only be decrypted within the well-being analysis systems operated by the healthcare professionals, client confidentiality is assured through the normal mechanisms.

Most importantly the clients must feel that they will benefit from having their well-being continuously monitored. Although these are people who the care professionals have judged to be infirm and at risk, many of them will nevertheless consider themselves in fine health and not in need of monitoring. This dilemma is addressed in part by ensuring that the monitoring methodology does not intrude on the clients or their way of life, which is one of the key tenets in our research. The remaining issues can only be addressed by earning the client's trust over time and demonstrating the value of continuous monitoring through positive experience.

14.5 Sensing Activities of Daily Living

Continuously monitoring well-being can be accomplished in a number of ways ranging from camera-based approaches to a suite of sensors that monitor activity around the home. A measure of well-being can be either determined directly from the sensor data or inferred from a secondary method such as a longitudinal trend analysis.

14.5.1 Inferring Well-Being Through Visual Sensing Technologies

At a purely technical level the use of closed circuit television is an ideal technology for providing a remote view into someone's home. If multiple cameras are deployed around the home, then almost every activity could be monitored. Installing video cameras and intelligent image-processing systems has many advantages over the use of simple discrete sensing devices. Only a few video cameras would be required to cover a whole house and its surroundings, and intelligent image processing could be used to extract behaviour patterns through smart tracking algorithms and even facial recognition of the people being monitored. Cameras can be easily installed in new and old houses (especially if used with wireless connectivity). However, as mentioned earlier, visual monitoring raises serious and controversial sociological issues. Many people are horrified at the thought of being monitored within their homes by video cameras. Even though very low-resolution cameras could be used (where an individual could not be recognised), and on-board processing could further ensure that no recognisable image is sent, the mere thought of a camera in the home is still of concern.

Despite advances in image processing and device size, cameras are inevitably seen as intrusive and that raises serious ethical concerns for their use as a well-being monitor. Even for those vulnerable groups who could genuinely benefit from the use of camera-based surveillance systems, ethical issues are still a constraint. Consequently, alternative technologies must be considered that can monitor the ADLs undertaken by people less intrusively than camera-based approaches.

14.5.2 Inferring Well-Being Through Non-Visual Sensing Technologies

Many ADLs have characteristics that can be exploited by using simple sensing techniques. For example, simple pressure sensors appropriately deployed can detect bed use, chair use, room occupancy, opening the front door, etc. These sensors provide a direct/primary indication of activity.

It is also possible to detect ADLs by sensing secondary indicators such as vibration or acoustic signatures. Vibration or acoustic sensors attached to water pipes will detect water usage, the activity of the central heating system, toilet flushes, etc. Most importantly, both of these approaches can be deployed at relatively low cost and with minimal disruption to the client's premises. This is crucial for any sensing methodology.

Conversely, ADLs such as managing medication and handling money are so complex in terms of the sensing methodology, and are so critical to life in some instances, that it is difficult at present to see how they can be safely and reliably included in a well-being monitoring system.

Even an apparently simple task such as making a cup of hot tea is relatively complex in terms of its sensing and knowing unambiguously that the task has been completed. To illustrate this consider the task of merely boiling water in a kettle, which we will assume to already contain sufficient water. A sensor on the mains cable monitoring the power being supplied to the kettle will signal when water is being heated. Suitable sensors can be readily retrofitted to any power cable and so are ideal for this purpose. To determine whether or not the water in the kettle has reached boiling point would require a temperature sensor attached to the kettle. Retrofitting a suitable sensor is not feasible in most instances, so we can only infer that the water was boiled based on the length of time that power was supplied to the kettle. The magnitude of this uncertainty grows when we consider the full range of actions involved in making a hot cup of tea: getting a cup from the cupboard, placing a tea bag in the cup, pouring in some milk, and then topping up with boiled water, and so on. As putting a sensor on every cup, milk bottle, and tea bag in the client's household is clearly impractical, indirect sensing is the only option. Nevertheless, by collecting data about water consumption, electrical power consumption, general movement around the house, etc, a reliable indicator can be deduced that all is well, or not, within the home.

14.6   Multiple Occupancy Issues

Implicit in our discussion thus far is that the client is the sole occupant of the setting and that sensors are caused to be triggered by that person. What if more than the one person is present? Indeed, how do we know that one of them is even the client? Without additional information we can only assume that if one person is in the client's setting, then that person is the client, and if more than one person is in the client's setting, one of them is the client.

A variety of technologies can be deployed to determine the number and identity of people in a client's setting. These include RFID (radio frequency identification) tags, passive and active infra-red sensors, short-range radio and infra-red pingers, bar codes, etc. Though effective at what they do, these techniques all require the people to wear a tag or some other unique identifier that must be readable under all circumstances. Some techniques do not require the tag to be visible, in which case it could be incorporated into a person's clothes, item of jewellery, spectacle frame, etc.

For any of these schemes to work, suitable readers must be deployed in the client's setting. To minimise the additional cost and complexity brought on by this, a single reader could be deployed at the client's main door, which would allow the number and identity of occupants to be determined as they enter or leave, but not where they are located within the home. Achieving the latter would require a reader in every room, perhaps several in some instances if we wish to know with near certainty that, of the two people in a particular room, it is the client who is sitting down and the guest who is standing, or the client is in bed while the guest is sitting at the bedside. That level of knowledge could be crucial for the care professionals who are monitoring the situation.

Designing a network of sensors that can cope with multiple occupancy presents many technical challenges, all of which have an impact to some degree on the accuracy and reliability of the sensor data generated, and of course cost. At the moment the pragmatic solution to the multiple occupancy problem is to consider tracking each individual around their home, either by direct means or through particular activity. The robustness and reliability of this approach could be increased by employing redundancy within the sensor network as well as collecting data from clusters of sensors.

14.7   Sensor Fusion

By clustering sensors so that their outputs are logically combined, the accuracy and reliability of detecting an event can be improved. Indeed some ADLs can only be inferred when a number of sensor events have occurred. With careful design it is possible to introduce a degree of redundancy into the system so that in the event of a sensor not picking up an important ADL, other sensors would capture the activity. System robustness would be enhanced if multiple sensors, possibly sensing different events relating to an activity, could corroborate their data. Certain alerts can then be much improved, particularly where the ADL in question is being monitored by indirect means. For example, we would know with greater certainty that the client has made a hot cup of tea if we could cluster sensors monitoring water usage, mains power, kettle temperature if available, cupboard usage, etc. This approach is commonly referred to as sensor fusion, examples of which are listed in Table 14.1, with each horizontal row indicating the array of sensors whose data can be fused to reliably detect a particular ADL.

Generally, the rule is, the more sensors there are within a cluster, the greater the accuracy and reliability of the alert. Consider, for example, the ADL of washing clothes in Table 14.1. Washing clothes can be sensed by monitoring water and electricity consumption, noise and vibration, client location and movement, room temperature and humidity, and others. Such a wealth of data ensures that that particular ADL can be identified with near certainty. Indeed, sufficient accuracy could be attained with only some of these sensor inputs. Similarly, the ADL of preparing food can be accurately identified, though it may be difficult to determine the precise nature of the food being prepared, what is being eaten, how much is being eaten, etc. That granularity of information will require many more sensors, and as discussed earlier in connection with the simple act of boiling water, even that may not deliver the desired level of accuracy.

Reading and relaxing are among many apparently benign ADLs that could in fact mask a serious medical condition. If we know from the sensor history that the client is sitting in a favourite chair at a time of day when the newspaper is usually read, how can we detect if the client has suddenly become ill during that period. An alert may only be triggered when the client has been sitting for a longer period than normal, which could be some hours after the onset of illness. By fusing sensors in the room, an earlier alert could be given. For example, if the client is not incapacitated, a call for help could be made or a panic button pressed. If, on the other hand, the client is incapacitated, then the absence of any motion in the chair (NB people constantly move when reading) fused with, for example, a change in room

Table 14.1   Mapping sensor domain to activities of daily living.

ADL	Water consumption	Electricity consumption	Noise/vibration	Gas consumption	Motion	Temperature	Mechanical movement	Pressure/weight	Telephone use	Location in room	Humidity
Toilet	✓		✓				✓			✓	
Bath/shower Washing/grooming	✓		✓			✓				✓	✓
Bed/sleeping			✓			✓		✓		✓	
Chair/sitting			✓			✓		✓		✓	
Dressing							✓			✓	
Light exercising			✓		✓		✓	✓		✓	
Walking			✓		✓			✓		✓	
Using stairs/steps			✓					✓		✓	
Reading/relaxing								✓		✓	
Watching television		✓	✓			✓		✓		✓	
Using the telephone			✓				✓		✓	✓	
Opening front door			✓				✓	✓		✓	
Feeding (drinking) Preparing hot food/drink	✓	✓	✓	✓		✓	✓	✓		✓	✓
Household tasks — washing clothes, vacuuming, etc	✓	✓	✓	✓	✓	✓	✓	✓			✓

temperature, could be used to trigger an early alert. Either way, sensor fusion could be an effective guard against sudden departures from the norm that might otherwise go undetected for a long time.

Sensor fusion can also be applied to clusters of the same type of sensor. Pressure sensors are a particularly good example as they are simple, are low-cost, and can be widely deployed throughout a client's setting — underneath carpets, on chair legs, and the like. The data they produce can be layered depending on the granularity of information required. For example, if all the pressure sensors throughout the client's setting are clustered as one, then any one being triggered will signal that the client is on the premises. Alternatively, clustering all the sensors within each separate room will allow the room the client is in to be determined, and removing all the clustering could allow location within the room to be determined if sufficient sensors have been deployed.

Sensor fusion at the hardware level can be achieved entirely within the sensors, or at a central hub within the client's setting, or a hybrid of both (see Fig. 14.1). All have their merits and trade-offs against cost, technical suitability, and complexity. Carrying out sensor fusion at the sensors might arguably minimise the totality of equipment deployed in the client's setting, particularly if that obviates the need for a hub and renders the network configuration highly adaptable. However, each sensor would need to incorporate sufficient intelligence to fuse its data with that of its sister sensors, and each of these sensors would require ubiquitous connectivity so that all could share each other's data. All of that might raise the power consumption of each sensor, which in turn will place a greater demand on the sensor's powering methodology. Sensor cost will also increase.

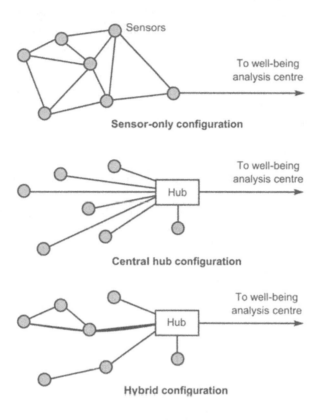

Fig. 14.1   Options for sensor fusion.

Conversely, employing a central hub could minimise the complexity and cost of the sensors by taking on board all the intelligence, data fusing, etc. However, some sensors could be located some distance from the hub and achieving connectivity could present challenges. Clearly, the hybrid scheme affords an attractive compromise in terms of connectivity and sharing the intelligence.

14.8   Sensor Networks

The purpose of a sensor network designed for healthcare is to obtain a broad range of data about clients and their local environment, then convey that data, either in raw form or partially processed on site, to a central well-being analysis centre operated by the local health authorities or support organisations. The sensor network itself plays no part in the decision process — all decisions are taken by professionals on the basis of the longitudinal trends made available to them by the well-being analysis centre.

Sensor networks of this kind typically comprise a number of self-contained sensing nodes that transmit information to a central processing unit. The sensors are required to be multifunctional, low-power, physically small and able to communicate over short distances [13]. With appropriate design it is possible to create self-organising sensor networks where individual sensor nodes interconnect autonomously and operate co-operatively [14]. Additionally, on-board processing can be incorporated into sensors to support sophisticated functions such as sensor fusion as discussed earlier, and caching real-time data in memory to be transmitted in a burst at regular intervals, or when there is a state change. The latter is one of many steps that can be taken to reduce the power budget of sensor nodes and increase their battery life.

Ultimately sensor networks in healthcare applications must have at least the following key attributes:

- ability to continuously monitor and provide reliable indicators of the well-being of clients in their own setting;

- wireless connectivity between sensors that is capable of creating a robust autonomous *ad hoc* network that can support a large number of sensor nodes — potentially hundreds or even thousands;

- sensors with an appropriate level of local processing for the purposes of data fusion, link reliability, security, etc;

- sensors with a very long battery life;

- easy installation and maintenance;

- low cost.

In the following sections we will see examples of how these specifications can be achieved.

14.8.1   Design Considerations

The development of low-cost, autonomous sensors that are capable of a variety of monitoring functions is crucial to the widespread deployment of continuous health monitoring systems. It is therefore necessary to pay close attention to sensor design and the underlying infrastructure that will be required to support the sensing devices. These important design aspects need to take into account the environment and local circumstances in which sensor nodes will be deployed. It is inadequate to assume that sensors can be readily attached to suitable appliances and anchorages around the client's home, and that these sensors can be reliably powered from the local mains supply. Sensor design must be agnostic to these factors. Indeed, some homes may not be suited at all to this kind of retrofit installation, particularly if structural alterations are required.

A further enabler for the widespread take-up of continuous health monitoring systems is keeping the cost of deployment low and eliminating the need for follow-up maintenance. It is therefore vital to design sensors and their supporting network elements for easy installation by relatively unskilled people, perhaps even the clients themselves. The sensors should be supplied ready to be easily switched on, ready to clip on to a suitable anchorage in the home, and able to self-calibrate if appropriate. Likewise the network elements (e.g. the hub and wireless connections between the sensors) should activate immediately and create the necessary connectivity to the remote healthcare provider over the national network. In addition, the battery life of the sensors should be sufficiently high, at least 1 year, to minimise the frequency of later changes, and the task of changing should require minimal skill. Better still, where feasible, sensors should scavenge their power from the local environment, whereupon they become powered for life, and for free.

All of these requirements can be met with the right technology and the right design.

14.8.2   Sensors

Our studies of ADLs and the various sensing methodologies that they require for continuous well-being monitoring have directed our attention to developing a suite of prototype sensors that all meet stringent requirements on cost and technical performance. Schematically each of our sensors comprises the key elements shown in Fig. 14.2.

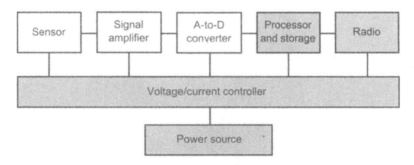

Fig. 14.2   Schematic of a sensor node.

The sensing element is a material/device that is sensitive to the parameter being monitored, for example, a piezo-electric crystal or sheet to monitor pressure, a bimetallic strip or thermistor to measure temperature, an acoustic pick-up to measure sound or vibrations, and so on. As, in some cases, the output signal from these devices is analogue and low level, they are followed by a low-noise signal amplifier. The amplified analogue signal is converted to a digital stream and then passed to the processor. It is here that the structure of the sensor data is defined — how many bits comprise each data packet, how the sensor is given a unique identifier, encryption is added if required, etc. The processor might also facilitate the sensor fusion techniques discussed earlier, because it is here that the inputs from other sensors in the cluster might be logically combined. Associated with the processor is a memory used by those sensors which cache their data over a period of time before transmitting it serially in a short burst via the radio element. The power source for the sensor can take a variety of forms, some of which deliver a clean steady voltage, while others not. The purpose of the voltage/current controller is to ensure that the sensitive electronics always receive a clean steady voltage, and the current drain is closely monitored.

The ability to monitor water usage is a particularly important sensing capability as it is integral to several important ADLs. Most commercial water usage sensors use inflow devices or ultrasonic transducers embedded in the pipe work. Although both are accurate at measuring water rate and volume, their installation is complex and costly, and they require local mains electricity. In contrast, our sensors are specifically designed to be retro-fitted to existing pipe work, employ no moving parts, are internally powered, and are fundamentally simple and low-cost. Monitoring water usage can be achieved most simply by detecting vibrations in the pipe work or by measuring temperature, or both. We elected to study both approaches.

Figure 14.3 shows our acoustic water flow sensor installed in a typical location, in this case on the main cold water inlet to our test home. Visually our temperature sensor is the same. All of the sensor electronics and battery are contained within the black box, and acoustic or thermal coupling to the pipe is provided via the white clamps. The radio antenna is visible on top of the box.

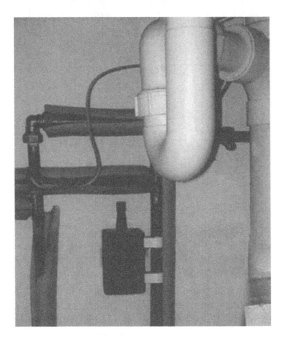

Fig. 14.3   Experimental water flow sensor.

Figure 14.4 shows a typical acoustic signal from the sensing element caused by water flowing through the pipe (over 150 seconds). The corresponding processed data from our sensor is shown in Fig. 14.5 (over 24 hours) where the timing of the spikes indicates when water has flowed.

Embedded in the amplitude and profile of these spikes is a richness of information that allows us to determine with reasonable accuracy the particular source of water usage within the client's setting. This is because different sources create different acoustic signatures that can be distinguished by the sensor's processor. For example, a toilet flush sounds different from filling a kettle or running a bath, and they all have different durations. A single sensor judiciously placed on the pipe work might therefore suffice for the entire client setting if accuracy, though desirable, is not essential; or by deploying perhaps only 2 or 3 sensors, the entire client setting could be monitored with high accuracy.

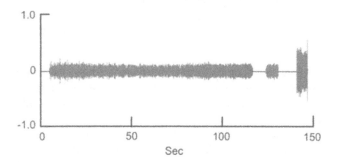

Fig. 14.4   Sound generated by water flowing in a pipe over 150 sec.

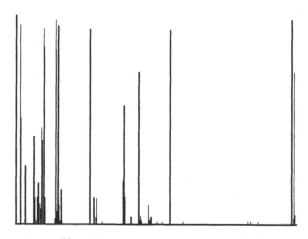

Fig. 14.5   Water usage over 24 hours.

The same sensing methodology can also be applied to gas pipes to monitor gas usage. For those clients with gas fires, central heating and cookers, this sensor can afford an indirect means of monitoring the use of these appliances.

Water flow can also be detected by a temperature change in the pipe work. In Fig. 14.6, the upper trace shows a typical temperature profile over a 24-hour period detected by our temperature sensor. The corresponding processed data from the sensor is shown on the lower trace. Temperature change is subject to the thermal mass of the pipe work and so is not as instantaneous as the acoustic signal in Fig. 14.4. However, this 'storage' effect can be exploited by the sensor since relatively infrequent samples of temperature will suffice for continuous monitoring. Power consumption within the sensor should therefore be minimal, thus maximising battery life. In contrast, monitoring water flow acoustically might necessitate a higher sampling rate and a greater processing overhead, all of which will have an impact on battery life. However, acoustic sensing is capable of detecting the short

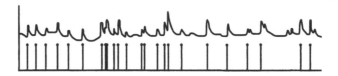

Fig. 14.6   Temperature change caused by water flow over 24 hours.

bursts of water flow that temperature sensing might miss, for example, filling a kettle to boil water and similar ADLs that give a useful indication of the client's well-being. Arguably the optimum design of water usage sensor combines elements of both approaches.

This temperature sensor is also suited to monitoring the use of the central heating system in the client's setting, which is another important factor in determining client well-being.

14.8.3   Sensor Connectivity

A highly reliable and robust means of wirelessly interconnecting sensor nodes in an *ad hoc* fashion is crucial to a sensor network for healthcare applications. A variety of high-performance radio modules for sensor applications are commercially available today, most of which operate in the 433-MHz and 869-MHz bands (these have been set aside for telemetry and social alarm applications) and support data rates approaching 100 kbit/s.

These modules achieve respectable ranges with small antennas, and thus give the sensor enclosure a compact form factor. Our work thus far has used these modules. However, they do not readily lend themselves to *ad hoc* networking without sophisticated onboard processing being introduced, and in situations where many wireless sensors are in close proximity (which is likely to be the norm) the resulting level of interference might be difficult to tolerate without further on-board processing. Nevertheless, these modules are very low-cost, have a very long battery life, and are extensively used in the current generation of healthcare systems in which networking and interference are minimal if any.

An emerging wireless scheme that comes closest to meeting all the requirements of a sensor network for healthcare is ZigBee [15]. It is designed to create *ad hoc* networks with up to 65,000 nodes, and can support a date rate approaching 250 kbit/s between nodes over a line-of-sight distance of some 30 m. It has a very fast wake-up time after long periods of inactivity, and operates on a very low duty cycle to achieve a long battery life. The one concern is that ZigBee operates in the same 2.4-GHz radio band as today's ubiquitous wireless LAN systems, and interference could be problematic. On the other hand, the underlying networking protocols that ZigBee uses belong to the IEEE802 family of international standards, as do wireless LAN systems, and therefore these protocols have been designed to be highly resilient in dense wireless environments. It is therefore reasonable to expect that ZigBee will perform reliably at all times, and that, coupled with its other features, is likely to make it the wireless scheme of choice in next-generation sensor networks for healthcare.

14.8.4   Sensor Powering Options

Supplying power to the various sensors deployed throughout the client's setting requires careful thought and planning, taking into account many broad factors, not the least being the wishes of the clients. Undoubtedly there will be instances when utilising the local supply is by far the most cost-effective solution, and, with the clients approval, it would be remiss not to exploit that option. However, it is vital that sensors are designed as autonomous, self-powered units, so that continued operation is assured under all circumstances. It could be disastrous if certain sensors become inoperative when the client removes the mains plug to connect a vacuum cleaner, and worse still if the client forgets to replace the plug. The principal rationale behind utilising the clients' mains supply is to constantly trickle charge the sensors' own internal power units. Beyond that, all sensors should be completely self-powered.

Table 14.2 lists examples of the current state-of-the-art in battery technologies with corresponding power densities. Commercial lithium ion (L-ion) devices feature prominently at typically $300 mAh/cm^3$, largely due to the mobile telephone and portable ICT industries, which have invested heavily in the development of that technology. To put that figure into perspective, a lithium ion device in the form of a 1-cm cube (about the size of a sugar cube) could deliver 300 milliamps continuously for an hour. Clearly, that is an idealised interpretation of what $300 mAh/cm^3$ means, but it will serve our purposes here. If we set an arbitrary target of sensor current not exceeding 1 mA (long-term average), then we can power a sensor continuously for

Table 14.2   Power density delivered by conventional bulk cells and from scavenging.

Energy source	Estimated power density	Information source	
Batteries (zinc-air)	1050–1560 mWh/cm^3	Manufacturer's data	
Batteries (lithium ion)	300 mWh/cm^3	Manufacturer's data	
Nickel cadmium	125 mWh/cm^3	Manufacturer's data	Available as commercial off-the-shelf devices
Nickel metal hydride	180 mWh/cm^3	Manufacturer's data	
Lithium-polymer	300–415 mWh/cm^3	Manufacturer's data	
Alkaline	347 mWh/cm^3	Manufacturer's data	
Silver oxide	500 mWh/cm^3	Manufacturer's data	
Lithium ion	550 mWh/cm^3	www.ee.ucla.edu/	
Solar (indoors — desk)	0.006 mW/cm^2	www.ee.ucla.edu/	
Vibrations	0.001–0.1 mW/cm^3	www.ee.ucla.edu/	
Acoustic (75 dBSPL) — 1m from a loud TV	3×10^{-6} mW/cm^2	Direct calculations from acoustic theory	Under development
Acoustic (100 dBSPL) — 1m from a small jack hammer	9.6×10^{-4} mW/cm2^2	Direct calculations from acoustic theory	
Thermal conversion	0.0018 mW @ 10°C gradient	www.ee.ucla.edu/mbs	
Nuclear reaction	80 mW/cm^3	www.ee.ucla.edu/mbs	
Fuel cells	300–500 mW/cm^3	www.ee.ucla.edu/mbs	

Note. Power density in Table 14.2 is quoted under perfect conditions and optimum drains/loads. A discharge rate too high for the design of the cell will significantly reduce these figures. The figures for scavenged power assume that power is stored in a suitable reservoir and can be released over time when required.

300 hours. We would therefore need to replace the battery every two weeks or so, which is clearly impractical in a real situation. However, most sensors need not run continuously. They can operate on a regime where most of the circuitry is in an idle state, only becoming active for short periods. Typically, a sensor might be active for 1 time period out of every 100 (i.e. a 1% duty cycle), in which case battery life increases to 200 weeks, about four years. Even allowing for optimism in these figures, it is nevertheless clear that the time span between battery changes is potentially significant. Ten years between battery changes might be a sensible target for deploying sensor networks on a commercial scale, in which case some improvements in the technology are still required. Research on L-ion devices promises to double today's power density in a few years, and even that might soon be overtaken by other technologies such as lithium-polymer. That, coupled with sensors and processors with improved power budgets that are coming along, means that 10 years between battery changes should be attainable, perhaps even stretching to zero change for the life of the system.

Power for sensors need not be limited to the bulk cells considered thus far. Reasonable powers can be scavenged from the local environment in the form of sunlight, heat, and vibration, examples of which are also listed in Table 14.2. It is clear that the power densities of these techniques are down on those for L-ion and the like, significantly so in some instances, but that should be tempered with the fact that scavenged power is free, constant (when coupled with suitable storage), ecological, and life long.

Indeed, some sensors are better suited to scavenged power than conventional bulk cells. For example, a pressure sensor could operate on the principle of a piezo-electric material being squeezed or released. Such material generates very high voltages over short periods when they are constricted, and in fact is commonly used to generate the spark in gas lighters for cookers and cigarettes. Not only will that material function as the sensing element, but it could also power the whole sensor for the brief period in which it transmits its data packet. We have constructed a number of prototype sensors that prove this principle [16].

Solar cells are another readily available scavenging technology, with commercial products capable of recharging mobile telephones and the like, provided the light level is relatively high. We are investigating the efficacy of this technology with realistic indoor lighting conditions and are encouraged by its potential. If a suitable method can be developed for a power reservoir so that power can be delivered to the sensor even in darkness, then it may prove to be a viable option. However, as always, the final decision depends on cost, and currently solar cells are notoriously expensive, particularly the high-efficiency devices that are likely to be required.

14.9 Experimental Work

Our study of ADLs highlighted their diversity and yet, conversely, the commonalities between the sensors required to monitor them. For example, a pressure sensor, one of the simplest of all sensor types, is integral to monitoring virtually all forms of movement around the client's setting, sitting in a chair, lying in bed, and many others. They can also be used to locate the clients within their setting, which is essential for monitoring the majority of ADLs. Similarly, an acoustic sensor, another simple device, will monitor all forms of water usage and potentially gas usage, which again covers a wide range of ADLs.

Our study of ADLs also highlighted the benefit of sensor fusion, where the outputs of several sensors are logically combined to obtain a more accurate determination of a particular ADL. From that it became evident that a relatively limited suite of sensors would adequately service many ADLs.

To investigate that further we developed two prototype devices, an acoustic sensor and a temperature sensor. When examining the efficacy of the acoustic sensor at detecting water flow, we discovered that the data, when appropriately processed, could distinguish between a variety of sources around the client's premises, such as toilet flushes, taking a shower, filling the bath, filling the kettle, etc. For such a simple device this is a remarkable richness of data.

Lastly we examined the power density of a selection of today's bulk chemical batteries such as lithium ion and found that they can power a typical sensor for potentially years. Anticipated improvements in batteries and low-power electronics promise a 10-year period, or perhaps even the life of the system. On the other hand, power scavenging techniques, although appealing on a number of grounds, have some way to go before they can match that performance.

All of this leads us to conclude that sensors and their powering regime are not a limiting factor in the development of commercially viable well-being monitoring systems.

Our ongoing research is examining in detail the richness embedded in the sensor data, looking particularly at local behavioural patterns and whether or not they can be reliably inferred or predicted. Studies conducted in this area [16] have discovered that the outcome is highly dependent on whether the client is co-operating with the monitoring system or rebelling against it, wilfully or otherwise. Either way, inferring or predicting sensor activity from behavioural patterns presents a number of interesting challenges.

We are also preparing for a number of our sensor networks to undergo trials in a UK local health authority. These will be deployed in a variety of client settings (e.g. residential, sheltered, and community) with connectivity back to a common location where the well-being analysis centre will be sited. That will be staffed by local care professionals and they will be responsible for all decisions involving client care.

14.10 Summary

We firmly believe that continuous well-being monitoring in the clients' setting is a credible proposition to reduce the UK's healthcare bill and ease the burden on carers and support organisations. But is continuous monitoring viable on a commercial scale? Simple reactive systems such as personal panic alarms are already commercially available and in widespread use. Continuous health monitoring, which is ostensibly a pro-active methodology, does not preclude the use of these reactive systems, and indeed would sensibly incorporate them in the overall design. The primary difference between reactive and pro-active health monitoring is the need for continuous sensing in the latter. The commercial viability of continuous health monitoring therefore rests heavily on developing low-cost sensors and associated networking systems.

In this chapter we have shown that experimental sensors can be constructed from very simple components that are capable of continuously monitoring some of the most common activities of daily living. We have also shown that these sensors can be autonomous, self-powered, and deployed with minimal disruption. With further development and refinement, we can reasonably conclude that our designs could form the basis of suitably low-cost, high-performance sensors for a commercially viable system.

For healthcare applications it is clear that the sensor network needs to be flexible, be fault tolerant, have a high-sensing fidelity, and be low cost. The development of very small sensor nodes will enable the rapid deployment of the sensor networks with minimal impact on the infrastructure in a home. The future of sensor networks for monitoring the well-being of individuals who are classed as vulnerable (through illness, age, or special needs) therefore looks very promising.

References

1. Scottish Executive. First Report for the Range and Capacity Review: Projections of Community Care Services Users, Workforce and Costs. Edinburgh, 2004.

2. Seed P and Kaye G. Handbook for Assessing and Managing Care in the Community. Jessica Kingsley, London, 1994.

3. Hayes T L et al. Unobtrusive Monitoring of Health Status in an Aging Population. UbiHealth 2003, The 2nd International Workshop on Ubiquitous Computing for Pervasive Healthcare Applications, Seattle, Washington, 2003.

4. Marks R et al. Hip Fractures Among the Elderly: Causes, Consequences and Control. Ageing Research Reviews, 2003:2:57–93.

5. McCormack P. Undernutrition in the Elderly Population Living at Home in the Community: A Review of the Literature. J of Advanced Nursing, 1997:26:856–863.

6. Fulmer T T et al. An Intervention Study to Enhance Medication Compliance in Community-Dwelling Elderly Individuals. J Gerontol Nurs, 1999:25:6–14.

7. Joseph A D et al. Security, Privacy and Health. IEEE Pervasive Computing, 2003:2:96–97.

8. Siebers M J et al. Coping with Loss of Independence. Singular Pub Group, San Diego, California, 1993.

9. Laybourne A. An Investigation into the Baseline Predictors of Older Peoples' Social Functioning after Participation in a Falls Rehabilitation Programme. Age Concern Institute of Gerontology, Kings College London, 2003.

10. Chin P et al. Rehabilitation Nursing Practice. McGraw-Hill Health Professional Division, New York, 1998.

11. Doward J. Hardcore Criminals to be Tagged. The Observer, London, October 2003.

12. Royal College of Nursing. The Privacy of Clients: Electronic Tagging and Closed Circuit Television. London, 1994.

13. Shen C et al. Sensor Information Networking Architecture and Applications. IEEE Personal Communications, 2001:52–59.

14. Estrin D et al. Instrumenting the World with Wireless Sensor Networks. Proceedings of the International Conference on Acoustics, Speech and Signal Processing (ICASSP), 2001.

15. The ZigBee Alliance — http://www.zigbee.org/

16. Paradiso J A and Feldmeier M. A Compact, Wireless, Self-Powered Push Button Controller. ACM UBICOMP Conference Proceedings, Atlanta GA, 2001:299–304.

17. Twidale M, Randall D and Bentley R. Situation Evaluation for Cooperative Systems. ACM Conf on Computer Supported Cooperative Work (CSCW '94), Chapel Hill, NC, 1994:441–452.

15

Segmentation and Tracking of Multiple Moving Objects for Intelligent Video Analysis

L-Q Xu, J L Landabaso, and B Lei

15.1   Introduction

In recent years, there has been considerable interest in visual surveillance of a wide range of indoor and outdoor sites by various parties. This is manifested by the widespread and unabated deployment of CCTV cameras in public and private areas. In particular, the increasing connectivity of broadband wired and wireless IP networks, and the emergence of IP-CCTV systems with smart sensors, enabling centralised or distributed remote monitoring, have further fuelled this trend. It is not uncommon nowadays to see a bank of displays in an organisation showing the activities of dozens of surveillance sites simultaneously. However, the limitations and deficiencies, together with the costs associated with human operators in monitoring the overwhelming video sources, have created urgent demands for automated video analysis solutions. Indeed, the ability of a system to automatically analyse and interpret visual scenes is of increasing importance to decision making, offering enormous business opportunities in the sector of information and communications technologies.

In monitoring a visual scene that is cluttered and busy, the importance of detection and tracking of any number of moving objects of interest can never be overestimated. This is the central element of an object-based intelligent video surveillance system, of which the two types of application are:

- to allow real-time detection of unforeseen events that warrant the attention of security guards or law enforcement officers to take preventive actions [1];

- to enable tagging and indexing of interesting (customer-defined) scene activities/ statistics into a meta-data database for rapid forensic analysis [2].

In addition, object detection and tracking are the building blocks of higher-level vision-based or assisted event monitoring and management systems with a view to understanding the complex actions, interactions, and abnormal behaviours of objects in the scene.

The range of applications include detection of criminal behaviours in banks [3], marketing data analysis in shopping malls [4, 5], and well-being monitoring at home [6].

15.1.1   Surveillance Systems — Challenges

Vision-based surveillance systems can be classified in several different ways, depending on the conditions in which they are designed to operate:

- indoor, outdoor, or airborne;
- the type and number of sensors;
- the objects and level of details to be tracked.

In this chapter we focus on processing videos captured by a single fixed outdoor CCTV camera overlooking areas where there are a variety of vehicle and/or people activities, though the techniques developed can be applied to indoor scenarios.

There are typically a number of challenges associated with the chosen scenario in a realistic surveillance application environment.

- Natural cluttered background

  A natural outdoor environment is usually noisy and difficult to characterise. The video sequences captured are also often subjected to a compression process such as MPEG or JPEG before being transmitted via a network or stored for analysis. This introduces coding-induced noise into the already noisy imaging sources.

- Dynamic background

  The scene background is not normally a fixed structure, but often changes with time. In the case of a swaying tree or flag, each pixel in the background cannot be fully characterised by a single colour; two or more different appearances could be alternating.

- Illumination changes

  Outdoor surveillance systems suffer heavily from the change of weather conditions. Rain, sunset, sunrise, as well as floating clouds can have a dramatic impact on the scene illumination. Hence, they will degrade the performance of object detectors and trackers if these factors are not accommodated properly.

- Occlusions

  In a typical outdoor scene with many moving objects, occlusion is a crucial issue that needs special treatment. The occlusion can happen in the following cases:

  — inter-object where objects occlude each other — this problem becomes acute when two or more objects enter into the scene while occluding each other;

  — thin scene structures — thin objects in the scene such as trees or streetlights break a moving object into several (typically two) separate parts;

  — large scene structures — because of large scene structures such as buildings, moving objects may disappear completely for a period of time, and then re-appear, e.g. a pedestrian walking behind a parked or moving van.

- Object entries and exits

  Before a newly detected object in the scene is confirmed, it is important to know if this is a new entry, and if so, how it is to be modelled, and equally important is the decision about how and when to delete an existing object after its track is lost from the scene for some time.

- Shadows and highlights

  These are more problematic when tracking is carried out in outdoor environments, as very strong shadows or long shadows, larger than the actual object, are not uncommon; in addition, there are two types of shadows that need different treatment:

  — cast shadows: these are areas in the background projected by an object in the direction of light rays, which can, without careful consideration, be easily taken as part of an object, causing difficulties to the ensuing object tracking and classification tasks;

  — self-shadows: these are parts of the object that are not illuminated by direct light, which a simple shadow-removal procedure is likely to get rid of, resulting in an inaccurate object silhouette.

15.1.2   Related Work

These technical challenges, together with the ever-increasing demand of intelligent video surveillance applications, have led over recent years to extensive research activities that propose various new ideas, solutions, and frameworks for robust object detection and tracking [7, 8]. Most adopt a type of 'background subtraction' technique to firstly detect foreground pixels. A connected component analysis (CCA) is then followed to cluster and label the foreground pixels into separate meaningful blobs, from which some inherent appearance and motion features can be extracted. Finally, there is the blob-based tracking process aiming to find persistent blob correspondences between consecutive frames. In addition, most application systems also deal with the issues of object categorisation or identification (and possibly detailed parts analysis) either before [7] or after [9] the tracking is established.

With regard to the 'background subtraction' technique, the background scene structures are usually modelled pixel-wise by various statistically based learning techniques using features such as intensities, colours, edges, textures, etc [10, 11]. The models employed can be a uni-modal Gaussian [12, 13], a Gaussian mixture [14, 15], a non-parametric kernel density function [16], or simply temporal median filtering [9].

The issues of evaluation and maintenance of background models are discussed by Gao et al [17] and Toyama et al [18].

One major issue in background subtraction concerns shadow detection and removal [19]. An effective shadow removal scheme should remove completely the cast shadows, but not distort a foreground object's shape by removing extremities or deleting possible self-shadows. The use of a colour constancy model for shadow detection has been well studied by Horprasert et al [20], assuming that the chromaticity be the same while only intensity differs between the shadow and background.

However, in the case where shadow removal based on colour properties alone may not be effective or colour information is not available, variants of gradient information can be exploited to fulfil the task [21].

Combinations of multiple cues (e.g. colour, normalised colour, gradient) were also considered by Javed et al [11] and McKenna et al [13]. Often, appropriate heuristic rules have to be adopted [21, 13] in order to accurately recover the true shape of an object.

Regarding the matching method and the choice of suitable metrics, the inherent heterogeneous nature of features extracted from the 2D blobs has motivated some researchers to use only a few features, e.g. the size and velocity [8] for motion correspondence, and the size and position with Kalman predictors [14]. Others using more features conducted the matching in a hierarchical manner, e.g. in the order of centroid, shape, and then colour as discussed by Zhou and Aggarwal [9]. Note that if certain *a priori* factors are known, e.g. the type of an object to be tracked is a single person, then a more complex dynamic appearance model of the silhouette can be employed [7].

Also, in Elgamal et al [16], the kernel density function was used to model the colour distribution of an object to help detect and track individual persons who start to form a group and occlude each other; McKenna et al [13] provide another relevant example where probabilistic object models were exploited. Furthermore, domain knowledge of a physical site can be built beforehand for more effective management of object entry and exit [22] and for better handling the object occlusion issues in some applications [23].

In this chapter we describe an effective multi-object detection and tracking system in which a few novel ideas are introduced to deal with these challenging issues. This leads to the enhancement of several aspects of state-of-the-art object detection and tracking techniques. In particular, we employ a technique to suppress the falsely detected foreground pixels, caused mainly by video compression artefacts. A novel framework is introduced for effective cast shadows/highlights removal while preserving the original object shape. An integrated matching strategy is discussed, using the scaled Euclidean distance metric, in which a feature set characterising a foreground object is used simultaneously, taking care of both the scale and variance of each of the features. This matching method is not only robust (in the sense of tolerating sudden speed change or direction change), but also allows an easy inclusion of more extracted features, if necessary, leaving room for future enhancement.

Figure 15.1 depicts schematically the block diagram of our proposed object detection and tracking system, which comprises two named major functional modules, each in turn containing a number of processing steps. The object classification module is included for completeness, though it will not be discussed in this chapter; interested readers are referred to Javed and Shah [8] or Zhou and Aggarwal [9] for more information.

The chapter is structured as follows. In the next section, techniques for pixel-domain analysis, leading to segmented foreground object blobs, are discussed, with emphasis on the introduction of a novel shadow removal scheme. Section 15.3 is devoted to discussion of multi-object tracking, including the use of a temporal object template, the adoption of a parallel matching procedure and the partial occlusion handling.

Section 15.4 presents the experimental studies of this system with various real-world test sequences undergoing a variety of video compression procedures. Section 15.5 concludes this chapter with a discussion of future research direction and system enhancement.

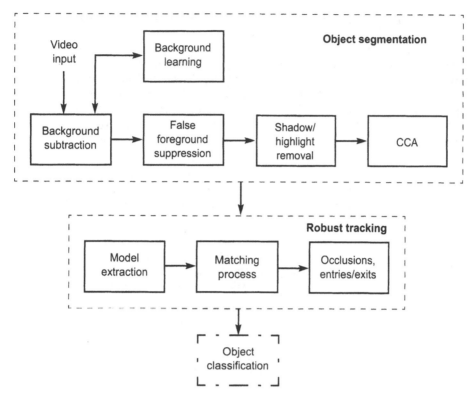

Fig. 15.1   The schematic system block diagram showing the two main functional modules.

15.2   Moving Objects Segmentation with Shadow Removal

As depicted in Fig. 15.1, the first issue to be addressed is 'background learning', designed for segmenting scene pixels forming part of the foreground moving objects via background subtraction. As in Javed and Shah [8], the adaptive background learning method proposed by Stauffer and Grimson [14] is adopted. At each pixel location, a Gaussian mixture model (GMM) is used to model the temporal colour variations in the imaging scene. The Gaussian distributions are updated with each incoming frame; the models are then used to determine if an incoming pixel is generated by the background process or a foreground moving object. This model allows a proper representation of the background scene undergoing slow and smooth lighting changes (but not suddenly turning on or off, e.g. caused by floating clouds) and momentary and random variations such as trees or flags swaying in the wind.

Considering that the foreground pixels thus obtained are likely to suffer from false detections due to imaging and compression noise as well as camera jitter, a false-foreground-pixel-suppression procedure is introduced to alleviate this problem. The idea is that, for each pixel $x = \{x, y\}$ initially classified as a foreground pixel, the GMMs of its eight connected neighbouring pixels are examined. If the majority of them (>5) agree that x is a background pixel, then x is considered as a false detection and removed from foreground.

15.2.1   A Novel Shadow/Highlight Removal Scheme

Once the foreground pixels are identified, a further detection scheme is applied to locate areas likely to be cast shadows or highlights. In the following, we discuss a novel scheme for effective shadow (highlights) detection using both colour and texture cues. Since in any shadow removal algorithm, misclassification errors often occur, resulting in distorted object shapes, the core of this scheme is the use of a technique capable of correcting these errors. The technique is based on a greedy thresholding followed by a conditional morphological dilation. The greedy thresholding removes all shadows together with some true foreground pixels. The conditional morphological dilation then aims to recover only those deleted true foreground pixels constrained within the original foreground mask.

The working mechanism of this novel scheme is shown in Fig. 15.2 and comprises the following four steps.

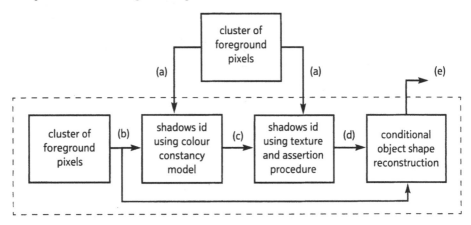

Fig. 15.2   The schematic diagram of the novel shadows/highlights removal approach made up of four main processing steps. The input and output of each block are as follows — (a) the adaptive background image; (b) initial foreground segmentation result; (c) shadows/highlights removal using colour constancy model; (d) the result after shadows assertion using gradient/texture information, generating a 'skeleton' image; and (e) final reconstructed foreground regions.

- Colour-based detection

    As the first step, a simplified version of the colour constancy model introduced by Horprasert et al [20] is employed. This model evaluates the variability in both brightness and colour distortions in RGB colour space between the foreground pixels and the adaptive background. The background reference image is obtained from the mean of the most probable Gaussian component of the GMM modelling each pixel. Possible shadows and highlights are then detected by certain thresholding decisions. It was observed though that this procedure is less effective in cases where the objects of interest have similar colours to those of presumed shadows.

- Texture-based detection

    The same regions with or without cast shadows tend to retain similar texture (edge) properties despite the difference in illumination. To exploit this fact, the

Sobel edge detector is used to compute the horizontal and vertical gradient for both the foreground pixels and their corresponding background ones. For each pixel, the Euclidean distance with respect to the gradients is evaluated over a small neighbourhood region, which is then employed to examine the similarity between the foreground and reference pixel. If the distance is less than a certain threshold, then a possible shadow pixel is suggested.

- Assertion procedure

Based on the detection results from the above two steps, an assertion procedure is introduced, which confirms a pixel as belong to foreground only if both the above two outputs agree. Output from this procedure is a seed 'skeleton' image (as shown in Fig. 15.4(c)) free of shadows and highlights.

- Conditional object shape reconstruction

The above processing steps are designed to effectively remove cast shadows and highlights, though they also invariably delete some foreground object pixels (self-shadows), causing the distortion of a real object's shape. Therefore, a morphology-based conditional region reconstruction step is employed to restore each object's original shape from the 'skeleton' image.

The mathematical morphology reconstruction filter uses an image called 'marker' as the seed to rebuild an object inside an original image called 'mask'. In our case, the 'marker' image (see Fig. 15.4(c)) is a binary image in which a pixel is set at '1' when it corresponds to a foreground, not a cast shadow/highlight, pixel. On the other hand, the 'mask' image (see Fig. 15.4(b)) is also a binary image where a '1' pixel can correspond to a foreground pixel, or a cast shadow/highlight pixel, or speckle noise.

It is highly desirable that the 'marker' image, $\tilde{M}$, contains only real foreground object pixels, i.e. not any shadow/highlight pixels so that those regions will not be reconstructed. Therefore, the use of very aggressive thresholds is necessary in the colour-based removal process to ensure that all the shadow/highlight pixels are removed. A speckle noise removal filter is also applied to suppress isolated noisy foreground pixels that remain and to obtain a good-quality 'marker' image, $\tilde{M}$.

The speckle removal filter is also realised using morphological operators as shown in Eq. (15.1):

$$\tilde{M} = M \cap (M \oplus N), \qquad\qquad \text{...... (15.1)}$$

where M is the binary image generated after shadow removal and assertion process; N denotes the structuring element, shown in Fig. 15.3, with its origin at the centre.

The dilation operation $M \oplus N$ in Eq. (15.1) identifies all the pixels that are four-connected to (i.e. next to) a pixel of M. Hence, $\tilde{M}$ identifies all the pixels that are in M and also have a four-connected neighbour, eliminating the isolated pixels in M.

As a result, only the regions not affected by noise which are clearly free of shadows/highlights (Fig. 15.4(c)) are subject to the shape reconstruction process shown in Eq. (15.2):

$$R = M_s \cap (\tilde{M} \oplus SE), \qquad\qquad \text{...... (15.2)}$$

Fig. 15.3   The 3 × 3 morphological structuring element used for speckles filtering.
Note that the origin is not included.

where M_s is the 'mask', $\tilde{M}$ the 'marker', and SE the structuring element whose size usually depends on the size of the objects of interest, although a 9 × 9 square element proved to work well in our tests.

Basically this process consists of a dilation of the 'marker' image, followed by the intersection with the 'mask' image. The underlying idea is that there should be a fairly large number of valid object pixels remaining after the shadow removal processing. These pixels are appropriate for leading the reconstruction of neighbouring points as long as they form part of the silhouette in the original blob (prior to the shadow removal as in Fig. 15.4(b)). The finally reconstructed blobs are shown in Fig. 15.4(d).

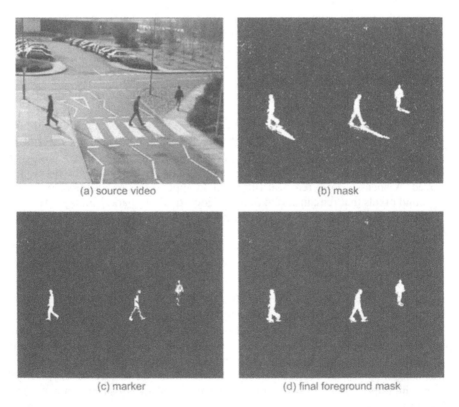

(a) source video   (b) mask

(c) marker   (d) final foreground mask

Fig. 15.4   (a) A snapshot of a surveillance video sequence, the cast shadows from pedestrians are strong and large; (b) the result of initial foreground pixels segmentation, the moving shadows being included; (c) the 'skeleton' image obtained after the shadow removal processing; and (d) the final reconstructed objects with erroneous pixels corrected.

This novel combined scheme gives favourable results compared to the current state-of-the-art ones to suppress shadows/highlights. Figure 15.4 illustrates an example of this scheme at various processing stages.

15.3   Multi-Object Tracking Using Temporal Templates

After the cast shadows/highlights removal procedure, a classic 8-connectivity connected component analysis (CCA) is performed to group all the pixels presumably belonging to individual objects into respective blobs. The blobs are temporally tracked throughout their movements within the scene by means of temporal templates. Figure 15.5 illustrates an example where the three objects (indexed by l) are tracked to frame t, which seek to match the newly detected candidate blobs (indexed by k) in frame $t+1$. One of these four candidates (near the right border) just enters into the scene, for which a new template has to be created.

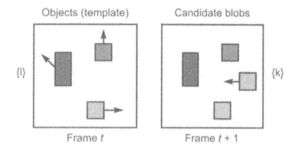

Fig. 15.5   The illustration of object tracking between two consecutive frames. On the left are the three objects already tracked, for which feature template models exist; on the right are the four newly detected candidate blobs in frame $t+1$, for which matching to the corresponding tracks are sought, noting the far right one just enters the viewing scene.

15.3.1   Temporal Templates

Each object of interest in the scene is modelled by a temporal template of persistent characteristic features. In the current studies, a set of five significant features is used, describing the velocity, shape, and colour of each object (candidate blob) as shown in Table 15.1.

Therefore, at time t, we have, for each object l centred at (p'_{lx}, p'_{ly}), a template of features:

$$M_l(t) = (v_l, s_l, r_l, \theta_l, c_l) .$$

There are two points that need special clarification as follows:

- prior to matching the template l with a candidate blob k in frame $t+1$, centred at (p'_{kx}, p'_{ky}) with a feature vector $B_k(t+1) = (v'_k, s'_k, r'_k, \theta'_k, c'_k)$, Kalman filters are used to update the template by predicting, respectively, its new velocity, size,

Table 15.1   The five significant features for each object.

$v = (v_x, v_y)$	the velocity at its centroid (p_x, p_y)
s	the size, or number of pixels contained
r	the ratio of the major and minor axis of the best-fit ellipse of the blob [24]; it is a better descriptor of an object's posture than its bounding box
θ	the orientation of the major axis of the ellipse
c	the dominant colour, computed as the principal eigenvector of the colour co-variance matrix for pixels within the blob [9]

aspect ratio, and orientation in $\hat{M}_l(t + 1)$ — the velocity of the candidate blob k is calculated as:

$$v'_k = (p'_{kx}, p'_{ky})^T - (p_{lx}, p_{ly})^T ;$$

- the difference between the dominant colour of template l and that of candidate blob k is defined in Eq. (15.3):

$$d_{lk}(c_l, c'_k) = 1 - \frac{c_l \bullet c_k}{\|c_l\| \cdot \|c_k\|} . \qquad \qquad ...... (15.3)$$

The mean $\overline{M}_l(t)$ and variance $V_l(t)$ vector of a template l are updated when a matching candidate blob k is found. And they are computed using the most recent L blobs on the track, or over a temporal window of L frames (e.g. $L = 50$). The set of Kalman filters, $KF_l(t)$, is updated by feeding with the corresponding feature value of the matched blob.

It is clear that the variance of each template feature should be analysed and taken into account in the matching process outlined in Section 15.3.2 to achieve a robust tracking result.

15.3.2   Matching Procedure

We choose to use a parallel matching strategy in preference to the serial matching ones such as that used by Zhou and Aggarwal [9]. The next issue is to employ a proper distance metric that best suits the problem under study. As described above, the template for each object being tracked has a set of associated Kalman filters, each of which predicts the expected value for one feature (except for the dominant colour) in the next frame. Obviously, some features are more persistent for an object, while others may be more susceptible to noise, and different features normally assume numerical values of different scales and variances. Euclidean distance does not account for these factors as it will allow dimensions with larger scales to dominate the distance measure.

One way to tackle this problem is to use the Mahalanobis distance metric, which takes account of not only the scale and variance of a feature, but also its correlation with other features based on the co-variance matrix. Thus, if there are correlated features, their contributions are weighted appropriately.

Though, for simplicity, in the current work, a scaled Euclidean distance shown in Eq. (15.4) is adopted to match the template l and a candidate blob k, assuming a diagonal co-variance matrix. For a heterogeneous data set, this is a reasonable distance definition:

$$D(l, k) = \sqrt{\sum_{i=1}^{N} \frac{(x_{li} - y_{ki})^2}{\sigma_{li}^2}} \,, \qquad \text{...... (15.4)}$$

where the index i runs through all the $N=5$ features of the template, and σ_{li}^2 is the corresponding component of the variance vector $V_l(t)$. Note exceptionally that, as discussed in Section 15.3.1, on the dominant colour feature, it can be viewed as $x_{li} - y_{ki} = d_{lk}(c_l, c'_k)$. The initial values of all components of $V_l(t)$ are either set at a relatively large value or inherited from a neighbouring object.

Having defined a suitable distance metric, the matching process can be described in greater detail as follows.

Given that in frame t, for each object l being tracked so far, we have:

$M_l(t)$	the template of features;
$(\overline{M}_l(t), V_l(t))$	its mean and variance vectors;
$KF_l(t)$	the related set of Kalman filters;
$TK(t) = n$	the counter of tracked frames, i.e. current track length;
$MS(t) = 0$	the counter of lost frames;
$\hat{M}_l(t+1)$	the expected values in frame $t+1$ by Kalman prediction.

- Step 1

  For each new frame $t+1$, all the valid candidate blobs $\{k\}$ are matched against all the existing tracks $\{l\}$ via Eq. (15.4) by way of the template prediction, $\hat{M}_l(t+1)$, variance vector $V_l(t)$ and $B_k(t+1)$. A ranking list is then built for each object l by sorting the matching pairs from low to high cost. The matching pair with the lowest cost value $D(l, k)$, which is also less than a threshold, THR (e.g.10 in our experiments), is identified as a match pair.

- Step 2

  If object l is matched by a candidate blob k in frame $t+1$, then the track length $TK(t+1)$ is increased by 1, and the normal updates for l are performed. We obtain $M_l(t+1) = B_k(t+1)$, as well as the mean and variance $(\overline{M}_l(t+1), V_l(t+1))$ respectively, as discussed in Section 15.3.1, and correspondingly the Kalman filters $KF_l(t+1)$.

- Step 3

  If object l has found no match at all in frame $t+1$, presumably because it is missing or occluded, then the mean of its template is kept the same, or

$\overline{M}_l (t + 1) = \overline{M}_l (t)$; the lost counter $MS(t+1)$ is increased by 1. The object l is carried over to the next frame, though the following rules apply:

— if object l has been lost for a certain number of frames, or $MS(t+1) \geq$ *MAX_LOST* (e.g. 10), then it is deleted from the scene; the possible explanations include becoming static (merged into background), entering into a building/car, or leaving the camera's field of view;

— otherwise, the variance $(V_l (t + 1)$ is adjusted according to Eq. (15.5) to assist the tracker to recover the lost object that may undergo unexpected or sudden movements:

$$\sigma_i^2(t + 1) = (1 + \delta)\sigma_i^2(t), \qquad\qquad ...... (15.5)$$

where $d = 0.05$ is a good choice. As no observation is available for each feature, the latest template mean vector is used for prediction, which states that $M_l (t + 1) = M_l(t) + \overline{M}_l (t)$.

Note that the MAX_LOST is measured in terms of number of frames; in actual applications the value should be adjusted in accordance with the video capture frame rate and maximum speed of a moving object, if possible.

- Step 4

  For each candidate blob k in frame $t + 1$ that is not matched, a new object template $M_k (t + 1)$ is created from $B_k (t + 1)$. The choice of initial variance vector $V_k (t + 1)$ needs some consideration — it can be copied from either a very similar object already in the scene or typical values obtained by prior statistical analysis of tracked objects. This new object, however, will not be declared (marked) until after it has been tracked for a number of frames, or $TK (t + 1) > =$ *MIN_SEEN* (e.g. 10), so as to discount any short momentary object movements; otherwise it will be deleted.

15.3.3   Occlusions Handling

In the current approach, no use is made of any special heuristics on areas where an object may enter (exit) into (from) the scene. The possible background structures that may occlude moving foreground objects are also unknown *a priori* [23]. Objects may just appear or disappear in the middle of the image, and, hence, positional rules are not enforced, as opposed to Stauffer [22].

To handle the occlusion issue with *a priori* information, a simple heuristic is adopted. Every time an object fails to find a matching candidate blob (step 3, Section 15.3.2), a test on occlusion is carried out. If the object's predicted bounding box overlaps a certain new candidate's bounding box, then this object is marked as 'occluded'. If this new candidate occludes more than one 'unmatched' object, it is deleted. The template of each 'occluded' object is blindly updated as discussed above from the previous tracking results until it gets matched again or removed after being missing for certain frames.

As discussed before, during the possible occlusion period, the object template of features is updated using the average of the last 50 correct predictions to obtain a long-term tendency prediction. Occluded objects are better tracked using the averaged template predictions. In doing so, small erratic movements in the last few frames are filtered out. Predictions of positions are constrained within the blob that occludes the current 'occluded' object.

15.4 Experimental Results

The system has been evaluated extensively on standard test sequences such as the set of benchmarking image sequences provided by PETS'2001 and a range of our own captured image sequences under various weather conditions and video compression formats.

For PETS sequences, original images are provided in JPEG format, and their frame size is 768 × 576 pixels. In our experiments though, the sub-sampled images of size 384 × 288 pixels were used. Also, an AVI video file was created for each image sequence using an XviD codec, introducing a second temporal compression. Apart from these compression artefacts, the imaging scenes also contain a range of difficult defects, including thin structures, window reflections, illumination changes due to slowly moving clouds, and swaying leaves in trees. Our system has dealt with all these problems successfully and handles very well the complex occlusion situations.

Figure 15.6 shows an example where the white van is occluded by a thin structure, or streetlight pole (left), and subsequently a group of people are largely blocked by the van for a few frames (middle).

Fig. 15.6   An example (from PETS'2001) illustrating one of the difficult tracking situations that the system handles successfully, in which the moving white van, first occluded by the thin streetlight pole, then partially occludes a group of walking people (from left to right): before, during, and after occlusion. The tracking labels have been correctly kept.

For the other sequences, a CIF-size image frame (352 × 288 pixels) is used. The original video was captured at 25 fps using Mini DV format, and then converted to MPEG-1, followed by an XviD compression. Figure 15.7 illustrates an example of a complex and difficult situation where large and strong shadows exist and three objects (two people and a van) pass by each other. Figure 15.8 gives another example displaying the results obtained after different processing stages of the system. The system runs at an average rate of 12 fps on a PC with a single 2-GHz Pentium-4 processor.

Fig. 15.7   Another example illustrating the success of the system in dealing with a severe shadow problem and a complex dynamic occlusion situation. Two people were walking towards each other across the pedestrian crossing, while a van is approaching and slowing down (from left to right) — before, during, and after their intersection.

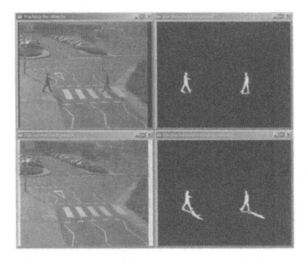

Fig. 15.8   Results showing different processing stages of the system (anti-clockwise from top left) — the source video image overlaid with objects being tracked; the learned background image; the foreground mask output from initial background subtraction and thresholding; the final restored foreground mask after noise suppression and shadow removal.

Some problems occurred when a few individually moving objects start to join each other and form a group. These objects are correctly tracked within the limit of predefined MAX_LOST frames as if they were occluding each other. Beyond this limit the system decides that they have disappeared and creates a new template for the whole group. Other problems may occur when objects abruptly change their motion trajectories during occlusions — sometimes the system is able to recover the individual objects after the occlusion, but on other occasions new templates are created.

The system copes with shadows and highlights satisfactorily in most cases, though very long cast shadows may not always be completely removed. A small defect of the algorithm is that the reconstructed region contains a small patch of shadow in an object's exterior where the cast shadow starts (see the feet of the people in Fig. 15.4(d)). This patch is about half the size of the structuring element used, and is produced during the conditional dilation. Intersection with the mask image cannot suppress this segment as all the shadowed regions form part of the mask.

15.5 Summary

In this chapter, we have presented a vision-based system for accurate segmentation and tracking of moving objects in cluttered and dynamic outdoor environments surveyed by a single fixed camera. Each foreground object of interest has been segmented and shadows/highlights removed by an effective scheme. The 2D appearance of each detected object blob is described by multiple characteristic cues including velocity, size, elliptic-fit aspect ratio, orientation, and dominant colour. This template of features is used, by way of a scaled Euclidean distance-matching metric, for tracking between object templates and the candidate blobs appearing in the new frame. In completing the system, we have also introduced technical solutions dealing with false foreground pixel suppression, and temporal template adaptation. Experiments have been conducted on a variety of real-world wide-area scenarios under different weather conditions. Good and consistent performance has been confirmed. The method has successfully coped with illumination changes, partial occlusions, clutters, and scale and orientation variations of objects of interest — and, especially, it is not sensitive to noise incurred by the camera imaging system and different video codec.

Having undertaken this first but significant step towards developing a fully functional intelligent video surveillance system, we will further explore several aspects to enhance the robustness and consistency.

- Shadow removal

  As previously noted, removing cast shadows while preserving self-shadows is always a conflicting goal. Thanks to the skeleton-based conditional re-construction method for error correction, we can start with a very greedy and simple shadow removal scheme. It works well most of the time, though in certain cases where a foreground object happens to have similar properties to that of the shadowed background, it would fragment the object into several smaller parts, thus causing problems for the tracking procedure. It is necessary to devise a new procedure to link those parts into a single object.

- Matching

  For the matching problem, currently all features involved are treated separately and identically. A further investigation could be done to evaluate the impact of each feature on the matching score, and then choose to use the more significant ones as well as determine their relative contributions in the final distance metric calculation.

- Occlusion

  As regards handling the occlusion problem, we have used a simple heuristic at the moment. It fails in dealing with more sophisticated multiple object occlusion or long total occlusions. The method can be improved if, during an object's presence in the scene, more tracking states than the current three ('matched', 'occluded', and 'disappeared') are introduced, plus employing more heuristic rules in the management of these state transitions. On the other hand, the use of a probabilistic texture [5] or colour appearance model [25] may help find a better solution to resolving occlusions, especially for people tracking indoor environments where more information is available concerning target objects and their interactions.

References

1. Lipton A J et al. Automated Video Protection, Monitoring and Detection of Critical Infrastructure. IEEE Aerospace and Electronic Systems Magazine, May 2003:18:5.

2. Perrott A J, Lindsay A T, and Parkes A P. Realtime Multimedia Tagging and Content-based Retrieval for CCTV Surveillance System. Proc of SPIE: Internet Multimedia Management Systems III, Boston, 2002.

3. Georis B et al. A Video Interpretation Platform Applied to Bank Agency Monitoring. Proc of IEE IDSS'04, London, February 2004:46–50.

4. Haritaoglu I and Flickner M. Detection and Tracking of Shopping Groups in Stores. Proc of IEEE CVPR'2001, Kauai, Hawaii, USA, December 2001.

5. Senior A. Tracking People with Probabilistic Appearance Models. Proc 3rd IEEE Intl Workshop on Performance Evaluation of Tracking and Surveillance (PETS'2002), Copenhagen, Denmark, June 2002:48–55.

6. Cucchiara R et al. Using Computer Vision Techniques for Dangerous Situation Detection in Domotics Applications. Proc of IEE IDSS'04, London, February 2004:1–5.

7. Haritaoglu I, Harwood D, and Davis L. W4: Real Time Surveillance of People and their Activities. IEEE Trans on Pattern Analysis and Machine Intelligence, August 2000:22:8.

8. Javed O and Shah M. Tracking and Object Classification for Automated Surveillance. Proc of ECCV'2002, Copenhagen, Denmark, May—June 2002:343–357.

9. Zhou Q and Aggarwal J K. Tracking and Classifying Moving Objects from Video. Proc of 2nd IEEE Intl Workshop on Performance Evaluation of Tracking and Surveillance (PETS'2001), Kauai, Hawaii, USA, December 2001.

10. Li L and Leung M K H. Integrating Intensity and Texture Differences for Robust Change Detection. IEEE Trans on Image Processing, 2002:11:2:105–112.

11. Javed O, Shafique K, and Shah M. A Hierarchical Approach to Robust Background Subtraction Using Color and Gradient Information. Proc of IEEE Workshop on Motion and Video Computing, Orlando, FL, December 2002.

12. Jabri S et al. Detection and Location of People in Video Images Using Adaptive Fusion of Color and Edge Information. Proc of ICPR'2000, Barcelona, Spain, September 2000.

13. McKenna S J et al. Tracking Groups of People. Computer Vision and Image Understanding, 2000:80:42–56.

14. Stauffer C and Grimson W E L. Learning Patterns of Activity Using Real-Time Tracking. IEEE Trans on Pattern Analysis and Machine Intelligence, August 2000:22:8.

15. Lee D S, Hull J J, and Erol B. A Bayesian Framework for Gaussian Mixture Background Modelling. Proc of IEEE ICIP'2003, Barcelona, Spain, September 2003.

16. Elgamal A et al. Background and Foreground Modelling Using Nonparametric Kernel Density Estimation for Visual Surveillance. Proc of the IEEE, July 2002:90:7.

17. Gao X et al. Error Analysis of Background Adaptation. Proc of IEEE CVPR'2000, South Carolina, USA, June 2000:503–510.

18. Toyama K et al. Wallflower: Principles and Practice of Background Maintenance. Proc of IEEE ICCV'99, Kerkyra, Greece, September 1999:255–261.

19. Cucchiara R et al. Detecting Moving Objects, Ghosts and Shadows in Video Streams. IEEE Trans on Pattern Analysis and Machine Intelligence, 2003:25:10:1337–1342.

20. Horprasert T, Harwood D, and Davis L. A Statistical Approach for Real-time Robust Background Subtraction and Shadow Detection. Proc of ICCV'99 FRAME-RATE Workshop, 1999.

21. Bevilacqua A. Effective Shadow Detection in Traffic Monitoring Applications. Proc of WSCG'2003, Plzen-Bory, Czech Republic, February 2003.

22. Stauffer C. Estimating Tracking Sources and Sinks. Proc of 2nd IEEE Workshop on Event Mining (in conjunction with CVPR'2003), Madison, WI, June 2003:4.

23. Xu M and Ellis T J. Partial Observation versus Blind Tracking through Occlusion. in Proc of BMVC'2002, Cardiff, September 2002:777–786.

24. Fitzgibbon A W and Fisher R B. A Buyer's Guide to Conic Fitting. Proc of 5th British Machine Vision Conference, Birmingham, 1995:513–522.

25. Balcells Capellades M et al. An Appearance Based Approach for Human and Object Tracking. Proc of IEEE ICIP'2003, Barcelona, Spain, September 2003.

16

An Attention-based Approach to Content-based Image Retrieval

A Bamidele, F W M Stentiford, and J Morphett

16.1   Introduction

Weiser's vision that ubiquitous or pervasive computing will overcome the problem of information overload [1] is on the verge of becoming a reality. The volume of digital images has been increasing dramatically in recent years and as a result a crisis is now taking place within a broad range of disciplines that require and use visual content. While storage and image capture technologies are able to cope with huge numbers of images, poor image and video retrieval is in danger of rendering many repositories valueless because of the difficulty of access. Many disciplines and segments in industry, including telecommunications, entertainment, medicine, and surveillance, need high-performance retrieval systems to function efficiently — and this requirement will grow as we continue moving forward in a world connected by both fixed and wireless networks.

It is envisaged that massive volumes of image and video content will be generated by the requirements for more pervasive applications. There is an increasing demand not only for reacting to people's requests, but also for monitoring people's intent and behaviour in a passive manner within intelligent spaces (iSpaces). Whether the visual material will describe a security status, the behaviour of a crowd, the emotion of a PC user, or the interests of shoppers, major advances in image interpretation are needed to make these applications viable.

Visual searches by text alone are ineffective on images and are haphazard at best. Descriptive text simply does not reflect the capabilities of the human visual memory and does not satisfy users' expectations. Furthermore, the annotation of visual data for subsequent retrieval is almost entirely carried out through manual effort. This is slow, costly, and error-prone and presents a barrier to the stimulation of new multimedia services. Much research is now being conducted into measures of visual similarity that take account of the semantic content of images in an attempt to reduce the human involvement during database composition. Indeed semantically associating related visual content will add value to the material by improving access and exposing new potential benefits to a wider market.

In addition to storing and interconnecting iSpaces, service and network providers need to be able to reduce costs in providing content and content management services to a range of devices. Doing so in a cost-effective manner, however, only makes sense when the effectiveness of the systems makes it attractive enough for consumers to want to pay for such services. It is posited that the potential lack of both effectiveness and efficiency in current image management systems prevents them from being a commercial alternative to free (albeit ineffective) text-based search engines. Here lies the proposed commercial benefit of the work. We are working jointly on making content classification, access, and retrieval effective for pervasive computing users, while, at the same time, seeking to remove many of the costs associated with manual data entry, thereby making the proposition commercially viable.

The academic perspective in this chapter stems from identifying what is perceived as relevant information to the user by the integration of mechanisms of content-based image retrieval (CBIR) and context-aware technologies [2, 3]. Visual content continues to represent the most important and most desirable communications medium and it is a challenge to deliver relevant visual data to users engaged in diverse and unpredictable activities.

Section 16.2 outlines relevant state-of-the-art research. Section 16.3 describes the current research and overviews the visual attention model. Section 16.4 describes an experiment using the model and presents the results. Section 16.5 briefly discusses the results, with Section 16.6 concluding the chapter and suggesting future work.

16.2   State of the Art

It is the job of an image retrieval system to produce images that a user wants. In response to a user's query, the system must offer images that are similar in some user-defined sense. This goal is met by selecting visual features thought to be significant in human visual perception and using them to measure relevance to the query.

Many image retrieval systems in operation today rely upon annotations that can be searched using key words. These approaches have limitations not least of which are the problems of providing adequate textual descriptions and the associated natural language processing necessary to service search requests.

Colour, texture, local shape, and spatial layout in a variety of forms are the most widely used features in image retrieval. Such features are specified by the user in the 'direct query on descriptions' retrieval method [4]. This approach makes great demands on the user, who must be aware of the technical significance of the parameters that are being used during the search.

Swain and Stricker [5] measured the similarity of images using colour histograms and the Manhattan metric. The PICASSO system [6] proposed by Del Bimbo and Pala uses visual querying by colour perceptive regions. Colour regions were modelled through spatial location, area, shape, average colour, and a binary 128-dimensional colour vector. A single region characterises the image with a colour vector retaining the global colour attributes for the whole image. Similarity between two images is then computed based on the modelled colour regions. Jain and Vailaya [7] utilised colour histograms and edge direction histograms for image matching and retrieval.

The MARS project [8] used a combination of low-level features (colour, texture, shape) and textual descriptions. Colour is represented using a 2D histogram of hue and saturation. Texture is represented by two histograms, one measuring the coarseness and the other one the image directionality, and one scalar for contrast. It was later enhanced using a shape-matching similarity algorithm [9]; although invariant to transformational effects in image content, it was deficient in taking account of perceptual similarity between images.

Phillips and Lu [10] address the problem of the arbitrary boundaries between colour bins, which can mean that closely adjacent colours are considered different by the machine. They applied a method of perceptually weighted histograms to weaken this effect in other approaches.

One of the first commercial image search engines was QBIC [11], which executes user queries against a database of pre-extracted features. The Virage system [12] generates a set of general primitives such as global colour, local colour, texture, and shapes. When comparing two images a similarity score is computed using the distance function defined for each primitive. Weights are needed to combine individual scores into an overall score, and the developer is left to select the weights appropriate to their application [13].

MetaSeek [14] also uses colour and texture for retrieval, but matching is carried out by other engines such as QBIC [11] and MARS [8]. MetaSeek uses a clustering approach for the locally extracted colour and texture features. The system was intelligently designed to select and interface with multiple Web-based image search engines by ranking their performance for different classes of user queries. Kulkami [15] used extracted texture feature values to formulate specific user-defined queries.

Region-based querying is favoured in Blobworld [16], where global histograms are shown to perform comparatively poorly on images containing distinctive objects. Similar conclusions were obtained in comparisons with the SIMPLIcity system [17]. VisualSEEk [18] determines similarity by measuring image regions by using both colour parameters and spatial relationships and obtains better performance than histogram methods that use colour information alone. NeTra [19] also relies upon image segmentation to carry out region-based searches that allow the user to select example regions and lay emphasis on image attributes to focus the search. Object segmentation for broad domains of general images is considered difficult, and a weaker form of segmentation that identifies salient point sets may be more fruitful [20].

Vinod [21] proposed an interactive method to identify regions in images, which can represent a given object based on colour features. Regions of interest are extracted based on sampling using a square window. This technique increased the efficiency of search by concentrating on the most promising regions in the image. The approach focused on just the upper bound of histogram intersection and assumed all matching was the same across all focused regions.

Relevance feedback is often proposed as a technique for overcoming many of the problems faced by fully automatic systems by allowing the user to interact with the computer to improve retrieval performance [22]. In Quicklook [23] and ImageRover [24] items identified by the user as relevant are used to adjust the weights assigned to the similarity function to obtain better search performance. PicHunter [25] has implemented a probabilistic relevance feedback mechanism that predicts the target image based upon the content of the images already selected by the user during the search. Related work is reported by Jose [26]. This reduces the burden on unskilled users to set quantitative pictorial search parameters or to select images that come closest to meeting their goals, but it does require the user to behave consistently as defined by the machine. Retrieval should not require the user to have explicit knowledge of the features employed by the system, and users should not have to reformulate their visual interests in ways that they do not understand.

Conventional approaches suffer from some disadvantages. Firstly, there is a real danger that the use of any form of predefined feature measurements will preclude solutions in the search space and be unable to handle unseen material. Secondly, the choice of features in anything other than a trivial problem is unable to anticipate a user's perception of image content. This information cannot be obtained by training on typical users, because every user possesses a subtly different subjective perception of the world and it is not possible to capture this in a single fixed set of features and associated representations.

An approach to visual search should be consistent with the known attributes of the human visual system and account should be taken of the perceptual importance of visual material as well as more objective attributes [27, 28].

This chapter describes the application of models of human visual attention to CBIR in ways that enable fast and effective search of large image databases. The model employs the use of visual attention maps to define regions of interest (ROIs) in an image with a view to improving the performance of image retrieval. The work will also involve the study of new database configurations that accommodate new metadata attributes and their associated functionality. The work may yield new metadata vocabularies and attributes that as yet are not encompassed by the MPEG-7 multimedia standards [29].

16.3   Current Research

The use of models of human visual attention in problems of visual search is attractive because it is reasonable to believe that this is the mechanism people actually use when looking for images [30]. The model [31] used in this chapter is favoured for its simplicity and the ease of implementation both in software and potentially in hardware. Initial work has concentrated upon demonstrating that knowledge of perceptually significant areas in an image improves search performance and that this can be automated through the application of an attention model.

Related work [32] using an eye tracker is exploring gaze behaviour and is using an attention model to anticipate users' search intentions during CBIR. This work will validate and at the same time refine the visual attention model for specific applications. For more detailed information, see Chapter 17.

16.3.1   Visual Attention Model

The visual attention mechanism used in this chapter is based upon ideas that have their counterpart in surround suppression in primate V1 [33]. Petkov and Westenberg [34] use a version of this model and confirm qualitative explanations of visual pop-out effects. This model assigns high values of visual attention when neighbouring pixel configurations do not match identical positional arrangements in other randomly selected neighbourhoods in the image. This means that textures and other features that are common in an image will tend to suppress attention values in their neighbourhood.

In this model, digital images are represented as a set of pixels, arranged in a rectangular grid in Fig. 16.1. The process of calculating the visual attention (VA) score for a pixel x begins by selecting a small number (m) of random pixels in the immediate neighbourhood (radius, ε) of *x*. Then another pixel *y* is selected randomly elsewhere in the image. The pixel configuration surrounding *x* is then compared with the same configuration around *y* and tested for a mismatch. If a mismatch is detected, the score for *x* is incremented and the process is repeated for another randomly selected *y*, for *t* iterations.

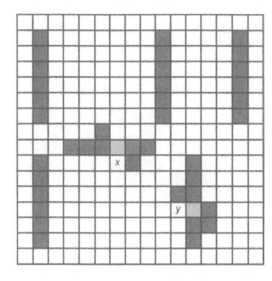

1. Create a random neighbourhood at *x*

2. Select a random second pixel *y* and compare

3. Increment score and repeat from 2 for a mismatch

4. Repeat from 1 for a match

Fig. 16.1   Neighbourhood at *x* mismatching at *y* ($m = 3$, $ε = 1$).

If the configurations match, then the score is not incremented and a new random configuration around *x* is generated. The process continues for a fixed number of iterations for each *x*. Regions obtain high scores if they possess features not present elsewhere in the image. Low scores tend to be assigned to regions that have features that are common in many other parts of the image. Such features may be dependent upon colour, shape, or both.

The visual attention estimator has been implemented as a set of tools that process images and produce corresponding arrays of attention values. The attention values are displayed in Fig. 16.2 as a map where VA scores are represented as false colours with the highest scores shown in the figure in a light tint and lower scores as darker shades. This map is used as a mask to indicate which areas of the image are to be analysed for comparison purposes, thereby suppressing background pixels from the computation.

Unweighted Mechanism
Let the colour histograms of images *A* and *B* be H_A and H_B each with *n* bins. The Manhattan global distance between the histograms is normalised by image area and is given by:

$$d(H_A, H_B) = \sum_{i=1}^{n} |H_A(i) - H_B(i)| ,$$

where $H_\alpha(i) = \dfrac{\text{number of pixels with hue } i}{\text{number of pixels in } \alpha} .$

| Red car | ROIs identified on red car |
| Red cars and trees | ROIs identified on red cars |

Fig. 16.2   Images and corresponding VA map.

A major disadvantage of the histogram and many other more sophisticated measures is their inability to distinguish foreground from background. This means that images with a dominant green background, for example, are very likely to be marked as similar regardless of the nature of the principal subject material, which might be a tractor in one image and a horse in another. The visual attention mask is introduced to combat this problem.

Let the visual attention mask for image α be given by:

$$M_\alpha(x, y) \begin{cases} = 1 \left(\text{if attention score at} (x, y) \geq T \right), \\ = 0 \text{ otherwise}. \end{cases}$$

The attention histogram distance between the images A and B is defined as:

$$d'(H_A, H_B) = \sum_{i=1}^{n} \left| H'_A(i) - H'_B(i) \right|,$$

$$H'_\alpha(i) = \frac{\text{number of pixels with hue } i \text{ and } M_\alpha(x, y) = 1}{\text{number of pixels in } \alpha \text{ and } M_\alpha(x, y) = 1}.$$

The new attention-based distance d' restricts the histogram calculation to pixels lying within areas that are assigned high values of visual attention by the model. This means that greater emphasis is given to subject material and hence retrieval performance should improve for those images possessing clear regions of interest, which are characterised by their colour histograms.

Weighted Mechanism

The attention-weighted colour histogram $\hat{H}_A(k)$ for image A and the attention-weighted distance $\hat{d}(H_A, H_B)$ between the images A and B are given by:

$$\hat{H}_A(k) = \frac{\sum\limits_{hue(i,j)=k} (i,j)S_A}{\sum\limits_{k}\sum\limits_{hue(i,j)=k} S_A(i,j)} \, , \qquad \hat{d}(H_A, H_B) = \sum_{k=1}^{n} \left| \hat{H}_A(k) - \hat{H}_B(k) \right| \, .$$

The new weighted similarity measure places more emphasis on hue histogram values that correspond to pixels possessing a high visual attention score. Pixels possessing low attention scores will not individually contribute as much to the histogram values, but large areas of similar background may be expected to be significant. This is in contrast to the unweighted approach where the background content has no effect on the similarity score.

16.3.2 Process Model

A similarity metric, when applied to the images in a collection, creates a network of associations between pairs of images each taking the value of the strength of the similarity. More generally, the associations can connect image regions to regions in other images so that images may still be strongly related if they contain similar objects in spite of possessing different backgrounds. It is this additional meta-data that provides the information to enable a convergent and intelligent search path.

Images in a collection are processed off-line to produce meta-data that is stored in the relational database. VA analysis is applied to a query image and the similarity of ROIs to others in the database is determined. A rank-ordered list of candidate retrieved images is returned to the user, as illustrated in Fig. 16.3. The precomputed network of similarity associations enables images to be clustered according to their mutual separations. This means that query images are matched first with 'vantage' images [35] in each cluster before selecting images from within the closest cluster groups.

16.3.3 Data Model

The data model encompasses regions of interest, images, clusters of images, and potentially a hierarchy of clusters of clusters. Similarity associations relate images and ROIs within clusters and images and ROIs in different clusters.

In addition, most images will be present in more than one cluster, for example, one on the basis of background content and another on the basis of foreground subject material.

Figure 16.4 illustrates an entity-relationship diagram (ERD) for the application. Two intermediate entities ('image to cluster mapping' and 'image to ROI mapping') are inserted to break the potential many-to-many relationship between:

- 'cluster' and 'image';

- 'image' and 'region of interest'.

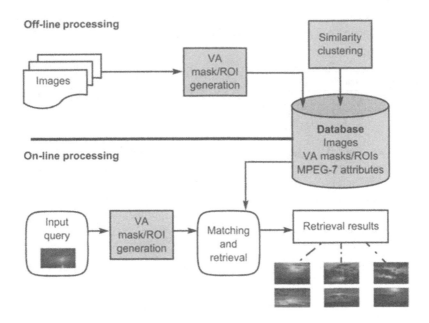

Fig. 16.3   Image entry and retrieval system.

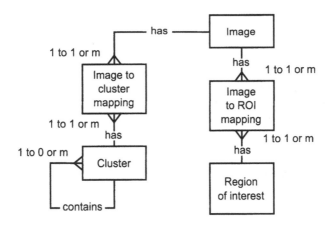

Fig. 16.4   Application entity relationship diagram.

16.4   Results

The method is illustrated by application to a small set of 12 images consisting of 6 pairs that are clearly similar. Figure 16.5 shows the 12 images together with their VA maps.

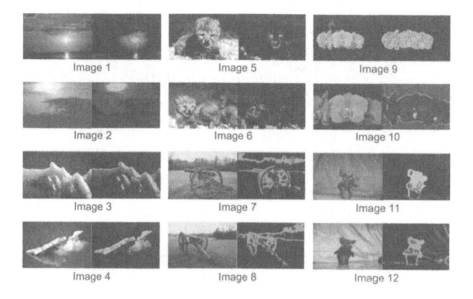

Fig. 16.5   Images and visual attention maps.

The VA maps were obtained using the parameter values $t = 50$, $m = 1$, and $\varepsilon = 4$. A mismatch is detected if any of the RGB values for the pixels being compared differ by more than 50. Each map yields a mask, which is used to construct the arrays $M_\alpha(x, y)$ [36].

The histograms are based upon the hue values at each pixel, which range from 1 to 360. Examples of global and attention-based histograms for image 9 are shown in Fig. 16.6. The difference is due mainly to the different colour profiles of the background and foreground.

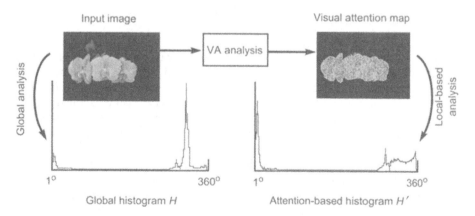

Fig. 16.6   Colour histogram models.

The distances $100d$ and $100d'$ between all 12 of the images using the global and attention-based similarity measures were computed. In order to compare the global (P_i) and attention-based (P_i') histogram performances on image i, the distances between the pairs of subjectively similar images (i, j) were compared to those between all the others, where:

$$P_i = \left\{ \frac{\left| \sum_{A \neq i,j} (d(H_A, H_i) - d(H_i, H_j)) \right|}{d(H_i, H_j)} \right\},$$

and, similarly:

$$P_i' = \left\{ \frac{\left| \sum_{A \neq i,j} (d'(H_A, H_i) - d'(H_i, H_j)) \right|}{d'(H_i, H_j)} \right\}.$$

The comparative performance is displayed in Fig. 16.7, where $100(P_i - P_i')/10$ is plotted for each image. Positive values indicate improvements in performance over the global similarity measure.

This was repeated for the weighted mechanism with $\hat{d}$ and for $\hat{P}_i$, where:

$$\hat{P}_i = \left\{ \frac{\left| \sum_{A \neq i,j} (\hat{d}(H_A, H_i) - \hat{d}(H_i, H_j)) \right|}{\hat{d}(H_i, H_j)} \right\}.$$

The comparative performances of the global and unweighted attention measures applied to the 12 images in Fig. 16.5 are displayed in Fig. 16.7, where the performance estimates $10P_i$ and $10P_i'$ are plotted for each image. In a similar fashion the comparative performance of the global and weighted measures applied to the same images is displayed in Fig. 16.8, where $10P_i$ and $10\hat{P}_i$ are plotted for each image. Figure 16.7 shows that the unweighted attention measure improves performance over a basic global histogram measure in all except images 7 and 8. Here the green background plays a major part in the good discrimination by the global measure, but is largely ignored through the use of the attention mask.

Figure 16.8 shows the performance of the weighted attention measure, which again yields general improvement when compared with the basic histogram distance measure, but again does not resolve images 7 and 8. Although the weighted scheme does give extra emphasis to the background regions [37], this is outweighed by much greater values assigned to salient regions and leads to a worse performance on these images.

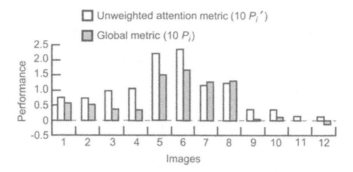

Fig. 16.7   Comparative performances of the global and unweighted attention metrics.

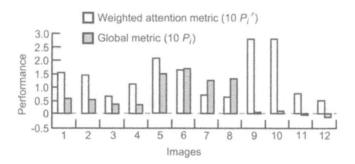

Fig. 16.8   Comparative performances of the global and weighted attention metrics.

16.5   Discussion

An improvement in separation is seen in 5 of the pairs of images, but images 7 and 8 are not separated from images 3 and 4 as well as by the global histograms. This is because the visual attention masks cover a high proportion of white and grey areas in all four images, at the same time as the background material being significantly different between the two pairs.

The green background is treated as important by the global histogram (Fig. 16.9) but is suppressed by the attention mechanism (Fig. 16.10). The background happens to be a distinguishing feature in this data set. Images 9 and 10 yield a significant improvement because the central subject material is very similar. It should be observed that the subjects in images 11 and 12 are identical but the background is substantially different.

In this case the attention model has been able to focus on the important image components and detect a high value of similarity. By the same token image 10 is a magnified and cropped version of image 9 and illustrates how an effective similarity measure might detect infringements of copyright in which parts of images have been replicated and distorted.

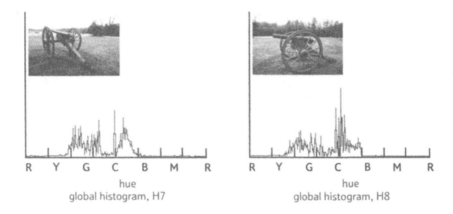

Fig. 16.9   Global histogram of images 7 and 8.

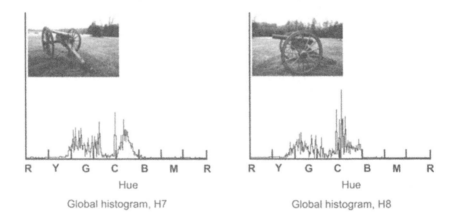

Fig. 16.10   Attention-based histogram of images 7 and 8.

Processing time on a 1.8-GHz machine for a 214 × 144 image is 543 ms for code written in C++. However, the score calculation in the VA algorithm is independent for each pixel and is therefore eminently suitable for parallel implementation.

Many images can be distinguished by analysing and comparing salient areas because the background is of no relevance or interest. However, it is clear that the colour histogram measure lays great emphasis on large areas of similar background material, which by chance can achieve discrimination. In most circumstances retrieval on the basis of background regions will lead to poor recall and precision. Furthermore, the histogram approach takes no account of structure and location and therefore is unable to abstract any discrimination arising from the relationship between foreground and background. A more powerful and embracing distance measure would yield more consistent results over a wider range of images. The exploratory results reported in this chapter are on the basis of a very small body of data and, although indicative, require extending to a larger database to test their statistical significance.

16.6   Summary and Future Work

There is good reason to believe that the saliency of images should play a major part in automated image retrieval, and this chapter has illustrated a way in which this might be achieved. The work has indicated that laying emphasis upon areas of images that attract high visual attention can improve retrieval performance. However, the histogram distance measure is very restrictive and limits the potential benefit that can be obtained by recognising saliency. The weighted visual attention mask did not yield a substantial improvement over a simpler mask, but a more powerful measure that encompasses features such as shape, orientation, and scale offers scope for better performance. Future experiments will make use of more meaningful measures of similarity that take account of image structure and other features. More work is also necessary on larger sets of images to obtain statistical significance in the results.

Future work on automating the selection of appropriate values for the VA parameters t, m, and ε are continuing to develop the VA pipeline into a 'black box' suitable for commercial deployment. Furthermore, expanding the current implementation from being a single-PC, multi-threaded process, to a multi-processor-based server cluster should see high returns as the algorithm is highly parallel in nature. This whole process will then need to be integrated with a commercially available content management system such as Interactive Content Factory (ICF) from Trans World International or Asset Manager from Asset House, for example. Equally content management workflows will need to be adapted to accommodate content ingestion from users and system analysis before distribution back to the user. Once achieved, the complete system will then be able to effectively serve a variety of ubiquitous devices in what we believe to be a cost-efficient manner.

A collaboration with Berkeley will provide a rich source of annotated images collected through mobile videophones on campus. This project [38] is revealing the communal benefits of mobile media creation, sharing, and reuse. It takes advantage of previously annotated media to make educated guesses about the content of newly captured media. Visual attention technology promises to add value to the associations that can be automatically deduced from image content.

Content-based image retrieval technology that can retrieve and even appear to anticipate users' needs will find huge application. It can be immediately applied to video retrieval through the medium of key frames. There is a growing demand for new video mobile services but which cannot become pervasive until accessibility bottle-necks are removed. Security and crime prevention applications are increasingly hoping to rely on new technology to deliver visual content that is relevant to the moment, none of which is currently possible without heavy manual involvement. Natural and intuitive access to multimedia content is a vision for anyone and everyone in the communications industry.

References

1.   Weiser M. The Computer for the 21st Century. Scientific American, September 1991.

2. Brown P J and Jones G J F. Context-Aware Retrieval for Pervasive Computing Environments. IEEE International Conference Proceedings on Pervasive Computing. Zurich, Switzerland, August 2002.

3. Lee D L and Lee W-C. Data Management in Location-dependent Information Services. Proc IEEE International Conference on Pervasive Computing. Zurich, Switzerland, August 2002.

4. Vendrig J. Filter Image Browsing: A Study of Image Retrieval in Large Pictorial Databases. Master's Thesis, Dept Computer Science, University of Amsterdam, The Netherlands, February 1997.

5. Stricker M and Swain M. The Capacity of Colour Histogram Indexing. IEEE CVPR. Seattle, 1994:704–708.

6. Del Bimbo A and Pala P. Visual Querying by Color Perceptive Regions. Pattern Recognition, 1998:31:1241–1253.

7. Jain A K and Vailaya A. Image Retrieval Using Color and Shape, Pattern Recognition, 1996:29:8:1233–1244.

8. Ortega M et al. Supporting Similarity Queries in MARS. Proceedings of Fifth ACM International Multimedia Conference. Seattle, USA, 1997.

9. Mehrotra S and Chakrabarti K. Similarity Shape Retrieval in MARS. IEEE International Conference on Multimedia and Expo. New York, 2000.

10. Lu G and Phillips J. Using Perceptually Weighted Histograms for Colour-based Image Retrieval. Proc of 4th Int Conf on Signal Processing, ICSP98, 1998:2.

11. Niblack W and Flickner M. Query by Image and Video Content: The QBIC System. IEEE Computer, September 1995:23–32.

12. Bach J et al. The Virage Image Search Engine: An Open Framework for Image Management. Proceedings of the SPIE Storage and Retrieval for Image and Video Databases IV. San Jose, CA, February 1996:76–87.

13. Veltkamp R C and Tanase M. Content-based Retrieval Systems: A Survey. March 2001 — http://www.aa-lab.cs.uu.nl/cbirsurvey/cbir-survey/

14. Beige M, Benitez A B, and Chang S F. MetaSeek: Content-based Meta-Search Engine for Images. Proceedings of the SPIE Conference on Storage and Retrieval for Image and Video Databases VI. San Jose, CA, January 1998 — http://www.informatik.un-trier.de/~ley/db/conf/spieSR/spieSR98.html

15. Kulkami S. Interpretation of Fuzzy Logic for Texture Queries in CBIR. In: Vision, Video and Graphics. Prentice Hall and Willis, 2003.

16. Carson C et al. Blobworld: Segmentation Using Expectation-Maximisation and Its Application to Querying. IEEE Trans PAMI, August 2002:24:8:1026–1038.

17. Wang J, Li J Z, and Wiederhold G. SIMPLIcity: Semantics-Sensitive Integrated Matching for Picture Libraries. IEEE Trans PAMI, September 2001:23:9:947–963.

18. Smith J R and Chang S-F. VisualSEEk: A Fully Automated Content-based Query System. Proc ACM Intl Conf Multimedia. Boston, MA, November 1996:87–98.

19. Ma W-Y and Manjunath B S. NeTra: A Toolbox for Navigating Large Databases. Multimedia Systems, 1999:7:184–198.

20. Smeulders A W M et al. Content-based Retrieval at the End of the Early Years. IEEE Trans PAMI, December 2000:22:12:1349–1379.

21. Vinod V and Murase H. Focused Color Intersection with Efficient Searching for Object Extraction. International Conference on Multimedia Computing and Systems, Pattern Recognition, 1997:30:10:1787–1797.

22. Rui Y, Huang T S, Ortega M, and Mehrotra S. Relevance Feedback: A Power Tool for Interactive Content-based Image Retrieval. IEEE Trans on Circuits and Video Technology, 1998:1–13.

23. Ciocca G and Schettini R. A Multimedia Search Engine with Relevance Feedback. Proc SPIE. San Jose, CA, January 2002:4672.

24. Taycher L, Cascia M La and Sclaroff S. Image Digestion and Relevance Feedback in the ImageRover WWW Search Engine. Proc 2nd Intl Conf on Visual Information Systems. San Diego, CA, December 1997:85–94.

25. Cox I J et al. The Bayesian Image Retrieval System, PicHunter: Theory, Implementation, and Psychophysical Experiments. IEEE Trans Image Processing, January 2000:9:1.

26. Innes M and Jose J M. A Personalised Information Retrieval Tool. 26th Int ACM SIGIP Conf on Research and Development in Information Retrieval. Toronto, 2003.

27. Stentiford F W M. An Attention-based Similarity Measure with Application to Content-based Information Retrieval. SPIE, Storage and Retrieval for Media Databases. Santa Clara, CA, January 2003.

28. Pauwels E J and Frederix G. Finding Salient Regions in Images: Non-Parametric Clustering for Image Segmentation and Grouping. Computer Vision and Image Understanding, 1998:75:73–85.

29. Salembier P. Overview of the MPEG-7 Standard and of Future Challenges for Visual Information Analysis. EURASIP Journal on Applied Signal Processing, 2002.

30. Bamidele A and Stentiford F W M. Image Retrieval: A Visual Attention-based Approach. Postgraduate Research Conference in Electronics, Photonics, Communications and Networks, and Computing Science. Hertfordshire, April 2004.

31. Stentiford F W M. An Estimator for Visual Attention Through Competitive Novelty with Application to Compression. Picture Coding Symposium. Seoul, April 2001.

32. Oyekoya O K and Stentiford F W M. Exploring Human Eye Behaviour Using a Model of Visual Attention. International Conference on Pattern Recognition. Cambridge, August 2004.

33. Nothdurft H-C, Gallant J L, and Van Essen D C. Response Modulation by Texture Surround in Primate Area VI: Correlates of 'Popout' under Anesthesia. Visual Neuroscience, 1999:16:15–34.

34. Petkov N and Westenberg M A. Suppression of Contour Perception by Band-Limited Noise and Its Relation to Nonclassical Receptive Field Inhibition. Biol Cybern, 2003: 88:236–246.

35. Vleugels J and Veltkamp R C. Efficient Image Retrieval Through Vantage Objects. Pattern Recognition, 2002:35:69–80.

36. Bamidele A and Stentiford F W M. A New Enhancement to Histogram-based Approaches in Content-based Image Retrieval Systems. London Communications Symposium, Multimedia Systems and Applications. University College London, September 2004.

37. Bamidele A. An Attention-based Model to Colour Histogram Indexing. European Workshop on the Integration of Knowledge, Semantics and Digital Media Technology. London, UK, November 2004.

38. Sarvas R, Herrarte E, Wilhelm A, and Davis M. Metadata Creation System for Mobile Images. 2nd International Conference on Mobile Systems, Applications and Services (MobiSys 2004). Boston, 2004.

17

Eye Tracking as a New Interface for Image Retrieval

O K Oyekoya and F W M Stentiford

17.1   Introduction

The best interfaces are the most natural ones. They are unobtrusive and provide relevant information quickly and in ways that do not interfere with the task itself.

The disappearance of technologies into the fabric of everyday life is as a result of human psychology rather than technology [1]. Many challenges in computing have to be overcome before the dream of integrating information technology with human users can be achieved.

This is still a distant vision, mainly because of hardware constraints [2], but also because there are serious human–computer interaction (HCI) issues to consider. Social and cognitive factors are just as important in making computers inconspicuous [3].

Eye-tracking and other natural methods such as voice and body gestures will play an important part in solving the cognitive issues of pervasive computing. Eye tracking offers a new way of communicating with human thought processes.

This chapter addresses the problem of retrieving images using a natural interface for search. Understanding the fixations and saccades in human eye movement data and its validation against a visual attention model suggests a new image retrieval interface that uses new eye-tracking technology. Such a model will not only have to identify the items of interest within the image but also characterise it according to its relative importance.

Section 17.2 describes related research and the key issues that are addressed. This is followed in Section 17.3 by a description of the current research with results from preliminary experiments. Section 17.4 discusses some outstanding issues including the cognitive factors that have to be overcome. The final section provides some conclusions and an indication of the future work.

17.2   State of the Art

Research activity in eye tracking has increased in the last few years due to improvements in performance and reductions in the costs of eye-tracking devices. The research is considered under three headings:

- eye-tracking technology;

- human behaviour;
- current applications.

17.2.1   Eye-Tracking Technology

A number of eye-gaze detection methods have been developed over the years. Invasive methods that required tampering directly with the eyes were mostly used before the 1970s. The search coil method [4] offers high accuracy and large dynamic range but requires an insertion into the eye! Non-invasive methods such as the DPI (Dual Purkinje Image) eye tracker [5] require the head to be restricted and are relatively expensive.

More recently systems have appeared that use video images and/or infra-red cameras. The FreeGaze system [6] attempts to limit errors arising from calibration and gaze detection by using only two points for individual personal calibration. The position of observed pupil image is used directly to compute the gaze direction, but this may not be in the right place due to refraction in the surface of the cornea. The eyeball model corrects the pupil position for obtaining a more accurate gaze direction. ASL [7], Smarteye [8], IBM's Almaden [9], Arrington's Viewpoint [10], SR's Eyelink [11], and CRS [12] eye trackers are examples of recent commercial eye trackers. A typical commercial eye tracker tracks the pupil and the first Purkinje image (corneal reflex) and the difference gives a measure of eye rotation. Section 17.1.3 describes LC Technology's Eyegaze system [13] used in this research in more detail.

Several methods of improving the accuracy of estimating gaze direction and inferring intent from eye movement have been proposed. The Eye-R system [14] is designed to be battery operated and is mounted on any pair of glasses. It measures eye motion using infra-red technology by monitoring light fluctuations from infra-red light and utilises this as an implicit input channel to a sensor system and computer. Mulligan and Beutter [15] use a low-cost approach to track eye movement using compressed video images of the fundus on the back surface of the eyeball. A technical challenge for these types of trackers is the real-time digitisation and storage of the video stream from the cameras. Bhaskar et al [16] propose a method that uses eye-blink detection to locate an eye, which is then tracked using an eye tracker. Blinking is necessary for the tracker to work well, and the user has to be aware of this.

17.2.2   Human Behaviour

Experiments have been conducted to explore human gaze behaviour for different purposes. Privitera et al [17] use 10 image processing algorithms to compare human identified regions of interest with regions of interest determined by an eye tracker and defined by a fixation algorithm. The comparative approach used a similarity measurement to compare two aROIs (algorithmically detected regions of interest), two hROIs (human identified regions of interest), and an aROI plus hROI. The prediction accuracy was compared in order to identify the best matching algorithms. Different algorithms fared better under differing conditions.

They concluded that aROIs cannot always be expected to be similar to hROIs in the same image because two hROIs produce different results in separate runs. This means that algorithms are unable in general to predict the sequential ordering of fixation points.

Jaimes et al [18] compare eye movement across categories and link category-specific eye-tracking results to automatic image classification techniques. They hypothesise that the eye movements of human observers differ for images of different semantic categories and that this information can be effectively used in automatic content-based classifiers. The eye-tracking results suggest that similar viewing patterns occur when different subjects view different images in the same semantic category. They suggested that it is possible to apply the Privitera's fixation clustering approach [17] to cluster gaze points.

Pomplun and Ritter [19] present a three-level model, which is able to explain about 98% of empirical data collected in six different experiments of comparative visual search. Pairs of almost identical items are compared requiring subjects to switch between images several times before detecting a possible mismatch. The model consists of the global scan path strategy (upper level), shifts of attention between two visual hemifields (intermediate level), and eye movement patterns (lower level).

Simulated gaze trajectories obtained from this model are compared with experimental data. Results suggest that the model data of most variables presents a remarkably good correspondence to the empirical data.

Identification and analysis of fixations and saccades in eye-tracking protocol are important in understanding visual behaviour. Salvucci [20] classifies algorithms with respect to five spatial and temporal characteristics. The spatial criteria divide algorithms in terms of their use of velocity, dispersion of fixation points, and areas of interest information. The temporal criteria divide algorithms in terms of their use of duration information and their local adaptivity. Five fixation identification algorithms are described and compared in terms of their accuracy, speed, robustness, ease of implementation, and parameters. The results show that hidden Markov models based on the dispersion threshold fare better in terms of their accuracy and robustness.

The Minimum Spanning Tree uses a minimised connected set of points and provides robust identification of fixation points, but runs slower due to the two-step approach of construction and search of the minimum spanning trees. The velocity threshold has the simplest algorithm and is thus fast but not robust. Areas of interest are found to perform poorly on all fronts. These findings are implemented in the EyeTracer system [21], an interactive environment for manipulating, viewing, and analysing eye movement protocols.

Stone and Beutter (from NASA) [22] focus on the development and testing of human eye movement control with particular emphasis on search saccades and the response to motion (smooth pursuit). They conclude that current models of pursuit should be modified to include visual input that estimates object motion and not merely retinal image motion as in current models.

Duchowski [23] presents a 3D eye movement analysis algorithm for binocular eye tracking within virtual reality. Its signal analysis techniques can be categorised into three — position-variance, velocity-based, and ROI-based, again using two of Salvucci's criteria. This is easily adapted to a 2D environment by holding head position and visual angle constant.

17.2.3   Current Applications

Eye-tracking equipment is used as an interface device in several diverse applications. Schnell and Wu [24] apply eye tracking as an alternative method for the activation of controls and functions in aircraft.

Dasher [25] is a method for text entry that relies purely on gaze direction. The user composes text by looking at characters as they stream across the screen from right to left. Dasher presents likely characters in sizes according to the probability of their occurrence in that position. The user is often able to select rapidly whole words or phases as their size increases on the screen.

Nikolov et al propose [26] a system for construction of gaze-contingent multi-modality displays of multi-layered geographical maps. Gaze-contingent multi-resolutional displays (GCMRDs) centre high-resolution information on the user's gaze position, matching the user's interest. In this system, different map information is channelled to the central and the peripheral vision giving real performance advantage.

Nokia [27] conducted a usability evaluation on two mobile Internet sites and discovered the importance of search on mobile telephones contrary to the initial hypothesis that users would not like to use search because of the effort of keying inputs. The research also showed that customers prefer any interface that produces a successful search. This evaluation confirms that users do have a need for information retrieval for mobile usage.

Xin Fan et al [28] propose an image-viewing technique based on an adaptive attention-shifting model, which looks at the issue of browsing large images on limited and heterogeneous screen zones of mobile telephones. Xin Fan's paper focuses on facilitating image viewing on devices with limited display sizes.

The Collage Machine [29] is an agent of Web recombination. It deconstructs Web sites and re-presents them in collage form. It can be taught to bring media of interest to the user on the basis of the user's interactions. The evolving model provides an extremely flexible way of presenting relevant visual information to the user.

Cognitive interest is hard to measure and so any steps taken to suggest user selection will improve performance and allow users to change their mind. Farid [30] describes the implementation and initial experimentation of systems based on a user's eye gaze behaviour. It was concluded that the systems performed well because of minimal latency and obtrusiveness. A zooming technique is adopted with a magnified region of interest and multiple video streams.

Eye tracking is being used successfully for various applications and experimental purposes, but outstanding issues include accuracy and interpretation. The research described in this chapter uses an attention model to assist in the interpretation of users' eye gaze behaviour when conducting a visual search, and it is hoped that this will lead to a more intimate and rapid interface for content-based image retrieval (CBIR).

17.3   Current Research Objectives

The aim of this research is to provide a rapid and natural interface for searching visual digital data in a CBIR system (Fig. 17.1). A pre-computed network of similarities between image regions in an image collection can be traversed very rapidly using eye tracking providing the users' gaze behaviours yield suitable information about their intentions. It is reasonable to believe that users will look at the objects in which they are interested during a search [31], and this provides the machine with the necessary information to retrieve plausible candidate images for the user. Such images will contain regions that possess similarity links with the gazed regions and can be presented to the user in a variety of ways. Dasher's text entry [25] and Kerne's Collage Machine [29] both provide promising CBIR interfaces for future investigation.

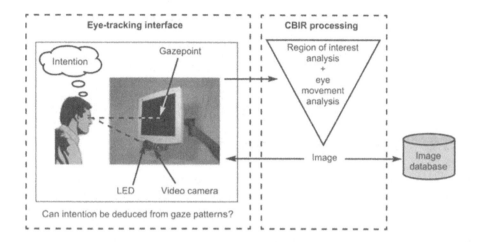

Fig. 17.1   Proposed system architecture.

Initial experiments have investigated the gaze behaviour of participants and compared it with data obtained through a model of visual attention (VA) [32]. This enabled possible differences in behaviour to be detected arising from varying image content.

Regions of interest are identified both by human interaction and prior analysis and used to explore aspects of vision that would not otherwise be apparent. Images with and without obvious subjects were used in this work to accentuate any behaviour differences that might be apparent.

17.3.1   System Overview

The system design is broken down into two major components, as shown in Fig. 17.2:

- algorithmic analysis of image to obtain visual attention scores;
- human identification of region of interest.

It should be noted that the analysis process is grouped with the eye-tracking process because the main goal is to carry out real-time analysis to identify objects of interest for use in real-world applications.

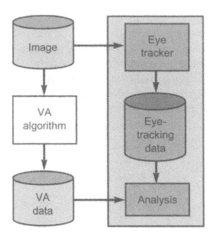

Fig. 17.2   Experimental process.

17.3.2   Eye-Tracking Equipment

The Eyegaze system [13] is an eye tracker designed to measure where a person is looking on a computer screen. The Eyegaze system tracks the subject's gazepoint on the screen automatically and in real time. It uses the pupil-centre/corneal-reflection (PCCR) method to determine the eye's gaze direction. A video camera located below the computer screen remotely and unobtrusively observes the subject's eye (as shown in Fig. 17.1). No attachments to the head are required. A small, low-power, infra-red light emitting diode (LED) located at the centre of the camera lens illuminates the eye. The LED generates the corneal reflection and causes the bright pupil effect, which enhances the camera's image of the pupil (Fig. 17.3).

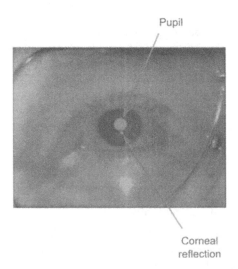

Fig. 17.3   Camera image of eye, illustrating bright image pupil and corneal reflection.

Specialised image-processing software in the Eyegaze computer identifies and locates the centres of both the pupil and corneal reflection. Trigonometric calculations project the person's gaze point based on the positions of the pupil centre and the corneal reflection within the video image. The Eyegaze system generates raw gaze-point location data at the camera field rate of 60 Hz.

The procedure to calibrate the Eyegaze system is robust yet fast and easy to perform. The calibration procedure takes approximately 15 sec and is fully automatic; no assistance from another person is required. The procedure does not accept full calibration until the overall gaze prediction accuracy and consistency exceed desired thresholds. To achieve high gaze-point tracking accuracy, the image-processing algorithms in the Eyegaze system explicitly accommodate several common sources of gaze-point tracking error such as nonlinear gaze-point tracking equations, head-range variation, pupil-diameter variation, and glint that straddles the pupil edge. A chair with a head rest provides support for chin and forehead in order to minimise the effects of head movements, although the eye tracker does accommodate head movement of up to 1.5 inches (3.8 cm).

17.3.3   Overview of the Visual Attention Model

The model used in this work [32] employs an algorithm that assigns high VA scores to pixels where neighbouring pixel configurations do not match identical positional arrangements in other randomly selected neighbourhoods in the image. This means, for example, that high scores will be associated with anomalous objects, or edges and boundaries, if those features do not predominate in the image. A flowchart describing this process is given in Fig. 17.4.

For display purposes the VA scores for each pixel are displayed as a map using a continuous spectrum of false colours with the scores being marked with a distinctive colour or grey level (as in Figs. 17.6 and 17.7 in Section 17.3.5).

17.3.4   Experiment Design

In this experiment the VA algorithm is applied to each image to identify regions of interest and obtain VA scores for each pixel. It should be noted that the parameter settings are the same for all the images used. The images are viewed by a human participant and eye-tracking data is gathered using the Eyegaze eye tracker. The VA and eye-tracking data is then combined and analysed by identifying the co-ordinates of the gaze points on the image and obtaining the VA scores from the corresponding pixel position. VA scores are then plotted against time for each image and subject as illustrated later in Figs. 17.6 and 17.7.

All participants had normal or corrected-to-normal vision and had no knowledge of the purpose of the study. Participants included a mix of graduates and administrative staff. Over the course of the experiment, four participants were presented 20 images for 5 sec each separated by displays of a blank screen followed by a central black dot on a white background (Fig. 17.5). These images were displayed on a 15-in LCD flat-panel monitor at a resolution of 1024 × 768 pixels. All participants were encouraged to minimise head movement and were asked to focus on the dot before each image was loaded.

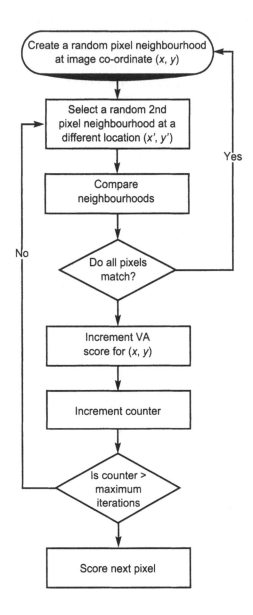

Fig. 17.4   Visual attention model.

Fig. 17.5   Display sequence.

17.3.5 Results

Figures 17.6 and 17.7 show two of the images used in the experiments together with corresponding VA maps and graphs for four subjects. The locations of saccades and fixations performed by the subjects on each of the images are recorded by the eye-tracking system. The VA score that corresponds to the pixel at each fixation point is associated with the time of the fixation and plotted as graphs for study in units of 20 ms. It is observed that there is considerable variation in behaviour over the four subjects, but all viewed the regions with the highest VA scores early in the display period.

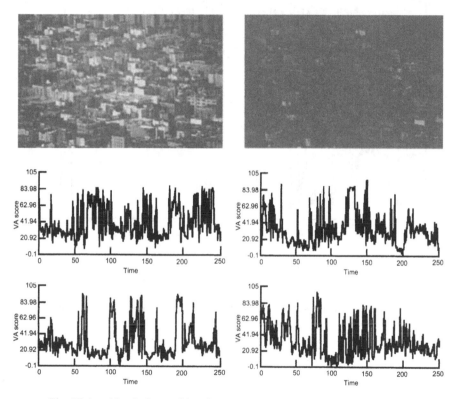

Fig. 17.6   No obvious subject image — VA map and plots for 4 subjects.

The variance measure has been selected to characterise the variability of the VA scores from the mean of the score distribution. The variance of the VA scores (x) over time is given by:

$$v = \frac{1}{n-1} \sum_{j=0}^{n-1} (x_j - \bar{x})^2 \; ,$$

where $x_j = j$th VA score in the data series $x_0, ..., x_{n-1}$ and $\bar{x}$ = mean of the VA scores $x_0, ..., x_{n-1}$.

The variance v measures the average spread or variability of the VA scores for the scan path and the image. The variances of the VA scores over six of the images for

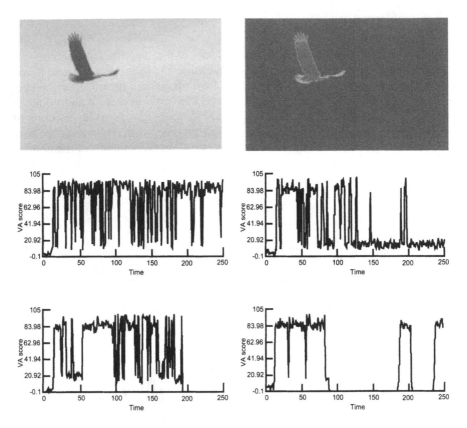

Fig 17.7   Obvious subject image –– VA map and plots for 4 subjects.

four subjects and the image variance of the VA scores for all pixels are presented in Table 17.1 and Fig. 17.8.

Table 17.1   Variance of VA scores.

Images		Image variance	Subjects			
			1	2	3	4
Unclear ROI	1	298	325	193	333	532
	2	500	479	496	328	629
	3	175	389	175	365	197
Obvious ROI	4	443	741	687	1094	857
	5	246	1432	1453	1202	1466
	6	378	1246	1226	862	1497

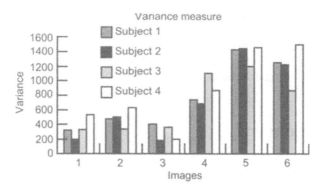

Fig. 17.8   Variance histogram.

17.4   Discussion

The goal of the initial experiment was to explore the relationship between gaze behaviour and the visual attention model in determining eye movement patterns during different stages of viewing. Results indicate that regions with high VA scores do attract eye gaze for those images studied. However, it was apparent that individual behaviours varied considerably and it was difficult to identify a pattern over such a small amount of data. Nevertheless, the results did show that there was a higher variance in VA score over time on images with obvious regions of interest due to gaze patterns shifting between areas of high visual attention and the background. This would seem reasonable in view of a natural inclination to make rapid visual comparisons between anomalous material and a relatively predictable background.

Interestly, the results also show that the variance of VA scores for the gaze path is higher than the variance of the VA scores for every pixel in the image. The subject may be gathering information by scanning between high VA regions and background material. This is substantiated by the high value of the variance of the VA scores for obvious-ROI images. The variance for the whole image, which is similar to the variance for unclear-ROI images, is significantly lower than the variance of the scores generated by the scan path of participants on obvious-ROI images. Hence, it is likely that the eye path may yield useful information for image retrieval, as clear regions of interest in images attract fixation.

Accurate interpretation of interest is necessary for a successful interface. Fixations above a certain threshold and pursuit movement above a set velocity are just some of the factors that can be interpreted as an indication of interest. The findings by Jaimes et al [18] suggest that similar viewing patterns occur when different subjects view different images in the same semantic category. Hence, discrimination within an image might yield useful interpretation of interest.

The accuracy of gaze location is an important factor in the results and some of the noise may be due to head and body movement as well as the basic accuracy of the equipment.

There is clear evidence [33] that users do not need to look directly at objects during covert attention.

This means that gaze direction does not necessarily indicate a current region of interest, only a general direction and could confound some conclusions.

Overall, the technical challenges still facing eye-tracking approaches include accuracy, simultaneous tracking and capturing of a visual scene, and most importantly interpreting gaze behaviour.

17.5   Summary

Preliminary experiments have confirmed that clear regions of interest in images lead to the attraction of eye gaze, which are not inconsistent with the visual attention model.

This gives credence to the belief that eye trackers can provide a new and exciting interface technology that promises to inspire a new range of computational tools that react to our thoughts and feelings rather than our hands.

Experiments are planned to investigate gaze behaviour in more constrained conditions in which users are focused on specific visual search tasks. This will reduce (but not eliminate) the confounding effects of users' prior interests and associated behaviours. The attention graphs should reveal details of gaze behaviour that can be utilised during CBIR operations.

References

1. Weiser M. The Computer for the 21st Century. Scientific American, 2003.

2. Satyanarayanan M. Pervasive Computing: Vision and Challenges. IEEE Personal Communications, 2001:10–17.

3. Lueg C. On the Gap Between Vision and Feasibility. Proceedings of the International Conference on Pervasive Computing, Springer Lecture Notes in Computer Science (LNCS 1414), 2002:45–57.

4. Robinson D A. A Method of Measuring Eye Movement Using a Scleral Search Coil in a Magnetic Field. IEEE Transactions on Biomedical Electronics, BME-10, 1963:137–145.

5. Crane H D and Steele C S. Accurate Three-Dimensional Eye Tracker. Applied Optics, 1978:17:691–705.

6. Ohno T, Mukawa N and Yoshikawa A. FreeGaze: A Gaze Tracking System for Everyday Gaze Interaction. Proceedings of the Eye Tracking Research and Applications Symposium, 2002:125–132.

7. ASL — http://www.a-s-l.com/

8. Smarteye — http://www.smarteye.se/

9. Almaden — http://www.almaden.ibm.com/cs/blueeyes/

10. Viewpoint — http://www.arringtonresearch.com/

11. SR Research — http://www.eyelinkinfo.com/

12. CRS — http://www.crsltd.com/

13. LC Technology — http://www.eyegaze.com/

14. Selker T, Lockerd A, and Martinez J. Eye-R: A Glasses-Mounted Eye Motion Detection Interface. CHI '01, Extended Abstracts on Human Factors in Computer Systems, Seattle, WA, 2001.

15. Mulligan J B and Beutter B R. Eye Movement Tracking Using Compressed Video Images. Vision Sciences and Its Applications: Optical Society Technical Digest Series, 1995:1:163–166.

16. Bhaskar T N et al. Blink Detection and Eye Tracking for Eye Localization. IEEE Tencon, India, 2003.

17. Privitera C M and Stark L W. Algorithms for Defining Visual Regions of Interest: Comparison with Eye Fixations. IEEE Transactions on Pattern Analysis and Machine Intelligence, 2000:22:9:970–982.

18. Jaimes A et al. Using Human Observers' Eye Movements in Automatic Image Classifiers. Proceedings of SPIE Human Vision and Electronic Imaging VI, San Jose, CA, 2001.

19. Pomplun M and Ritter H. A Three-Level Model of Comparative Visual Search. In: Hahn M and Stoness S C (editors). Proceedings of the Twenty-First Annual Conference. Cognitive Science Society, 1999:543–548.

20. Salvucci D D and Goldberg J H. Identifying Fixations and Saccades in Eye-Tracking Protocols. Proceedings of the Eye Tracking Research and Applications Symposium, New York, ACM Press, 2000:71–78.

21. Salvucci D D. An Interactive Model-based Environment for Eye-Movement Protocol Analysis and Visualization. Proceedings of the Symposium on Eye Tracking Research and Applications, Palm Beach Gardens, FL, 2000:57–63.

22. Stone L and Beutter B et al. Models of Tracking and Search Eye-Movement Behaviour. NASA, 2000.

23. Duchowski A T et al. 3D Eye Movement Analysis. Behavior Research Methods, Instruments and Computers (BRMIC), 2002:34:4:573–591.

24. Schnell T and Wu T. Applying Eye Tracking as Alternative Approach for Activation of Controls and Functions in Aircraft. Proceedings of the 5th International Conference on Human Interaction with Complex Systems (HICS), Urbana, Illinois, USA, 2000:113.

25. Ward D J and MacKay D J C. Fast Hands-Free Writing by Gaze Direction. Nature, 2002:418:838.

26. Nikolov S G et al. Gaze-Contingent Multi-Modality Displays of Multi-Layered Geographical Maps. Proc of the 5th Ihtl Conf on Numerical Methods and Applications (NM&A02), Symposium on Numerical Methods for Sensor Data Processing, Borovetz, Bulgaria, 2002.

27. Roto V. Search on Mobile Phones. Nokia Research Centre, 2002.

28. Fan X et al. Visual Attention-based Image Browsing on Mobile Devices. IEEE International Conference on Multimedia and Expo I, Baltimore, MD, USA, 2003:53–56.

29. Kerne A. CollageMachine: An Interactive Agent of Web Recombination. Leonardo, 2000:33:5:347–350.

30. Farid M, Murtagh F, and Starck J L. Computer Display Control and Interaction Using Eye-Gaze. Journal of the Society for Information Display, 2002:10:3:289–293.

31. Oyekoya O K and Stentiford F W M. Exploring Human Eye Behaviour Using a Model of Visual Attention. International Conference on Pattern Recognition, Cambridge, UK, 2004.

32. Stentiford F W M. An Estimator for Visual Attention Through Competitive Novelty with Application to Image Compression. Picture Coding Symposium, Seoul, 2001.

33. Itti L and Koch C. A Saliency-based Search Mechanism for Overt and Covert Shifts of Visual Attention. Vision Research, 2000:40:10–12:1489–1506.

18

The Implications of Pervasive Computing on Network Design

R Briscoe

18.1   Introduction

Mark Weiser's late-1980s vision of an age of calm technology with pervasive computing disappearing into the fabric of the world [1] has been tempered by an industry-driven vision with more of a feel of conspicuous consumption. In the modified version, everyone carries around consumer electronics to provide natural, seamless interactions both with other people and with the information world, particularly for eCommerce, but still through a pervasive computing fabric.

Based on cost trends, trillions of devices globally have been predicted. Using a high-level economic argument we predict that most will be globally connected, at least at a rudimentary level. To a casual outsider, a global network of either form of pervasive computing would seem to require a major redesign of the world's communications systems. However, to a reasonable extent, assumptions made during the development of the Internet's architecture took into account the more obvious issues that pervasive computing would raise. For instance, the packet abstraction allows for brief one-way datagrams that are ideally suited for reporting changes in the physical environment, and IPv6 has sufficient address space for perhaps 10^{18} addresses per square metre of the earth's surface.[1] Also, the Internet protocol is deliberately designed to abstract away from the creation of new link layer technologies (IP over everything), such as those appropriate for wireless links to battery-powered sensors or devices in hostile environments.

However, when one delves a little deeper, problems surface. The Internet architecture had substantially crystallised out just before Weiser's vision was articulated. Perhaps as a result, the Internet was largely built on assumptions of relatively stable, fixed but slightly unreliable connectivity, where availability of plentiful mains electricity was never questioned. Pervasive computing breaks these assumptions, requiring a redesign.

We focus on the more fundamental issues, such as addressing and routing, progressing to likely changes to traffic profiles that have implications on control of congestion and how to assure reliable delivery. We address security issues throughout. Before drawing the chapter to a close, we consider how the technical changes we have outlined will affect the business of networking, and vice versa. But before we start on any of the above issues we give a reasoned argument for why the

---

[1] The IPv6 address space accommodates 3×10^{38} different IPv6 addresses. But depending on allocation efficiency [2], this would lead to anything from 1.5×10^3 to 4×10^{18} addresses per square metre of the earth's surface.

prevalent mode of communications for pervasive computing will be publish-subscribe rather than primarily request-reply.

18.2   Architecture

18.2.1   Conceptual Model

No prediction of the impact of pervasive computing on network design can be undertaken without some characterisation of likely applications. Chapters 5, 6, 7, and 8 survey expected applications, including case studies of its use in the automotive sector, for care in the community, and in the home. The MIT Internet Zero project [3, 4] has built lights in flexible office spaces containing Internet-connected switches through which they are connected to mains power, while touch sensors that look like light switches can be programmed to instruct the actual switches over the Internet in order to alter their state. Probably the application closest to widespread deployment is the use of identity tags in the supply chain to replace bar codes, while sensors on work tools and materials offer the promise of automating the recording of daily activity for workers, particularly in the service industries.

We believe we can abstract all these pervasive computing applications into a single conceptual model, which we will use throughout the rest of this chapter. Pervasive computing devices allow the creation and use of models in information space that represent various aspects of our changing physical space. We can create information models that track changes in the physical world and conversely arrange to change the physical world when we modify our virtual models of it.

As a concrete example, the switch within an Internet Zero light socket contains a simple (two-state) information model of the light, and touch sensors hold the addresses of the lights they control within their connectivity model. When a touch sensor is pressed, it uses its connectivity model to determine which light it requests to change its state. In reality, the entire world's Internet Zero lights and touch sensors are physically connected to the Internet. But each connectivity model is a logical mask programmed into each touch sensor that limits its logical connectivity to only a few lights. The connectivity model in any touch sensor can itself be reprogrammed to allow it to control different lights (or an Internet hi-fi, for that matter). For instance, when a 'screwdriver' (in reality an authorised ID tag and reader in a screwdriver-like casing) is touched against a light then a touch sensor, it might reprogram the touch sensor's connectivity model so that in future it switches that particular light.

Thus, pervasive computing devices, in their role as the interface between physical and information worlds, have two complementary roles:

- to translate the state of the physical world into information (via sensors), and vice versa (actuators), collectively termed digital transducers;
- in concert with many other transducers, to share (i.e. communicate) information about the physical world with other computers in order to collectively build more comprehensive models of the real world to be used for various purposes.

This chapter focuses nearly exclusively on communications driven by sensing the world. A full treatment of our subject would include actuators, but we choose a scope that brings out at least most of the major issues, as sensors tend to be more diffuse and the load from them far greater. Wide-area tight feedback loops between the physical and information worlds would have been even more challenging but will have to be set aside for future work.

Every sensor creates an information model of the part of the physical phenomenon it covers, but usually such localised models serve little useful purpose alone. Many of these localised models need to be composed into a more comprehensive model, requiring communication from the sensors, then processing to correlate the parts into a greater whole. This process is illustrated on the left of Fig. 18.1, where the visual model is created from multiple photographic scenes.

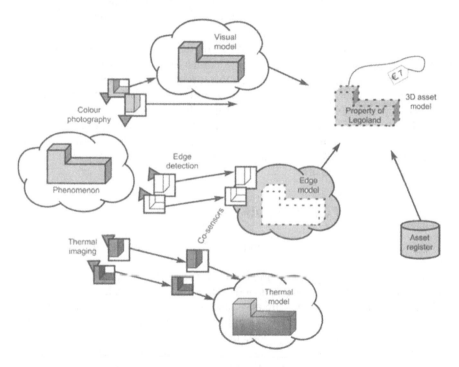

Fig. 18.1   Information models of the environment.

Also, multiple information models of different aspects of the same physical thing may be required. For example, referring again to the left of Fig. 18.1, its visual appearance, its thermal properties, its extent in 3D space (an edge or vector model), etc. The creation of certain information models might be within the capabilities of the computing power of the network of sensors themselves. The way the visual model's creation is depicted in Fig. 18.1 works this way, composing a wide, high-resolution 3D visual scene across a 'sensor network' of simple devices, each connected to a simple camera. Other models might require more computing power than is available within the sensor network. In this case sensors (or networks of sensors) would have to report their findings to 'co-sensors' (or co-sensor networks), which are computational processes running on more powerful computers (or across many computers). The illustration in Fig. 18.1 shows the co-sensor case for thermal and edge models of the same original physical phenomenon.

Parts of each newly created model may in themselves recursively form part of a more comprehensive information model of reality — Fig. 18.1 shows the visual model and the edge models being combined into a model of the 3D extent and appearance of the original phenomenon. Further, these models may be combined with non-physical information, such as ownership, value, etc, extracted from on-line databases, as shown on the right of the diagram.

Note that there is no implication of some grand plan leading to the ultimate model of everything. Each of the millions of mini-models will be required in its own right and each by some different interested party, who may or may not be willing to pass on the model to help build other models. But we can expect some owners of these models to exploit them both for their own purposes and to sell to others for theirs — retailing and wholesaling, respectively.

Continuing the example of the Internet Zero light switches as an illustration, behind each touch sensor might be multiple connectivity models — a default and one for each of those who had ever chosen to reprogramme the lighting system for their office space (assuming the touch sensor was arranged to also detect the identity behind each touch). A further model correlating all these separate models together could be built, also encompassing a model of the presence of individuals built from other sensor inputs. So the office lighting could adapt, trying to satisfy every occupant, given potentially conflicting requirements where some people turned lights on that others turned off.

18.2.2   Layered Connectivity

In the above scenarios, connectivity is implicit. Physical and logical connectivity has been deliberately arranged so that each stage in the system can connect to and be understood by the next stage in the model. It is true that humans will often deploy sensor networks for specific purposes and ensure that their wireless transmissions can all reach each other, that they are all transmitting on the same frequencies, with the same codings and with the same application-level languages and formats. However, many applications will include the creation of connectivity as part of the application. It will also be desirable to be able to use existing devices and models to create new applications. So we have to allow devices to find each other and form into networks in the first place.

A classic, well-worn scenario is where individuals walk up to shop windows with their personal digital assistants (PDAs), which connect to a monitor in the window to give them access to more screen space. Behind this simple idea lies a host of problems. There are dozens of radio link standards in fashion at any one time (Bluetooth, the WiFi family, etc), using different frequencies in each region, and hundreds of legacy standards still in use across thousands of different devices. To find each other by radio contact, the PDA would have to scan many frequency ranges and try all common coding, link, and message formats (e.g. Jini, SLP, Twine, JESA).

The chances of such an approach leading to reliable seamless connectivity, any time, anywhere, are slim unless only one or two link standards predominate for all time.

An alternative approach would be to arrange at least the first stages of connectivity over a network common to any randomly chosen pair of devices, which was the purpose of introducing the Internet protocol — an intermediary between different link technologies ('IP over everything'). So both the PDA and the monitor use their own link technologies to connect to their respective points of presence on the Internet. The monitor advertises its location on a geographical extension of the Web (e.g. geographic mark-up language or SensorML), and the PDA, knowing its own location and coverage, uses a geographical search engine to find suitable monitors within range.

Clearly, the indirect approach to connectivity may also fail to connect our two devices due to lack of mutually understood standards at the application level (e.g. the XML format of the appropriate geographical search responses). However, the direct link approach has the same chances of mismatch at the application layer on top of the chances of mismatch at the physical, link, and transport layers.

A logical model of the physical world has been created here in order to bootstrap creation of connectivity back in the physical world. Once the two devices have found each other in the information world, they can look up whether they have compatible interfaces in order to initiate a direct link. Failing that, they may have a good enough path to drive the graphics display through their Internet connection. Indeed, the monitor in our scenario may not have had any wireless connectivity at all, only having a fixed link to the Internet. Another advantage of the indirect connectivity approach is that devices can find each other in logical space even if the radio range of either of them is insufficient or not in line-of-sight.

A more far-reaching advantage is that logical objects can be placed in a model of the physical world even if they are not located there in the real world. That is, a form of augmented reality, but within a model of reality, rather than the real thing (e.g. to test contingencies). If changes to the model were also able to drive events in the real world, it would be possible to test the response of the real world to simulated events.

On top of Internet connectivity, a further prerequisite for bootstrapping physical and logical connectivity in pervasive computing applications like that above will be comprehensive information models of the location of things in the physical world [5, 6]. Again, we see the pattern where we start with potential connectivity to everything, then logically reduce connectivity to that possible within a confined geographical scope, then further reduce connectivity to that required for an application. Effectively, we are creating overlay networks over overlay networks.

18.2.3   Modes of Communications

Asynchronous Communications

Impressive work has been done compressing common communications protocols into tiny devices. For instance, Shrikumar has implemented a Web server and all the protocols beneath it using 256 B of code [7] (Fig. 18.2). However, this example highlights a need to carefully consider what mode of communication is appropriate when interfacing with the physical environment. The Web works in request-reply mode. A client asks and the server responds. But this is not how we sense the physical world. We do not ask the grass what colour it is. Photons arrive from the grass unsolicited. If we want to know whether it is dark yet, we do not keep asking a light sensor whether it is dark yet. It is far more efficient to configure the sensor to tell us when it is dark and, importantly, we will find out as soon as it gets dark, rather than the first time we happen to ask after it has become dark — timely notification of events. Thus, request-reply is appropriate for actuators, but less so for sensors.[2]

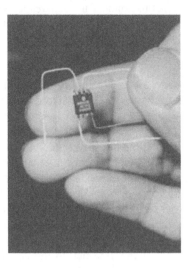

Fig. 18.2   The iPic Web server.
[Photo courtesy of UMass News Office]

Thus, a more appropriate mode of communication for sensors will be based on asynchronous events, a point Shrikumar himself made about the applicability of his miniature Web server with respect to his earlier work on event notification embedded in devices [8]. An event should trigger in a sensor as its environment[3] changes, the magnitude of the necessary change determining the sensing granularity. An event notifies a change in the state of an object, allowing other copies or models of that object to update themselves, which in turn may require them to generate further events. Event notification requires the publish-subscribe (pub-sub) mode of communications (Fig. 18.3), where an object publishes its potential to generate events to a logical channel, then listeners may subscribe to be notified when they occur. This model was popularised by Usenet and first commercialised by Teknekron Systems [9] (which became The Information Bus Company, or TIBCO).

In terms of the conceptual model built in the previous section, some information models will need to be physical-event-driven and continuous, requiring pub-sub feeds into them, while others will be created to fulfil one specific request, requiring request-reply. So each arrow representing communications between adjacent models in Fig. 18.1 might involve either push or pull. However, an event-driven model can only receive genuinely timely events if all the models it depends on are also event-driven,[4] right back to the physical phenomenon itself. On the other hand, a request-reply model will still be valid if it makes a request into a real-time model lower down the chain. Thus, all pervasive computing systems should support pub-sub.

---

[2] Request-reply has its place when a model is rarely used and can be stable between times.

[3] Time being part of a sensor's environment, which may be used to trigger scheduled reports on the rest of the sensor's environment.

[4] At the same or at a finer granularity.

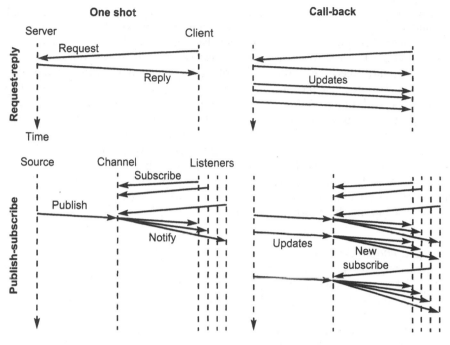

Fig. 18.3   Communication modes.

In fact, when one decomposes a request-reply service into its more rudimentary parts, one finds a pub-sub service is necessary within it. The request-reply service is merely a special event listener that holds state, which it updates dependent on each event. It can then respond to requests for its latest state (Fig. 18.4).

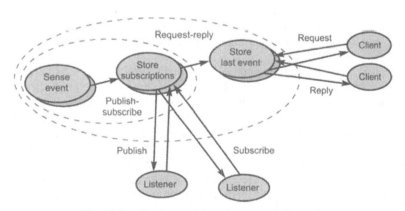

Fig. 18.4   Decomposition of request-reply mode.

A common composition of both request-reply and pub-sub modes is where a pub-sub session is dynamically created (and eventually torn down) on request, with regular responses fed back to the requestor. This is an example of the call-back mode of communications (Fig. 18.3). Later we will discuss an approach called directed diffusion [10] that works this way, with a request diffusing through a sensor network to the most appropriate sensors and regular responses following the same path in reverse to the requestor. We implemented another useful composition termed 'look up and watch' using our generic announcement protocol (GAP [11]), where the initial request gives an immediate reply, but also sets up a call-back session to notify future changes, the address of which is also published so others can join.

Having introduced the main modes of communication relevant to pervasive computing, we single out pub-sub for special attention below, examining two further features beyond timely notification that are particularly relevant to pervasive computing — group communications and no listening at the source. Before moving on, we should clarify that we do not envisage the pub-sub mode being prevalent for machine-to-human communications, as few people want or need continual interruption (evident from the lack of take-up of Web push in the mid-1990s). Humans prefer the hybrid messaging mode where communications are queued until the recipient's attention is ready to turn to them. We only expect pub-sub mode to predominate for machine-to-machine communications.

Group Communications

Whereas request-reply is inherently point to point, pub-sub's inherent point-to-multipoint nature allows multiple parties to maintain the models they need. The underlying feeds from the real world may then contribute to a plethora of different views of the world.

But it would be unscalable to expect a sensor to remember a list of everyone interested in its output, because it would have no control over how much interest there might be. Also, every device listening for sensor events would have to remember to tell the sensor of any changes to its notification address while it was waiting.

Two approaches solve this problem. One provides a bare logical communication channel where those interested join the channel (e.g. IP multicast [12]). The other simply moves the problem to a proxy service for the sensor (e.g. the distributed event mediator service in the Cambridge Event Architecture [13]). In either approach, a sensor only has to remember one channel address and send just one message to it for each event, rather than overloading already challenged sensors with multiple requests.

Under the covers, both approaches are essentially similar. They are both generally implemented as numerous software objects, which are addressed collectively as a logical channel. Listeners declare their interest to their neighbouring instance of the channel, which remembers their interest and in turn subscribes onwards to other instances. When an event occurs, the source sends it to its neighbouring instance of the channel, which distributes it onwards towards wherever interest has been declared (for more detail, see Fig. 18.9 in Section 18.3.3 later).

However, the fundamental difference is that the mediator provides a bundle of event-related services while the bare communications channel deliberately only provides dumb forwarding. So a bare channel could as easily be implemented either as a radio channel or as a collection of software subscription lists as described above. The bare channel approach follows end-to-end design principles [14], deliberately keeping the common communications service rudimentary and complementing it with other services such as event archiving and recovery, but only if required. If recall of previous events were required, perhaps to help late joiners or those temporarily disconnected, the event mediator would provide this service itself, whereas without knowing why, the bare channel would simply forward the information to an archiving node because it had joined the channel in order to provide this service. Other approaches sit at intermediate points on this spectrum. For instance, Microsoft's SCRIBE [15] is a bare channel service, but it also offers reliable delivery (discussed in Section 18.3.5).

Of course, we cannot expect everyone to share their data freely. Chapter 11 discusses how confidentiality may be required to protect trade, individual privacy, or other differences of interest. Again the above two approaches differ in how they offer confidentiality. An event mediator service includes an access control function that acts fully on behalf of the sensor. This requires each listener to give appropriate credentials before being allowed to join, while the dumb channel again leaves confidentiality to another service. The sensed data would have to be encrypted before sending to the channel, while another service would control access to the decryption key. So anyone could join the channel, but they would not understand it without the key. The merits of each approach are discussed in the sections on function placement (Section 18.2.4) and on security (Section 18.3.6).

Announce or Listen

A further advantage of the pub-sub mode is that the sensor has no need to listen for requests in 'server mode'.[5] Wireless sensors would very quickly run down their batteries if they had to leave their radio receiver running to listen for arbitrary incoming requests. It is far less power-consuming to leave only the sensing mechanism running, 'listening' for changes to the physical environment, which can then trigger power up of the radio circuitry only to send notification of the event.

But, when discussing our conceptual model earlier, we emphasised that pervasive computing systems need to be able to respond to arbitrary requests as well as asynchronous notification of events. Does this not mean that their radio receivers will have to remain powered up anyway? The answer lies in separating event memory from event communication. In order to answer requests for the current temperature, or the current state of a touch sensor, the sensor itself does not need to remember its own state. As long as something else (connected to mains power) receives events from the sensor, it can respond to requests for the sensor's current state between times.

Proving many of the points so far, Shrikumar's tiny Web server was soon taken off the Internet, as its serial link was continually overloaded with requests from curious browsers. Its content is now served from a larger mirror server.

18.2.4   Function Placement

Evolvability

A system's evolvability is highly sensitive to the placement of communications functions, which is the chief concern of the Internet's end-to-end design principle [14]. The need for evolvability of today's communications infrastructure is obvious, given large investment costs require future-proofing. But one may wonder why evolvability of pervasive computing devices is a concern, given the growth of pervasive computing is based on projections of plummeting device costs [1]. Can we not assume each device is disposable, only ever being used for the purpose for which

---

[5] The term 'server' relates to any process able to respond to arbitrary incoming requests, irrespective of whether it runs on a large machine often called a 'server' or on a tiny sensor.

it was first deployed? The issue here is that the equipment is only a part of the cost of a new application. Deployment is a major cost consideration, so it is highly desirable to put devices deployed for one purpose to use for others. For instance, to add a one penny wireless sensor beneath the drum of your washing machine costs a lot more than remotely reusing the one already there.

Open by Design, Closed by Choice

In Section 18.2.2 on layered connectivity we recursively create confined connectivity within wider potential connectivity. We argue that the value of global connectivity greatly outweighs the cost. Metcalfe showed that the value of the connectivity of each device rises with the number of other devices it could potentially connect to, making global connectivity highly valuable, whereas the cost of fully standards-compliant Internet connectivity is about a mere 200 B of code [7][6] plus the running cost of the processing and bandwidth required for the extra header layer (compressible to a byte or so). Devices might not carry an Internet stack, but instead connect to a hub that does. However, the added complexity of arranging and managing a hub hardly seems worthwhile given the low cost of direct Internet connectivity. Therefore, economies of volume manufacture are likely to lead to every device design including an Internet stack, whether or not it is needed for every application.

Global connectivity is also highly desirable for evolvability; otherwise, new uses will be constrained by locality. For example, initially it may not seem necessary to give light switches global connectivity, but one day you might appreciate the facility to turn your lights off from your mobile phone while on holiday. However, more controversially, others may be able to remotely control or monitor your lights. One approach to this privacy problem is to place inherent accessibility limits in the design (e.g. to design a car door lock so it can only be opened within a limited range). But this only limits the first hop, which cannot be prevented from networking onward globally. A safer approach is to assume global accessibility might exist, and to close off undesirable uses logically rather than physically. To fully stress network design, we take the 'assume open then close' approach. However, we accept that designers of car security systems and the like will care more about present security than future evolvability. This dilemma is further explored in Chapter 11, which specifically deals with maintaining privacy in pervasive computing networks.

Dumb Relays

Whether or not the devices themselves should be evolvable, it is certain that the rest of the systems they work with should be. All too often, principles of evolvable system design are too readily set aside in pervasive computing demonstrators. Rather than designing for messages from sensors to be transmitted to and from any other computer in the world, functions are often embedded in the base stations that interface between the sensor and the rest of the world, perhaps doing some address or protocol conversion (e.g. from sensor-local to global). We discuss some cases ahead where intelligent base stations can be justified on principle. But if intelligent relays are necessary to a design, the end-to-end design principle teaches us that it is worth taking a long, hard look at alternative designs that confine intermediate relays to dumb forwarding.

---

[6] 2.5% of the memory of a Berkeley mote, which is likely to grow in capacity and shrink in size in line with Moore's law.

Ideally, the sensors themselves should be first-class Internet citizens. But failing that, the remote end-points they communicate with should supplement their limited capabilities, not neighbouring relays (so the fate of a communication depends only on state and trust shared between the end-points of the communication). Tying higher-layer functions to specific instances of equipment operated by specific parties will limit flexibility, especially for new business models.

Power conservation can be a valid reason to relax the end-to-end principle, with base stations taking on additional functions by virtue of their role as the first mains-powered node in the path. But this need not be an excuse to open the floodgates to more functions than necessary. For instance, strong encryption is possible on challenged devices (see Section 18.3.6), so sensors should encrypt their data for confidentiality and the base station should merely relay the encrypted data to another destination. Functions such as retransmission can be achieved without access to encryption keys, the goal being to limit access to as few parties as possible. For instance, it would be inadvisable to embed an event mediator service in the base station, which decrypted events and controlled further access to them itself. This would limit future uses of the system to ones where the base-station operator was trusted by everyone who might want these future uses.

However, it may be more efficient for the sensors themselves to behave as intelligent infrastructure (relays) for the nodes around them — multi-hop sensor networks. Taking the sensor network as a whole, it has been proven that combining data aggregation with the relay function within each sensor saves considerable battery power for typical diffuse sensing applications [16]. When battery power is paramount relative to evolvability, it seems we have to compromise and make infrastructure more application-specific — counter to end-to-end design principles. We return to this subject in Section 18.3.3 on routing.

18.3   Component Services

So, faced with all the choices above and more to come below, which course should a wireless sensor manufacturer or network equipment vendor take? Is there a generic design for communications with miniature devices? Which communications services should service providers be considering? Of course, the detailed answer might depend on the specifics of the application or the devices required for it. But, the following sections discuss progress towards defining generic component services so that as many specific requirements as possible can be satisfied by building applications over these components.

To start the discussion we propose a straw-man design for the communications systems of a miniature device. We believe that a large range of applications could be satisfied by this apparently strange proposal. We briefly outline the reasoning behind the proposal, but we do not intend to imply that any other approach must be inferior in all circumstances. The architectural discussion above was necessarily conducted at a fairly abstract level. We put up a straw-man at this point to deliberately force a change of pace in the chapter. As we proceed through the following sections, the choices widen further for each aspect: routing, addressing, reliable delivery, congestion control, traffic profiles, security, and other ancillary communications services. We hope the straw-man will provoke thought while reading those subsequent sections, and remind the reader that the economies of scale necessary for the pervasive computing vision require device manufacturers to commit to a design that will survive a large production run.

18.3.1   A Straw-Man Proposal

We would recommend a configuration-free device (Fig. 18.5) that powered up its radio transmitter whenever it sensed a threshold change to its environment. It could then send a 'fire-and-forget' datagram to a hard-coded multicast address[7] and immediately power down its transmitter. It would also send heartbeat messages, confirming the previously sent event at regular intervals.[8] The device would have to be one hop from its base station. It should be relatively tamper-resistant, at least outputting a warning if tampered with, so that it could hold an internally stored key, which it would use to seed a regularly changing pseudo-random sequence of keys used to encrypt its messages.

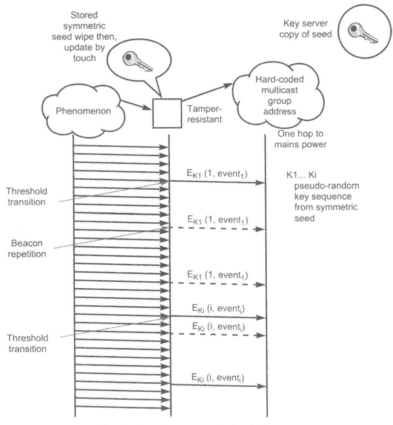

Fig. 18.5   Straw-man device design.

---

[7]Preferably IP multicast, but otherwise a multicast medium access control (MAC) address, with a different one in each device.

[8]Slow changes to the interval could be arranged with repeated advance warnings.

Our reasoning for choosing this design is that, although a sensor may only be able to perform one simple function, to bring down its cost of production, it should be manufactured in volume. So its single function will need to be applied in many different ways. So the device must be secure to some degree even though it may not always need to be. And we have deliberately chosen to allow it to be repurposed pre- and post-deployment but without reconfiguration, so that the device need have no server listening for configuration changes, saving battery power and improving inherent security (for instance, proofing it against the sleep deprivation torture attack [17], which leaves any node that responds to arbitrary requests vulnerable to rapid exhaustion of its battery).

We have recommended multi-cast addressing, as otherwise a device hard-coded to send to a unicast address is permanently tied to a specific corresponding node. Multi-cast addresses have no topological significance, so the receiver of each message can be changed without involving the sender, instead only requiring potential receiver(s) to be configured to listen. Multi-cast addresses need only be loosely unique, as a multi-cast transmission can be locally scoped, to prevent clashes with transmissions to the same address. Any receiver could re-multi-cast with a wider scope if necessary.

The device's multi-cast event notifications could be limited to just one receiver, by not revealing the seed key more widely. Or the seed key could be published if there were no need for confidentiality. Between these two extremes, time-bounded parts of the pseudo-random sequence could be revealed to selected groups by a separate key management server (as in our own MARKS key management scheme [18]).

At least one receiver (perhaps the only authorised receiver) could maintain the sensor's state, acting as its proxy for arbitrary incoming requests, and archiving events for late joiners. The sensor would not be able to receive acknowledgements for anything it sent, so, if a receiver missed a heartbeat, it would need to rely on other receivers for a retransmission (as in SRM [19]) or, if there were no other successful deliveries, wait until the next heartbeat.

This straw-man proposal is intended to cover a wide set of circumstances, but only where each sensor alone has sufficient radio range to reach a mains-powered communications device. Multi-hop networks of sensors would not be possible with send-only sensors. Multi-hop sensor networks come up repeatedly in the rest of this chapter, being a major focus of the research agenda. But that does not make this straw-man proposal irrelevant, given single-hop wireless sensors may turn out to be more prevalent in practice.

18.3.2   Unusual Link Technologies

Given power constraints, communications links to pervasive computing leaf nodes often use highly constraining technology. Connectivity may be the exception rather than the rule [20, 21], due to line-of-sight issues as much as power conservation. Link availability may have to be pre-scheduled or opportunistic. Error rates may be high even when connected.

Further, the range of one end-point may be much greater than that of the other (typically where one end is connected to mains power), implying that often connectivity will be unidirectional. Nonetheless, novel technologies have been built to scavenge energy from communications in one direction, modulating it in order to respond in the other. Radio frequency identity tags work this way, capturing the excitation energy in the reader's radio transmission until sufficient energy has been built up to respond by modulating the incoming signal. Micro-electro-mechanical (MEM) fabrication has been used at UC Berkeley to build corner cube reflectors on 'smart dust' devices (Fig. 18.6). It is projected that smart dust will be small enough to float in air or water. The reflectors work on the same principle as roadway cat's eyes, but the angle of one face can be varied slightly to modulate the reflection of an incoming optical beam back to its source [22]. The team has manufactured a sub-millimetre cube and achieved 400 bit/s over 180 m with good signal-to-noise ratio [23], while their analysis claims many kbit/s are possible over hundreds of metres in bright sunlight.

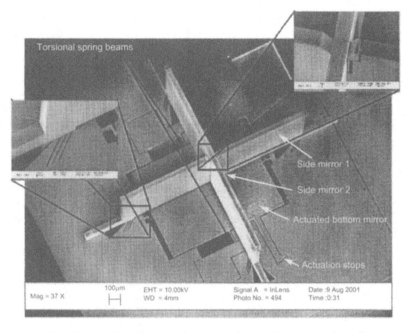

Fig. 18.6   Scanning electron microscope picture of a corner cube reflector.
[Photo courtesy of UC Berkeley, EECS]

Such power-scavenging technologies seem more suited to request-reply mode, where a reader base station requests a reading and the sensor responds. However, smart dust is equipped with hybrid communications technology, so that it can hail the base station with a short burst of radio broadcast. The base station then shines its optical beam in order to pick up the message the sensor has for it [22], giving the sensor on-demand access to the link for minimal energy cost.

Even with more conventional wireless link technologies, there is considerable scope for improving power efficiency by designing medium access [24, 25] and transport protocols [26] to minimise energy use, with only minor compromises in traditional performance metrics necessary.

All this novel link technology helps, but it does not remove the problem of poor connectivity, which changes the rules for designing all the layers built over it, right up to the application. In our own index-based event-messaging system [27], eventual message delivery over disconnections is provided by the managed messaging layer on announcers and listeners. Messages are clustered into groups based on interest, and indexes of the current version of messages in each cluster are beaconed at regular intervals. As nodes regain connectivity, their managed messaging layer transparently finds which messages they have missed and accesses them from an event archive.

18.3.3   Routing

The task of routing messages through an *ad hoc* network of mobile battery-powered nodes is hard enough when the nodes are allowed large, rechargeable batteries. A 2003 review of practical progress [28] revealed most research was still stronger in theory than practice. Just one implementation (as opposed to simulation) of a routing protocol (AODV [29]) was able to reliably route packets over more than one hop. These were results from the Internet Engineering Task Force's (IETF's) Mobile *Ad Hoc* Networks (MANET) working group, which has been chartered since 1995/6 to focus on standardising protocols that are near to market.

To realise the vision of pervasive computing, far more challenging scenarios are envisaged. Routing protocols have been implemented for large numbers of tiny, dust-sized devices with very short range, where each second of battery use is one second closer to death. In such scenarios, few nodes are within range of a gateway giving access to wider networks, but collectively a network of sensors should be able to relay most nodes' messages to a gateway.

Routing Hierarchy
Routing research for sensor networks has rightly separated routing within the sensor network from the routing beyond it. Although there may be a choice of routes out of the sensor network, it is rarely necessary to consider optimising routes across both networks at once, as the sensor network leg is far more resource-critical (Fig. 18.7). However, ensuring that messages destined for the sensor network enter it from the most efficient gateway requires a model of the sensor network to be held by routers outside the domain. Baker [30] has argued that if routing nodes are relatively powerful (e.g. MANETs being considered by the IETF), popular link-state routing protocols can be sufficient. They can be tuned to allow the combination of fixed and mobile nodes to work together effectively, without too much power and memory consumption within the MANET.

System-Wide Energy Conservation
Routing protocols are generally designed to be agnostic about which route cost-metrics to use. So it is relatively straightforward to replace traditional hop metrics with power-aware metrics. Singh et al [31] show mean time to battery exhaustion for a whole mobile *ad hoc* network could be considerably improved by using such metrics.

Chang et al [32] prove analytically that battery lives across a whole network of fixed but wireless devices could be maximised with no need for global co-ordination, only requiring an algorithm local to each node that ensured local energy consumption was proportional to local energy reserves. However, often the lifetimes of critically placed nodes become the determining factor for the lifetime of the whole network (e.g. those close to a base station).

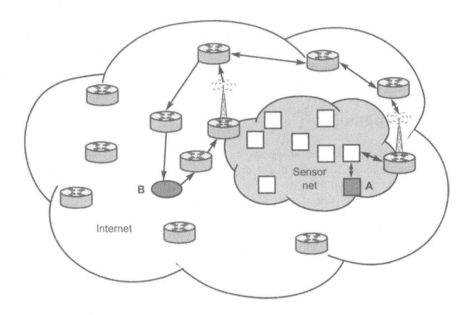

Fig. 18.7   Hybrid mains-/battery-powered routing with a deliberately tortuous mains-powered path, to avoid concerning Internet routing with power optimisation.

Application-Specific Concast

In Section 18.2.3 we explain the need for pub-sub mode of communications and introduced the requirement for routing events to multiple parties. However, sensor network routing has avoided multi-casting, as it is more power efficient to relay events across sensor nodes to a single gateway rather than duplicating the message and the power required to transmit it. From there, the multi-cast model can be offered, with multiple parties subscribing to a logical event channel.

In 2001, researchers at the Internet Sciences Institute (ISI) showed that when on-net capacity (within the sensor network) is critical, it is more efficient to hold back sensor data until it can be aggregated with other readings while routing them (Fig. 18.8), rather than sending each reading immediately and separately to an off-net reader to be aggregated there [16]. This proved the correctness of their seminal earlier work called 'directed diffusion' [10].

Directed diffusion was a radical departure. Traditionally, routing is based on node addresses, ensuring everywhere in the network maintains routes to any other address so that applications can send messages to other nodes by their addresses. Instead, directed diffusion addressed messages by the content of the question that required answering. And nodes advertised the answers they could give by the content of the questions they could answer. Thus, for a sensor reading such as 'temperature = 17' the relevant content name is 'temperature'. This was the first instance of what came to be termed content-addressable networks (CANs).[9] However, unlike subsequent CANs, directed diffusion worked without the benefit of any underlying routing. Sensors capable of answering 'temperature' questions would advertise this fact to

---

[9]CANs became prevalent during the next year for routing in peer-to-peer overlay networks for file-sharing and related applications.

their neighbours, who would flood this fact outwards. Queries about 'temperature' could then be routed to the correct sensors, leaving behind a trail of 'bread-crumbs' so return messages could be reverse-routed to the original place the query had entered the network. While return messages were relayed across the sensor network, the temperature values could be aggregated. For instance, the weighted mean might be calculated before forwarding the result.

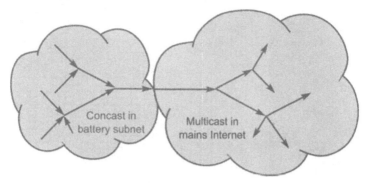

Fig. 18.8   Energy shortage makes concast, not multi-cast, the most efficient communications mode.

The aggregation functions to use and the routing logic of each directed diffusion session were highly application-specific. As explained earlier, evolvability has to be compromised if other factors (e.g. power conservation) are paramount. But then, in 2002, researchers from the database community at UC Berkeley generalised the ideas in directed diffusion, using common aggregation primitives found in commercial databases (COUNT, MIN, MAX, SUM, and AVERAGE) [33]. Thus, a more generic routing capability has been implemented in the TinyOS operating system built for the Berkeley motes (see Fig. 18.12 later in Section 18.3.6). It is called TinyDB, given it involves the rather unexpected inclusion of database aggregation primitives within a routing protocol.

In fact, generic aggregation functions at merge points in a network were recognised as important outside the sensor networking field in the late 1990s, appearing in Cisco's generic router assist (GRA) technology [34] — a generalisation of all concast modes of communications. In concast, multiple messages converge, with some combination function at each merge point (Fig. 18.9). In the mid-1990s, concast was recognised as a valid communications mode, used primarily when data traversed a multi-cast tree in reverse, for functions like aggregating multi-cast feedback or merging bandwidth reservations.

We should add that both directed diffusion and TinyDB allow for a time series of responses to an initial query. In this respect, they use the call-back mode of communications introduced in Section 18.2.3, creating a logical pub-sub channel (e.g. on the 'temperature' topic) in response to a session initiation request.

Unusual Routing for Unusual Links

Beyond designing for challenging power requirements, routing protocols are also having to be redesigned to cope with inconsistent link availability (see Section 18.3.2 earlier). If sensor nodes are acting as relays in multi-hop networks but can only power up intermittently, then they all have to synchronise to get any relaying done.

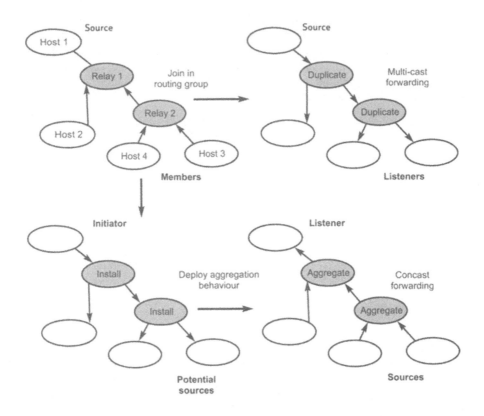

Fig. 18.9   Multi-cast and concast group formation and forwarding.

Also, routing is notoriously difficult with unidirectional links (as routing inherently concerns passing advertisements of downstream connectivity to upstream nodes). Routing over unidirectional links has been solved for the classic example of satellite down-links, by creating a tunnelled virtual link along a back channel, through which routing messages can be passed [35]. However, routing over links that become unidirectional unpredictably is still a research issue.

Routing Security

If all the above research issues were not enough, routing in *ad hoc* networks presents numerous further unsolved security challenges. Already authentication of route advertisements is a difficult area if there is a high churn of network operators. It is unrealistic to expect trillions of devices to appear in the next decades unless billions of networks also appear to connect them together, implying extremely rapid appearance of new network operators (unless all networking is outsourced to the few existing operators, which seems hopelessly optimistic).

In order to validate routing message authentication, any one network must know from whom it would expect to receive advertisements. So authentication of routes through newly appearing networks will require trusted third parties to introduce the new players. Also, just because a route advertisement is authenticated does not mean it is honest, as pointed out by Perlman in 1988 [36]. Commercial networks have an incentive to understate the cost metrics of their routes to attract extra custom. So unless the cost of an advertised route can be objectively tested (as, for example, in feedback-based routing [37]), authentication means little.

Although problems of authentication are hard, the range of possible attacks on the availability of *ad hoc* networks are even harder to solve. We have already mentioned sleep deprivation torture attacks on power constrained nodes. Law et al list a range of further attacks in their excellent introduction to this area [38] — black-holing, flooding, detours, loops, wormholes, blackmailing, and hijacking (Fig. 18.10). Each node's finite battery power makes it vulnerable to any attack that requires it to use its energy before it can determine whether it is being attacked.

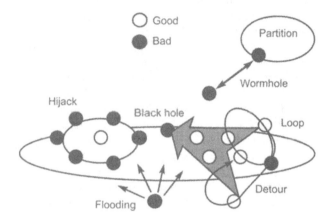

Fig. 18.10   Types of attack on routing (from Law et al [38]).

Clearly, if any section of society takes a dislike to certain wireless devices in their environment, they will only need to identify one of these vulnerabilities to attack them. The send-only sensor in the straw-man proposal above is a pragmatic way to avoid many of the vulnerabilities, although it is still susceptible to physical-layer attacks such as channel jamming and the like.

18.3.4   Naming and Addressing

To a casual observer, the size of the required address space for a computing network should relate to the number of hardware devices in the world. However, if pub-sub communications become predominant, the size of the problem will be determined by the number of software objects that have an audience of other software objects watching for updates to their state — potentially far more numerous than the trillions of devices on which they sit.

Encapsulation

Hierarchy has invariably been used to ensure addressing schemes can scale. For instance, variable names used within a programme resolve to memory addresses, but the same variable name or memory address used in two programmes (or even two instances of the same programme) are distinguished by the identity of the process in which they run (strictly the identity of the interface to the process). Continuing up the hierarchy, processes are identified relative to the interfaces of the machines on which they run. Machines are identified relative to their sub-network and so on.

Address Aggregation

However, large distributed processes like environment monitoring sit across machines rather than within one machine, inverting the 'normal' hierarchy.[10] Sharing the variables of the process across machines causes the scaling problem introduced above. Imagine a large set of sensors also acting as relays for each other. Imagine that a sub-set comprises temperature sensors, which, along with those interested in their readings, all hold a common interest in the group-name 'temperature'. We explain earlier (Section 18.2.3) why the only practical approach here is for each sensor to send to a logical channel — pub-sub mode — rather than each hold a list of interested listeners. The logical channel is created by the interest of the listeners and the combined routing of all the relays. So every relay has to remember the list of those logical neighbours to which to forward messages concerning the temperature question. This list consumes a small amount of memory on each relay.

Another subset of the same sensors may be gathering road traffic statistics. So each relay also has to set aside memory to route messages for the 'road-traffic' group. If there are a large number of network-wide processes being supported across the sensor network, there could be a routing group for each variable in each process — potentially one routing group for each software object on the network. Alternatively, many groups can be combined into one, so that some end-points have to filter out messages in which they are not interested (a problem familiar to people who use e-mail lists). However many groups there are, each relay will have to store a different neighbour list for each group.

Unfortunately, there is no generic way for each relay to aggregate the per-group neighbour lists it holds, so the memory required on each relay grows linearly with the number of routing groups. Each pair (group-name, neighbour-list) bears little relation to any other pair. Even if numbers are uniquely assigned to each group, in a numeric order that helps one node to group its neighbour-lists efficiently, this order is unlikely to help any others. In 2001, this problem was articulated formally as the 'channelisation problem' [39], also applying to radio channel allocation. Given we believe pub-sub will be the predominant mode of communications in pervasive computing, the channelisation problem puts inherent limits on the economic viability of pervasive computing. The designers of directed diffusion and TinyDB have not had to worry about this problem, because current sensor networks are application-specific, requiring only a few routing groups. However, if our conceptual model of pervasive computing (Section 18.2.1) becomes prevalent on a global scale, the channelisation problem will arise in the (mains-powered) networks connecting together the physical and information worlds. We predict that events from the physical world will spread out across a web of listeners around the globe, with little correlation by location.

Until recently, only limited group aggregation potential was considered feasible on relays [40]. A naive solution is to use one coarser logical channel to replace many more granular ones and just expect receivers to filter out what does not concern them. Some of the filtering burden can be carried by the network, even using commercially available Internet routing products. Hop-by-hop filtering can be added

---

[10] Distributed processes will be the norm in the future.

to these products [41] using their support for generic concast functions [34] (see Section 18.3.3).

Our own solution to this problem [27] takes an end-to-end[11] rather than hop-by-hop approach. We use an addressing scheme where any object may take a globally unique[12] and meaningless address for the sequence of events it will generate as its state changes. Then it gives each event within the sequence an incrementing version number. Our aim was to solve the address scalability problem, but without revealing any more than necessary to intermediate parties, given messages will often contain commercial or private information.

We create routing state on relays for very granular routing groups (one for each event sequence) but only for the brief time it is needed to pass a message, which at first sight seems to make sending anything impossible. But we introduce indexers that regularly beacon a list of related event identifiers along with their latest versions. Listeners monitor the index or indexes of their choice in order to hear when a message arises for them. So the persistent routing groups for the indexes will only be held open on relays for those indexes with an audience.[13] Indexes beacon regularly for reliability as listeners come and go (see Section 18.3.5). The indexing function may itself be distributed. Changes to indexes are notified to end-points interested in them using the same messaging system as for the events themselves, and indexes may themselves be further indexed recursively. When an event source has a message to send, it first asks the indexer to send out an update (Fig. 18.11(b) or (e)). Those listening then send join requests to their closest relays, creating the

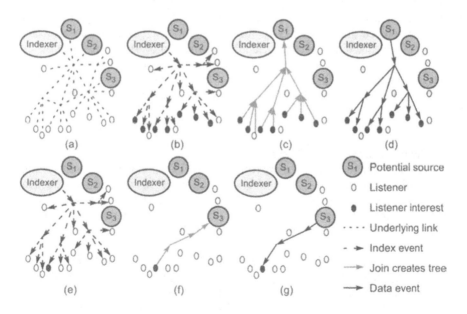

Fig 18.11   Index-based event messaging.

---

[11] Throughout the chapter, the term 'end-to-end' is used in its technical sense to mean 'involving only the end-points to provide the function in question'.

[12] Messages contain only a locally unique sub-range of the addresses to reduce overhead.

[13] On a longer time-scale, listeners reveal all the sequences in which they are interested so that indexers can optimise which sequences are announced in which index, around how listener interest is clustered.

group's routing structure (Fig. 18.11(c) or (f)) only for the brief time required to send the event (Fig. 18.11(d) or (g)). The solution makes memory usage scalable as more groups are required, but can trade this off against the greater need for messages to co-ordinate the indexes.

An approach using similar intermediate structures to the above indexes was proposed by Kulik at MIT [42]. However, in Kulik's approach every relay stores the relevant parts of the directed acyclic graphs relating indexes together, whereas in our scheme listeners store the relevant branches of the graph. Kulik's approach clearly speeds up event notification at the expense of more storage on relays.

Topographical Addressing

We have already briefly discussed requirements for mapping between physical space and the logical addresses of processes on computing devices (Section 18.2.2). In order for two software objects to establish whether they are close in a modelled co-ordinate space, the most efficient approach is to create further objects to represent each volume of space.

The model of each space holds the identifiers of objects placed within it and announces whenever an object enters or leaves it. Then, any object has to monitor the object representing the space it occupies in order to find other nearby objects, rather than having to continually interrogate the position of all objects in the world in case any one of them passes close by. [14]

Thus, we can immediately see a scenario where every space (of varying volume) in the physical world is represented by an object in the information world, which many other objects that have placed themselves in that space are continuously monitoring. Just this single proximity application would be sufficient to cause the group address aggregation scaling problems we have outlined — when trillions of objects are watching for changes in trillions of other objects. Further, many service providers will maintain space models requiring co-ordination between multiple models of the same space.

Internetworking Beyond the Internet

As networks of computing devices are formed, they may all inherit their networking characteristics from the evolving Internet architecture. However, new independent forms of network may develop without any overarching architecture common to all the networks. Overlays that work across multiple network architectures are perfectly feasible, the Internet itself being the classic example. But federations of different network architectures are fraught with problems.

The Plutarch proposal [43] considers what is necessary to federate multiple addressing architectures, also making some inroads into wider federation issues. But address resolution differences can be confined to end-points and clearly identifiable gateways between architectures (cf IPv4 to IPv6 gateways). The hard problems start when federating data handling along the whole network path: detecting routing loops or congestion, or controlling priority, capacity reservation or routing. The gain from not using an Internet-wide architecture would have to override the pain suffered dealing with such a wide range of issues.

---

[14] Recall that any object might jump to anywhere in cyberspace.

18.3.5   Data Transport Issues

Traffic Profiles
If computing does become pervasive, one might assume that a majority of traffic flows would consist of just a few packets, with single datagram flows being common. But we cannot predict whether these bursts would constitute a large proportion of total traffic volume. In the last half of the 1990s, due to the rise in popularity of the Web, flows of a few packets (< 20) constituted the large majority of the flows (95%) and a sizeable proportion of the volume of traffic on the Internet (see, for example, Brownlee and Ma [44]). The rise in the popularity of peer-to-peer file sharing between 2000 and 2004 has seen longer lasting flows take over in prominence. Thus, not only would it be foolish to try to predict the future traffic mix, it would be reckless to design networks and protocols without contingency for a range of scenarios.

Even our intuition about the traffic implications of current uses of the Internet can be misguided. Most people imagine multi-cast is used to stream long-running sessions. Although this use does indeed constitute a large volume of multi-cast traffic, a study of nearly four million native multi-cast flows [15] [45] found over 75% consisted of just one packet. Closer investigation found a large proportion of these consisted of co-ordination messages to announce the existence of other sessions through various multi-cast indexing tools. The same bimodal distribution caused by the division in human behaviour between managing and doing (whether work, social interactions, or whatever) is seen in unicast traffic [46]. But, past behaviour (mostly from human-attended sessions) is not a reliable guide to the future traffic mix if unattended sessions come to predominate.

For instance, we might see huge avalanches of messages firing across the Internet following major changes in the real world (road-traffic accidents, battles, security advisories, etc). Network management event avalanches already create problems that are hard to quantify until they happen. Once the information world is much more tightly coupled to the real world, the complex chains of dependency between messages (that may also get lost during such events) may become near impossible to design for.

Congestion Control
If the large majority of Internet traffic volume does turn out to consist of little bursts of packets between uncorrelated end-points, current congestion control techniques will be largely useless. In order to pace its rate, a sender should mimic the behaviour of the transmission control protocol (TCP-friendly), which relies on congestion feedback from routers on the path. When a sender starts a new flow, it carefully introduces packets to the network, sending two for every one that gets acknowledged by the receiver, until it senses congestion. However, brief flows finish long before they discover the rate they could have used, because they have to proceed so cautiously.

If the traffic mix is mainly short flows, there may be insufficient long-running flows to use up the remaining network capacity. So there will come a time when further increases in network capacity will not bring any benefit. TCP-friendly slow-

---

[15] Monitored throughout July 2001 on MCI/WorldCom's backbone.

start algorithms will become the limiting factor for network capacity. Of course, the contrary approach would not work either, where everyone agrees that TCP should be allowed to ramp up more aggressively. We could then return to the episodes of persistent congestion collapse that led to the introduction of TCP in the 1980s.

Further, in the pervasive computing vision, distributed computations will always be fighting against unavoidable propagation delays due to the speed of light. Already many GRID applications use parallelism extremely judiciously, because the messaging delays between computers are so great relative to local delays. TCP's 'slow-start' puts an inherent limit of $O(\log(n))$ on the latency of a short burst of n packets, whereas often a whole burst could have been served in one round trip, but that can only be discovered in retrospect.[16]

The Data Rate of Reality

As we have mentioned, sensor networks can tend to generate event avalanches. The Anderson project at Columbia University has proposed a novel congestion control mechanism, tailored to the particular problems of sensor networks [47]. The problem is that traditional congestion control only exerts back pressure on the sender's transmission rate. Herein lie two problems:

- the ultimate sender is the real world — it is obviously not possible to slow the data rate of reality;

- often, there is no backlog of messages at the sender, which may have only contributed one message — congestion only arises at certain unfortunate relays in the sensor network.

By definition, congestion implies a high probability of not being able to service a request due to high utilisation of resources. So, again by definition, if a relay is congested, it will have no spare buffer space up its sleeve. So, once a relay is congested, it has very little room for manoeuvre, given all the data has probably already left the sources that caused the congestion. All that can be done is to ask upstream relays to hold back data, and sources to buffer any new data arriving 'from reality'. Clearly though, as events continue to unfold in the real world, if congestion persists, there will come a point where data has to be dropped.

We should emphasise that some messages, no matter how tiny, might carry very important information. But the importance will rarely be understood by the sensor or relay — often it will only be possible to establish how important a message is once its meaning has been extracted by the receiver.[17] As with the quality-of-service question in public networks, the dilemma lies between adding capacity (which will rarely be sufficient in all circumstances) and introducing complex prioritisation or multi-path routing schemes. Both increase the size and cost of the devices, just to provide cover against unlikely eventualities, which may never happen.[18] But catastrophes are exactly the time when reliable data is most required.

---

[16] Our current research solves these 'slow-start' problems by reversing the incentive structures of the Internet's congestion control mechanisms. A publication is in preparation.

[17] In the physical world, this problem is solved by transmitting information in analogue form. For instance, an arbitrarily large volume of information can pass through the lens of the eye and the retina, in order to be prioritised during processing by the brain.

[18] Aggregation of data within a sensor network (Section 18.3.3) might alleviate most potential congestion problems.

As messages cross the Internet at large, these problems can be ignored if the 'data rate from reality' is dwarfed by the data rate between entities in the information world. The latter is more elastic, so it can hold back to allow for fluctuations and avalanches of data from reality.

Delivery Reliability

Having introduced the possibility of dropping messages (whether as a result of congestion or wireless channel fade), this leads us directly into a further challenge to conventional thinking. How does a receiver know a message has been lost when it was not expecting it anyway?

Usually a receiver can detect a missing message when a sequence of packets stops arriving, or the next in the sequence arrives revealing a gap. Asynchronous events are not expected by definition. So the receiver can only detect a loss when the next event arrives, which may be anything from microseconds to years later. If using positive acknowledgement (ack) this is not a problem, because the sender can detect a lack of ack, and resend. But if a large number of listeners want to be informed of each event, the source can be overwhelmed by what is termed an 'ack implosion'. Therefore, for scalability, the pub-sub model is deliberately arranged to hide the comings and goings of listeners from the source. So how can the source know how many listeners are interested, and therefore how many acks it should have received?

Negative acknowledgement (nack), where receivers only complain if they miss a message, is preferred in multi-cast streaming scenarios. So nacks can be aggregated on their way to the source if more than one receiver misses a message (Cisco provides the pragmatic general multi-cast (PGM) capability [48] on their routers to aggregate nacks, which is a specific type of concasting within their generic router assist framework discussed in Section 18.3.3). This still leaves the above problems where no one can nack a missed message that they were not expecting.

Our own index-based event-messaging system (introduced in Sections 18.3.2 and 18.3.4 in the context of intermittent links and address aggregation) was also designed to solve this problem. Because its indexes beacon regularly, it is clear when one is missed. And the indexes list the version number of the latest message on each message channel. So receivers can nack a missed message, even being able to catch up if they have been disconnected for some time.

Hop-by-hop ack or nack handling can be used for reliable delivery. PGM aggregates nacks [48], while SCRIBE [15] uses the acks of a long-running TCP session between each intermediate system. However, an early insight during the design of the Internet was that hop-by-hop acknowledgement did not remove the need for end-to-end acknowledgement (e.g. during re-routing or router failures) [14]. The situation is no different for asynchronous events. We have to check delivery end-to-end, so hop by hop is redundant, hence justifying our choice of beaconing indexes.

The above concerns reliable multi-cast delivery across global networks, originating from a sensor just one hop from mains power as in our straw-man proposal (Section 18.3.1). When messages arise in a multi-hop sensor network, we have already (Section 18.3.3) recommended avoiding duplication of power consumption, aggregating with concast, rather than duplicating with multi-cast until a node with mains power is reached. How reliability mechanisms should most efficiently span the two parts of the message transport in these cases is a matter for further research.

18.3.6   Security

All distributed applications require some degree of trust between the devices comprising the system. Chapter 10 discusses an approach to allow pervasive devices to determine whether they hold sufficient trust in their correspondents for the risk associated with the action in hand. Such systems require rudimentary primitives for secure communications.

Pervasive placement of computers in the environment breaks many traditional communications security assumptions. Most importantly, storage of keys on a device assumes the device is physically secured against those who do not know the key, which is not the case for many sensor networking applications spread liberally throughout the environment.

Verifiable Location

However, many other applications of pervasive computing involve devices within business or residential premises. Recent research at UC Berkeley has introduced a technique to establish whether a device is located where it claims to be [49], although a trusted node close to the device is a prerequisite. Techniques that do not rely on a nearby trusted node are far more complex, as described in Gabber's excellent survey of the field [50]. If it can be established that a device is within, rather than outside, a physically secured building, immediately more trust can be placed in messages from that device. Also, it may be possible to authenticate that a device is what it says it is, because it is located where it is meant to be.

Tamper Resistance and Challenged Hardware

If security-sensitive devices must be subject to general access, it may be sufficient to use mildly tamper-resistant casings (as in our straw-man proposal in Section 18.3.1), as long as the limitations are understood [51]. The sheer numbers of devices can be used to offer sufficient protection by designing the whole system to be resistant to compromise of a minority of devices. SPINS [52] is an example of this approach, which has been implemented on Berkeley motes (Fig. 18.12). It consists of two message security primitives — SNEP for confidentiality and µTESLA for message authenticity and integrity. Both are designed to provide strong protection despite extremely limited hardware, ruling out the exponentiation required for asymmetric cryptography. Further, each data source needs to authenticate its communications to a large group of receivers, ruling out the use of shared keys too. So µTESLA[19] derives a new form of asymmetry for its keys from the one-way passage of time (Fig. 18.13). In SPINS, these primitives are built up into a secure sensor network system bootstrapped from an association with a base station.

Key Management

Public key (asymmetric) cryptography requires considerable computing resources, so it is considered infeasible on miniature devices for the foreseeable future. Even on high-speed computers, asymmetric keys tend to only be used to bootstrap lighter-

---

[19]µTESLA is based on TESLA, our own joint work with Carnegie Mellon University, UC Berkeley, and IBM for lightweight, per-packet authentication of broadcast multimedia streams. It is currently in the process of standardisation through the IETF [53].

Fig. 18.12   A Berkeley mote — generic sensor node manufactured by Crossbow.
[Photo courtesy of UC Berkeley, EECS]

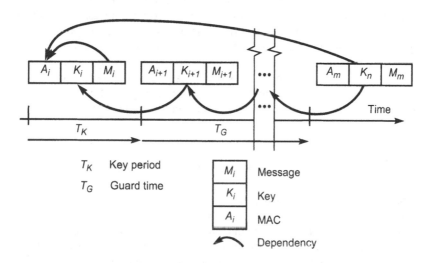

Fig. 18.13   TESLA source authentication for group communications. A key and a message authentication code (MAC) accompany each message. But they both depend on future keys not known to receivers. In advance the source generates a sequence of keys by repeating a simple one-way function. Each key period, it reveals a new key back along the sequence. But, for the MAC, it uses a key it will reveal later, thus committing to a key it guarantees no one else will know for at least the guard-time (typically 500 ms). As the source reveals each key commitment, every receiver can be sure earlier messages were authentic, giving slightly delayed but strong authentication for challenged hardware.

weight symmetric cryptography by exchange of a symmetric key. Without the ability to use public keys, it is hard to bootstrap a secure system of miniature devices by authenticating that the source of the initial keys is trusted. This is why SPINS (above) cannot bootstrap its authentication with any trusted identity, being limited to having to trust the base-station owner, which it authenticates by locality.

Stajano and Anderson [17] propose that a useful key establishment primitive for miniature devices would be physical touch. That is, a master key can be established in a device when it is placed in contact with a mother device. This key cannot then be overridden by the touch of another device. Only the original mother can release the device from its mother's binding, after which it can be bound to the first new mother that touches it. The reliance on touch can be relaxed to include proximity [54]. Chan et al [55] establish keys by giving each of a set of sensors a different sub-set of a large set of random keys prior to deployment. It uses the increased probability of any two nodes sharing common keys to bootstrap key establishment.

Once initial keys are established, key management procedures must be used to refresh the keys actually employed for message cryptography [56], reducing the time attackers have to guess the keys in use by brute-force methods (as in our straw-man proposal in Section 18.3.1). However, when broadcasting secrets to a constrained group, traditional key management techniques developed for one-to-one communications cannot be used, because the authorised membership of the group may change over time.

One approach is to assume the presence of a stable set of trusted event mediator nodes (see Section 18.2.3). Then messages are sent to these mediators and group members form a one-to-one security association with any one of these mediators. However, trust in stable intermediaries is neither generic nor necessary in pervasive computing scenarios (or across the Internet at large). A preferred approach is for the message to be encrypted with a group key (using that classic oxymoron, the secret shared over a large group) at source, and remain encrypted throughout its end-to-end journey, at least avoiding sharing the key unnecessarily with intermediate nodes. As end-points join and leave the group, the group key is changed. Moyer et al provide a useful overview of the issues in group key management and a survey of solutions at the time [57].

18.3.7   Ancillary Communications Services

Throughout the chapter so far, we have kept our focus on the rudimentary functions necessary for communications to realise a pervasive computing vision. Beyond these, a richer set of ancillary communications services may be necessary for each specific application: search and discovery, group forming, session co-ordination, certification, transactional messaging, causal message ordering, and so on.

There are two schools of thought on how to achieve all but the most rudimentary function of forwarding and routing:

- bundled — functions embedded within routers and relays throughout the messaging network (e.g. the event mediation service[20]);

- unbundled — communications services separately provided by third parties (e.g. event archives) or by the joint efforts of peer end-points (e.g. authentication and confidentiality).

Both approaches are distributed, they merely differ in whether the act of relaying is unavoidably bundled with other functions or not. In the unbundled approach, relays act as common carriers, irrespective of the messages being passed.

Our instincts are to always try to design unbundled functions (which can then optionally be collocated with the relaying function). But each case must be taken on

---

[20] This may itself be an overlay network built on more rudimentary primitives, but it consists of message relays itself.

its merits, and reasoned justifications given, rather than following the end-to-end design principle as a religion. We have given these reasoned arguments throughout.

But once we move from rudimentary to higher-level functions as listed above, there is no question that they are best designed so that they can be separated from the basic networking service. In this respect, they have less impact on network design, justifying ruling their detailed discussion out of the scope of this chapter.

18.4   Business Implications

18.4.1   Trends

Over the last couple of decades asynchronous programming has become prevalent, at least for non-networked code local to the machine's own bus (e.g. an event listener is set for a mouse click event and, when it triggers, the code checks where the mouse pointer is and calls the relevant function). This trend will extend to distributed programming, though initially through the use of intermediary message servers rather than direct peer-to-peer remote procedure calls. As computing becomes more interfaced to the wider physical world, we can expect distributed asynchronous programming to become commonplace. Crowcroft envisages 10^{10} event messages per second worldwide [41]. We have already explained that, if we expect trillions of devices, there will be orders of magnitude more event sources and listeners (Section 18.3.4). This warns us that the potential growth of pervasive computing will be dependent on the successful deployment of the pub-sub mode of group communications, whether directly in the network infrastructure (e.g. as IP multi-cast [12]) or using overlays [15, 58].

The Value of Group Forming
Metcalfe's law predicts that the value of a network is $O(n^2)$, because each of n users has the potential to communicate with $n-1$ other users. Reed's law goes beyond this, pointing out that n users[21] have the potential to create 2^n different groups between themselves [59], making the value of a network that supports formation of groups rise exponentially $O(2^n)$. Although neither law is intended to be a guide to prediction of actual market size, they give a feel for what shape the market growth curve should take in each case. They certainly show that a business that allows unfettered creation of groups ('Yahoo Groups for machines') will tend to be popular. If growth in computing device numbers remains exponential (the predicted doubling time is about 0.6 years), then growth in group numbers will be doubly exponential, that is $O(2^{2^t})$. Or put another way, if we are to create thousands of trillions of groups by 2020, worldwide group creation facilities will have to have been capable of creating millions of groups every second.

Whose Business? Which Customer?
If devices are spread throughout the fabric of our lives, in shared office blocks, in industrial units, in public places, and in private dwellings, up to a point, networks of

---
[21] Or processes?

devices will be able to act as their own infrastructure. But part of the capacity of global networking infrastructure and all the capacity of ancillary services dedicated to asynchronous messaging will also be required. Why would anyone invest in this infrastructure? For the public good? For private gain? What socio-economic mechanisms will cause these prerequisites of the pervasive computing vision to happen?[22]

Because the impact of each device is so small, the question of who is responsible for its share of infrastructure becomes blurred. Many assume that infrastructure operators will cover their costs by cross-subsidising infrastructure from higher-level services. But it is unrealistic to expect any company to be successful enough at these very different businesses for one to sustain the other, given competition from specialists in services for pervasive computing.

So, if a washing machine detects new fabrics in its wash-load and looks up their washing instructions over the Internet, who should arrange for the required infrastructure and its maintenance? The manufacturer? The retailer? The house-holder? Who should pay for the service engineer to come out to a faulty washing machine only to discover the fault is due to the householder's not paying their Internet bill? If sensor A is measuring light levels for one application, but also relaying for sensor B, they may both need global connectivity, but should relay A charge sensor B for its services?

Clearly, there will be many informal acts of give and take over what will often be trivial issues. But many tiny acts of take without any give mount up. Solutions to these free-rider problems must be found if the vision of pervasive computing is to be realised.[23]

Pricing

Assuming someone (probably not the end user) will take responsibility for paying the bills for the communications infrastructure necessary to support pervasive computing, how will it be priced? The casual observer would expect event messaging services to be flat charged (irrespective of usage). Usage charging[24] would incentivise responsible use of resources, but we have seen that miniature devices already have good reason to be parsimonious, particularly to conserve battery power.

Our intuition is that flat charging will prevail wherever pervasive computing is 'scavenging' resources provided for other purposes (e.g. the wider Internet). But where messaging services are provided specifically, the potential sheer volume of messaging will tend to force the introduction of usage charging. We have also explained that many applications will be part of vital business processes, their communications requiring priority over more optional messages during surges in demand. Clearly, priority service will attract premium charging. Given priority will rarely have to be exercised, premiums are unlikely to be levied only when priority is needed (usage). Rather they will be paid regularly in advance for the right to priority as a contingency (flat).

---

[22] The wider question of who will have the incentive to invest in deployment of the devices themselves is just as valid, but outside the scope of this chapter.

[23] See http://www.mmapps.org/ for our collaborative research on motivations in peer-to-peer communities.

[24] In bulk — it goes without saying that itemisation is out of the question.

Pub-Sub Business Model

Traditionally, multi-cast has been associated with efficient distribution of streamed media, but it is also suitable for the timely delivery of asynchronous events. The sessions are just considerably shorter. One of the reasons pub-sub has not been widely deployed for media distribution is the desire to re-create content distribution business models over it that mimic those used today, by both the content and the network industry. Specifically, they expect the distribution network to charge the sender proportionately to the number of receivers.

Therefore, the full potential of pervasive computing will not be realised unless we can establish a viable separation between the business models for media distribution and for event notification. It is clearly not feasible to charge for event notification messaging per session (i.e. per event), but, if pub-sub were charged flat rate, it would be hard to prevent the same mechanisms being used to bypass media distribution pricing.

To Bundle or to Unbundle?

When we discussed function placement (Section 18.2.4), we recommended that functions should not be assigned to specific equipment. Rather, we advised that the system should be designed open. Then, it is still perfectly possible to bundle functions together into a piece of equipment (e.g. if a vendor believes the business model is advantageous). But bundling is chosen, not inherent to the technical design.

Throughout, we have shown that there are rarely technical reasons to lock in even rudimentary communications services with the business of operating a dumb pub-sub network.[25] But, despite having no inherent lock-in, we can predict that messaging services will make good business for network operators in the next few years. However, as the pervasive computing scenario develops, we predict that all, or at least most of these services, will be self-provided more competitively by distributed software across the pervasive computing base. Therefore, the technology should be designed for this transition from closed to open from the outset ('Design for Tussle' [60]), justifying our intuition of an open design closed by policy choice.

18.5 Summary

We have given controversial but reasoned explanations for why most pervasive computing will largely be connected globally and for why it will rely heavily on models of the physical world within the information world. It is infeasible to imagine that any arbitrary pair of computing devices will be able to talk directly to each other just because they are in physical proximity. Instead physical devices will be bound to information models of themselves, which will meet in cyberspace, communications between devices taking place across cyberspace, as often as by direct wireless connectivity. Continuous co-ordination between the physical and information worlds will lead to a web of tens of billions of messages per second across the world's networks. We have explained why we predict that asynchronous event messaging using publish-subscribe will be the predominant mode of communications for pervasive computing. Pub-sub will mostly be based on the

---

[25] Message aggregation and duplication — concast and multi-cast — being exceptions.

multi-cast mode (whether native or overlay), once messages from the physical world have hit the first gateway to the rest of the Internet (the first connection to mains power). But, if there is a multi-hop wireless network between the physical world and that first gateway, in order to conserve power, concast will be the most likely communications mode up to that gateway.

We have questioned the assumption that tiny cheap computing devices will be considered disposable and application-specific. Economies of scale in volume device manufacturing will always favour reuse of the investment in generic device designs, whether each unit is disposable or not. Also, the investment in deploying devices will be higher than their cost, tending to encourage new ways to combine deployed devices to novel ends. Therefore, working out the most generic communications facilities for miniature devices is a central part of the research agenda.

Having set out the grand challenge, we have surveyed its implications on each rudimentary element of communications — routing, addressing, congestion control, reliable delivery, security, etc. We have described the problems precisely and the various main approaches being adopted by the research community to solve them, giving rationale.

We have exploded some myths particularly explaining why it is often more effective and less complex to create an x-like system from un-x-like parts (e.g. a reliable system from unreliable parts, or a secure system from insecure parts). We have also corrected some misunderstandings that the research community seems to have carried over from their previous research areas. For instance, it is fruitless to try to control congestion by varying the data rate of reality and it is fruitless to expect receivers to know when they have missed an asynchronous message, which by definition they were not expecting anyway.

Finally, we have introduced the implications of pervasive computing on the business of communications, explaining the trouble the commercial community has with the pub-sub model and emphasising the importance of group creation services. Many open questions remain, particularly concerning how to promote investment in pervasive computing infrastructure, given the benefits are so thinly spread, making collection of return on investment costly, even with flat pricing models. We have explained why 'open by design but closed by policy choice' will still be the appropriate commercial approach, given communications designs will still need to be generic, even though the devices on which they are implemented will be disposable.

References

1. Weiser M. The Computer for the 21st Century. Scientific American, September 1991:265: 3:94–104.

2. Durand A, Huitema C. The Host-Density Ratio for Address Assignment Efficiency: An Update on the H Ratio. Request for Comments 3194, Internet Engineering Task Force, November 2001.

3. Gershenfeld N and Krikorian R. Building Intelligence. June 2002 — http://www.media. mit.edu/physics/projects/IP/bldg/bi/

4. Krikorian R. Internet 0: Bringing IP to the Leaf Node. April 2003 — http://www.bitwaste.com/wasted-bits/blog/conferences/et2003/I0-oreilly.pdf

5. Yokoji S, Takahashi K, and Miura N. Kokono Search: A Location-based Search Engine. Proc Tenth International World Wide Web Conference (WWW10) poster, May 2001 — http://www10.org/cdrom/posters/contents.html#a5

6. Buyukkokten O et al. Exploiting Geographical Location Information of Web Pages. (Informal) Proc Workshop on Web Databases (WebDB'99), ACM, June 1999 — http://citeseer.ist.psu.edu/buyukkokten99exploiting.html

7. Shrikumar H. IPic — A Match Head Sized Web Server. October 2002 — http://www-ccs.cs.umass.edu/shri/iPic.html

8. Shrikumar H. Connecting Absolutely Everything. White Paper WP010308, Ipsil, 2001 — http://www.ipsil.com/resources/whitepapers/connecting.pdf

9. Oki B el al. The Information Bus: An Architecture for Extensible Distributed Systems. Proc 14th ACM Symposium on Operating Systems Principles, 1993 — http://www.cs.utah.edu/~retrac/cs7460/infobus.pdf

10. Intanagonwiwat C, Govindan R, and Estrin D. Directed Diffusion: A Scalable and Robust Communication Paradigm for Sensor Networks. Proc ACM International Conference on Mobile Computing and Networks (MobiCOM'00), ACM, August 2000 — http://www.isi.edu/scadds/projects/diffusion.html#publications

11. Soppera A et al. GAP: The Generic Announcement Protocol for Event Messaging. Proc London Communication Symposium (LCS'03), UCL, September 2003 — http://www.ee.ucl.ac.uk/lcs/papers2003/103.pdf

12. Deering S E. Multicast Routing in Internetworks and Extended LANs. Proc ACM SIGCOMM'88, August 1988.

13. Bacon J et al. Generic Support for Distributed Applications. IEEE Computer, March 2000 — http://www.cl.cam.ac.uk/Research/SRG/opera/publications/prc-2002.html#2000

14. Saltzer J H, Reed D P, and Clark D D. End-to-End Arguments in System Design. ACM Transactions on Computer Systems, November 1984:2:4:277–288 — http://web.mit.edu/Saltzer/www/publications/endtoend/endtoend.pdf (An earlier version appeared in the Second International Conference on Distributed Computing Systems, April, 1981:509–512.)

15. Rowstron A et al. SCRIBE: The Design of a Large-Scale Event Notification Infrastructure. In: Crowcroft J, Hofmann M (editors). Proc 3rd International COST264 Workshop on Networked Group Communication (NGC'01), Springer LNCS 2233, November 2001:30–34 — http://link.springer.de/link/service/series/0558/bibs/2233/22330030.htm

16. Heidemann J et al. Building Efficient Wireless Sensor Networks with Low-Level Naming. Proc Symposium on Operating Systems Principles, ACM, October 2001:146–159 — http://www.isi.edu/~johnh/PAPERS/Heidemann01c.html

17. Stajano F and Anderson R. The Resurrecting Duckling: Security Issues for *ad hoc* Wireless Networks. In: Christianson B, Crispo B, Roe M (editors). Proc 7th International Workshop on Security Protocols, Springer LNCS 1796, April 1999:172–194 — http://citeseer.ist.psu.edu/227971.html

18. Briscoe B. MARKS: Zero Side Effect Multicast Key Management Using Arbitrarily Revealed Key Sequences. Proc 1st International COST264 Workshop on Networked Group Communication (NGC'99), Springer LNCS 1736, November 1999 — http://www.btexact.com/publications/papers?doc=70250

19. Floyd S et al. A Reliable Multicast Framework for Lightweight Sessions and Application Level Framing. Proc ACM SIGCOMM'95, Computer Communication Review, October 1995:25:4:342–356 — http://www.acm.org/sigcomm/ccr/archive/1995/conf/floyd.html

20. Fall K. Delay Tolerant Networking Research Group. Working group charter, Internet Research Task Force, 2002 — http://www.dtnrg.org/

21. Fall K. A Delay Tolerant Network Architecture for Challenged Internets. Proc ACM SIGCOMM'03, Computer Communication Review, October 2003:33:4:27–34 — http://portal.acm.org/citation.cfm?id=863960&dl=ACM&coll=portal

22. Kahn J M et al. Emerging Challenges: Mobile Networking for 'Smart Dust'. Journal of Communications and Networks, September 2000:2:3:188–196 — http://citeseer.ist.psu.edu/kahn00emerging.html

23. Zhou L et al. Corner-cube Retroreflectors Based on Structure-assisted Assembly for Freespace Optical Communication. IEEE Journal of Microelectromechanical Systems, June 2003:12:3:233–242 — http://www-ee.stanford.edu/~jmk/pubs/ccr.jmems.pdf

24. Chlamtac I, Petrioli C, and Redi J. Energy Conservation in Access Protocols for Mobile Computing and Communication. Microprocessors and Microsystems Journal, March 1998:1:20–32.

25. Chockalingam A and Zorzi M. Energy Efficiency of Media Access Protocols for Mobile Data Networks. IEEE Transactions on Communications, November 1998:46:1:1418–1421 — http://citeseer.nj.nec.com/259740.html

26. Kravets R and Krishnan P. Application-Driven Power Management for Mobile Communication. Wireless Networks, 2000:6:263–277 — http://citeseer.nj.nec.com/kravets98applicationdriven.html

27. Soppera A, Burbridge T, and Nekovee M. Index-based Event Messaging. Proc International Workshop on Large-Scale Group Communication, October 2003 — http://srds2003.cnuce.cnr.it/papers/soppera.pdf

28. Tschudin C, Lundgren H, and Nordström E. Embedding MANETs in the Real World. Proc Conference on Personal Wireless Communications (TWC'03), IFIP, September 2003 — http://www.it.uu.se/research/group/core/publications.php?pub_id=41

29. Perkins C, Belding-Royer E, and Das S. *Ad hoc* on-demand distance vector (AODV) routing. RFC 3561, Internet Engineering Task Force, July 2003 — http://www.tcs.hut.fi/~anttit/manet/aodv/

30. Baker F. An Outsider's View of MANET. Internet Draft, Internet Engineering Task Force, March 2002 — http://bgp.potaroo.net/ietf/old-ids/draft-baker-manet-review-01.txt

31. Singh S, Woo M, and Raghavendra C S. Power-Aware Routing in Mobile *ad hoc* Networks. Proc ACM International Conference on Mobile Computing and Networks (MobiCOM'98), 1998:181–190 — http://citeseer.nj.nec.com/singh98poweraware.html

32. Chang J H and Tassiulas L. Energy Conserving Routing in Wireless Ad-hoc Networks. Proc IEEE Conference on Computer Communications, 2000:22–31 — http://citeseer.nj.nec.com/chang00energy.html

33. Madden S R et al. Supporting Aggregate Queries over Ad-hoc Wireless Sensor Networks. Proc Workshop on Mobile Computing and Systems Applications, 2002 — http://www.cs.berkeley.edu/~madden/madden_aggregation.pdf

34. Cain B, Speakman T, and Towsley D. Generic Router Assist (GRA) Building Block: Motivation and Architecture. Internet draft, Internet Engineering Task Force, March 2000 — http://bgp.potaroo.net/ietf/old-ids/draft-ietf-rmt-gra-arch-01.txt

35. Duros E et al. A Link-Layer Tunneling Mechanism for Unidirectional Links. RFC 3077, Internet Engineering Task Force, March 2001.

36. Perlman R. Network Layer Protocols with Byzantine Robustness. Technical Report 429, MIT, Based on PhD thesis, October 1988 — http://www.lcs.mit.edu/publications/specpub.php?id=997

37. Zhu D, Gritter M, and Cheriton D R. Feedback-based Routing. Computer Communication Review, January 2003:33:1:71–76 — http://portal.acm.org/citation.cfm?id=774774&dl=ACM&coll=portal

38. Law Y et al. Assessing Security-Critical Energy-Efficient Sensor Networks. In: Gritzalis D, Vimercati S D C D, Samarati P, Katsikas S (editors). Proc 18th TC11 Intl Conf on Information Security. IFIP, Kluwer, May 2003:459–463 — http://www.ub.utwente.nl/webdocs/ctit/1/00000087.pdf

39. Adler M et al. Channelisation Problem in Large Scale Data Dissemination. Proc IEEE International Conference on Network Protocols (ICNP'01), 2001 — http://www.cs.umass.edu/~micah/pubs/channelization.ps

40. Thaler D and Handley M. On the Aggregatability of Multicast Forwarding State. Proc IEEE Conference on Computer Communications (Infocom 2000), March 2000 — http://www.ieee-infocom.org/2000/papers/632.ps

41. Crowcroft J et al. Channel Islands in a Reflective Ocean: Large Scale Event Distribution in Heterogeneous Networks. IEEE Communications Magazine, September 2002:40:9:112–115 — http://www.cl.cam.ac.uk/Research/SRG/opera/publications/2002-pubs.html

42. Kulik J. Fast and Flexible Forwarding for Internet Subscription Systems. Proc 2nd Intl Workshop on Distributed Event-based Systems, ACM Press, June 2003:1–8 — http://doi.acm.org/10.1145/966618.966635

43. Crowcroft J et al. Plutarch: An Argument for Network Pluralism. SIGCOMM FDNA'03, ACM, 2003 — http://www.cl.cam.ac.uk/~jac22/out/plutarch.pdf

44. Brownlee N and Ma A. NeTraMet Flow Lifetimes and Implications for Routing Context. Data in and out of UC San Diego Supercomputer Center collected June 2002 — http://www.caida.org/analysis/workload/netramet/lifetimes/

45. Beverly R and Claffy K. Wide-Area IP Multicast Traffic Characterisation. IEEE Network, January/February 2003 — http://www.caida.org/outreach/papers/2003/mcastworkchar/

46. Crovella M and Bestavros A. Self-Similarity in World Wide Web Traffic: Evidence and Possible Causes. IEEE/ACM Transactions on Networking, 1997:5:6:835–846 — http://citeseer.ist.psu.edu/22080.html

47. Wan C Y et al. CODA: Congestion Detection and Avoidance in Sensor Networks. Proc First International Conference on Embedded Networked Sensor Systems, ACM, 2003:266–279 — http://comet.ctr.columbia.edu/armstrong/

48. Speakman T et al. PGM Reliable Transport Protocol Specification. RFC 3208, Internet Engineering Task Force, December 2001.

49. Sastry N, Shankar U, and Wagner D. Secure Verification of Location Claims. Proc Workshop on Wireless Security (WiSe 2003), ACM, September 2003 — http://www.cs.berkeley.edu/~nks/locprove/

50. Gabber E and Wool A. On Location-Restricted Services. IEEE Network, 1999:13:6:44–52.

51. Anderson R and Kuhn M G. Tamper Resistance — A Cautionary Note. Proc Second USENIX Electronic Commerce Workshop, November 1996:1–21 — http://www.cl.cam.ac.uk/users/rja14/#Reliability

52. Perrig A et al. SPINS: Security Protocols for Sensor Networks. Proc ACM International Conference on Mobile Computing and Networks (Mobicom'01), July 2001:189–199 — http://citeseer.ist.psu.edu/568886.html

53. Perrig A et al. TESLA: Multicast Source Authentication Transform Introduction. Internet draft-ietf-msec-tesla-intro-03.txt, Internet Engineering Task Force, August 2004.

54. Juels A. 'Yoking-proofs' for RFID Tags. In: Sandhu R, Thomas R (editors). Proc First International Workshop on Pervasive Computing and Communication Security. IEEE Press, 2004 — http://www.rsasecurity.com/rsalabs/staff/bios/ajuels/publications/rfidyoke/

55. Chan H, Perrig A, and Song D. Random Key Predistribution Schemes for Sensor Networks. Proc IEEE Symposium on Security and Privacy, 2003 — http://www.ece.cmu.edu/~adrian/publications.html

56. Basagni S et al. Secure Pebblenet. Proc International Symposium on Mobile Ad Hoc Networking and Computing (MobiHoc'01), ACM, October 2001:156–163 — http://www.ece.neu.edu/faculty/basagni/publications.html

57. Moyer M J, Rao J R, and Rohatgi P. A Survey of Multicast Security Issues in Multicast Communications. IEEE Network, 1999:13:6:12–23 — http://www.comsoc.org/

58. Ratnasamy S et al. Application-Level Multicast Using Content-Addressable Networks. Proc 3rd International COST264 Workshop on Networked Group Communication (NGC'01), Springer LNCS 2233, November 2001:LNCS2233:14–29 — http://link.springer.de/link/service/series/0558/bibs/2233/22330014.htm

59. Reed D P. That Sneaky Exponential — Beyond Metcalfe's Law to the Power of Community Building. Online Supplement to Article in Context magazine, 1999 — http://www.reed.com/Papers/GFN/reedslaw.html

60. Clark D et al. Tussle in Cyberspace: Defining Tomorrow's Internet. Proc ACM SIGCOMM'02, Computer Communication Review, August 2002:32:4 — http://www.acm.org/sigcomm/sigcomm2002/papers/tussle.pdf

19

Autonomic Computing for Pervasive ICT — A Whole-System Perspective

M Shackleton, F Saffre, R Tateson, E Bonsma, and C Roadknight

19.1   Introduction

Pervasive ICT [1] heralds a world full of vast numbers of devices and software entities that are able to communicate with one another. For devices, the communication will typically be via wireless networking technologies such as WiFi, Bluetooth, or 3G. A key challenge to realising the pervasive ICT vision, or at least to make it a truly useful vision, is the development of an associated set of technologies that will allow these underlying components to be assembled in real time, to provide useful applications and services. Initial progress towards this goal is proceeding under several initiatives such as Web Services, GRID computing, and peer-to-peer (P2P) computing. These areas in fact have many fundamental underlying concerns in common.

Even if we leave pervasive ICT to one side for a moment, there is already a recognition that existing ICT systems are growing in complexity to such an extent that they are becoming unmanageable [2]. This complexity stems from the sheer scale of current and envisaged ICT deployments, the heterogeneity of their infrastructural components, and the unanticipated interactions between these components that may lead to failures or sub-optimal system behaviour. The cost of the hardware itself continues to fall, but the cost of trouble-shooting this complexity and fixing the associated problems is increasingly dominating the total cost of ownership (TCO) of large ICT deployments. All of the major IT companies have programmes seeking to address these underlying issues, but perhaps it is IBM that has enunciated the issues and its approach to addressing them most clearly by launching its 'Autonomic Computing' initiative [3]. This initiative is one example of a 'nature-inspired' approach in that it draws inspiration from the human autonomic nervous system where many functions, such as breathing or heart rate, are regulated by the system itself without conscious effort. By analogy, IBM is seeking to create ICT systems that are more 'autonomic' (self-managing) in the following ways:

- self-configuring — adaptation to IT system changes such as new nodes becoming available, or going off-line;

- self-optimising — tuning resources and load balancing;

- self-protecting — guard against damage from attacks or failures;

- self-healing — recovery from, or work around, failed components.

The manner in which IBM is seeking to achieve its goal of dealing with system complexity and making systems that are increasingly autonomic, and thus significantly reducing the TCO of ICT deployments, is described in its autonomic computing blueprint [4], roadmap [5], and associated documents [6]. We agree that these are important challenges for research in ICT today and would go further to assert that the vision of pervasive ICT could not be realised at the scales envisaged without the development of these associated new technologies. In addition, such self-managing solutions will play an important role in making the pervasive environment 'invisible' so that users need not become full-time system administrators to their pervasive home environment and devices. In this chapter we describe four example systems exhibiting behaviour and associated engineering approaches that cover each of the self-managing characteristics listed above. We introduce these example systems for two reasons. Firstly, they tackle problems with real-world relevance that begin to highlight design heuristics/principles that have proved useful to realising autonomic and adaptive solutions. We expect that this class of approach to designing autonomic solutions will similarly prove useful in tackling other problems and will, after further refinement, become part of mainstream ICT system design methodologies in the future. Secondly, the example systems highlight the importance of certain approaches to design that are not yet very well addressed by the existing autonomic computing initiative (or associated research). However, we expect they will prove to be important to realising future robust, large-scale, and self-managing ICT deployments. In particular, these approaches to system design seek to tackle the relative importance of the interactions between components on the overall whole-system (or global) behaviour. This is illustrated in Fig. 19.1.

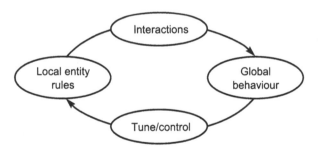

Fig. 19.1   A view of how components within a complex system interact to produce overall global behaviour. The diagram also shows how the design can be iteratively refined, by observing global behaviour and tuning local rules accordingly, with complex systems analysis playing a useful role in this cycle.

19.2   Illustrative Example Systems

The four following examples describe systems that have successfully tackled real-world problems in the diverse application domains of mobile networks, network security, P2P information management, and adaptive service provision. Referring back to the IBM autonomic classifications, these examples address problems involving, respectively, self-optimising resource allocation, self-protecting security management, a self-configuring information space, and self-optimising (load-balanced) service provision. Several of the examples also exhibit self-healing behaviour, in that they can cope robustly with individual components/nodes that fail while maintaining appropriate overall system-level behaviour.

19.2.1   'Flyphones' — Channel (Resource) Allocation

The allocation of channels in a mobile telephone network is one example of a range of problems involving allocating resources in geographically or logically dispersed systems. The operator of the mobile network must decide which base stations will be permitted to use which channels. This choice is constrained by the conflicting desires to provide each base station with sufficient channels to meet peak call demand, while avoiding situations in which the channels in use at neighbouring base stations cause interference and hence low quality of calls.

Channel allocation, in common with most problems of this type, has traditionally been solved by centralised optimisation. Information about the network, gathered over some representative period of time (e.g. one month), is fed into an optimisation algorithm such as a simulated annealer. Simulated annealing, and related techniques, rely on the idea that an example solution to the problem can be assigned a 'score' based on the predicted performance of the entire network if this solution was adopted. By producing a series of subtly different solutions and comparing their scores, such algorithms are able to find their way to better solutions.

However, this approach relies on the ability to accurately model the network such that every proposed solution can be given a score. In situations where accurate models are not available, because information is either unavailable or outdated, and particularly if the network is changing rapidly such that good solutions themselves quickly become useless, it is desirable to have a dynamic channel allocation strategy that can provide good performance without global knowledge.

We have produced such an algorithm by drawing inspiration from nature. The cells in developing animals are able to produce a highly detailed and accurate macro-structure (the adult form of the animal) without any global knowledge. The cells rely on interactions with their immediate and mid-range neighbours to self-organise. One example is bristle formation in the fruit fly *Drosophila melanogaster*. Many cells in the developing larva have the ability to form bristles, and they send inhibitory signals to their neighbours indicating that those neighbours (who may be sending such signals of their own) should not form bristles. This mutually inhibitory 'conversation' continues for a few hours, by the end of which most cells have abandoned the ability to make bristles, leaving a few 'winners' to go ahead and produce these structures in the adult fly.

To produce a channel allocation algorithm inspired by this process requires two steps. Firstly, it is necessary to sacrifice central control and allow the base stations the same level of autonomy enjoyed by the fruit fly cells. The base stations can decide for themselves which channels they will use. Then we provide the base stations with the 'mutual inhibition' logic (local rules) for interacting with their neighbours (see Fig. 19.2). Put simply, each base station must send signals to its neighbours attempting to stop them from using its 'favourite' channels, and it must respond to such signals from its neighbours by reducing its 'preference' for their favourite channels. Sometimes there will be a 'clash' whereby two base stations both

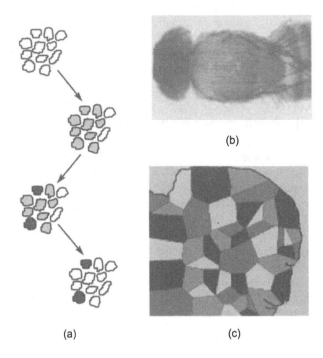

Fig. 19.2   (a) The mutual inhibition process that limits the number of cells adopting the neural 'bristle-making' fate. Many have the potential (grey) but only a few realise that potential (black) while inhibiting their neighbours (white). (b) The pattern of bristles that results in the adult fly. (c) A map of East Anglia in the UK, with the coverage areas of base stations in a mobile telephone network shaded as if there were only four frequencies to allocate.

want a particular channel, and then just as in the fruit fly, this will be resolved with one base station emerging victorious and the other relinquishing that channel.

The algorithm has been tested in network simulations of both civilian and military wireless communications networks spanning the range from fairly simple to rather complex scenarios [7–9]. It successfully self-configures to provide good solutions to the global problem. More importantly, it brings with it the ability to continue to function well even in a network that is losing or gaining nodes, where nodes themselves may move and hence encounter new neighbours, and where accurate up-to-date information about the overall network is not available. In this sense it is also self-healing. The algorithm also evades scaling problems since it relies on the elements of the network to perform their own local decision making — hence as the network gets bigger, its processing power increases exactly in step with this growth.

19.2.2   'ADDICT' — Adaptive Response to Threat

Network security in general, and intrusion detection (IDS) and response in particular, provide another striking example of a context where the cost and practical limitations of centralised management become more evident by the day. The combination of ever-increasing network speed/capacity with the rapid evolution of new, more efficient 'cyber-threats' (e.g. ultra-fast worms) has created a very volatile situation. Even if methods for monitoring network activity are available, it is a fact of life that data cannot be analysed, tactical decisions made, and defensive measures implemented in time to contain a developing threat if all these processes are taking place centrally.

Of course, pervasive computing, in the form of enhanced mobility, portability, and diversity of interacting devices, is making this situation worse. Seamless connectivity and ubiquitous access effectively signal the end of any permanent distinction between secure and insecure network environments, a phenomenon that has been adequately named 'the disappearing perimeter' [10]. In practice, unless a third way can be found, we are facing a bleak alternative between denying services by default (which goes against the very principles of pervasive ICT and somewhat defeats its purpose) and leaving our networks wide open to attack.

Concretely, what is needed is a method to bridge the gap between a host-based (HIDS) and a network-based (NIDS) intrusion detection system. The former typically scales well because every device is in charge of monitoring its immediate neighbourhood (and so processing power grows linearly with network size). On the other hand, it is incapable of recognising suspicious global activity patterns, because scattered data does not allow for the distinction between 'security noise' (e.g. the odd probing of IP addresses) and a concerted attack by a malicious entity. The latter is an archetypal example of the shortcomings of centralised management — if infinite processing power were available, NIDS would in theory be capable of immediately picking up subtle correlations between events happening throughout the network and identify a serious threat. However, in practice, this ideal case is obviously never realised and so network-based intrusion detection is usually conducted off-line, which turns it into a sophisticated forensic tool rather than a real-time protection system.

We have proposed that a biologically inspired form of inhibitory signalling between hosts could be used to overcome both difficulties. In 'ADDICT' [11], individual devices compute an 'alert level' on the basis of locally detectable network activity (equivalent to HIDS), and then exchange beacon signals with other nodes, which are effectively a digest of security-relevant information (i.e. the alert level, but also identity, internal state, etc). The collected beacons are then used by every member to update its own alert level x as per Eq. (19.1):

$$\frac{dx}{dt} = \frac{x(1-x)}{N}\left(N - n + \alpha \sum_{i=1}^{n} x_i\right) - \beta x , \qquad \text{......} (19.1)$$

where N is the number of perceived devices (sources of network traffic), n is the number of identifiable/trusted devices among them, and α and β are tunable parameters. This creates a feedback loop allowing the community of peers to rapidly converge towards a state reflective of the globally perceived threat level (similar to NIDS).

Once the alert level is mapped on to predefined security stances (probably involving use of a personal firewall), ADDICT should be capable of rapid adaptation to changing conditions and real-time redrawing of the trusted domain boundary. This dynamic perimeter defence can accurately be described as an enabler for self-configuring, self-protecting, and self-healing pervasive networks as it could allow for immediate reaction to security breaches as they are forming (e.g. aggressive scanning by a rogue device) and spontaneous containment of the corresponding threat through isolation of all sources of suspicious activity.

19.2.3 'SWAN' — Self-Organised Information Management

The peer-to-peer (P2P) paradigm fits autonomic computing very well. P2P infrastructures contain many nodes and lack centralised control. There can be large variations in the capabilities of the peer nodes. They are typically unreliable, and nodes can join and leave the system at any time. Despite this, P2P applications can be built that function reliably, automatically adapt to changes, optimise their configuration, and are able to cope with node failure and malicious attacks. This is made possible by various P2P technologies. One such technology is the small world adaptive network (SWAN) [12]. It is a distributed look-up system for P2P networks that can be used to find out the address of a node, given the key under which it is published. Nodes here can be anything that can be accessed through an underlying communications network, including computers, documents, services, and users. An important property of SWAN is that it is fully decentralised. This is done to make the system robust to failure and to ensure that the load is shared fairly across the computing nodes that contribute and participate in the look-up system.

SWAN is able to provide look-up functionality without resorting to centralised tables by letting nodes self-organise into a virtual network. Each node simply maintains a limited number of links to other nodes in the network. These links are used for handling look-up queries. For each incoming query, a node examines its links to find the node with a key that is closest to that of the target query. It then forwards the query to this neighbouring node, unless its own key is actually closer to the query. In the latter case, the receiving node replies with its own address. So each node uses only simple, local rules for handling incoming queries. Whether or not queries can be successfully answered this way, and the number of messages that are on average required per query, depends on the links that the nodes maintain. SWAN is engineered so that nodes self-organise into a network that meets specific properties. When these properties are met, queries are guaranteed to succeed and the number of messages that are required scales well with the total number of nodes.

More specifically, nodes self-organise into a 'small world network' [13]. Each node maintains a limited number of short-range links to nodes with different but similar keys. These links ensure that all nodes can be found. If, however, only these links were used, the number of messages that is needed does not scale well. There-fore, nodes also maintain a fixed number of long-range links to nodes with keys that differ more. Although these links are randomly chosen, the random process is designed such that the long-range links meet the distribution of lengths that is recommended by Kleinberg, which he mathematically proves to be optimal [14, 15]. This way, the number of messages required to find a node is proportional to $(\log N)^2$, where N is the total number of nodes.

The SWAN system illustrates that a good way to build a decentralised system is to base it on a solid theoretical foundation. In this case Kleinberg's theoretical work showed what the global properties of the small world network needed to be for nodes to effectively route queries using only local knowledge. Obviously, engineering the system may still involve tackling difficult issues. In the case of SWAN, for instance, the question of how nodes can self-organise into a network with the desired global properties, using only local knowledge and interactions, still had to be solved.

19.2.4   'Bacterial Plasmids' — Adaptive Service Provision on an Active Network

Data networks are continually growing and changing. Management and control of these networks will also need to change if they are to deliver an acceptable quality of service. External human control becomes untenable in most envisaged scenarios, especially if the network becomes more 'active'. Positioning the right active software in the right place at the right time is a combinatorially explosive problem.

We have proposed and tested a scalable solution to adaptive management of active service networks [16, 17] which suggests that a bacterium-inspired software distribution algorithm is well suited to the task. The approach treats mobile software and associated execution constraints as bacterial RNA (ribonucleic acid), and the execution environment in which it is run as the bacterium itself. The RNA decides how suited the bacterium is to its current location. So if the code is profitable, sections of the RNA (plasmids) spread around the network in search of further profitable locations. Alternatively, if the code is unused or unprofitable, its fitness declines until it is replaced or modified by RNA from a more successful organism. Figure 19.3 shows a possible future environment where active code inhabits a network of dynamic proxy servers. Requests for the services that the software provides are handled if the code is present and the subjective criteria (workload,

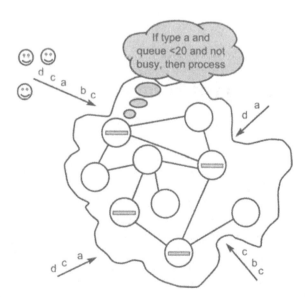

Fig. 19.3   Future 'active' network model. Dynamic proxy server nodes with active code have a bar, those without are empty. Incoming requests (a,b,c,d) are routed to the nearest live node by an underlying transport network.

queue lengths, cost, price, etc) are matched. The combination of code present on the device and the subjective criteria for use of this code amounts to the RNA of the node.

Mimicking the unmatched haste of bacterial evolution gives the network the required adaptability, while its distributed nature is inherently more robust than a centralised management approach. Genetic diversity is created in at least two ways, namely mutation and plasmid migration. Mutation involves the random alteration of just one value in a single rule. Plasmid migration involves genes from healthy individuals being shed or replicated into the environment and subsequently being absorbed into the genetic material of less healthy individuals. This intra-generation (bacterial) evolution adds a level of short-term adaptation over the longer-term inter-generation (Darwinian) evolution.

As load balancing and the distribution of new software are implicit parts of the reproductive and evolutionary nature of the algorithm, it is no surprise that these functions are performed so readily [17]. More complex functionality, such as allowing some varied quality of service, some payment-based security, and the ability to handle realistic traffic streams, were also demonstrated [16].

While external management is not required, it is supported in the guise of injectable policies. Active software can be manually placed on the network, with associated policies for its use; its adoption and proliferation will depend on user behaviour and this initial placement. The configuration can also be manually modified by injecting new fitness functions, e.g. instating a fitness function that gives no reward for running software would soon purge the network. This combination of 'hands-off' management with simple methods to enable intervention is a key requirement for the adoption of autonomic solutions, as it supports policy-driven management.

Ad hoc networks can also benefit from this kind of approach. The lower bandwidths, CPU power, and storage capacity of mobile devices make their automated optimal configuration a priority [18]. A real-world application of this method to a subset of *ad hoc* networks, and sensor networks, is now well under way [19, 20].

19.3   Discussion of Example Systems

The example systems discussed above cover a wide range of application and problem domains. However, each example exhibits one or more of the 'autonomic' self-managing characteristics — self-configuring, self-optimising, self-protecting, and/or self-healing. We will now consider certain common features that are highlighted by the examples that may prove useful as design heuristics for the creation of future autonomic ICT systems. It is probably worth noting that autonomic computing defines a series of maturity levels [21] — basic, managed, predictive, adaptive, autonomic. The examples we have described should best be considered as 'adaptive' (i.e. takes action itself based on the situation) or possibly fully 'autonomic' (i.e. policy-driven system activities, such as resource allocation).

Clearly, the autonomic computing initiative is biologically inspired in origin, in that it explicitly refers to (and aspires to mimic) the characteristics of the human autonomic nervous system. This natural system regulates many bodily functions in humans, such as heart rate. It is worth noting that three out of the four examples given earlier are themselves 'nature-inspired systems' (NISs). In fact, we have found nature to be a rich source of design principles for robust and decentralised architectures [22]. By looking at analogous natural systems that exhibit desirable properties, we can often gain insights into how artificial systems may be constructed that exhibit similar properties. For example, the mammalian immune system has been used as inspiration to devise novel, self-protecting mechanisms for computational systems [23]. However, it is also possible to use analogous design heuristics regardless of a specific natural analogy, as was done for the design of the 'SWAN' information management example described earlier.

So what design heuristics might we draw from the examples we have given? We suggest that the following are some key principles:

- local rules — wherever possible use local rules and decision making to achieve overall behaviour;

- interactions — by combining local decision making with carefully crafted interactions between neighbourhood nodes/entities, the desired global behaviour can often be achieved;

- positive and negative feedback — in the same way that biological systems make extensive use of feedback to control processes and achieve robust design of structure and behaviour, similar principles can be used in artificial systems, e.g. Flyphones and ADDICT use inhibitory signalling;

- decentralised solutions — often a given problem is in essence a decentralised problem (cf Flyphones), where a decentralised solution may be well matched, since, in addition, nodes in a decentralised system often 'bring their own resources', which can help provide a scalable solution;

- engineered-in behaviour versus explicit external control — where possible, it is preferable to embody some management within the system itself, as policy-based management is still appropriate and possible via tuning parameters and via the system's in-built adaptability;

- complex systems — the analysis tools of complex systems research are likely to prove increasingly important, e.g. this approach helped with the design of the SWAN system.

These design heuristics are already useful for creating autonomic solutions, as can be seen from the example systems discussed earlier. We can speculate that it may be possible to begin to formalise such heuristics as design patterns [24] for pervasive ICT systems in the future.

In fact, some well-known existing systems make use of a number of these principles, whether implicitly or explicitly. For example, peer-to-peer applications (such as KaZaA) create a decentralised architecture that makes use of local rules and neighbourhood interactions to create an autonomic system that is clearly self-healing and self-protecting.

The IBM Autonomic Computing initiative has a strong focus on managing the components in a system. These 'managed elements' are controlled through associated sensors and effectors [25]. We believe that currently there is insufficient focus on the nature of interactions between the components. While 'autonomic manager collaboration' is explicitly mentioned in the IBM autonomic computing blueprint [4], it simply says that the '... autonomic managers can communicate with each other in both peer-to-peer and hierarchical arrangements'. It notes that the '... autonomic managers for the various contexts will need to co-operate' using a 'matrix management protocol'. In a pervasive ICT context with many interacting components, it is unclear how this management will be effectively resolved.

The research field of complex systems deals specifically with systems of many interacting components and helps explain how overall system behaviour arises as a result of these interactions. It offers the potential to allow the behaviour of systems to be analysed, tuned, and bounded appropriately via analytical, modelling, and simulation-based approaches and tools. It also highlights that in many cases the interactions are a greater determinant of global system behaviour than the individual components themselves. Complex systems theory can help assess and quantify the robustness and dependability of solutions, such as specific network architectures [11]. It can also suggest how local rules may be created to achieve the desired global behaviour (e.g. this approach was used in the 'SWAN' example above to engineer an efficient solution). We also note that some others have observed that complex systems theory has a role to play in realising autonomic systems [26].

Just as for the design of current ICT systems, designers of autonomic solutions will have to ask themselves whether there may be some unintended side effect or interaction between sub-systems or components that may lead to failure conditions or inefficiencies. For these reasons complex systems theory and modelling tools are likely to prove important in engineering robust and adaptive solutions in a pervasive ICT context that by definition includes many interacting components. The next section discusses this in more detail.

19.4   The Need for 'Complex Systems' Theory and Modelling

Traditional engineering starts by specifying desirable system-wide characteristics and then designs/selects individual components under the assumption that the whole is only the sum of its parts. In the domain of pervasive computing, this approach is unlikely to deliver viable solutions due to the scale and complexity of the overall system. The mobility of participating devices and diversity of available services adds an additional dimension to the already arduous problem of managing large distributed systems. However, despite being aware of this difficulty, many technologists seem reluctant to cross the cultural barrier between a proven and immensely successful paradigm (inherited from the industrial revolution) and the 'new' science of complexity, which is less well understood by engineers.

Complexity science provides powerful methods for dealing with probabilistic predictability and describing systems comprised of individually unpredictable elements in a rigorous and useful way. Over the last three decades, it has been extensively demonstrated that variability in the individual response of its constituents does not necessarily translate into the frequency distribution of a system's states exhibiting a similar amount of 'noise'. On the contrary, the huge number of interactions and the presence of intricate feedback loops often mean that the system as a whole can only exist in a limited number of configurations, despite the largely random behaviour of individual units. The science of complexity mainly consists of identifying these configurations, determining their probability of occurrence, and understanding/characterising transitions between them and trajectories leading to them (e.g. bifurcation).

The sheer size of a large network comprised of many thousands of components means that the state of a pervasive computing environment will virtually always be the result of an unforeseeable combination of many events, and so can only be described probabilistically. While there may be an increased recognition of this situation, there is a poor awareness of the methods capable of dealing with it. The heterogeneity of the underlying infrastructure (in terms of purpose, capability, and ownership) precludes a centrally imposed set of rules defining the function and privileges of every participant. Instead, we must find ways to engineer autonomic principles, like self-configuration, into individual elements and their interactions, so as to allow them to deal with unexpected situations, requests, combinations of events, etc.

Complex systems theory and modelling can and must help us understand which macroscopic behaviour is more or less likely to emerge from the many interactions between heterogeneous devices. The real challenge is not to cope with microscopic unpredictability — the conceptual tools required to handle its macroscopic effects are readily available. The difficulty resides in identifying and weighting the factors involved, so that the purpose of fine-tuning the local rules is not defeated by the presence of 'hidden variables' capable of pushing the entire system into an unexpected/undesirable state.

19.5   Summary

The existing trends of ICT systems are already considered to be unsustainable in the long run [2]. This is because the complexity and scale of ICT deployments are outstripping the capabilities of our existing design tools and manual management practices. The impact is experienced in the form of increasing total cost of ownership (TCO) of large ICT deployments, as well as reliability issues and application down-time. All of the major IT companies have programmes seeking radical solutions to these problems, including IBM's Autonomic Computing research initiative [6]. As we enter the world of pervasive ICT, the envisaged scale and complexity make autonomic self-managing solutions not only desirable, but essential.

This chapter makes explicit a number of design heuristics that are particularly useful for implementing autonomic solutions. These principles have been illustrated in the context of four example systems that address specific real-world problems in ICT. Note that three of the four systems are directly nature-inspired, while the remaining example uses similar design principles in a fully engineered solution. The use of the appropriate principles leads to efficient solutions with self-managing properties and real-time adaptive and resilient behaviour. By implication, this is helping to address the issue of reducing the TCO of ICT deployments, and coping with system complexity.

In addition to presenting design principles that can be used right now to engineer-in autonomic behaviour, we also point towards the key role that complex systems analysis should play in the design of future systems. Pervasive ICT will have vast numbers of individual components interacting together in extremely complicated ways. Complex systems analysis provides modelling and simulation tools that can provide a link between the design of the local rules and component interactions, and the resulting global behaviour of the whole system.

References

1 Waldrop M. Pervasive Computing — An Overview of the Concept and Exploration of the Public Policy Implications. Publication 2003-3, Foresight and Governance Project, Woodrow Wilson International Center for Scholars — http://wwics.si.edu/news/docs/pervcomp.pdf

2 Horn P. Autonomic Computing: IBM's Perspective on the State of Information Technology (also known as IBM's Autonomic Computing Manifesto), IBM, 2001 — http://www.research.ibm.com/autonomic/manifesto/autonomic_computing.pdf

3 Kephart J O and Chess D M. The Vision of Autonomic Computing. IEEE Computer Magazine, January 2003:41–50.

4 IBM. IBM and Autonomic Computing: An Architectural Blueprint for Autonomic Computing. IBM Publication, 2003 — http://www.ibm.com/autonomic/pdfs/ACwpFinal.pdf

5 Chase N. An Autonomic Computing Roadmap. IBM DeveloperWorks, 2004 — http://www-106.ibm.com/developerworks/library/ac-roadmap/

6 IBM's Autonomic Computing Web site — http://www.research.ibm.com/autonomic/

7 Tateson R. Self-Organising Pattern Formation: Fruit Flies and Cell Phones. In: Proceedings of the Fifth International Conference on Parallel Problem Solving from Nature. Berlin: Springer, 1988:732–741.

8 Tateson R et al. Nature-inspired Computation — Towards Novel and Radical Computing. BT Technol J:18:1:73–75.

9 Tateson R, Howard S and Bradbeer S. Nature-Inspired Self-Organisation in Wireless Communications Networks. In: Marzo D, Karageorgos A, Rana O F, and Zambonelli F (editors). Engineering Self-Organising Applications. Post-Proceedings, Springer, Berlin, 2004.

10 Erlanger L. 21st Century Security. Internet World Magazine — http://www.internetworld.com/

11 Saffre F. Adaptive Security and Robust Networks. Information Security Bulletin, 2002:7:11.

12 Bonsma E. Fully Decentralised, Scalable Look-up in a Network of Peers Using Small World Networks. Proc of the 6th World Multi Conf on Systemics, Cybernetics and Informatics (SCI2002), Orlando, July 2002:6:147–152.

13 Watts D J and Strogatz S H. Collective Dynamics of 'Small-World' Networks. Nature, 1998:393:440–442.

14 Kleinberg J M. The Small-World Phenomenon: An Algorithmic Perspective. Technical Report 99-1776, Department of Computer Science, Cornell University, Ithaca, NY, 1999.

15 Kleinberg J M. Navigation in a Small World. Nature, August 2000:305:845.

16 Marshall I W and Roadknight C. Adaptive Management of an Active Services Network. BT Technol J, October 2000:18:4:78–84.

17 Marshall I W and Roadknight C. Provision of Quality of Service for Active Services. Computer Networks, April 2001.

18 Roadknight C and Marshall I W. Emergent Organisation in Colonies of Simple Automata. ECAL 2001:349–356.

19 Sacks L et al. The Development of a Robust, Autonomous Sensor Network Platform for Environmental Monitoring. Sensors and their Applications XXII, Limerick, Ireland, 2003.

20 Roadknight C et al. A Layered Approach to *in situ* Data Management on a Wireless Sensor Network. ISSNIP 2005 (in press).

21 Worden D. Understand Autonomic Maturity Levels. IBM DeveloperWorks, 2004 — http://www-106.ibm.com/developerworks/library/ac-mature.html

22 Shackleton M and Marrow P (editors). Nature-Inspired Computing. Special Issue. BT Technol J, October 2000:18:4.

23 Kephart J O. A Biologically Inspired Immune System for Computers. In: Brooks R A and Maes P (editors). Artificial Life IV. Proceedings of the Fourth International Workshop on Synthesis and Simulation of Living Systems, Cambridge, MA, MIT Press, 1994:130–139.

24 Gamma E et al. Design Patterns: Elements of Reusable Object-Oriented Software. Addison-Wesley Pub Co, 1995.

25 Bell J. Understand the Autonomic Manager Concept. IBM DeveloperWorks, February 2004 — http://www-106.ibm.com/developerworks/library/ac-amconcept/

26 Hall T. Autonomic Computing: It's About Making Smarter Systems. An Interview with Vaughn Rokosz, LDD Today. The Technology Journal for Lotus Software, 2003 — http://www-10.lotus.com/ldd/today.nsf/lookup/autonomic_computing

20

Scale-Free Topology for Pervasive Networks

F Saffre, H Jovanovic, C Hoile, and S Nicolas

20.1   Introduction

20.1.1   Scale-Free Networks

Scale-free networks have become a major research topic in recent years, after it was discovered that many large and complex networks, such as the Internet and World Wide Web, exhibit scale-free (instead of previously assumed random) topology [1, 2]. In short, the most fundamental property of scale-free networks is that the probability that a node has k connections $P(k)$ follows a power-law distribution $P(k) \sim k^{-\gamma}$, as opposed to random networks where $P(k)$ obeys an exponential law (see Fig. 20.1).

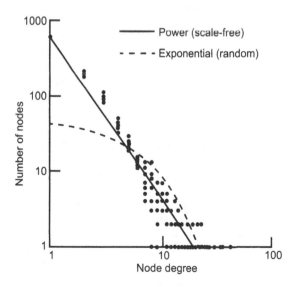

Fig. 20.1   Node degree distribution in a scale-free network built by applying the preferential attachment rule in standard simulation (sequential addition on nodes).

The two aspects of great importance to understand the emergence of a scale-free topology [3] are detailed below.

- Progressive addition

  Firstly, scale-free networks appear to be typically grown via the progressive addition of new nodes, which are connected to the already existing structure. For example, the World Wide Web has grown exponentially over time through the addition of new pages, and the Internet's size is increasing continuously as new users subscribe to the service.

- Preferential attachment

  Secondly, the rules presiding for a newcomer establishing a connection with the network involve the so-called preferential attachment principle. In effect, the probability to select a particular node as a parent is a linear function of its degree, compared to that of other possible candidates. This results in a 'rich becomes richer' process, whereby highly connected nodes tend to attract increasingly more newcomers (positive feedback). For example, it is likely that a new Web page will be linked to an existing page with many previously existing links, rather than to one of its less popular counterparts.

The resulting structure is a network that contains a few nodes with a high number of links and many nodes with fewer connections, hence the power-law signature previously mentioned.

However, the fact that scale-free topology usually results from a growth process, where nodes are sequentially added and connected to a parent selected using the preferential attachment rule, creates major difficulties when attempting to generate scale-free *ad hoc* networks. This work is an attempt at solving this problem.

20.1.2   *Ad Hoc* Networks

An *ad hoc* network is usually defined as a short-lived, self-organising group of devices, typically interacting via wireless or temporary plug-in connections [4]. Member devices can only be part of the network for the duration of a single communication session, or while in close proximity to the rest of a group (for example, in the case of mobile/portable devices).

Being capable of autonomous operation is often regarded as an intrinsic property of *ad hoc* networks. For example, most applications would require the system to function without being connected to any fixed infrastructure. Furthermore, member devices should be able to define their own role in the network all by themselves (via some kind of negotiation process). Finally, because its hosting device's capabilities should be considered unpredictable by default, pervasive applications should probably favour a peer-to-peer (instead of hierarchical) architecture.

If adding mobility, one has to cope with the extra difficulty of managing dynamic topology. This usually means that member devices have to collaborate heavily to keep the network alive by constantly re-organising it into a coherent whole, despite ever-changing node distribution. As the best candidate applications for *ad hoc* connectivity typically involve low-powered devices, the range of communication is often very short. As a result, interaction between distant members would usually require many hops, meaning that a considerable fraction of the node's activity has to do with relaying transmissions between others.

20.1.3   Scale-Free *Ad Hoc* Networks?

The objective of this chapter is to emphasise that, if one wanted to build a scale-free network in an *ad hoc* context, a number of precautions should be taken in order to deal with some trivial yet easily overlooked effects of a straightforward implementation of the preferential attachment rule. On a higher level, we wish to contribute to linking the very theoretical field that has come to be known as the study of complex networks to that of actually engineering their physical counterparts.

Though this places us in the somewhat difficult position of having to face criticism on two fronts, we are convinced that it is the best and possibly only way to stimulate discussion between these two research communities.

Despite this not being our main focus, we wish to briefly discuss the potential advantages of 'forcing' an *ad hoc* network to adopt scale-free architecture. The reader should keep in mind, however, that we do not suggest that this topology is necessarily desirable and are fully aware that there are actually a number of counter-arguments to its utilisation.

Some of the best-known examples of *ad hoc* networks are sensor arrays, automotive networks, and 'rapid deployment' military communication systems. All of these networks involve mobile devices and/or variable or unpredictable topology (e.g. parachuted sensor arrays).

Communication between units is achieved through specific routing procedures where nodes communicate with each other using other nodes' information about the rest of the network.

We believe that some characteristics of scale-free networks can be adapted to meet the constraints of a variety of *ad hoc* systems. Several studies have been devoted to identifying ways of improving efficiency in similar environments [5, 6]. One of them, more specifically targeted at reducing transmission power, suggests that one possible strategy would consist of actually increasing the number of hops, in order to eliminate long-range transmissions, which consume a lot of energy [7].

Though we recognise the fact that power-saving measures designed to minimise energy consumption homogeneously (i.e. for all member devices) can be useful in a number of cases, we argue that it is not always so.

For example, in some distributed sensor array deployment scenarios, it may be advantageous to make sure that a small number of units do take on the role of relaying most of the traffic, so that maintenance efforts (e.g. battery replacement) can be focused on those alone. A similar approach could be useful for some pervasive computing applications, where differentiation of a sub-set of participating devices into 'temporary hubs' can help in solving QoS issues. Indeed, it can be beneficial to the system as a whole that a more permanent and/or reliable member device is 'forced' into taking on the role of communication relay, while more 'transient' resources are left in charge of background processes that do not require real-time interactions.

Though admittedly addressing only part of a complex problem, identifying ways of generating scale-free topology, so as to increase the probability that a small sub-set of highly connected devices are in charge of relaying most of the traffic, seems a possible first step toward such mission-specific differentiation.

20.2   Methodology

20.2.1   Standard Simulation

Most recent work about scale-free networks has used standard simulation techniques, where newcomers are added sequentially and select a parent among the already connected nodes in accordance with the preferential attachment rule [8]. Typically, no constraints on range or power are taken into account. Similarly, the possibility that timing and/or limited locally available information could disturb the 'normal' growth process is often completely ignored.

One of the most preoccupying artefacts of this ideal sequence of events, where only one node is allowed to join at a time, is that it guarantees that all candidate members will ultimately be included in a single network [9]. Achieving the same result while taking into account realistic constraints requires considerable refinement of the connection rules.

20.2.2   STAN Simulation

A 'simulation tool for *ad hoc* networks' (STAN) has been developed internally by BT to improve the realism of *ad hoc* network simulation [4]. It is written in the Java programming language.

Several characteristics make STAN a particularly suitable simulation tool for this kind of research, but fundamentally they all come down to the fact that STAN accurately models the behaviour of, and interaction between, individual nodes, instead of adopting a 'bird's-eye view' of network operations.

In STAN, all nodes are modelled as very simple devices performing very basic tasks. The only thing a node is allowed to 'know' is when a message is received and what is its nature (which closely mimics real *ad hoc* communications).

A second, very important characteristic is that STAN is an event-driven simulation platform, and thus completely asynchronous. In short, nodes receive messages and are required to act on the exclusive basis of the information they contain (i.e. without any artificial knowledge of what their peers are doing and/or when). Nodes' actions themselves are considered as events and added to the sequence at the appropriate location. Simulation time and processing time are therefore effectively disconnected from one another, resulting in a considerable increase in realism and flexibility. Finally, STAN can also include constraints on range and handle signal collisions during communication between nodes.

All of these features are of great importance to this work, as accurate modelling of *ad hoc* communications and accompanying constraints is an absolute prerequisite if one is to conduct a proper study of scale-free topology in this specific context.

20.3   Results

20.3.1   Three Message Types

Description
As previously mentioned, STAN is based on directly simulating all communications between nodes. Since the type and content of the message(s) received directly

influence a node's action, it is necessary to define as accurately as possible the different kind of messages that are going to be used when nodes negotiate connections between themselves

In our first attempt at creating an approximation of scale-free topology in an *ad hoc* context, we used a connection protocol based on three message types: 'neighbour request' (NR), 'neighbour reply' (NRp), and 'connection report' (CR). At this stage, constraints on range were not taken into account.

- Neighbour request

  NR is a broadcast message, meaning that it does not refer to any specific receiver as its intended target, but is implicitly addressed to all simulated devices. The only information conveyed by NR messages is in fact the ID of the node that sent it (sender). The purpose of this message type is merely to announce that the sender is willing to join the network. Candidate members send this message periodically until they have identified a parent and connection has been successfully established. Therefore, NR messages can be assimilated to a 'beacon' signal.

- Neighbour reply

  NRp is a point-to-point message, meaning that it is intended for a specific receiver. Members are required to send NRp if they have received NR messages(s). NRp contains the ID of the sender, the ID of its target as well as data about the number of connections (degree k) already maintained by the sender. So in effect, when collecting NRp messages (over a predefined period), a candidate member (target) collects information about senders that will allow it to select a parent by applying the preferential attachment rule.

- Connection report

  CR is used to inform an existing member (target) that it has been selected as a parent by a newcomer (sender). It is also a point-to-point message, so it obviously contains both the sender's and the target's ID. It is emitted after the sender has chosen a member to connect to, by applying the preferential attachment rule.

The first step involves candidate members broadcasting NR messages. As already mentioned, every node that is not yet connected to the network (degree $k = 0$) is assumed to send a message of this type periodically until it has found a parent. When a member (degree $k \geq 0$) receives an NR message, it puts the ID of the sender in a list of requests (neighbourRequest).

Periodically, every member picks up one ID from that list, selected at random, and sends an NRp message to this particular candidate member. After this, the list is reinitialised.

The rule whereby any member is only allowed to answer one of all the NR messages received over one cycle (randomly selected) is made necessary by initial conditions. Indeed, if a parent was allowed to 'adopt' more than one child at a time (and range and interference are not taken into account), it would be expected to answer all NR messages. As the root is the one and only one member during the first cycle, all candidate children would have no choice but to select the sender of the single NRp message received as their parent, resulting in a 'pathological' star configuration.

A member's degree is increased by one unit each time it receives a CR message, while, obviously, a newcomer's degree is set to 1 when it selects a parent and itself becomes a member.

Properties and Comparison with Standard Scale-Free Topology

The most important footprint of scale-free networks is that the frequency distribution of nodes as a function of their degree obeys a power law. Surprisingly, the architecture obtained using our simulation, despite being based on the application of the preferential attachment rule, does not exhibit this primary characteristic. Instead, the frequency distribution appears to be between that expected for a random graph (exponential) and that of the standard scale-free topology (see Fig. 20.2).

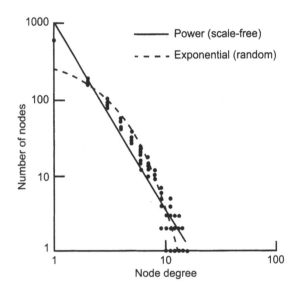

Fig. 20.2   Node degree distribution in a network obtained by applying the preferential attachment rule in STAN (asynchronous simulation), with three message types.

Similarly, two other key global variables, network diameter and average path length, are also different. Their mean values were, respectively, 14.6 and 7.6 for networks produced with STAN, and 20 and 8.3 for standard scale-free topology.

Finally, when considering the upper limit of degree distribution (i.e. the degree of the most connected node, averaged over 10 simulations), we find it to be only ~14, which is less than half the expected value for a scale-free network of this size (~31). This can easily be seen on the graphical representation of the topology shown in Fig. 20.3.

The cause of these striking differences is to be found in the information actually available to candidate members when they select their parent using the preferential attachment rule. When examining simulation records more closely, we found that most of them (~80%) had no choice at all when choosing their parent, as they had only received one NRp message over the cycle, at the end of which the decision was made. The explanation lies in the fact that when the number of candidate parents is lower than that of non-members, the probability that several of them randomly select

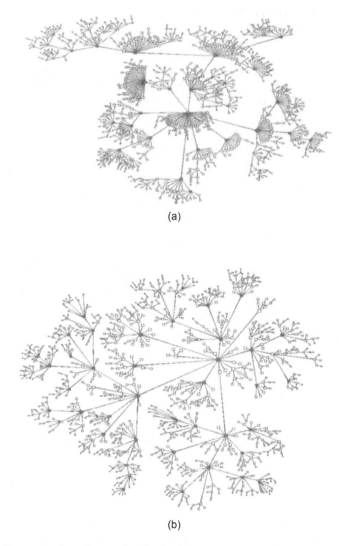

(a)

(b)

Fig. 20.3 Representation of networks obtained by applying the preferential attachment rule in standard simulation (a), and in STAN (asynchronous simulation) with three message types

the same candidate child for adoption (effectively giving it the choice of its parent) is actually very low. It is only at the end of the network growth process that the still 'unadopted' nodes (now a minority) obtain a relatively good picture of the degree distribution among members, and can apply the preferential attachment rule properly. In short, in its early stage, the connection process resembles that of a random graph, then progressively turns into that of a scale-free network, hence the hybrid signature.

To solve this problem, we had to ensure that candidate members are given more options from the very beginning of the network growth process, but still without allowing members to adopt more than one child per cycle. In order to achieve this, we had to switch to a four-message-type scenario.

20.3.2   Four Message Types

Description

The four-message-type protocol is quite similar to that of its predecessor. It still includes 'neighbour request' (NR), 'neighbour reply' (NRp), and 'connection report' (CR), but one additional message type, 'connection approved' (CA), is added:

* NR is identical to the one described in Section 20.3.1;

* NRp is now a broadcast message, meaning that it still contains the ID of the sender and its number of connections (degree k), but is not intended for a particular recipient. In that sense, like NR, it can now be seen as a beacon signal that is sent periodically as long as the neighbourRequest queue is not empty;

* CR messages are unchanged in format, but they are now temporarily stored by the receiver (selected parent) in a connectionReport queue, which is reset at the end of each cycle;

* CA is a point-to-point message sent by a member to its chosen new child — it can be regarded as a response to one of the CR messages received over the last cycle, randomly selected in the connectionReport queue.

Node behaviour associated with sending/receiving these messages is similar to that described in the three-message-type scenarios. The main difference is that the candidate child does not update its status and degree when sending the CR message for an obvious reason — there is no guarantee that it will indeed be accepted by its chosen parent (which may have received several requests). Instead, the responsibility of confirming the link now lies with the parent and is associated with sending the final CA message, concluding the transaction. Finally, it is necessary that candidate children who have sent a CR message but not received the corresponding CA after one cycle resume the procedure from the start (i.e. send a new NR beacon).

Properties

Despite the addition of a fourth message type and constraints on range still not being taken into account, initial results again showed a surprisingly different outcome from the standard application of the preferential attachment rule. This time, it is attributable to the massive variation in growth rate between the early and late stages of the connection process. Indeed, because of the various constraints imposed on the nodes, the number of newcomers joining the network per cycle peaks when the total population is about evenly distributed between the two categories (members and non-members).

In the beginning, the demand far exceeds the offer (many candidate children, only a handful of eligible parents). The opposite holds when only a small number of unconnected nodes are still available to adopt. In other words, the growth process cannot be assimilated to a sequential addition of new members, each of them applying the preferential attachment rule to select a parent in a new, recently updated network. Instead, there is a phase during which many candidate children make their choice on the basis of the same information, indirectly reducing the intensity of the positive feedback favouring highly connected nodes.

A final adjustment therefore consisted in lowering the maximum growth rate by 'artificially' reducing the number of adoptions per cycle. This was achieved by forcing newcomers to perform a random test against a fixed threshold of 0.1 before sending the CR message. As a result, only an average 10% of all candidate members immediately inform their chosen parent of their decision, while in effect, the remaining 90% give themselves a chance to collect up-to-date information and revise their decision by delaying their own adoption.

Adding this extra refinement finally produced the desired scale-free topology in terms of the final node degree distribution (see Fig. 20.4), despite a significant difference in the values of other global variables (diameter and average path length — see Table 20.1 for details).

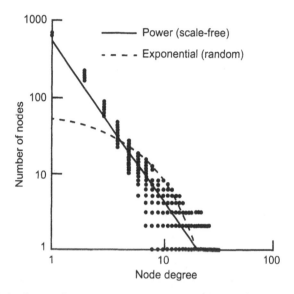

Fig. 20.4   Node degree distribution in a network obtained by applying the preferential attachment rule in STAN (asynchronous simulation) with four message types plus 'artificial' noise (see text for details).

An example of a network obtained by applying this latest version of the connection protocol is shown in Fig. 20.5. Comparison with Fig. 20.3(a) clearly demonstrates this topology to be a closer relative to a 'real' scale-free network than in previous attempts (Fig. 20.3(b)).

Adding Range Constraints

With a satisfactory protocol to generate scale-free topology in a fully asynchronous context now in place, it becomes possible to study the effect of environmental factors on the network produced. Among these, the most immediately relevant is probably the interplay between node density and maximum communication range, which would have a strong influence on the system's ability to self-organise, for example, in the case of an *ad hoc* network of sensors.

We simulated systems comprising 1000, 500, and 250 nodes, with a maximum communication range of 5, 10, 20, and 100% of the maximum possible distance

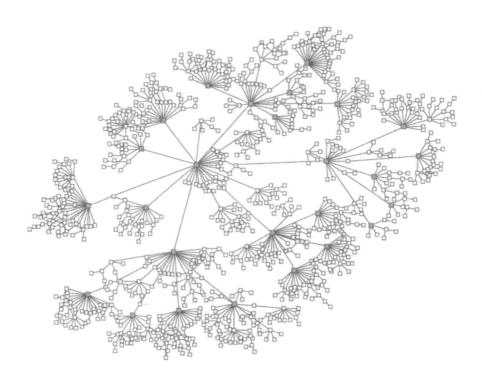

Fig. 20.5   Representation of a network obtained by applying the preferential attachment
rule in STAN (asynchronous simulation), with four message types plus 'artificial' noise.

between two nodes ($2^{1/2}$ times the edge of the square-shaped environment in which
the network is being deployed). Results presented here correspond to 50 realisations
for each combination of parameter values.

As could be expected, lowering the communication range without changing the
population density results in the scale-free signature being progressively lost (results
not shown here). This is attributable to the fact that increasingly strong constraints
on the maximum distance between possible parents and children effectively limits
the competition between members to 'attract' newcomers.

Interestingly though, only when combined with very low density (250 nodes)
does a 5% range result in the network's failing to develop altogether. Even though
short-range communication and/or small population size do affect network topology
(scale-free signature disappears and degree distribution becomes progressively
exponential), they do not prevent most nodes from successfully establishing a
connection with the growing structure.

So, in practice, the main effect of reducing communication range is a rapid
increase in diameter and average path length (see Fig. 20.6), together with the
disappearance of the scale-free topology, not a failure of the network to self-organise
into a single, coherent structure. Moreover, 'limited' constraints on range appear to
have virtually no effect. Indeed, results obtained for a maximum communication
distance of 20% are remarkably similar to those corresponding to 100% (i.e. no
range constraints). The data is summarised in Table 20.1.

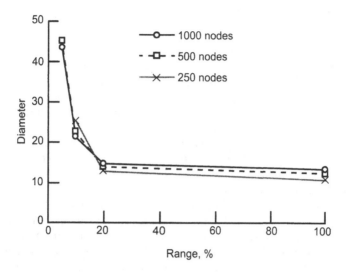

Fig. 20.6   Evolution of network diameter as a function of communication range (averaged over 10 realisations). Average path length follows a similar curve.

Table 20.1   Evolution of the diameter and average path length for the four message types protocol plus 'artificial' noise, three different network sizes and four ranges. The 'x' in the line corresponding to 5% range and low population density (250 nodes) indicates that the values were irrelevant due to the low success rate (network fails to develop, see text for details).

			1000 nodes			
Range	Diameter	Average path length	σ diameter	σ apl	Max degree	σ max
100%	13.3	6.437994	0.674949	0.038722	27.29412	1.868626
20%	14.6	7.2214	0.699206	0.475718	23.11111	3.297535
10%	21.4	9.9965	2.01108	0.971066	16.79167	2.790244
5%	43.6	19.4485	6.113737	2.151734	10.46939	1.002124
			500 nodes			
Range	Diameter	Average path length	σ diameter	σ apl	Max degree	σ max
100%	12.3	5.8851	1.05935	0.383064	24	1.833495
20%	13.9	6.5588	1.197219	0.509989	19.73469	3.005381
10%	22.6	10.6361	2.716207	1.180218	12.82	2.076988
5%	45.2	19.6795	5.884065	1.774996	8.166667	0.930187
			250 nodes			
Range	Diameter	Average path length	σ diameter	σ apl	Max degree	σ max
100%	10.8	5.1367	1.032796	0.140677	20.74	3.544527
20%	13	6.3038	1.490712	0.430033	15.26	2.388835
10%	25.3	10.9665	3.020302	1.260496	9.6	1.293626
5%	×	×	×	×	×	×

20.4   Summary

In this work, we originally intended to demonstrate that it is theoretically possible to obtain an approximation of scale-free topology by applying the preferential attachment rule locally and asynchronously. We discovered, however, that a variety of side effects from observing these realistic constraints tend to disturb the 'normal' growth process, which results in the structure produced often being closer to a random graph than to a scale-free network. However, by progressively increasing the complexity of the negotiation phase leading to the creation of a new link, we managed to overcome this difficulty and successfully developed a protocol of interaction capable of producing the intended topology, with the notable exception of average path length and diameter.

One of the most intriguing difficulties that we encountered in this study turned out to be caused by the extremely strong influence of keeping growth rate constant throughout network history, an implicit property resulting from the way the preferential attachment rule is usually applied in more theoretical models. In our view, this problem is not unrelated to the criticism voiced several years ago by Huberman and Adamic [10] about the 'realism' of such a scenario. Indeed, the indirect but crucial role played by the system's history is easily overlooked, resulting in a biased, and quite possibly mistaken, understanding of the amplification mechanism presiding on the emergence of scale-free topology in real networks.

This can be of extreme consequence if practically implementing the preferential attachment rule as part of an attempt to generate a desired global architecture in the absence of central control. In short, protocols used to govern node behaviour in a real, possibly dynamic, *ad hoc* network should be designed to address the specific problems posed by such deployment, not simply duplicate abstract rules found to produce the adequate topology in a theoretical set-up. The present study suggests that intentionally disturbing the normal growth dynamics (which would otherwise be characterised by an exponential signature) could be the only way to generate an approximation of a scale-free network through asynchronous interaction between the constituent units, in a simulated environment. This opens fascinating perspectives in terms of the opportunity to actually take advantage of naturally occurring perturbations in a pervasive computing environment in order to improve the topological characteristics and increase the overall predictability of the emerging design in a real deployment scenario.

Future developments of our work will include exploring this direction, by taking the influence of several aspects of wireless communication explicitly into account. For example, we will introduce elements like message collision, line-of-sight (as opposed to range only), and node mobility. We anticipate that submitting existing protocols to these additional physical constraints, while simultaneously retaining the overall objective of generating specific network topologies, will lead to significant progress in developing successful decentralised management techniques for *ad hoc* architectures.

In parallel, we intend to investigate how temporary specialisation could benefit pervasive computing applications and which forms of differentiation could take advantage of scale-free topology, in the context of a self-structuring community of co-operative hosts.

References

1. Faloutsos M, Faloutsos P, and Faloutsos C. On Power-Law Relationships of the Internet Topology. ACM SIGCOMM '99, Computer Communications Review, 1999:29:251.

2. Albert R, Jeong H, and Barabási A L. Diameter of the World-Wide Web. Nature, 1999:401:130–131.

3. Barabási A L, Albert R, and Jeong H. Mean-Field Theory for Scale-Free Random Networks. Physica, 1999:A272:173–187.

4. Nicolas S. Ad Hoc Network and Protocol Simulation Tool. Aston University, Birmingham, Department of Electronic and Electrical Engineering, MSc Telecommunications Technology, 2001/2002.

5. Kim B J et al. Path Finding Strategies in Scale Free Networks. Phys Rev, 2002:E65:027103.

6. Jost J and Joy M P. Evolving Networks with Distance Preferences. Phys Rev, 2002:E66:036126.

7. Gomez J et al. Conserving Transmission Power in Wireless Ad Hoc Networks. 9th International Conference on Network Protocols (ICNP), 2001.

8. Albert R, Jeong H, and Barábasi A L. Error and Attack Tolerance of Complex Networks. Phys Rev, 2002:E66:036126.

9. Saffre F and Ghanea-Hercock R. Simple Laws for Complex Networks. BT Technol J, April 2003:21:2:112–119.

10. Huberman B and Adamic L. Growth Dynamics of the World-Wide-Web. Nature, 1999:401:131.

21

NEXUS — Resilient Intelligent Middleware

N Kaveh and R Ghanea Hercock

21.1   Introduction

Service-oriented computing, a composition of distributed-object computing, component-based, and Web-based concepts, is becoming the widespread choice for developing dynamic heterogeneous software assets available as services across a network. One of the major strengths of service-oriented technologies is the high abstraction layer and large granularity level at which software assets are viewed compared to traditional object-oriented technologies. Collaboration through encapsulated and separately defined service interfaces creates a service-oriented environment, whereby multiple services can be linked together through their interfaces to compose a functional system. This approach enables better integration of legacy and non-legacy services, via wrapper interfaces, and allows for service composition at a more abstract level especially in cases such as vertical market stacks. The heterogeneous nature of service-oriented technologies and the granularity of their software components makes them a suitable computing model in the pervasive domain.

Figure 21.1 shows how a service provider advertises its available services (software assets) with a known service broker. This allows entities interested in the services of a service provider, namely service requesters, to query a service broker for the existence and location of such services. Using the obtained broker information, a service requester can make a direct service request to the identified service provider.

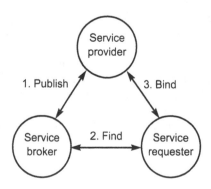

Fig. 21.1   Service-oriented architecture.

21.2   Motivating Scenario

In this section we present a typical use case scenario in which the NEXUS system is envisaged to be utilised. This scenario highlights the motivation behind this project and serves as a source for the system's functional and non-functional requirements.

- Situation — a single user needs to perform an information fusion task

    An intelligence officer, Jane, is constructing a report on hostile force movements in region X. Due to the textual nature of the task she decides to access NEXUS through a Web browser rather than the NEXUS visual application. This causes the creation of a NEXUS node and agent automatically within the network. Having been authenticated successfully, Jane's node entry is placed into her assigned group, giving her access to all capabilities and services offered by the other group members.

    Once Jane has instructed her agent with the details of the report that she would like compiled, that agent breaks that request into multiple tasks. A task may be carried out locally or it may need to be sent to another agent for processing. For example, most sections of the report require up-to-date field information, which must be requested from their respective remote sources, whereas any textual transformation of the results can be done locally. Five minutes later Jane is presented with a list of the reporting tasks carried out along with their respective results and possible defence data channels in the form of a hyperlinked Web page. She is then in a position to select the most relevant information from the result set for the compilation of the report. One of the defence data channels is a territory image database from which Jane would like to include images. Jane clicks on the link and is provided with the search parameters that can be used for searching and selecting images from the database. Once her search parameters have been provided, her agent takes over the task of connecting, authorising, and fetching relevant images from the database.

    Figure 21.2 shows a UML sequence diagram of Jane requesting the retrieval of images based on provided parameters from her agent as discussed in the above scenario. The tasks of locating an appropriate database and retrieving related images is done by the NEXUS agent, transparently from Jane's viewpoint. Note that the messages shown being passed and the entities are abstract and for modelling the use case. The UML sequence diagram does not contain details of all entities and messages involved; these will be discussed in more detail in the following sections.

    The UML sequence diagram in Fig. 21.2 shows Jane's initial request is automatically broken up by the delegate's agent and the way in which it interacts with NEXUS to discover services that are required to accomplish Jane's request. As a new user, Jane would have to register herself by providing general identification details, as well as information to determine her level of authorisation. Jane can then log on to NEXUS via a username and password mechanism (via a network authorisation function) and edit her details at any time. A local repository of user information is then updated to reflect any changes. The main interaction by Jane will be either to initiate a direct search for specific information provided by service(s) on the network (resolved by a discovery function), or to delegate a more general, high-level information retrieval task to her local agent.

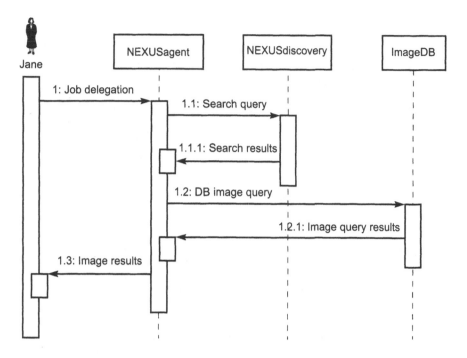

Fig. 21.2   Image fetching sequence diagram.

21.3   NEXUS Architecture

As mentioned in the introduction, the NEXUS project provides an architecture framework for the service broker role for service-oriented architecture (SOA) systems. This role should be undertaken transparently to the service requester and service provider entities to minimise coupling. This section outlines the architecture framework we propose, taking into account the requirements detailed in the previous section.

Figure 21.3 shows the topology of the NEXUS network. This hierarchical architecture is composed of three interconnected tiers. The bottom 'discovery' tier provides a decentralised mechanism for registering access details of a public service belonging to a service provider entity as well as a search facility for locating access/ location details of a given Web service for service requester entities. The discovery layer takes on the responsibilities of the service broker entity depicted in Fig. 21.1. This layer is composed of a set of discovery groups where each group is responsible for storing and searching for location details of a set of service-provider facilities. Each discovery group is responsible for providing services to a group at the service layer, as depicted in Fig. 21.3. The differentiation of groups at the service layer commonly represents business concerns such as organisational boundaries, trust groups, or different layers of a vertical market sector. The NEXUS architecture allows for mirroring the groupings of the service layer at the discovery layer in order to maintain the desired business boundaries. This mirroring is done dynamically to reflect the continual changes at the service layer. Such a facility helps in the

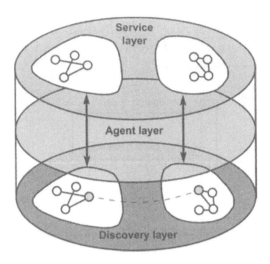

Fig. 21.3   NEXUS three-tier topology.

introduction of hierarchy to the system and the overall access control. The registration, discovery, and request of a service can be bound to a specific group or set of groups. Further details of the discovery layer are discussed later in this section.

The service layer represents service-provider and service-requester entities as illustrated in Fig. 21.1. It is an application layer that uses the underlying NEXUS middleware for locating desired services (discovery layer) and automation of certain activities (agent layer). Once a service-requester entity has used NEXUS to locate access details for a particular service, it can make a binding to the desired service-provider entity and use available services. As the binding and service utilisation activities preceding the discovery process are performed outside the scope of NEXUS, the service-requester and service-provider entities can communicate via any agreed technologies, such as SOAP. This clear separation of responsibility makes the introduction of the NEXUS middleware into existing and legacy systems simpler and more transparent to all parties involved. Moreover, this approach improves the scalability and non-reliance of NEXUS on any particular technology. As mentioned above, entities at the service layer are clustered into separate groups that represent different business-level boundaries. There can also be overlaps between groups representing cross-business boundary interaction. These group boundaries serve as a scoping mechanism for possible interactions between service-requester and service-provider entities, thus allowing the representation of the service layer organisational and logical boundaries within the NEXUS discovery service. The agent layer can be seen as an optional intermediary between the service and discovery layers.

An example of the agent layer in action was presented in the motivating scenario in Section 21.2, when Jane, operating at the service layer, instructed an agent to carry out an image search-and-retrieval task for her. Agents use domain-specific knowledge to make decisions on behalf of their users and may collaborate with other agents to accomplish a goal.

Interaction with the agent layer is optional due to circumstances where simple tasks only require direct interaction between the service and discovery layers. The usage of the agent layer is not essential since simple tasks can be achieved through direct interaction of the service and discovery layers. In the future we plan to add an intelligent agent layer, to make NEXUS useful in more complex task-intensive environments where greater automation is required.

By having clearly defined interfaces between each of the three layers, we ensure that there is minimal dependency between one another, thus allowing us to modify the inner workings of each layer without disruption to the others.

A key requirement of the NEXUS architecture framework is its modularity and non-dependability on any specific technology. Figure 21.4 shows how this is achieved in the NEXUS architecture, through the use of a dynamic module plug-in system. In Fig. 21.4, modules are represented as cubes, whereby desired run-time modules are plugged into the NEXUS middleware through a standard interface. The modules situated above the middleware operate at the service layer while those on the bottom row provide implementation for the discovery layer. These lists are non-exhaustive and the open standards utilised allow for future technologies to be plugged in without disruption to existing systems.

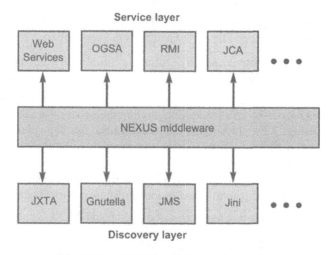

Fig. 21.4   NEXUS middleware integration.

The NEXUS middleware seamlessly supports the service-layer modules by replacing their proprietary service registration and discovery mechanism with a chosen discovery module. The loose coupling between a service and discovery module combination promotes modularity and non-dependency. The separation of the NEXUS discovery middleware and its client applications is analogous to the clean separation exhibited between the user interface display of a device and the device itself.

21.4   NEXUS Prototype

A prototype reference implementation of the NEXUS middleware platform has been developed. In this instance, the reference implementation employs the peer-to-peer JXTA protocol set at the discovery layer.

The ServiceBrowser, shown in Fig. 21.5, is a client application for discovering, displaying, and invoking currently available services that are advertised within NEXUS. Before the main application window of ServiceBrowser is displayed, NEXUS will attempt to discover currently available services, using the following process:

- instantiate itself as a NEXUS peer by initialising the JXTA platform;
- searching its local cache for JXTA module specification advertisements (MSAs) to check whether any previously discovered services can be retrieved;
- connecting, via JXTA, to its local rendezvous (or indexing) node;
- retrieve any additional or newly discovered service advertisements registered on the local rendezvous node;
- each service advertisement is then de-serialised in order to obtain the NEXUS Web service descriptor;
- from the Web service descriptor, URI links are obtained to a local or remote JAR file containing the client invocation GUI for each service;
- retrieve each client GUI and either display in the ServiceBrowser or launch a separate application (depending on the nature of the service).

Services that become registered and live after the initial discovery period can be added to the main service list in two ways:

- each ServiceBrowser is registered as a NEXUS discovery listener, and when a new service is registered on a rendezvous peer on the network and the registration propagates (using JXTA's own loosely coupled rendezvous algorithm) to the local rendezvous peer, this will fire a discovery event to all registered discovery listeners including the ServiceBrowser;
- if in any circumstance a newly registered service is not picked up by the ServiceBrowser, the user can initiate the above discovery process at any time.

Figure 21.5 shows a service that has been discovered using NEXUS and displayed in the ServiceBrowser.

The discovered RSS service parses RSS, RDF, and XML news feeds to present up-to-date news and information in a tabular format. The service advertisement contains a link for downloading a Java JAR file containing all files and resources for rendering the client application that connects to the RSS service and displays the news items. The link for each news item opens a browser displaying the additional news item. The news feeds are located using a URL, meaning that they are automatically updated. Service properties such as service name, SOAP end-point, and timestamp are shown in the properties table to the left.

21.5   Related Work

The Open Grid Services Architecture (OGSA) is a ratified Global Grid Forum (GGF) standard that was put in place to develop the original, proprietary grid system architecture into one that supports Web service (WS) concepts and standards. OGSA defines a grid service, which is a Web service that conforms to a set of conventions

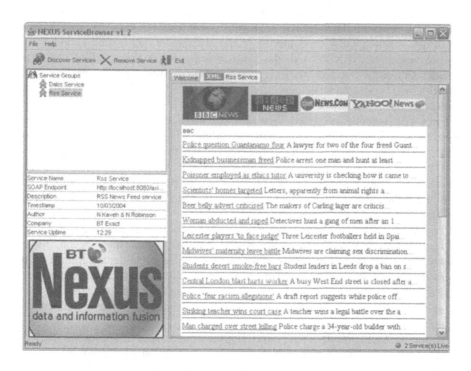

Fig. 21.5   NEXUS client ServiceBrowser prototype.

for such purposes of service lifetime management, inspection, and notification of service state changes. At a basic level, OGSA specifies a set of WSDL interfaces and schemata consistent with defining a grid-service interface. The latest version of the Globus Tool-kit, GT3, provides a reference implementation of the grid services specification, allowing Java objects to be deployed as open grid services infrastructure (OGSI) services. However OGSI, under the name WS-ResourceFramework, is re-factored into a set of new Web-service-conforming specifications. In summarising the high-level functionality of OGSA, and its base OGSI, and WS-RF specifications, a difference in purpose can be highlighted in comparison to the NEXUS middleware platform. OGSA is an architecture for enabling grid-service standards concerned with creating and managing grid-service instances such as Web Services. In comparison, NEXUS is a generic, distributed service broker architecture used for discovering such services, grid-enabled or otherwise. OGSA represents an evolution of grid functionality from early grid-specific contexts to Web service specifications — for OGSA to develop into a more commonly used standard is good for all; and these standards do not conflict with the functionality provided by NEXUS. The two are complementary technologies, operating in different application domains. This is highlighted because OGSA makes assumptions about reliability and service availability which are not compatible with the *ad hoc*, highly decentralised, peer-to-peer networks on which NEXUS is designed to operate. Within the Web service framework, OGSA provides standard interfaces for registering a grid service to a UDDI registry. It is the centralised nature of UDDI that NEXUS aims to circumvent by promoting a service registry based on a loosely consistent peer architecture. Thus OGSA can operate on the service layer of the NEXUS architecture and use NEXUS for grid-service discovery. Where OGSA (and more specifically the WS-RF specifications) can provide benefit to NEXUS is in the grid-service-specific functionality that they provide. Currently, services that are deployed on to the NEXUS platform are stateless, and consequently there could be scope for using service lifetime management capabilities.

There is a recently proposed Web services protocol that defines a multi-cast discovery for locating services on a network, while using a minimum of networking services (such as DNS or UDDI). However, should, for example, a UDDI service exist, WS-Discovery will make use of this to reduce network traffic. This discovery can occur on either managed or *ad hoc* networks for peer-to-peer applications (i.e. including devices and services that are not always connected to the network). Using WS-Discovery, a client can search for services either by name, type, or scope by sending multi-cast probing messages. Repeated probing is minimised by new services announcing their presence on the network when they become live. However, this discovery process in not mandated — if a client detects a third-party discovery proxy, it will not only attempt to automatically route the discovery request using this protocol, it can act as a bridge between more permanent (managed) and *ad hoc* service networks. This suppression of multi-cast requests is used as a device to provide scalability.

As for NEXUS, WS-Discovery has similar aims to provide dynamic service broker capabilities. However, as a Web services specification it is irrevocably tied to the Web services stack. NEXUS has been designed specifically to abstract over any particular discovery- or service-layer technology, and thus could potentially employ WS-Discovery in circumstances where it is appropriate (for example, where deployed Web services are requested). Thus NEXUS can employ 'best-of-breed' technologies both on the service-requester and service-provider components of the SOA-based architecture.

21.6   Summary

The NEXUS project shares the aims and objectives of a number of technologies such as those in the service space (e.g. Web services) and those related to grid (e.g. OGSA), which aspire to the SOA model. However, the dynamic and real-time requirements of the defence sector and an increasing trend in the mainstream market make the centralised approach used in current service-oriented deployments less than effective.

More crucially they are not amenable to a diverse network environment of legacy systems and thin devices that need to form dynamic and often volatile *ad hoc* networks for an undetermined period of time. Specially when in this time duration, members should dynamically discover and utilise each other's services, and collaborate in order to accomplish a group task. To address these issues, the proposed NEXUS architecture framework attempts to support existing SOA-based technologies and enhance their capabilities with a decentralised, scalable, and robust dynamic discovery mechanism.

Bibliography

Allsopp D et al. Coalition Experiment: Multiagent Cooperation in International Coalitions. IEEE Intelligent Systems, May 2002.

Bonsma E and Hoile C. A Distributed Implementation of the SWAN Peer-to-Peer Look-up System Using Mobile Agents. Proceedings of the International Workshop on Agents and Peer-to-Peer Computing, Autonomous Agents and Multi-Agent Systems, Bologna, Italy, 2002.

Capra L, Emmerich W, and Mascolo C. CARISMA: Context-Aware Reflective Middleware System for Mobile Applications. IEEE Transactions on Software Engineering, 2003:29:10: 929–945.

Chappell D A and Jewell T. Java Web Services: Using Java in Service-Oriented Architectures. O'Reilly, USA, 2002:13–24.

Denker G et al. Accessing Information and Services on the DAML-enabled Web. Whitepaper, SRI International, Menlo Park, CA, January 2001 — http://www.daml.org/

Foster I ct al. The Physiology of the Grid: An Open Grid Services Architecture for Distributed Systems Integration. Open Grid Service Infrastructure WG, Global Grid Forum, 2002.

Foster I and Iamnitchi A. On Death, Taxes, and the Convergence of Peer-to-Peer and Grid Computing. 2nd International Workshop on Peer-to-Peer Systems, Berkeley, CA, 2003.

Ghanea-Hercock R A. Phobos: An Agent-based User Authentication System. IEEE Intelligent Systems, 2003:18:3:67–73.

Global Grid Forum. Open Grid Services Architecture, v1.0. April 2003 — http://www.globalgridforum.org/

Gnutella — http://www.gnutella.com/

Gokhale A, Kumar B, and Sahuguet A. Reinventing the Wheel? CORBA vs. Web Services. The Eleventh International World Wide Web Conference, May 2002.

Groove Whitepaper, 2003 — http://www.groove.net/pdf/backgrounder-product.pdf

Howes T A and Smith M. A Scalable, Deployable Directory Service Framework for the Internet. Technical Report, Center for Information Technology Integration, University of Michigan, HTTP/1.0 — Informational RFC 1945, 1995 — http://www.w3.org/Protocols/rfc1945/

Kazaa — http://www.kazaa.com/

IBM DeveloperWorks — http://www-106.ibm.com/developerworks/

LDAP v3 protocol — RFC 2251— http://www.ogre.com/

Mizrak A. Structured Superpeers: Leveraging Heterogeneity to Provide Constant-Time Lookup. Proceedings of the IEEE Workshop on Internet Applications, San Jose, CA, 2003.

Pallickara S and Fox G. NaradaBrokering: A Distributed Middleware Framework and Architecture for Enabling Durable Peer-to-Peer Grids. Proceedings of ACM/IFIP/USENIX International Middleware Conference (Middleware-2003), Rio Janeiro, Brazil, June 2003.

Papazoglou M P, Krämer B J, and Yang J. Leveraging Web Services and Peer-to-Peer Networks. In: Eder J and Missikoff M (editors). Proceedings of Advanced Information Systems Engineering 15th International Conference. CAiSE'03, Klagenfurt, Austria, June 2003:485–501.

Resource Description Framework (RDF) Model and Syntax Specification, W3C — http://www.w3.org/TR/REC-rdf-syntax/

Rowstron A and Druschel P. Pastry: Scalable, Decentralized Object Location and Routing for Large Scale Peer-to-Peer Systems. Proceedings of 18th Conference on Distributed Systems Platforms, Heidelberg, 2001.

Saffre F. Adaptive Security and Robust Networks. Information Security Bulletin, November 2002:7:11.

SAML — Organization for the Advancement of Structured Information Standards — http://www.oasis-open.org/committees/security/docs/draft-sstc-saml-spec-00.PDF

Tuecke S et al. Grid Service Specification. Global Grid Forum, 2002 — http://www.ggf.org/ogsi-wg/

UK Ministry of Defence Expenditure Plans 2003-04 to 2005-06 — http://www.mod.uk/publications/expenditure2003/staff.htm

Wang F. Self-Organising Communities Formed by Middle Agents. Proceedings of the First International Conference on Autonomous Agents and Multi-Agent Systems, Bologna, Italy, 2002:1333–1339.

Zhao B, Kubiatowicz J, and Joseph A. Tapestry: An Infrastructure for Fault-Tolerant Wide-Area Location and Routing. Technical Report UCB/CSD-01-1141, Computer Science Division, UC, Berkeley, CA, 2002.

22

Intelligent Data Analysis for Detecting Behaviour Patterns in iSpaces

D D Nauck, B Majeed, and B-S Lee

22.1 Introduction

Pervasive ICT or ubiquitous computing is a vision for the near-term future where computing and communications devices, services, and software agents act together seamlessly in order to support human users anywhere and at any time. The nature of ubiquitous computing was defined by Weiser as the type of computing that is invisible, and docs not live on a personal device of any sort, but is in the woodwork everywhere [1]. In order to fulfil the vision of pervasive ICT [2], three main objectives have to be met.

- Awareness

  Services and devices need to be aware of their environment, events taking place in their environment, and the presence and intentions of users, in order to put agents into context.

- Adaptive context modelling

  In order to provide useful services, software agents need a model of the context they are working in. The model must be adaptive such that agents can react to changes in their environment and in user requirements and discover new services.

- Autonomy

  Software agents must have the ability to access services and influence their environment on behalf of the user.

This chapter focuses on the first objective — awareness — in the context of intelligent environments or iSpaces. An iSpace is an environment that is aware of its inhabitants and offers services, such as re-routing telephone calls, displaying information, or adjusting air conditioning based on what it knows about its inhabitants and their intentions.

In order to collect information about inhabitants and environmental conditions an iSpace requires sensors. We suggest that these sensors should be organised into a logical sensor network that is independent from the physical embodiment of the sensors and their networking. A logical sensor network allows designers to fuse sensor data streams into structures that represent higher-level events or complex states.

The readings from a sensor network are fed into an intelligent data analysis (IDA) process that derives the required information to interpret the current context. The

IDA process must be able to run automatically and adapt to changing conditions. We show how automatic IDA can be used to derive information from a logical sensor network to achieve awareness and possible re-configuring the sensor network. As an example we will discuss our work in a telecare project where we use automatic IDA in sensor networks for well-being monitoring.

This chapter discusses how automatic intelligent data analysis can be used within iSpaces that use sensor networks as data source. In the following section we give a short overview of different iSpace approaches. In Section 22.3 we discuss our approach to automatic data analysis and how it works in logical sensor networks. Section 22.4 then discusses an application example in the area of telecare, and we conclude the chapter in Section 22.5.

22.2   Approaches to iSpaces

The field of iSpaces has naturally developed from ubiquitous computing, and it is used in literature to describe a variety of application categories. As an example, the MavHome is an agent-based smart home that aims to maximise the inhabitant's comfort and productivity and to minimise costs [3]. The MavHome system is capable of predicting the location of the inhabitant [4], and of automating a number of tasks on their behalf (it orders milk, turns sprinklers on and off, follows the person with multimedia items to the bathroom, etc).

Another example is the University of Massachusetts's Intelligent Home project which involves designing and implementing a set of distributed autonomous home control agents that are capable of negotiation over shared resources [5]. An application that aims at energy-efficiency manages the thermal resource distribution in a building [6]. This system is implemented using a multi-agent environment in which the agents represent individual temperature controllers that bid to buy or sell cool or warm air.

Intelligent environments have attracted a number of collaborators working towards marketable solutions under the umbrella of the Centre for the Integrated Home Environment, a UK-based research centre that is concerned with the development of an integrated services environment to improve the quality of life for the consumer [7]. The work reported by Lee and Hashimoto [8] describes using a sensor network to control mobile robots that replace the automated guided vehicle (AGV) in factories. In traditional architecture for mobile robots, the biggest challenge is localisation and obstacle avoidance; hence robots have many sensors and large processing power. In this application the intelligent space (sensor network) does the monitoring. Obstacles, including humans, can be detected, and the information is passed to the robots. These examples show the intelligent environment as a means of controlling appliances and devices for the purpose of increased comfort and productivity.

Intelligent environments have also been popular for health-centred applications and in particular the area of care for the elderly and the ill. The Independent Life Style Assistant (ILSA) is a project run by Honeywell, and it looks at how an agent-based home environment can aid elderly people to live longer in their homes [9, 10]. The long-term behavioural monitoring of elderly people using a network of passive sensors is reported by Ogawa et al [11], while an alarm-raising system that detects falls and abnormally long periods of immobility of an elderly inhabitant is discussed by Sixsmith [12]. BT has an established research track record in telecare and telemedicine, which began in 1994, investigating whether life-style monitoring could be used to provide a proactive support service to older or vulnerable people in the community [13, 14].

22.3   Intelligent Data Analysis in Sensor Networks

In order to make a space intelligent and aware of its inhabitants and their activities and intentions without demanding direct input from its occupants, the iSpace must collect large amounts of data. The majority of this data will come from networked sensors that measure a variety of relevant features. The presence and activities of persons, for example, can be detected by sensors as diverse as passive infra-red sensors, pressure sensors on furniture, consumption of energy or water, door sensors, light sensors in cupboards, etc. It is also possible to detect people because their clothes may be enhanced by RFID tags or because their PDAs or mobile telephones interact with the iSpace. The sensors must be networked so they can work together and exchange information. Readings from one sensor could trigger changing modes of operation in other sensors like switching from one reading per minute to one reading per second.

In order to make sense of the data produced by the sensor network, intelligent data analysis (IDA) is required. Obviously, the analysis must be fully automatic and carried out in real time. When we design an iSpace we will typically not know which type of analysis method is the appropriate one to obtain a particular answer from the sensor data at a particular time. For example, imagine that the iSpace has detected the presence of a person and must now try to identify this person in order to offer services. If the person is not tagged and advanced identification based on camera images is not appropriate because of privacy reasons, then other methods must be found.

The iSpace can gather evidence about the person by analysing information like low-resolution infra-red images, readings from pressure sensors (weight) or gait sensors.

Depending on which type of information is currently available, the analysis methods that are used to identify the person may vary. For example, if infra-red and gait information were available, identification may be most reliable if a neural network were used. If readings from pressure sensors and gait were available, then maybe a decision tree would provide the best result.

We could also assume that, for some analysis methods, certain types of data pre-processing (discretisation, averaging, outlier detection, missing values handling, etc) would be required.

When a person has been successfully identified or if certain services have been accepted or rejected, then the internal models of the iSpace must adapt and learn from the experience. This learning process must happen automatically, i.e. the analysis engine of the iSpace must have certain meta-knowledge about how to learn from data and how to improve particular models.

22.3.1   Automatic Intelligent Data Analysis

In the area of automatic IDA we are looking for new approaches to handle large amounts of data by going beyond standard data mining approaches. IDA takes domain knowledge and knowledge about the analysis process into account. Important research issues are how to provide intelligent algorithms for model selection depending on the questions a user wants to be answered about the data. The final goal is a knowledge-based, completely automated analysis process from pre-processing over model selection and evaluation to application. Depending on the analysis requirement given by the application area, IDA uses data analysis methods that can create models on a range from comprehensible and simple to complex and precise — soft computing methodologies are ideal candidates for this task.

Today, we have modern intelligent algorithms based on computational intelligence and machine learning. Soft computing methods like neuro-fuzzy systems [15] and probabilistic networks, or AI methods, such as advanced decision trees and inductive logic programming, provide new, intelligent ways for analysing data. The advantage of these IDA methods is that they allow both the inclusion of available knowledge and the extraction of new, comprehensible knowledge about the analysed data.

We have developed an approach to automatic IDA that we are currently applying to a telecare project where the iSpace is the home of a person who potentially requires care (see next section). This approach has been implemented in a software platform called SPIDA (Soft Computing Platform for IDA) [16]. SPIDA is capable of fully automatic model creation based on IDA processes.

SPIDA selects suitable data analysis models based on requirements that must be met by the analysis results. These requirements can be, for example, accuracy, speed, simplicity, and adaptability of the model. The requirements can be vague (high accuracy, low speed, etc), and therefore fuzzy logic is used to implement a knowledge base for selecting analysis methods [17].

In its current implementation SPIDA contains analysis methods such as neuro-fuzzy systems, neural networks, support vector machines, fuzzy cluster analysis, multiple linear regression, and decision trees. All these methods have certain individual capabilities and produce models with different features that can be useful in different contexts. Neural networks, for example, can provide very accurate function approximation models, but they are black boxes and cannot be interpreted. In the same context (function approximation) neuro-fuzzy systems can learn an interpretable fuzzy rule base from data, but may be less accurate than a neural network.

Depending on the context that is described by the data to be analysed, the user requirements and the known features of the available analysis methods, SPIDA will select appropriate methods.

The selected methods will be configured and executed automatically to create the required models for the given analysis context such as function approximation, prediction, classification, segmentation, etc. SPIDA can change parameter settings of analysis methods if machine learning processes seem unstable, or if it turns out at the beginning of the model generation process that the result will probably not match the requirements. After a model has been created SPIDA can automatically re-run a particular method with refined parameter settings in order to obtain an improved solution that is, for example, more accurate or less complex.

For the automatic selection of data analysis methods, SPIDA employs fuzzy knowledge bases that provide it with the necessary guidelines for selecting, applying, and evaluating analysis methods and the models created by them. Several basic categories help us to identify the type of data analysis to be run:

- prediction (classification, function approximation, time-series analysis);

- clustering (segmentation, concept description);

- dependency description (associations, deviations, statistical models, probabilistic models).

In each category, several analysis methods are applicable. Which methods should be selected depends on the requirements and the available data. In an iSpace scenario the requirements are usually accuracy, reliability, speed, and adaptability. If the analysis results must be inspected by humans, such as in cases where safety critical features must be confirmed or the results must be checked for plausibility, then requirements like simplicity, interpretability, integration of prior knowledge, or user-friendliness are of interest. Most of these features are fuzzy in nature. Interpretability, for example, measures how easy it is to understand a model. Assume a rule-based model like a fuzzy system or a decision tree — the level of interpretability then depends on factors like the number of rules, the dimension of antecedents and, in the case of fuzzy systems, on the shape of fuzzy sets. It is also possible to define real-valued measures [18].

Nevertheless, since measures usually depend on many factors, they might be quite difficult to understand for non-expert users. Also, it does not seem sensible to distinguish similar values. For example, it would not make much of a difference for the interpretability of a solution if a rule base contains 20 or 21 rules. We assume that most users would rather prefer a coarse granular differentiation like *very easy*, *easy*, *medium*, *difficult*, or *very difficult*. In order to be able to interpolate between these coarse values, they can be modelled as fuzzy sets, i.e. if the value of the real-valued measure slightly changes, the fuzzy value is gradually shifted [17, 19].

Most of the categories, e.g. accuracy, adaptability, can be used to characterise requirements on the one hand, and data analysis method properties on the other hand. For instance, adaptability of a method to new data can be an important requirement because the iSpace must adapt its models to new sensor data. On the other hand, data analysis methods have different levels of adaptability (e.g. neural network — highly adaptive, neuro-fuzzy system — slightly adaptive, decision tree — not adaptive). The actual selection of an appropriate data analysis method in SPIDA is based on a fuzzy knowledge base for method selection (KBMS) that links fuzzy requirements with fuzzy method properties. The KBMS and the inference mechanism are based on the fuzzy system described in Spott [20].

The designer of an iSpace can specify the importance of features like adaptability or the possibility to integrate prior knowledge, as well as the level of required accuracy, simplicity, etc. The KBMS contains rules that can match the required degrees of adaptability, simplicity, etc, to features of analysis methods. If adaptability of a model is an important feature, then a method like induction of decision trees would be less suitable than a neural network, because the latter can be continuously trained with new data, while a decision tree would have to be completely rebuilt.

The KBMS is applied to the requirements, inferring a fuzzy profile of data analysis methods that reflects the requirements. This fuzzy profile will be matched against the fuzzy profiles of all methods. Based on the degrees of match, SPIDA generates a ranked list of data analysis methods. Based on the computational resources, one or many suitable methods can be executed.

Once SPIDA has decided that some data analysis method is appropriate, another knowledge base, the knowledge base for automated intelligent modelling (AIM), controls the data analysis process of model creation (learning). AIM contains heuristics about model creation represented by a mixture of exact and fuzzy rules. Since exact rules are a special case of fuzzy rules, AIM is, like the KBMS, a fuzzy knowledge base. Rules in this knowledge base are method-specific. Using neuro-fuzzy techniques as described in Nauck, Klawonn, and Kruse [15], rules in AIM can be adapted to the particular requirements and features of an iSpace that uses SPIDA as its IDA engine.

22.3.2   Data Analysis in Sensor Networks

An iSpace collects information from sensors. We propose that the sensors are organised in a logical sensor network that abstracts from the physical sensor and provides means for management and data transfer. A sensor network collects information about inhabitants and their environmental conditions. This provides the implicit input required for intelligent environments. The word 'inhabitant' can be used to refer to the humans in the environment, but also to animals, robots, or other types of machine. Sensor network research in relation to ubiquitous computing has been a very active area of research. Recent reviews of existing technology, new developments, and future trends of sensor networks can be found in Chong and Khumar [21] and Akyildiz et al [22].

In order for the intelligent environment to have 'context awareness', its sensors should be organised in a way that provides it with the ability to reason about activity-specific events. Consider the case where the environment needs to know about the sleeping patterns of its occupant. In this case it must be equipped with a group of sensors that detect sleep-related events. This leads to the notion of a logical sensor network that is independent from the physical embodiment of the sensors and their network topology.

A logical sensor network provides means to represent knowledge provided by domain experts. Their knowledge about relevant activities is reflected by activity-based sensor groups. Rather than gathering data from all sensors and carry out an overall data mining algorithm, a focused and more efficient algorithm can be applied to each of the activities according to the available knowledge and the data collected by the corresponding sensor group. This way more robust activity-based reasoning can be implemented that is capable of dealing with missing data from individual sensors within a sensor group. The sensors can be fixed inside the iSpace or they can be mobile and worn by the person.

The sensors form an *ad hoc* network that allows plug-and-play insertion and removal of sensors at any time. A management module allows the administrator of the iSpace to organise the physical sensors into a logical network and to configure them. A logical sensor network allows the fusion of sensor data streams into structures that represent higher-level events or complex states. Figure 22.1 shows the logical sensor organisation tool that has been developed in our telecare project (see Section 22.4). The sensor objects are organised in a tree structure that can be easily manipulated using the menu commands provided. All sensor objects have associated methods that allow the triggering of pre-processing algorithms (such as noise filtering) on their data streams.

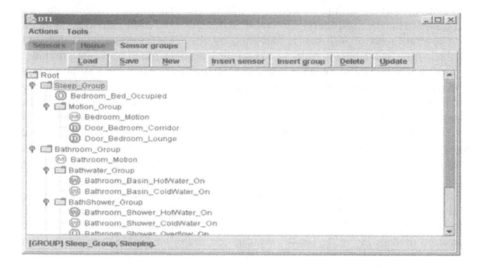

Fig. 22.1   Managing a logical sensor network.

The IDA engine of the iSpace can access the sensor network and retrieve the data for analysis. Based on the current context, the available data, the requirements, and the individual capabilities of the sensors, the IDA engine can reconfigure the logical network in order to retrieve additional or different information.

For example, when the iSpace detects the presence of a particular person and has information about the preferred room temperature, the IDA engine could decide to increase the temperature reading from an hourly average to a reading per minute in order to better control the heating system and the air conditioning. The iSpace could also decide to temporarily integrate a wearable sensor of the present person and fuse its data with PIR sensors in order to obtain better location information. When the person leaves the iSpace, the wearable sensor is removed from the configuration.

22.4   Detecting Unusual Patterns

As a part of the Care in the Community project within BT, we are developing an intelligent data analysis unit that is responsible for monitoring the long-term changes in the well-being indicators of people with care needs. The higher-level domain knowledge required for such analysis is developed by a partner group within the project (namely the domain-specific modelling (DSM) group), while installing the physical sensors and providing raw data for analysis are assigned to the sensor network group. We use 'long-term' to describe a period of time over which it is possible to observe subtle changes in the way activities of daily living are carried out, rather than an alarm system that indicates immediate problems (such as a fall detector).

The analysis of well-being is very challenging, as abnormal patterns of behaviour are difficult to obtain. Additionally, what is considered to be normal for one person can be abnormal for someone else. Moreover, people have a tendency to change the way they do things without necessarily being affected by deterioration in their physical or mental abilities. Therefore, interactive and adaptive algorithms are necessary to handle such analysis with the particularities of each individual in mind. The several facets of well-being, identified by the DSM group, require different methods for data analysis in order to answer the questions posed by a care provider.

In this project the iSpace is the home of a person whose well-being is monitored. The users and iSpace designers of the system are care professionals who require predictions about the development of the person's well-being. In this application domain we mainly require analysis methods that have a high degree of accuracy and adaptability. Accuracy is essential to reduce the number of false alarms. This would have a negative impact on the acceptance of the telecare concept by potential clients. Adaptability of models is required because of the earlier-mentioned fact that people happen to change their life-style patterns for no 'negative' reason.

In addition, we will also require simple and interpretable models, especially in the area of reporting. The IDA engine will build models that explain why the well-being of a person is about to deteriorate. These explanatory models will use input from the detection models. By using SPIDA we can configure the KBMS appropriately so that the correct analysis method can be automatically selected given a detection or explanation context. Figure 22.2 shows an overview of the data analysis environment, where the activity groups are those identified by the care experts.

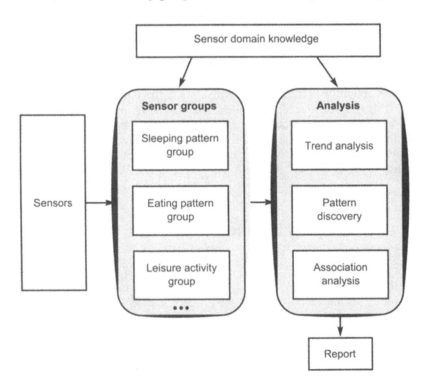

Fig. 22.2   Data analysis overview.

As an example of how the current system answers the questions posed by the care professionals, let us consider one of the activities identified as being an important indicator to the well-being of elderly people or those with care needs, namely their level of social interaction. Care experts working with the DSM group have identified a number of aspects of social interaction, which are measurable using the network of sensors and appropriate analysis of their data. Two of these aspects are the general pattern of 'going out' of the house whether for social purposes or to carry out other business (e.g. shopping) and having visitors at home.

For the first aspect, a tool was required to monitor the frequency of 'going out' events, the duration of these events, and the pattern of preparation prior to them. The last of these is particularly important in determining the ability of people to carry out physical activities and to look after their general state of grooming/hygiene. As a result, it was necessary to equip the data analysis unit with a feature that allows the carer to monitor any changes in the pattern of these three issues.

The first step was to look at the real data coming from the home of a person with care needs. We had access to motion and door sensor data, shown in Table 22.1, obtained from a current telecare trial (BT and Liverpool City Council). At a later stage of this project richer sensor information will be available. However, it was still possible to obtain useful results on the available limited data.

Table 22.1 Sample of sensor data.

	Sensor	Start time	Duration
1	Hall	10:43:57	00:01:18
2	Front door	10:44:00	00:01:14
4	Utility	10:46:38	00:00:19
5	Back door	10:47:00	00:00:00
6	Utility	10:47:00	00:00:17
8	Hall	10:48:35	00:03:01
9	Front door	10:51:13	00:00:13

It is evident from Table 22.1 that the start time and duration of the events cover a wide range of values, which makes it difficult to extract meaningful observations for the purpose of monitoring the overall pattern of events. For example, in order to look at the frequency of 'going out' events, should the system include all such events no matter how long they take or what time they occur? It is important to distinguish between significant and insignificant episodes depending on the life-style of the client. For this purpose, the events were classified into more useful groups using fuzzy sets. As an example, in this application, the start time data was fuzzified by dividing the time of day into fuzzy intervals as shown in Fig. 22.3 for the early part of the day.

There are several ways of obtaining a suitable fuzzy partitioning of a domain. If domain knowledge is available, then a domain expert can suggest appropriate boundaries. It is also possible to use data-driven approaches such as fuzzy cluster

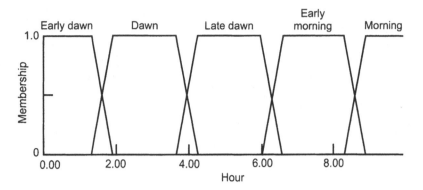

Fig. 22.3   Start time membership functions.

analysis [23] or neuro-fuzzy learning [15]. Fuzzy cluster analysis is an unsupervised learning method that looks for clusters appearing naturally in the data and represents each cluster as a fuzzy set [23]. Neuro-fuzzy learning is supervised and would require classified data describing for example 'normal' and 'abnormal' situations. A neuro-fuzzy algorithm would then construct fuzzy sets that are optimal for distinguishing the different classes [15]. Ideally, a data-driven approach and expert supervision are combined either by generating fuzzy sets that are validated by an expert or by refining fuzzy sets that are pre-defined by an expert during a subsequent learning process.

It should be noted that fuzzy partitions are domain- and application-dependent. One advantage of using fuzzy systems is typically given by the fact that they can be intuitively understood by domain experts. This facilitates the modelling of domain knowledge. Fuzzy systems also provide robust models because fuzzy sets overlap, and thus anomalies at set boundaries that are known from crisp rule-based systems are less likely to occur [19].

After fuzzifying the attributes of these events, the data analysis unit first discovers the significant 'going out' episodes within the daily events according to criteria that can be set automatically, and fine-tuned manually by the system user. By significant episodes, we mean those that are reasonably long and are preceded by a reasonable amount of 'getting ready' activities. In this way, a significant 'going out' episode would involve some sort of social interaction as opposed to those that may not involve such interaction. This is achieved by mining the data, for the duration of interest, and building a fuzzy knowledge base that provides a fuzzy classification of all the discovered episodes according to their significance.

At this stage the user is able to apply trend analysis to the duration and frequency of episodes that are selectable by their significance factor, for example, the user might only be interested in looking at very significant episodes for the last month, or in medium- to high-significance occurrences over the last six months, and so on. The trend analysis procedure employs a number of moving average views (weighted or non-weighted) that give the user flexibility in customising the analysis according to their expertise. Non-expert users can have default views generated automatically by the knowledge base.

Firstly, the data analysis engine applies its preprocessing (fuzzy) filters in order to determine the significant 'going out' episodes in the daily sensor data from the client's home, and then a plot of the aggregate amount spent outside the home is produced as shown in Fig. 22.4 for one of the clients during a four-month period. Figure 22.5 shows the same data processed using a moving average filter to iron out the sharp variation and to emphasize the repeating periodical behaviour. It is evident here that the overall graph shows a repetitive pattern where clients spend a regular amount of time outside their home. However, it is noticeable that there is a reduction

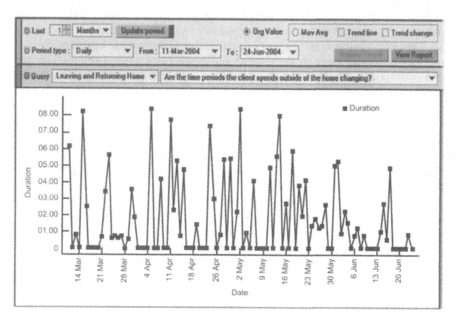

Fig. 22.4   'Going out' duration raw data.

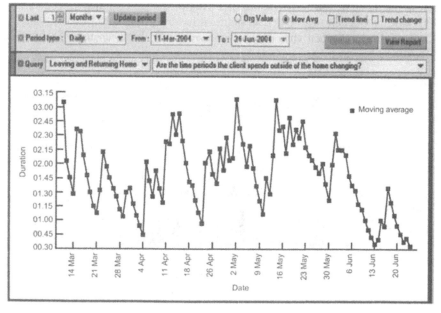

Fig. 22.5   Moving average of 'going out' duration.

of this time towards the end of the period. This observation may (or may not) indicate a general deterioration of health, ability, or desire to go out (the latter is usually exhibited by people suffering from depression). Here the system requires input from the expert user to decide whether to accept the situation and to adapt its internal models, or to raise an alarm condition. Users of the system must be provided with adequate training to help them interpret the result and take appropriate action.

Although this type of trend analysis can provide a suitable indication for monitoring the changes in the frequency and duration of the 'going out' episodes, it is not useful for analysing the pattern of preparation prior to these episodes. Work is currently progressing towards developing additional pattern recognition techniques that would allow us to determine the normal patterns of the person's behaviour in preparation to leaving the home. The system will then monitor how these patterns are changing with time in order to establish a link to the person's well-being status. The well-being status is based on a number of indicators that describe the way in which activities of daily living are being carried out by the client at home, and how the patterns of these activities change as a result of the deterioration in the client's health and well-being. This represents the research domain of the DSM project team as mentioned earlier in this section.

Receiving visitors at home is the second facet of social interaction being addressed in this study. Carers would like to know if the client is regularly receiving visitors at home, whether the client is active during the visit (e.g. opening doors, accompanying visitors). Current trials by the Liverpool City Council have so far made use of passive infra-red (PIR) sensors to pick up occurrences of motion in various rooms, supplemented by a few toggle switch sensors to detect when windows and entrances are open. Although this provides a very restricted data set consisting of few specific details about household events, plenty of information can still be inferred as to the general level of activity within the home, and hence the likelihood of a visitor's being present. The data in Fig. 22.6 shows motions detected (black) during a one-hour period in the home of a single occupant studied in the current Liverpool City Council trial. The data segment has been split into three regions (A, B, C) according to the entrance events observed, such that each region denotes a

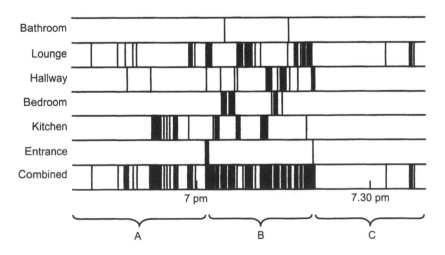

Fig. 22.6   An example of household motion data.

time during which the number of persons in the home should remain constant. By comparing the behaviours exhibited in regions neighbouring an entrance event, it is possible to determine those likely to correspond with people arriving, leaving, or simply indicating that the client is interacting with someone on the doorstep.

As a result of the reliance on limited types of sensors, and in the absence of client identification means (e.g. tags), it is not possible to determine with certainty whether there is a visitor in the house. The role of fuzzy logic is important in these situations as it provides means for making decisions with an associated confidence factor that the carer can use to form a general view about the visitor activity. The output of the data analysis in this case is presented in the abstract activity view shown in Fig. 22.7. Here the carer can see the activities of daily living and can point at them with the mouse to display the numeric value of the associated degree of confidence. For example, the 'Sleep' and 'Out' activities have a confidence level of 1 (i.e. 100%) due to the absence of any ambiguity in the analysis. This is not the case for the visitor activity for the reasons mentioned above, and as a result the user is presented with periods of time describing the visit activity with a colour scheme that is dependent on the confidence level. As the confidence in the decision increases, the colour of the visit activity changes from dark orange to bright yellow (in Fig. 22.7 a higher confidence level is represented by a lighter grey shade). It is important to emphasise that colour changes can give the user of the system a better appreciation of the variations of the level of the visit activities that the client is experiencing than a scheme that displays numbers and percentages.

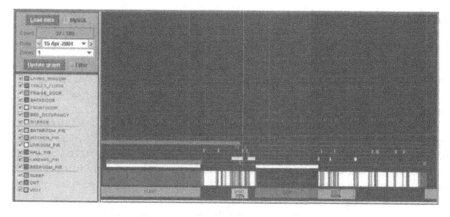

Fig. 22.7   Abstract activities view.

Other analysis views that the system provides present the user with trends of the aggregate visit activity in order to determine whether these are changing significantly with time.

Another example that demonstrates the capability of the system in developing normality models and using these to indicate the advent of abnormal behaviour is looking at sleep patterns. The system builds a model of a normal sleep pattern by observing the nightly events over a reasonably long period of time. Such a model takes the form of fuzzy rules that relate sleep duration, waking up frequency and duration, movement pattern in and out of the bedroom to the 'normality' of sleep of the client. Fine-tuning is provided by care experts who can make modifications to the fuzzy rules and to the fuzzy sets that describe the sleep-related variables. Figure 22.8

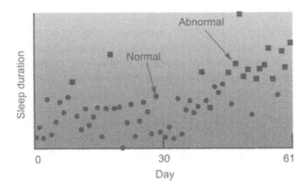

Fig. 22.8   Monitored sleep patterns — abnormal episodes are
not only due to longer sleep duration.

shows the changing trend in sleep pattern from normal to abnormal in relation to the sleep dur-ation variable. It can be seen that the sleep pattern is not only a function of sleep duration, which is evident in the abnormal event that falls within the normal sleep duration region (the grey area). This can be due to a larger than usual level of disturbance and movement during the night.

22.5   Summary

We have discussed how automatic intelligent data analysis in logical sensor networks can be used to achieve some degree of awareness by an iSpace. We have shown how this approach can be used in the area of telecare, where the iSpace is the home of a person whose well-being needs to be monitored. The home is fitted with a sensor network capable of capturing the events of daily activities.

We have started to adapt our automatic IDA platform SPIDA to data analysis in logical sensor networks and reported some initial results that we have achieved in the 'Intelligent Data Analysis in Sensor Networks' project within BT's Care in the Community Centre. Fuzzy reasoning and trend analysis were the algorithms used to provide a well-being status at the early part of the work. As more data becomes available, including a more varied range of sensor types, other data analysis techniques will be incorporated. Currently we are developing tools based on association rule discovery and sequential/temporal pattern recognition to deal with the more demanding aspects of well-being monitoring, such as preparing meals and dealing with multi-occupancy homes. One of the main difficulties in establishing 'normal' models of behaviour in a telecare application is that every client has a unique pattern of performing daily living activities. While some clients exhibit a very regular and repeatable activity pattern, others tend to change in a seemingly erratic manor. By nature, engineers and computer scientists deal with systems that exhibit repeatable response to external or internal triggers. This usually causes a problem when they try to apply their knowledge to people's behaviour monitoring. We have found that the role of care professionals is crucial here in order to bridge the gap between the data analysis community and the requirements of telecare. The input of care professionals is very important in designing user interfaces that provide just the right level of reporting to the system user without causing unnecessary harm by initiating unnecessary alarm events.

References

1. Weiser M. The World Is Not a Desktop. ACM Interactions, 1994:1:8:7–8.

2. Abowd G, Mynatt E, and Rodden T. The Human Experience. IEEE Pervasive Computing, 2002:48–57.

3. Cook D et al. MavHome: An Agent-based Smart Home. Proceedings of the First Intl Conf on Pervasive Computing and Communications (PerCom'03), 2003:521–524.

4. Das S et al. The Role of Prediction Algorithms in the MavHome Smart Home Architecture. IEEE Wireless Communications, 2002:77–84.

5. Lesser V et al. The UMASS Intelligent Home Project. Proceedings of the Association for Computing Machinery International Conference on Autonomous Agents, 1999:291–298.

6. Huberman B and Clearwater S. A Multi-agent System for Controlling Building Environments. Proceedings of First International Conference on Multiagent Systems. AAAI Press, 1995:171–176.

7. Centre for the Integrated Home Environment, December 2003 — http://www.cihe. lboro.ac.uk/

8. Lee J and Hashimoto H. Controlling Mobile Robots in Distributed Intelligent Sensor Networks. IEEE Transactions on Industrial Electronics, October 2003:50:5:890–902.

9. Haigh K, Phelps J and Geib C. An Open Agent Architecture for Assisting Elder Independence. First International Joint Conference on Autonomous Agents and MultiAgent Systems (AAMAS), Bologna, Italy, July 2002:578 586.

10. Miller C, Haigh K, and Dewing W. First Cause No Harm: Issues in Building Safe, Reliable and Trustworthy Elder Care Systems. AAAI 02 Automation as Caregiver Workshop, July 2002:80-84.

11. Ogawa M et al. Long-term Remote Behavioral Monitoring of the Elderly Using Sensors Installed in Domestic Houses. Proceedings of the Second Joint EMBS/BMES Conference, Houston, TX, USA, October 2002:1853–1854.

12. Sixsmith A. An Evaluation of an Intelligent Home Monitoring System. Journal of Telemedicine and Telecare, 2002:6:63–72.

13. Garner P et al. The Application of Telepresence in Medicine. BT Technol J, October 1997:15:4:181–187.

14. Barnes N et al. Lifestyle Monitoring — Technology for Supported Independence. Computing and Control Engineering Journal, August 1998:9:4:169–174.

15. Nauck D, Klawonn F and Kruse R. Foundations of Neuro-Fuzzy Systems. Wiley, Chichester, 1997.

16. Nauck D, Spott M, and Azvine B. SPIDA — A Novel Data Analysis Tool. BT Technol J, October 2003:21:4:104–112.

17. Zadeh L A. Soft Computing and Fuzzy Logic. IEEE Software, 1994:11:48–56.

18. Nauck D. Measuring Interpretability in Rule-based Classification Systems. Proc IEEE Intl Conf on Fuzzy Systems, St Louis, MO, 2003:196–201.

19. Kruse R, Gebhardt J, and Klawonn F. Foundations of Fuzzy Systems. Wiley, Chichester, 1994.

20. Spott M. Efficient Reasoning with Fuzzy Words. Proc Intl Conf on Fuzzy Systems and Knowledge Discovery, Singapore, 2002.

21. Chong C and Khumar S. Sensor Networks: Evolution, Opportunities, and Challenges. Proceedings of the IEEE, August 2003:91:8:1247–1256.

22. Akyildiz I et al. Wireless Sensor Networks: A Survey. Computer Networks, 2002:38:14.

23. Höppner F et al. Fuzzy Cluster Analysis. Wiley, Chichester, 1999.

23

xAssist — Inferring User Goals from Observed Actions

J Allen, S Appleby, and G Churcher

23.1   Introduction

The vision of intelligent spaces — iSpaces (also known as ambient intelligence [1] or ubiquitous computing [2]) — is that of computers being pervasive, yet unobtrusive. They will assist us in our tasks in such a natural way that we may not even be aware of their presence.

MIT Media Lab [3] defines iSpaces as follows:

Space-centred computation embedded in ordinary environments defines intelligent spaces populated by cameras, microphones, displays, sound output systems, radar systems, wireless networks, and controls for physical entities such as curtains, lighting, door locks, soda dispensers, toll gates, and automobiles. People interact in intelligent spaces naturally, using speech, gesture, drawing, and movement, without necessarily being aware that computation is present.

This is in sharp contrast to today's computing environment where we are only too well aware that computation is present. The computation is the bit that delivers unintelligible messages, stops working for no apparent reason, and makes a simple job needlessly complicated. It is also the part that does not know what we are doing, why we are doing it, and when we would least appreciate a small paper-clip leaping on screen to ask us if we are writing a letter. So how do we get from where we are to where we want to be?

An iSpace uses observations of an individual's behaviour and the context of that behaviour. The behaviour is considered to be the set of observable events triggered by the actions of the individual concerned (since an iSpace can only act on observable events). The context will be any other information, such as time or date, temperature, weather conditions, or any behaviour-independent information relevant to the iSpace.

Individuals may have active or passive goals. Active goals will be expressed through an individual's behaviour, since the individual is actively working towards these. Passive goals, on the other hand, are not indicated by behaviour. For example, an iSpace may order milk when users run low, thus satisfying a goal for which there was no expressed behaviour. The individuals did not, necessarily, carry out any action to indicate that they wanted milk — the action would have been triggered by the context alone.

A number of problems need to be solved before the iSpace vision can become a technical, or commercial, reality. Some of the problems relate to cost and infrastructure, such as making devices small enough, cheap enough, and able to communicate with one another. However, the focus of our work is on the inference of an individual's goals from observed behaviour, i.e. we are focusing on an individual's active goals. Previous attempts at this have at best been only partially successful. This is a very difficult problem to solve and has history in the fields of both psychology and artificial intelligence. We believe that until we are able to infer user goals from observed actions, with sufficient accuracy, the iSpace vision cannot become a reality. If we were able to infer user goals, we could develop systems that are able to provide timely and useful help, successfully take the initiative in interactions with humans, and generally make the process of interacting with computers much less painful than is currently the case.

To investigate the problem of inferencing goals from observed behaviour, we have selected an application domain that provides a realistic and useful test bed but avoids the problems of having to deal with physical iSpaces. We are developing xAssist, a framework for implementing applications to assist with a range of typical office automation tasks. xAssist thus operates within the desktop PC environment, which avoids many of the practical difficulties of dealing with sensors and physical spaces, yet provides a sufficiently rich set of observations of user behaviour to allow us to investigate the goal-inference problem outlined above. Specifically, the xAssist framework provides an architecture for building assistants and provides an implementation of the common components, such as:

- merging events from different sources into a timeline;

- mapping differing events to a consistent format;

- managing a knowledge base.

The xAssist applications are produced by populating the inferencing components within the xAssist framework. This chapter describes one specific application within the xAssist framework, namely that of e-mail attachment tracking.

23.2   Reasoning and Action Selection

In this section we present a discussion of some of the general issues involved in interpreting human behaviour and, specifically, the issues related to both inference of an individual's goals from observed behaviour and selection of the appropriate action.

23.2.1   Human Behaviour

Human behaviour is essentially unpredictable. While philosophers disagree as to how far computers can gain intelligent behaviour [4, 5], and therefore how far they can react to humans intelligently, it is true that in limited domains computers can give the impression of understanding human needs.

We have already suggested that iSpaces will fail to be 'intelligent' if we cannot adequately solve the problem of inferring the correct action to take based on direct or indirect evidence of user goals. If we do not solve this problem, we will either find our iSpace too obtrusive, and we will switch it off, or it will simply not offer timely help, and therefore be of little benefit.

In order to make any progress, we need to make some assumptions regarding the mapping between unobservable intentions and observable behaviour. We take as the starting point the following principle [6]:

... assume the actions of [the user] indicate what they want to communicate.

In our case we assume users will not be deliberately trying to fool the system and that it is reasonable to judge their intentions based on their actions.

In fact, this assumption that users are not going to deliberately deceive a system is liable to be a more general principle, taking on a sort of corollary to the 'Grice Maxims' [7]. Grice assumed that in conversations 'rational agents' should follow four rules relating to quality (speak truth), quantity (brief), relevance (orderly), and manner (unambiguous). Additionally, violation of these maxims generated implications about the actual meaning of the speaker. It is likely that a new set of maxims need to be developed for the iSpaces area following these lines. As most systems appear to be aiming for 'natural' interaction, a little philosophical work on what 'natural' behaviour involves could reap large benefits.

Implicit within the mapping from observations to intentions, there is also the requirement to take into account 'observational uncertainty' [8]. Where this is the case, several possible interpretations of the observation may have to be taken into account, including the possibility that the observation is simply an artefact of the observer.

However, simply understanding human behaviour is not enough. If an expert was writing a letter, they would not appreciate a small paper-clip jumping on screen. In this case the system may have correctly judged intentions but not requirements. Anything that distracts from the task at hand will tend to cause aggravation, anything that gives inappropriate behaviour once can be tolerated, anything that repeatedly demonstrates the same inappropriate behaviour rapidly becomes annoying.

It is clear that, in order to supress unhelpful behaviour, the reasoning component should be adaptable. In current systems, this adaptation trivially takes the form of user preferences. A dialogue box may appear giving the user various options, one of which may be 'never do this again'.

However, such an approach is still intrusive, and to be truly capable of providing timely assistance, the reasoning component must be capable of more subtle adaptation.

23.2.2 Input

There are many potential problems with input, e.g. the system may not know for sure whether it has received input or whether it has correctly interpreted the input it has [8]. Speech input in particular is known for giving problems in this regard. Other issues for input devices include availability of device, self-starting, capabilities of device, and resource contention [9]. More inputs may be better in most cases, but this does lead to issues in combining disparate inputs and a new layer of complication and combination before they can be fully utilised [3].

23.2.3   Reasoning

We have so far discussed the role of the reasoning component as the means to map from observations to goals and actions. We will now discuss the nature of the reasoning mechanism itself.

A number of different types of inference are candidates for the reasoning component. These include deductive, abductive, and inductive inference.

In deductive reasoning, we would typically hand-code rules of inference that map from evidence on to propositions. These propositions would essentially be that some plan is being executed with the intention of achieving a particular goal. Deductive reasoning is sound in the sense that, if the observations are correct, and the inference rules are valid, then the deduced propositions are true. Deductive systems can be very unstable, in the sense that adding a new inference rule can lead to behaviour that is difficult to predict [10].

In abductive reasoning, again rules tend to be hand-coded. Abductive inference is rather like reversing the normal deductive process in that we are trying to infer which propositions are consistent with a particular observation. An example of abductive reasoning is that of a doctor trying to diagnose an illness from symptoms. Abductive reasoning is unsound since there may be alternative 'explanations' for a given set of observations.

Deductive and abductive systems are often the foundation of the traditional AI approach. These are normally characterised by building domain knowledge by hand, based on the assumption that this knowledge is needed to 'understand' human behaviours. For example, Allen [11] states that behaviours only make sense if they:

> ... rely heavily on the 'discourse context', that collection of knowledge and beliefs that describe the state of the interaction.

Systems with this kind of architecture have been constructed in the past, e.g. TRAINS [12]. The foundation of these plans is encoded by the programmers and relies heavily on implicit knowledge of what the tasks are that the system should carry. In the terminology of the area, the plans rely on the 'discourse context' — that collection of knowledge and beliefs that describe the state of the interaction [11].

The requirement to build such knowledge bases would be a severe restriction on the practical feasibility of iSpaces, since a large quantity of knowledge would have to be compiled for each application. However, we reject the notion that it is necessary to understand human behaviour in order to predict it. Therefore, we do not believe that such a body of background knowledge is necessary for the success of iSpaces.

As an alternative to deductive and abductive approaches, inductive reasoning provides a means to generalise from specific examples. Here we are typically trying to achieve a generalisation over sets of propositions (e.g. evidence, goals, and actions) [13]. This means creating new rules of inference. In the xAssist case, inductive reasoning can be achieved by using a machine learning technique to generalise over examples [14].

It is desirable to use some degree of machine learning since we wish to provide a framework for the system to adapt its behaviour in response to user actions. For example, the system could generalise the conditions under which it will carry out some action by observing that two 'similar' sets of conditions typically led to that action.

In view of this, we have decided to adopt an inductive approach derived from case-based reasoning (see Rich and Knight [15] for an overview). We believe case-based reasoning is particularly appropriate where there are a relatively small number of possible goals, yet a large space of evidence that might be used to imply these goals. Further, the case-based approach does not suffer from the 'instability' of deductive systems mentioned above. This stability is essentially at the expense of inferencing ability. However, in this application, it is better to have a system that errs on the side of caution. It was felt that other statistical approaches (decision trees, neural nets, IR-type techniques) would need more data than we could provide resources to train. Case-based reasoning allows us to use limited training data without being forced to use brittle hand-crafted rules.

In case-based reasoning, our rule base consists of a number of 'cases'. These are examples of evidence and the appropriate user goal for each case. Effectively, the timeline of evidence represents the plan that leads to the goal. The evidence can be generalised by allowing similar sequences of evidence (perhaps similar plans) to be represented by a single template. In fact, this provides one route for inclusion of machine learning — the induction of templates from specific examples. This also provides an easier framework for either the correction of automatically inferred rules, or explicit training, since the route from evidence to actions is explicit.

23.2.4   Output

The output can often be seen as the easy part — indeed after the input and inference, it does seem a relatively simple proposition. However, large-scale iSpaces could have many applications each competing for output devices, which may themselves have limits on what they are able to display [9]. In our case output was directed to screen in a conventional manner. Though even then there is the question of how to present information unobtrusively. If every few moments a user is interrupted by new messages flashing on screen or taking over control from their current application to request input, then even screen display can lead to problems.

23.3   xAssist framework

The xAssist framework is designed to allow us to readily investigate how the user interacts with a variety of applications and to draw inferences about their overall goals. The framework is based around three main components — the relation inferencer, the active assist, and the event conduit. The relation inferencer and active assist are both streamed events via the event conduit, which, in turn, takes its events from a range of components that watch applications such as Outlook and MS Word. The event conduit can take events from components that represent a wide range of sources, put them into a common format, and then place them on to a timeline. The timeline is made available to any components that have registered an interest in any of the events (see Fig. 23.1).

Currently, the components that provide input events fall into three categories —
MS Office applications (including Outlook), a window title watcher, and a local file
system watcher. The MS Office components are designed to use component object
model (COM) call-backs to detect events in which we are interested. Unfortunately,
COM does not have an event model as such. It simply has a convention for passing
interfaces whose methods may be invoked in response to an event. This convention
is not always followed precisely, which means that while the APIs that are present
for each application appear feature-rich, their unconventional support for events
means that only a sub-set of events can be detected reliably. Hence, components such
as the relation inferencer must work on a range of information from a spectrum of
sources, such as the window title and the file system watcher components. Although
this makes life harder for the developer, it does present issues that are relevant to
iSpaces, namely, that only indirect evidence of user activities will be available. This
is discussed in more detail in the following section about a specific application.

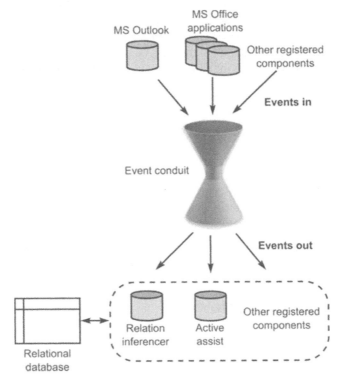

Fig. 23.1   The event conduit framework showing input events
passed through to registered components.

Referring to Fig. 23.1, the event conduit maintains two internal structures, which
are accessible by all components that are registered as either event sources or event
sinks. These structures are:

- a timeline of the (standardised) events;
- a database of objects, properties, and relations.

Both the composition of the events on the timeline and the semantics of the entries in the relational database are dependent on the issues addressed by any individual implementation.

The timeline is a finite-length list of events that operates as a stack, where the most recent event is on top of the stack. As components push events into the event conduit, they are automatically added to the timeline. For practicality, the timeline has a limited memory, so that the oldest events are discarded.

Once an event has been recorded on the timeline, it is then automatically pushed to those components that have registered an interest in it. While there can be any number of components to which the event conduit could push event information, we shall describe the two key components of the framework in more detail — the relation inferencer and the active assist. These two components rely on the relational database maintained by the event conduit. The database has been structured to be as flexible as possible for representing objects, their properties, and the relationships between them. With this in mind we have adopted the entity-relationship-value triple representation, which is the basis of description logic, and underlies the resource description framework (RDF) used by the Semantic Web [16]. This gives us the advantage of being able to use the tools and search engines associated with the RDF syntax as they are developed in support of the Semantic Web.

The actual role of the relation inferencer depends heavily on the specific problem that is trying to be solved within the xAssist framework. On receiving an event in which it has registered an interest, it then accesses both the event timeline and the relational database in order to make inferences. This can lead to the component's generating further events and modifying or adding to the relational database.

The active assist component is designed to perform actions based on received events and has access to both the timeline and the relational database in a similar fashion to that of the relation inferencer, but is much simpler in that it only requires an event and a specific context, for example, key features in a timeline, and need not perform complex inferencing. This component provides just-in-time assistance to the user, relying on the intelligence from the relation inferencer to detect overall tasks, or to make connections between events, depending on the specific problem tackled.

The next section portrays a particular application within the framework that addresses a specific problem and describes the interaction of these key components in detail.

23.4 Example xAssist Application

To investigate the practicality of the xAssist framework, while providing a useful application in its own right, we have implemented a system that allows us to focus on a specific problem often faced by users who receive a number of attachments in their e-mail that are then either left in the inbox or edited and saved on to a local disk. The user is faced with searching through both the inbox and the local disk to find the relevant file. Often the documents are re-saved with different names, making it increasingly difficult for the user to locate the exact version required. This was chosen because it is a specific and well-defined problem area that also allows us to try out the inference of a task through examining multiple events from multiple sources.

The xAssist implementation observes a number of events across MS Outlook and MS Office applications and attempts to infer relationships between viewed e-mails, their attachments, and edited/saved versions on disk. It can then present the user with what is effectively a version history of each attachment and provide an easy-to-use interface to manage the appropriate file. Users can then find files using one of two methods — just-in-time (JIT) activation and user-driven searching.

Just-in-time activation again relies on observing the user's interaction with the system. As users open e-mails containing attachments that have previously been edited/saved to local disk, it presents an information panel showing a version history for the attached files. While it is synonymous with the office assistant's popping up to ask them whether they are writing a letter and offering 'assistance', the system avoids the so-called 'paper-clip syndrome', since it does not interrupt a user's flow of interaction (see Fig. 23.2 for an example of the JIT aspect in operation). The panel also allows the user easy access to the associated e-mail and provides facilities to edit the file or browse the directory where the file is located. Figure 23.3 shows the version history for the returned file. Each individual file version can be selected and opened.

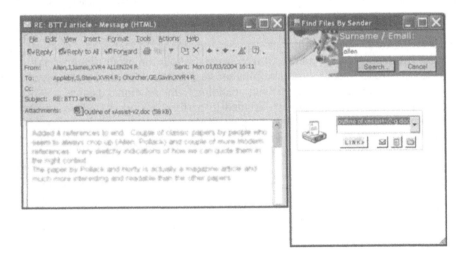

Fig. 23.2   An e-mail opens, and the user is presented with
a version history of the attachments.

The ability to infer relationships between e-mails, attachments, and documents on disk also allows the user to find documents according to this additional information. For instance, a file on disk can be retrieved according to the name of the person who originally sent it in an e-mail, according to keywords in the subject line, or according to surrounding body text. This can be more helpful than the properties of say, a Word document, since authorship information and other general properties are often inaccurate. To take an example, most BT-generated PowerPoint presentations have 'BT' as the author, and this obviously does not help in distinguishing among the numerous documents. The xAssist system therefore provides methods for searching for files based on information that is more useful to the user who is trying to retrieve them. The results that are returned are automatically grouped according to document history (as shown in Fig. 23.3).

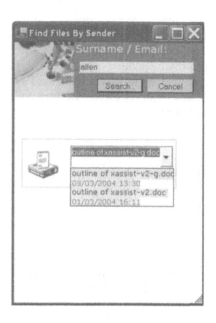

Fig. 23.3   The document history is available, and each individual file can be opened.

As detailed above, the relation inferencer is designed to take an input event and infer relations between objects and their properties based on the event timeline. In this implementation, the main relationship it needs to infer is that between a file that has been saved on disk and an e-mail to which it was originally attached. Hence, the component initially triggers when it receives the event that indicates that a file has been created on a local disk. There are two contexts of this happening in which the inferencer needs to make a connection — when the user has saved the attachment to disk directly from the e-mail, and when a previously saved attachment is edited and resaved as a new file on to disk. In the first instance, the inferencer examines the event timeline maintained by the event conduit and looks for evidence that the user was reading an e-mail containing an attachment that was then selected and saved to disk. This takes the form of a combination of an event of reading an e-mail, then a 'Save Attachment' window title, followed by a file creation event. If these conditions match, then the inferencer can add to the database entries to link that e-mail to the file on disk.

The user is then free to edit the saved file on disk and re-save it as a new file. This implementation attempts to track the history of files as they are saved to disk. On receiving an event indicating that a new file has been created, it consults the event timeline. To enable tracking of documents, the Office suite components that feed events into the event conduit use the COM callback for the 'Before Save' method. This is triggered every time the user saves a document and contains the document's file name and path. The relation inferencer, therefore, is triggered by a new file created on disk and it then looks through the timeline to see whether there is a 'Before Save' event in the recent past. The file name in this event is matched with those that appear in the database to see whether it is either an attachment or a descendent of one. If there is a match, the relation inferencer can update the database linking the new file with the original attachment and e-mail.

The semantics of the relational database depend heavily on the application area. In this implementation the database maintains objects for e-mails and for files.

The properties that are recorded for each enable the system to either make suggestions to the user or provide additional search terms to the user. For instance, the e-mail object has the properties of sender, date, and subject line. The database then ties a document to an e-mail, allowing the user to effectively search for a document based on the e-mail properties.

23.5   Discussion

In terms of the technical environment, it is clear that the desktop operating system is not the environment envisioned for iSpaces. So what will the iSpaces operating system of the future look like?

It would seem likely that the reasoning engine is a centralised component, where observations (sensor inputs and any other relevant information) are made available to a single process. The OSGi [17] (or similar) platform would be a convenient place for such a reasoning engine to reside. However, this is not to say that all intelligence will be sited centrally. For example, an iSpace may well require speech recognition. There is no architectural requirement for the recognition engine to be centrally located.

iSpaces must be able to gather information locally from many sensors. Primarily, this will be over wireless channels, such as Bluetooth [18] or even WiFi [19]. To provide advanced services, the iSpace will need to access a public network through a control interface. This is the role of OSA/Parlay [20].

There are a considerable number of problems to overcome to integrate these disparate technologies at all levels so that they behave as if they were a single, intelligent application environment. The FP6 project, ePerSpace [21], has been set up to explore some of these issues.

23.6   Summary

The key message of this chapter is that iSpaces will not become a reality until we can provide assistance to users that is more appropriate than that made available by current helper systems. To this end, the reasoning engine that infers user requirements will be a critical component.

The iSpace concept is so general and flexible that the reasoning engine will need to cope with a wide variety of situations and tasks and input events. We would argue that machine learning is probably the only way to achieve this in practice, as hand-coding any significant number of rules will be too expensive and inflexible.

We have developed the xAssist framework as a means to investigate the ability to provide appropriate and timely assistance in a desktop environment. The choice of the desktop environment allows us to isolate the inference issues, without simplifying them to an unrealistic degree.

A very significant issue in the attempt to infer needs from indirect observations is the unpredictability of human behaviour and the range of requirements for different individuals. It is difficult to categorise individuals in advance, and therefore, adaptability will be a key factor in the success of iSpaces.

References

1. Ambient Intelligence — http://www.research.philips.com/InformationCenter/Global/FArticleSummary.asp?1NodeId=71

2. Ubiquitous Computing — http://www.ubiq.com/weiser/

3. MIT Project Oxygen — http://oxygen.lcs.mit.edu/E21.html

4. Dreyfus H L. What Computers Can't Do — The Limits of Artificial Intelligence. Harper & Row, 1972.

5. Hofstadter D R. Godel, Escher, Bach: An Eternal Golden Braid. John Spears, 1979.

6. Elzer S et al. Extending Plan Inference Techniques to Recognize Intentions in Information Graphics. 9th International Conference on User Modeling, 2003:122–132.

7. Grice H P. Utterer's Meaning, Sentence Meaning and Word Meaning. Foundations of Language, 1968:4:225–242.

8. Pineau J et al. Towards Robotic Assistants in Nursing Homes: Challenges and Results. Robotics and Autonomous Systems, 2003:42.

9. Gajos K, Weisman L, and Shrobe H. Design Principles for Resource Management Systems for Intelligent Spaces. 2nd International Workshop on Self-Adaptive Software, 2001.

10. Hobbs J et al. Interpretation as Abduction. 26th Annual Meeting of the Association for Computational Linguistics, 1988:95–103.

11. Allen J, Ferguson G and Miller B. Trains-95: Towards a Mixed Initiative Planning Assistant. Proceedings of AIPS-96, 1996.

12. Allen J et al. A Robust System for Natural Spoken Dialogue. 34th Annual Meeting of ACL, 1996.

13. Muggleton S and Raedt L D. Inductive Logic Programming: Theory and Methods. The Journal of Logic Programming, 1994:19 and 20:629–680.

14. Mitchell T. Machine Learning. McGraw-Hill International, 1997.

15. Rich E and Knight K. Artificial Intelligence. McGraw-Hill, 1991.

16. Resource Description Framework — http://www.w3.org/RDF/

17. OSGi Alliance — http://www.osgi.org/

18. Bluetooth — http://www.bluetooth.com/

19. The WiFi Alliance — http://www.wi-fi.org/

20. The Parlay Group — http://www.parlay.org/

21. Information Society Technologies — http://www.cordis.lu/ist/

24

Programming iSpaces — A Tale of Two Paradigms

V Callaghan, M Colley, H Hagras, J Chin, F Doctor, and G Clarke

24.1   Introduction

'iSpace, the final frontier' — this parody of *Star Trek* encapsulates many of our aspirations for this area as, in the longer term, iSpaces are likely to be the key to mankind's successful exploration of deep space. In outer space, or hostile planetary habitats, it is inevitable that people will survive in wholly technologically supported artificial environments [1]. Such environments will contain numerous communicating computers embedded into a myriad of devices, sensing, acting, delivering media, processing data, and providing services that enhance the life-style and effectiveness of the occupant and, in outer space, preserving human life. Such environments will also include robots [2]. In today's iSpaces, while human life will not normally be at stake, the underlying principles and technology are much the same. Today our homes are rapidly being filled with diverse types of products ranging from simple lighting systems to sophisticated entertainment systems, all adding to the functionality and convenience available to the home user. The iSpace approach envisages that, one day soon, most artefacts will contain embedded computers and network connections, opening up the possibility for hundreds of communicating devices, co-operating in communities serving the occupant(s). The seeds of this revolution have already been sown in that pervasive technologies such as the Internet and mobile telephones already boast over 200 and 680 million users, respectively [3]. Today embedded computers account for 98% of all computer production, with an annual production of around 8 billion microprocessors [4], most being integrated into domestic appliances such as video recorders, washing machines, mobile telephones, and all manner of everyday electronic appliances. Furthermore, nanotechnology is opening up new possibilities such as embedding dust-particle-sized computers into hitherto unconventional mediums such as clothing fibres, paint pigments, etc. Thus, the embedded market is massive and ripe for the addition of networking to realise the iSpace vision. While these technological advances are fuelling significant changes in both the high-tech market-place and living environments, the most radical paradigm shift perhaps originated from the way these technologies can be applied. Firstly, communities of appliances can collaborate to provide new synergetic functionalities (e.g. a telephone ringing can be made to interact with other devices, such as pausing the TV), creating higher-order 'virtual appliances'. Secondly, the nature of the device is being questioned; is it a traditional appliance with multiple prefixed functionalities or is it an appliance with

its constituent sub-functionalities, logically or physically decomposed (functional decomposition is intrinsic to the pervasive computing world). Thirdly, programming of key functionalities (e.g. co-ordinated community actions) is transferred from the manufacturer to the user, empowering end users to design novel functionalities that match their individual needs. When users are given the freedom to choose combinations of devices, then they can create unique and novel functionalities, some of which may not have been envisaged by the manufacturers, making preprogrammed solutions virtually impossible. One challenge, and the focus of much of the discussion in this chapter, is how to manage and configure (program) such co-ordinated pervasive computing devices to do the end user's bidding, without the user's incurring prohibitive cognitive loads — a task that, without support, could quickly become prohibitive and an obstacle to the achievement of the pervasive home-networking environment vision. This chapter explores the issue of programming iSpaces by examining two possible approaches to supporting programming in the end user's environment — the use of autonomous intelligent embedded agents and the application of programming by example.

24.2   Degrees of Intelligence and Autonomy

For the iSpace vision to be realised in domestic environments, people must be able to use computer-based artefacts and systems in a way that gives them some control over aspects of the system, while eliminating cognitive awareness of parts of the system in which they have no interest and are happy to leave to automation or implicit programming processes. Where the line between fully autonomous intelligent systems and manual programming should be drawn is a subject of much research and argument. At the University of Essex we have chosen to provide an approach that allows the full spectrum of possibilities to be experimented with; we have therefore developed a range of autonomous intelligent embedded agents and some user-centric techniques. In this chapter we present a review of all these techniques, although we shall start by describing our test beds for intelligent spaces — the iDorm and the new iDorm-2.

24.3   The iDorm

The intelligent dormitory (iDorm) shown in Fig. 24.1 is a real pervasive computing test bed comprised of a large number of embedded sensors, actuators, processors, and networks in the form of a student bed-sitting room. The iDorm is a multi-use, multi-user space containing areas for different activities such as sleep, work, and entertaining. It contains the normal mix of furniture found in a typical student study/ bedroom environment, including a bed, a work desk, and a wardrobe.

A common interface to the iDorm and its devices is implemented through Universal Plug and Play (UPnP), which is an event-based communication middleware that allows devices to plug and play, thus enabling automatic discovery and configuration. A gateway server is used to run the UPnP software devices that interface with the hardware devices on their respective networks. Our experimental

Fig. 24.1   The iDorm.

agent mechanisms are built on top of the low-level UPnP control architecture enabling it to communicate with the UPnP devices in the iDorm and thus allowing it to monitor and control these devices. Figure 24.2 shows the logical network infrastructure of the iDorm.

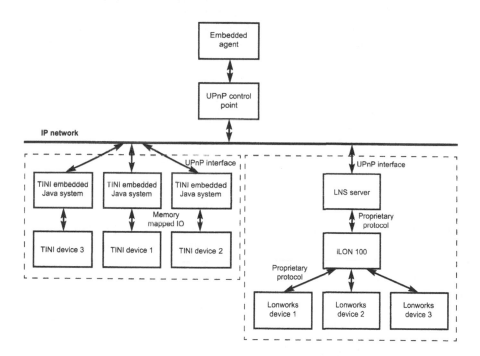

Fig. 24.2   The iDorm logical network infrastructure.

Entertainment is one of the behaviours used as a benchmark in the iDorm for performance assessment. There is a standard multimedia PC driving a flat-screen monitor and a video projector which can be used for both working and entertainment (see Fig. 24.3).

Fig. 24.3   Entertainment and work in the iDorm.

Any networked computer that can run a standard Java process can access and control the iDorm directly. Thus, any PC can also act as an interface to control the devices in the room. Equally interfaces to the devices could be operated from wearable artefacts that can monitor and control the iDorm wirelessly such as a hand-held PDA supporting Bluetooth wireless networking or a mobile telephone as shown in Fig. 24.4. In principle, it is possible to adjust the environment from anywhere and at any time subject to user and device privileges. There is also an Internet fridge in the iDorm (see Fig. 24.4(d)) that incorporates a PC with touchscreen capability, which can also be used to control the devices in the room. Control can of course still be exerted directly on the devices themselves via conventional switches, buttons, etc.

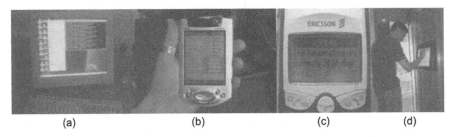

(a)   (b)   (c)   (d)

Fig. 24.4   PC interfaces.

There are a variety of computers in the iDorm, which are used to interface with sensors and actuators and run agents, all of them being configured as Java environments. At the low-performance end we use TINI [5] and SNAP [6] embedded Internet boards; these are mainly used for sensors and actuators. There are also more powerful processor boards capable of running agents such as jStik [7] and ITX [8]. For experiments where maximum flexibility is required, it is also possible to run agents on UPnP enabled workstations. This allows the granularity of agent to device to be varied, from an agent controlling an entire environment, down to one-to-one mappings between devices and agents.

24.3.1   The iDorm-2

With the success of the iDorm, Essex University is currently constructing a new test bed to support R&D in pervasive ICT. The new facility, funded by the HE SRIF programme, takes the form of a domestic apartment and has been called iDorm-2.

The iDorm-2 has been built from the ground up to be an experimental pervasive computing environment with many special structural features such as cavity walls/ceilings containing power and network outlets together with provision for internal wall-based sensors and processors, etc. There are numerous networks in place ranging from wired and power-line, through wireless, to broadband and high-bandwidth multi-mode fibre connections to the outside world. All the basic services are electrically controlled wherever possible (e.g. heating, water, doors). The basic layout of the apartment is show in Fig. 24.5. Opened in June 2005 at the international 'Intelligent Environments 05' workshop, it is one of few such facilities in the world.

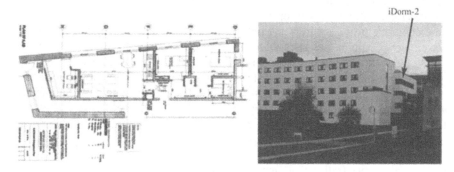

Fig. 24.5   iDorm-2.

24.4   Embedded Agents

The principal argument in support of utilising artificial intelligence (AI) in support of the creation (programming) and management (control) of intelligent pervasive computing-based spaces is that much of the cognitive load associated with using the technology (which is an obstacle to market penetration) can be off-loaded from the user to software processes. However, this is far from easy as such 'intelligent entities' operate in a computationally complex and challenging physical environment that is significantly different to that encountered in more traditional PC programming or AI. Some of the computational challenges associated with creating systems of intelligent artefacts are discussed below.

24.4.1   Embedded Intelligence

Embedded intelligence can be regarded as the inclusion, in an artefact, of some of the reasoning, planning, and learning that people possess. An intelligent artefact would normally contain only a minimal amount of 'embedded intelligence', sufficient to do the artefact task in question. Embedded computers that contain such an intelligent capability are normally referred to as 'embedded agents' [9]. Intelligent artefacts would, in effect, contain an embedded agent. Individually, such an embedded agent can harness intelligence to undertake such tasks as enhancing device functionality (i.e. enabling the artefact to do more complex control tasks), as well as reducing configuration or programming complexity and costs by enabling the pervasive computing system to autonomously learn its own program rules, or alternatively assisting the lay end user to program rules in a non-technical way (see Section 24.6.3).

24.4.2   Embedded Agents and Intelligent Spaces

There are a variety of approaches to this problem, perhaps the most relevant being those originating from the context-aware and embedded-agent communities. In embedded-agent work the goal is to utilise some form of AI to relieve the cognitive loading associated with setting up and running an iSpace system (i.e. transfer some of the cognitive processes from the person to the computer). Typically, researchers have employed approaches such as neural networks, based on traditional machine learning theory, to control the users' environment. However, these approaches utilise objective functions that either aim to derive a minimal control function that satisfies the needs of the users' 'average' or are aimed at optimising between a number of competing needs (e.g. energy efficiency and user comfort). In both cases the user has little control over the system and has to accept some degree of discomfort, or adapt to the conditions determined by the iSpace agents [10].

A contrasting agent-based paradigm is 'The User Rules', which creates agents that '... particularise (rather than generalise) to a specific user's needs, and respond immediately to whatever the end user demands (providing it does not violate any safety constraints)' [11, 12].

Work at Essex University (as part of the EU's Disappearing Computer programme and the UK Government's UK-Korean Scientific fund) has addressed this problem using behaviour-based systems (pioneered by Brooks [13]) and soft computing (fuzzy logic, neural networks, and genetic algorithms). This approach stems from our finding that embedded agents used in pervasive computing are equivalent to robots, experiencing similar problems with sensing, non-determinism, intractability, embodiment, etc [11]. Our earlier work [12, 14, 15] was in the field of robotics, which has allowed us to recognise the underlying similarities between robotics and intelligent artefacts. Models in both robotics and pervasive embedded computer devices have proved difficult to devise, mainly because of the intractability of the variables involved (and in the case of modelling people, non-determinism). A principal advantage of behaviour-based methods is that they discard the need for an abstract model, replacing it by the world itself — a principle most aptly summarised by Brooks as '... the world is its own best model' [13].

24.4.3   Agent Learning

Learning can be viewed as the process of gathering information from the environment and encoding it to improve the efficiency of a system in achieving a certain goal. However, the difficulty that arises concerns finding the most appropriate learning algorithm/technique to use. Most learning algorithms use a measure of the quality of the solution, given either by examples of the desired behaviour of a system, or by an assessment of the quality of the internal and/or external state.

The learning algorithm very much depends on the characteristics of the 'problem' itself. The best choice of learning algorithm can be made by comparing the problem characteristics against the learning-algorithm characteristics. The following describes a limited number of these characteristics.

- Problem characteristics

  Dynamics — to what degree do the environment variables change during the learning?

  Complexity — is the set of all possible solutions, search space, finite/countable?

  Uncertainty — does the information regarding the state contain noise, and are the actions performed noisy?

  Pre-acquired knowledge — can some knowledge about the solutions be acquired before learning starts?

  Observability — are the current/past states known to the learning algorithm?

  Type of data — is the data provided discrete-valued, real-valued, and complex-structured or state and transition?

  Feedback type — should the learning algorithm respond as an immediate, on-demand, delayed, or no-response feedback?

  Physical limitations — what is the processing capability or memory size of the system where the learning algorithm runs?

- Learning-algorithm characteristics

  Internal parameter type — what type of parameter does the algorithm contain, and how does it change?

  Input data — what kind of input data can the learning algorithm deal with, and can it adapt to noisy data?

  Solution/goal type — can the learning algorithm produce approximations in real-valued functions?

  Dynamics — can the solutions be changed during the environment's execution, or can the learning algorithm only change the solutions off-line?

  Parameter change — what parameters change in each phase of the learning cycle, and do they change all at the same time or only a small subset?

Another important distinction in learning agents is whether the learning is done on-line or off-line. On-line learning means that the agent performs its tasks and can learn or adapt after each event. On-line learning is like 'on-the-job' training and places a severe requirement on the learning algorithm. It must not only be fast but also very stable and fault-tolerant. Other hotly debated issues are whether supervised or unsupervised learning is best. Later we present the ISL and the AOFIS as examples of the unsupervised agent. The general challenges faced by designers of embedded-agents for such an environment were discussed at a recent workshop in the Ubiquitous Computing in Domestic Environments Conference [12].

24.4.4   Application-Level Emergent Behaviour

In pervasive computing systems, the embedded-agent host (frequently an appliance) has a network connection allowing the agents to have a view of their neighbours, thereby facilitating co-ordinated actions from groups of embedded agents. The key difference to isolated appliances is that those participating in groups not only have their individual functionality (as designed by the manufacturer), but they also assume a group functionality that can be something that was not envisaged by the manufacturers. In fact, if there are only weak constraints on association of appliances, it is possible for the user to program unique co-ordinated actions (i.e. unique collective functionality) that was not envisaged by the different manufacturers offering the component appliances. This enables an application-level emergent behaviour or functionality (something that, while enabled by the system, was not specified by the system). This naturally gives rise to questions such as the balance between prespecified functionality and emergent functionality, and what or who is responsible for the association between devices and the programming of the basic behaviours. Later in this chapter we discuss various approaches to this challenge. TOP provides an explicit means of directly harnessing user creativity to generate emergent applications while the ISL and AOFIS involve various degrees of user interaction using both supervised and unsupervised learning paradigms to generate emergent application-level functionality.

24.4.5   Machine-Level Emergent Behaviour

In the behaviour-based approach to AI, the equivalent to reasoning and planning in traditional AI is produced by arranging for an agent to have a number of competing processes that are vying for control of the agent. The 'sensory context' determines the degree to which any process influences the agent. Thus, as sensing is derived from what is effectively a non-deterministic world, the solutions from this process are equally non-deterministic and result in what is termed 'emergent behaviour' (behaviours or solutions that emerged but were not explicitly programmed). Anything that affects the context can thus have a hand in this machine-level 'emergent behaviour'. For example, the connections (associations) between devices critically affect the sensed data. Thus, agent-driven associations, or user-driven associations, will be closely associated with emergent behaviour. Emergent behaviour is also sometimes described as emergent solutions. The freedom to make *ad hoc* associations is an important factor in this process, as without them it is difficult to see how emergent functionality could be achieved. At the University of Essex we are researching into what we term promiscuous association — the freedom for agents to form their own associations in as open a way as possible. This approach opens up the possibility of using formally specified ontologies of devices and groups of devices.

It is important to understand that being autonomous and promiscuous (open to making associations with other artefacts) does not imply undirected or unsafe behaviour. Agents can have basic fixed rules built into them that prevent their taking specified actions deemed unsafe.

24.4.6   Multi-Agents

The underlying paradigm of all Essex agents is that they are associated with actuators (they are essentially control agents rather than information processing agents). In the underlying agent model, multi-agent operation is supported via three modes. In the first, sensory and actuator parameters are simply made available to other agents. In the second mode, agents make a 'compressed' version of this information (or their internal state) available to the wider network. In a behaviour-based agent, such as the ISL, the compressed data takes the form of which behaviours are active (and to what degree). The general philosophy we have adopted is that data from remote agents is simply treated in the same way as all other sensor data. As with any data, the processing agent decides for itself which information is relevant to any particular decision. Thus, multi-agent processing is implicit to this paradigm, which regards remote agents as simply more sensors (albeit more sophisticated sensors).

We have found that receiving high-level processed information from remote agents, such as 'the iDorm is occupied', is more useful than being given the low-level sensor information from the remote agent that gave rise to this higher-level characterisation.

This compressed form both relieves agent processing overheads and reduces network loading. A third approach we have developed is the use of inter-agent communication languages. Standardised agent communication languages (e.g. KQML and FIPA) tend to be too big to use on embedded computers (many tens of megabytes) and are not well matched in terms of functionality to them. We have generated research that has looked at the problem of developing a lightweight agent communication language; the interested reader is referred to our description of the distributed intelligent building agent language (DIBAL) [16]. Finally, in the home environment (rather than a general unconstrained pervasive environment), because the number of connected appliances is relatively tractable (no more than a few hundred), a widely adopted approach, at a network level, is to fully connect all the appliances, relegating the issue of what appliance will collaborate with any other to the application level. This approach has been successfully applied by the University of Essex group [17, 18].

24.4.7   Knowledge in Rule-based Agents

One reason we have opted for fuzzy logic rather than neural networks is that the knowledge acquired by the agent is gathered in human linguistic terms. A typical rules set from the iDorm is presented in Fig. 24.6. It is made up of simple, if somewhat large *IF–THEN–ELSE* rule sets. Such rules are intrinsically well structured, as they are based on mathematical logic sets.

Meta-structures can also be used. For example, at the meta-level, rule sets can also be characterised according to context such as rule sets for Mr A relating to Context B (e.g. a bedroom). Thus, from such rule sets it is possible to perform meta-functions such as deriving the closest rule set for a new user — Ms C — based upon rule sets from others users in the same context.

IF **InternalLightLevel** *is* **VVLOW** *AND* **ExternalLightLevel** *is* **VVLOW** *AND*

InternalTemperature *is* **VVHIGH** *AND* **ExternalTemperature** *is* **MEDIUM** *AND*

ChairPressure *is* **OFF** *AND* **BedPressure** *is* **ON** *AND* **Hour** *is* **Evening** *THEN*

ACTION_LIGHT1_value *is* **VHIGH** *AND* **ACTION_Light2_value** *is* **HIGH** *AND*

ACTION_LIGHT3_value *is* **LOW** *AND* **ACTION_Light4_value** *is* **VVLOW** *AND*

ACTION_Blind_state *is* **CLOSED** *AND* **ACTION_Bedlight_state** *is* **ON** *AND*

ACTION_DeskLight_state *is* **OFF** *AND* **ACTION_Heater_state** *is* **OFF** *AND*

ACTION_MSWord_state *is* **STOPPED** *AND* **ACTION_MSMediaPlayer_state** *is*

RUNNING

Fig. 24.6   Example of rule representation.

24.5   Embedded-Agent-based Approaches

At the University of Essex we have developed a number of agents that can deal with the problems discussed above. The main approaches we have developed are based on fuzzy logic. Fuzzy logic is particularly appropriate as it can describe inexact (and analogue) parameters using human-readable linguistic rules, offering a framework for representing imprecise and uncertain knowledge. Thus, it is well suited to developing control on the basis of inexact sensing and actuation that, when coupled to behaviour-based agent architectures, can deal with the non-determinism that sometimes characterises human behaviour. We believe this has similarities to the way people make decisions as it uses a mode of approximate reasoning, which allows it to deal with vague and incomplete information. We have shown that fuzzy logic can be applied well to a pervasive computing environment [19–21], such as the iDorm [22, 23], and have developed and tested two fuzzy-based embedded agents in the iDorm, namely the incremental synchronous learning agent [24] and the adaptive on-line fuzzy inference system agent [25, 26]. These agents have been run on commercial and in-house produced hardware. The photograph in Fig. 24.7 shows a hardware networked agent platform produced at the University of Essex and used to manage the iDorm pervasive computing community.

Fig. 24.7   Agent prototype.

24.5.1   The Incremental Synchronous Learning (ISL) Agent

In general terms, the ISL embedded agent[1] work is broadly situated within the behaviour-based architecture work pioneered by Brooks at MIT, consisting of many simple co-operating sub-control units. Our approach differs to other work in that we use fuzzy-logic-based sub-control units, arranging them in a hierarchy (see Fig. 24.8) and employing a user-driven technique to learn the fuzzy rules on-line and in real time. It is well known that it is often difficult to determine parameters for fuzzy systems. In most fuzzy systems, the fuzzy rules were determined and tuned through trial and error by human operators. It normally takes many iterations to determine and tune them. As the number of input variables increases (intelligent space agents develop large numbers of rules due to particularisation), the number of rules increases disproportionately, which can cause difficulty in matching and choosing between large numbers of rules. Thus, the introduction of a mechanism to learn fuzzy rules was a significant advance. In the ISL agent, we implement each behaviour as a fuzzy process and then use higher-level fuzzy process to co-ordinate them. The resultant architecture takes the form of a hierarchical tree structure (as depicted in Fig. 24.8). This approach has the following technical advantages:

- it simplifies the design of the embedded agent, reducing the number of rules to be determined (in previous work we have given examples of rules reduction of two orders of magnitude via the use of hierarchies);

- it uses the benefits of fuzzy logic to deal with imprecision and uncertainty;

- it provides a flexible structure where new behaviours can be added (e.g. comfort behaviours) or modified easily;

- it utilises a continuous activation scheme for behaviour co-ordination that provides a smoother response than switched schemata.

The learning process involves the creation of user behaviours. This is done interactively using reinforcement where the controller takes actions and monitors these actions to see if they satisfy the user or not, until a degree of satisfaction is achieved. The behaviours, resident inside the agent, take their input from sensors and appliances and adjust effector and appliance outputs (according to pre-determined, but settable, levels). The complexities of learning and negotiating satisfactory values for multiple users would depend upon having a reliable means of identifying different users.

It is clear that, in order for an appliance-based agent to autonomously particularise its service to an individual, some form of learning is essential [12]. In the ISL, learning takes the form of adapting the 'usage' behaviour rule base, according to the user's actions. To do this we utilise an evolutionary computing mechanism based on a novel hierarchical genetic algorithm (GA) technique that modifies the fuzzy controller rule sets through interaction with the environment and user.

The hub of the GA learning architecture is what we refer to as an Associative Experience Engine [27]. Briefly, each behaviour is a fuzzy logic controller (FLC) that has two parameters that can be modified — a rule base (RB) and its associated

---

[1] A detailed account of this agent, including the supporting theory and testing, can be found elsewhere [19–21].

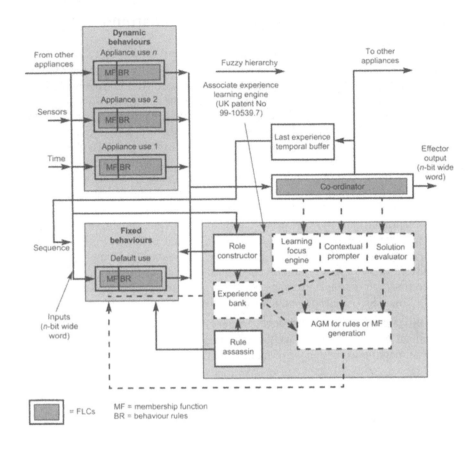

Fig. 24.8   ISL embedded-agent architecture.

membership functions (MFs). In our learning we modify the rule base. The architecture, as adapted for pervasive computing embedded agents, is shown in Fig. 24.8. The behaviours receive their inputs from sensors and provide outputs to the actuators via the co-ordinator that weights their effect. When the system fails to have the desired response (e.g. an occupant manually changes an effector setting), the learning cycle begins.

When a learning cycle is initiated, the most active behaviour (i.e. that most responsible for the agent behaviour) is provided to the learning focus from the co-ordinator (the fuzzy engine, which weights contributions to the outputs), which uses the information to point at the rule set to be modified (i.e. learnt) or exchanged. Initially, the contextual prompter (which gets a characterisation of the situation, an experience, from the co-ordinator) is used to make comparison to see whether there is a suitable behaviour rule set in the experience bank. If there is a suitable experience, it is used. When the past experiences do not satisfy the occupant's needs, we use the best-fit experiences to reduce the search space by pointing to a better starting point, which is the experience with the largest fitness. We then fire an adaptive genetic mechanism (AGM) using adaptive learning parameters to speed the search for new solutions. The AGM is constrained to produce new solutions in a certain range defined by the contextual prompter to avoid the AGM searching options where solutions are unlikely to be found. By using these mechanisms we narrow the AGM search space massively, thus improving its efficiency. After generating new solutions the system tests the new solution and gives it fitness through the solution evaluator. The AGM provides new options via operators such as crossover and mutation until a satisfactory solution is achieved.

The system then remains with this set of active rules (an experience) until the user's behaviour indicates a change of preference (e.g. has developed a new habit), signalled by a manual change to one of the effectors when the learning process described above is repeated. In the case of a new occupant in the room, the contextual prompter gets and activates the most suitable rule base from the experience bank or, if this proves unsuitable, the system re-starts the learning cycle above. The solution evaluator assigns each stored rule base in the experience bank a fitness value. When the experience bank is full, we have to delete some experiences. To assist with this, the rule assassin determines which rules are removed according to their importance (as set by the solution evaluator). The last experience temporal buffer feeds back to the inputs a compressed form of the $n-1$ state, thereby providing a mechanism to deal with temporal sequences.

24.5.2   Adaptive On-Line Fuzzy Inference System (AOFIS) Agent

Like the ISL agent, AOFIS is based on fuzzy logic. We utilise an unsupervised data-driven one-pass approach for extracting fuzzy rules and membership functions from data to learn a fuzzy logic controller (FLC) that will model the user's behaviours when using iDorm-based devices. It differs from the ISL in that it not only learns controller rules, but it also learns membership functions (a significant advance on the ISL, which has fixed membership functions). The data is collected by monitoring the user's occupation of the iDorm over a period of time. The learnt FLC provides an inference mechanism that produces output control responses based on the current state of the inputs. The AOFIS adaptive FLC will therefore control a pervasive computing community, such as the iDorm, on behalf of the user and will also allow the rules to be adapted on-line as the user's behaviour changes over time. This approach aims to realise the vision of ambient intelligence and support the aims of pervasive computing in the following ways:

- the agent is responsive to the particular needs and preferences of the user;

- the user is always in control and can override the agent at any time;

- the agent learns and controls its environment in a non-intrusive way (although users may be aware of the high-tech interface, they are unaware of the agent's presence);

- the agent uses a simple one-pass learning mechanism for learning the user's behaviours, and thus it is not computationally expensive;

- the agent's learnt behaviours can be adapted on-line as a result of changes in the user's behaviour;

- learning is life-long in that agent behaviours can be adapted and extended over a long period of time as a result of changes in the pervasive computing environment.

AOFIS involves five phases — monitoring of the user's interactions and capturing input/output data associated with their actions, extraction of the fuzzy membership functions from the data, extraction of the fuzzy rules from the recorded data, the agent control, and the life-long learning and adaptation mechanism. The last two phases are control loops that once initiated receive inputs as either monitored sensor changes that produce appropriate output control responses based on the set of learnt rules, or user action requests that cause the learnt rules to be adapted before an appropriate output control response is produced. These five phases are illustrated in Fig. 24.9.

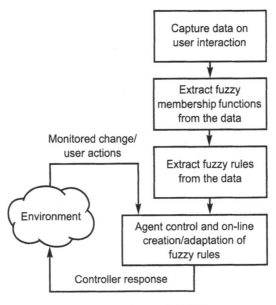

Fig. 24.9   Phases of AOFIS.

The agent initially monitors the user's actions in the environment. Whenever the user changes actuator settings, the agent records a 'snapshot'of the current inputs (sensor states) and the outputs (actuator states with the new values of whichever actuators were adjusted by the user). These 'snapshots' are accumulated over a period of time so that the agent observes as much of the user's interactions within the environment as possible. AOFIS learns a descriptive model of the user's behaviours from the data accumulated by the agent. In our experiments in the iDorm, we used 7 sensors for our inputs and 10 actuators for our outputs with a user spending up to three days in the iDorm. The fuzzy rules that are extracted represent local models that map a set of inputs to the set of outputs without the need for formulating any mathematical model. Individual rules can therefore be adapted on-line, influencing only specific parts of the descriptive model learnt by the agent.

It is necessary to be able to categorise the accumulated user input/output data into a set of fuzzy membership functions that quantify the raw, crisp values of the sensors and actuators into linguistic labels. AOFIS is based on learning the particularised behaviours of the user and therefore requires that these membership functions be defined from the user's input/output data recorded by the agent. A double clustering approach, combining Fuzzy-C-Means (FCM) and hierarchical clustering, is used for extracting fuzzy membership functions from the user data. This is a simple and effective approach where the objective is to build models at a certain level of information granularity that can be quantified in terms of fuzzy sets.

Once the agent has extracted the membership functions and the set of rules from the user input/output data, it has then learnt the FLC that captures the human behaviour. The agent FLC can start controlling the pervasive computing community on behalf of the user. The agent starts to monitor the state of the pervasive community and affect actuators based on its learnt FLC that approximate the particularised preferences of the user. Figure 24.10 illustrates the FLC, which consists of a fuzzifier, rule base, fuzzy inference engine, and defuzzifier.

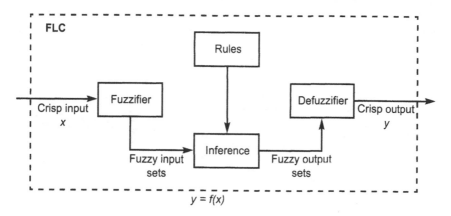

Fig. 24.10   AOFIS FLC.

In conformity with the non-intrusive aspect of intelligence [25, 26], whenever the user is not happy with the behaviour of the pervasive computing device or community, the agent's control responses can always be overridden by simply altering the manual control of the system. When this occurs the agent will adapt its rules on-line or add new rules based on the new user preferences. This process incorporates what we term 'learning inertia', where the agent delays adapting its learnt rules until the user preference for changing a particular set of actuator values has re-occurred a number of times. This prevents the agent from adapting its rules in response to 'one-off' user actions that do not reflect a marked change in the user's habitual behaviour (this 'learning inertia' parameter is user-settable). As rules are adapted, it is sensible to preserve old rules so they can be recalled by the agent in the future if they are more appropriate than the current rules. Whenever the user overrides the agent's control outputs and overrides any of the controlled output devices, a snapshot of the state of the environment is recorded and passed to the rule adaptation routine. The AOFIS agent supports the notion of life-long learning in that it adapts its rules as the state of the pervasive community and the user preferences vary over a significantly long period of time. Due to the flexibility of AOFIS, the initially learnt FLC can be easily extended to both adapt existing rules as well as add new rules. The fuzzy nature of the rules permits them to capture a wide range of values for each input and output parameter. This allows the rules to continue to operate even if there is a gradual change in the environment. If, however, there is a significant change in the environment or the user's activity is no longer captured by the existing rules, then the agent will automatically create new rules that satisfy the current conditions. The agent will therefore unobtrusively and incrementally extend its behaviours, which can then be adapted to satisfy a pervasive device and community user.

24.5.3   Benchmarking and Comparative Performance

We have also implemented other soft computing agents, namely genetic programming (GP), the adaptive neuro-fuzzy inference system (ANFIS), and the multi-layer perceptron neural network. The data set obtained from the iDorm (Fig. 24.11) during the AOFIS monitoring phase comprised 408 instances and was randomised into six samples. Each sample was then split into a training and test set consisting of 272 and 136 instances, respectively. The performance error for each technique was obtained on the test instances as the root mean-squared error, which was also scaled to account for the different ranges of the output parameters.

Fig. 24.11   User gathering experimental data in the iDorm.

The GP used a population of 200 individuals evolving them over 200 generations. The GP evolved both the rules and the fuzzy sets. Each individual was represented as a tree composed of 'AND' and 'OR' operators as the internal nodes and triangular and trapezoidal membership functions as terminal nodes. The parameters of the membership functions were also evolved in parallel with the structure. The search started with a randomly generated set of rules and parameters, which were then optimised by means of genetic operators. The GP-based approach for optimising an FLC was tested with different numbers of fuzzy sets. In ANFIS, subtractive clustering was used to generate an initial TSK-type fuzzy inference system. Back propagation was used to learn the premise parameters while least-square estimation was used to determine the consequent parameters.

An iteration of the learning procedure consisted of two parts, where the first part propagated the input patterns and estimated optimal consequent parameters through an iterative least-squares procedure, and the second part used back propagation to modify the antecedent membership functions.

We tested ANFIS with a range of different cluster radii values. The multi-layer perceptron (MLP) back-propagation neural network was tested with different numbers of hidden nodes in a single hidden layer. We tested the AOFIS with different numbers of fuzzy sets and the membership function overlap threshold was set to 0.5, as this gave a sufficient degree of overlap while also allowing the system to distinguish between the ranges covered by each fuzzy set. Tables 24.1 and 24.2 illustrate the scaled root mean-squared error (RMSE) and scaled standard deviation (STD) for each technique averaged over the six randomised samples, and corresponding to the values of the variable parameter tested for each approach. The

Table 24.1   Average scaled RMSE.

Average scaled root mean squared error (SRMSE) for six randomised samples of the data set							
AOFIS		GA		ANFIS		MLP	
Number of fuzzy sets	SRMSE	Number of fuzzy sets	SRMSE	Cluster radii	SRMSE	Number of hidden nodes	SRMSE
2	0.2148	2	0.1235	0.3	1.3269	2	0.2129
3	0.1476	3	0.1156	0.4	0.9229	4	0.1718
4	0.1461	4	0.1189	0.5	0.2582	6	0.1732
5	0.1364	5	0.1106	0.6	0.1661	8	0.1571
6	0.1352	6	0.1210	0.7	0.1669	10	0.1555
7	0.1261	7	0.1193	0.8	0.1418	20	0.1621
8	0.1326	8	0.1173	0.9	0.1213	30	0.1705
9	0.1472	9	0.1202	1.0	0.1157	40	0.1667
10	0.1537	10	0.1235	1.1	0.1201	50	0.1768
11	0.1696	11	0.1110	1.2	0.1168	60	0.1711
12	0.1999	12	0.1201	1.3	0.1131	70	0.1712
13	0.2246	13	0.1169	1.4	0.1131	80	0.1770
14	0.2337	14	0.1120	1.5	0.1118	90	0.1767
15	0.2460	15	0.1089	1.6	0.1130	100	0.1924
16	0.2459	16	0.1225	1.7	0.1115	200	0.2027
17	0.2732	17	0.1146	1.8	0.1137	300	0.2258
18	0.2747	18	0.1188	1.9	0.1182	400	0.2365
19	0.2771	19	0.1159	2.0	0.1189	500	0.2424
20	0.2839	20	0.1143				

Table 24.2   Average scaled STD.

Average scaled standard deviation (SSTD) for six randomised samples of the data set							
AOFIS		GA		ANFIS		MLP	
Number of fuzzy sets	SSTD	Number of fuzzy sets	SSTD	Cluster radii	SSTD	Number of hidden nodes	SSTD
2	0.1896	2	0.1128	0.3	1.2839	2	0.1499
3	0.1350	3	0.1063	0.4	0.9001	4	0.1299
4	0.1354	4	0.1094	0.5	0.2440	6	0.1277
5	0.1277	5	0.1026	0.6	0.1522	8	0.1193
6	0.1280	6	0.1121	0.7	0.1518	10	0.1160
7	0.1200	7	0.1107	0.8	0.1257	20	0.1198
8	0.1266	8	0.1085	0.9	0.1038	30	0.1229
9	0.1409	9	0.1117	1.0	0.0972	40	0.1234
10	0.1472	10	0.1145	1.1	0.1007	50	0.1245
11	0.1626	11	0.1026	1.2	0.0961	60	0.1234
12	0.1912	12	0.1115	1.3	0.0920	70	0.1222
13	0.2133	13	0.1084	1.4	0.0924	80	0.1283
14	0.2218	14	0.1031	1.5	0.0906	90	0.1272
15	0.2323	15	0.1007	1.6	0.0911	100	0.1333
16	0.2318	16	0.1128	1.7	0.0891	200	0.1366
17	0.2557	17	0.1063	1.8	0.0909	300	0.1503
18	0.2568	18	0.1090	1.9	0.0951	400	0.1674
19	0.2588	19	0.1075	2.0	0.0937	500	0.1676
20	0.2646	20	0.1051				

results in Tables 24.1 and 24.2 show that the optimum number of fuzzy sets for AOFIS was 7, and on average AOFIS produced 186 rules. The GP in comparison gave a marginally lower error for 7 fuzzy sets. Both ANFIS and the MLP on average gave a higher error than AOFIS. The ANFIS only learns a multi-input–single-output (MISO) FLC and had to be run repeatedly for each output parameter. The FLC produced was therefore only representative of an MISO system. Another restriction with ANFIS was that it generates TSK FLCs, where the consequent parameters are represented as either linear or constant values, rather than linguistic variables as is the case with Mamdani FLCs.

These linguistic variables are very important to understanding the human behaviour. It should be noted that the AOFIS generates multi-input–multi-output (MIMO) Mamdani FLCs representing rules in a more descriptive human-readable form, which is advantageous for pervasive computing communities or other ambient intelligent systems, as they deal with people whose behaviours are more easily described in such linguistic terms. The iterative nature of the GP makes it highly computationally intensive; this also applies to both ANFIS and the MLP, which are also iterative-based approaches.

AOFIS is far less computationally intensive due to the one-pass procedure it employs and is therefore more favourable for an embedded agent. Neither ANFIS nor the GP-based approach can easily be adapted on-line, as this would require their internal structures to be re-learnt if either new rules were to be added or existing rules were adapted.

Therefore, the AOFIS method is unique in that it can learn a good model of the user's behaviour that can then be adapted on-line in a life-long mode, in a non-intrusive manner, unlike other methods that need to repeat time-consuming learning cycles to adapt the user's behaviour.

Hence, in summary, the AOFIS agent proved to be the best for on-line learning and adaptation; moreover, it was computationally less intensive and better suited to on-line learning than the other approaches compared. Finally, at the outset of our work it was not clear how long (if any time at all) it would take for such learning in this type of environment to reach a steady state. Our initial results (see Fig. 24.12) indicate this is possible within a day although we would need to conduct experiences over much longer periods to catch other cycles, such as annual climate-related variations.

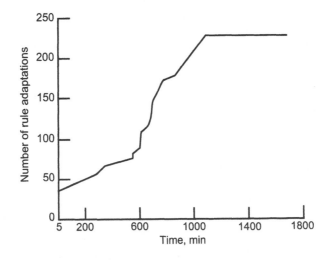

Fig. 24.12   Typical learning rate of FLC-based agent.

24.6 An End-User Programming-based Approach

24.6.1 Discussion

While autonomous agents may appeal to many people, their acceptance is not universal. Some laypeople distrust autonomous agents and prefer to exercise direct control over what is being learnt, when it is being learnt, and to whom (or what) the information is communicated. These concerns are particularly acute when such technology is in the private space of our homes. Often, end users are given very little, if any, choice in setting up the system to their likings, but rather, they are required to 'surrender their rights' and 'put up with' whatever is provided [28].

Moreover, there are other reasons advanced in support of a more human-driven involvement, such as exploiting the creative talents of people by providing them with the means to become designers of their own 'pervasive computing spaces', while at the same time shielding them from unnecessary technical details. To explore this aspect of our inhabited intelligent environment work, we have recently opened up a complementary strand of research, which we refer to as task-oriented programming (TOP) based on a combination of programming by example (PBE) (sometimes referred to as programming by demonstration — PBD), pioneered by Smith in the mid-1970s, learning from the user (LFU), the paradigm Essex University has been developing for many years [29], and ontologies (the latter mainly drawn from research work on the Semantic Web) [30]. It is based on a vision to put the user at the centre of the system programming experience by exchanging implicit autonomous learning for explicit user-driven teaching. In this approach a user defines a community of co-ordinating pervasive devices and then 'programs' it by physically operating the system to mimic the required behaviour, i.e. 'programming by example' [31].

24.6.2 Programming by Example

Programming by example (PBE) was introduced by Smith in the mid-1970s, where the algorithms for the system functionalities were not described abstractly but rather demonstrated in concrete examples [29]. Henry Lieberman later described PBE as '... a software agent that records the interactions between the user and a conventional direct-manipulation interface and writes a program that corresponds to the user's actions', where '... the agent can then generalise the program so that it can work in other simulations similar to, but not necessarily exactly the same as, the example on which it is taught' [32]. Thus, PBE reduces the gap between the user interactions and the delivered program functionality by merging the two tasks. The main area of PBE work has focused on graphical user interfaces running on PCs. By way of example, PBE has been applied to computer application development, computer-aided design (CAD) systems, children's programs, World Wide Web related technologies, and home automation [33–41]. The underlying principles in PBE are generic and transportable to the pervasive computing world. In addition to the underlying scientific principle, PBE shares the same motivation of empowering lay end users to utilise what would otherwise be prohibitively complex technology.

However, to date PBE has not been applied to programming tangible physical objects, nor to any other aspect of pervasive computing. Thus, TOP is the first application of PBE to this area.

24.6.3   Task-Oriented Programming

TOP was proposed and developed in 2003 as a means to address the issues of privacy and creativity in iSpaces [28]. In the TOP approach, the system is explicitly put into a learning mode and taught (by demonstration) how to behave by the lay end user. For example, the TV or sitting room light could be made to react to an incoming call on the telephone. Thus, the telephone, TV, and light co-ordinate their actions to form a new meta-(virtual) appliance. The vision goes beyond linking only conventional appliances. For instance, if a network capability is added to an appliance, it becomes possible to allow its functional units to be shared with others. Thus, in this notion, the audio amplifier in a TV could be made use of by the HiFi system, or vice versa. Consequently, 'virtual appliances' could be created by establishing logical connections between the sub-functions of appliances, creating replicas of traditional appliances, or inventing altogether new appliances. This decomposition of traditional appliances into their atomic functionalities (either physically or logically) and later allowing users to re-compose 'virtual appliances' (nuclear functions), by simply reconnecting these basic atomic functionalities together, is the paradigm we called 'the decomposed appliance' model. The key to creating 'virtual appliances' from decomposed functions is that of making connections between sub-functions so that a closed set of interconnected functions becomes a global set of functions (i.e. it becomes a 'community', or a collective of co-ordinating devices with a meta-functionality). To facilitate this it is necessary to have some standard way of describing the functionality of the devices and connections — for TOP we have therefore devised an ontology, dComp (see Section 24.6.4). Clearly, this concept of 'community' is not limited to decomposed appliances, but relates to any set of co-ordinated pervasive entities, whatever their functional or physical level (e.g. it could also relate to nano-scale or even macro-scale building-to-building environments). In general, a richer pool of sub-functions will lead to greater combinations or permutations for the user to create new virtual appliances.

As TOP has the notion of working with communities, the system supports setting up communities (if they do not already exist) (see Fig. 24.13). Then, by selecting any community that the user wishes to program, a set of co-ordinated actions is taught to the system by simply using the home networked devices in a role-play mode, supported by some on-screen activities. An action causes an appliance to generate an associated event, and this event is then used to generate appropriate rules (based on a 'snapshot' of the environment state). To be more general, co-ordinating actions (i.e. tasks) are performed by a community (i.e. one or more devices). A device can be involved in more than one community (i.e. performing one or more actions). The designer (user) interface with TOP is via an editor called 'TOPeditor'. This editor provides a means for:

- setting up/amending communities;

- holding teaching sessions so that tasks can also be taught (via the editor) as well as via physical usage of networked devices.

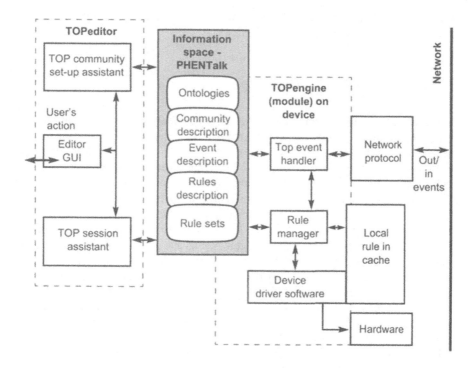

Fig. 24.13   The TOP architecture.

The TOP architecture has two distinct modules — a 'TOPeditor' (to program the systems) and a 'TOPengine' (to execute the user-generated rules). The TOPeditor has two main components. The first component, a 'TOP community set-up assistant', allows the user to set up groups (communities) of devices that can communicate and co-ordinate their actions to produce some desired meta-function (or virtual appliance). The second component, the TOPengine, is a process that runs inside each and every networked device and executes the taught rules. It has three main components:

- a 'TOP event handler' that monitors connected devices, forming rules based on a user's interaction with the networked devices (interactions generating 'events' managed by an underlying UPnP middleware) — user interactions can be direct (e.g. activating a control) or indirect (e.g. activating a telephone by dialling in from another phone);

- the second component, a 'rule manager', manages the addition and removal of rules from memory, which includes removing dormant rules to make space for newer rules, and checking for duplication or conflicts;

- the third module, a 'local rule cache', acts as a temporary rule buffer while rules are being built by the user (i.e. while the user is still designing and experimenting with creating community functionality).

To facilitate the information to be used within and beyond the community, data needs to be standardised so that it can be understood by all other parties in the network. For this aspect of work, the semantics in the TOP dComp ontology supports information interoperability between applications, providing a common machine 'understanding' knowledge framework.

24.6.4   The dComp Ontology

TOP leverages ontology semantics as the core vocabulary for its information space, generating ontology-based rule sets when a user demonstrates their desired tasks to the system in a 'teaching' session. As explained in the previous section, these rule sets are then interpreted and executed by a back-end execution engine — the 'TOPengine'. Ontology allows information to be conceptually specified in an explicit way by providing definitions associated with names of entities in a universe of discourse (e.g. classes, relations, functions, or other objects) that are in both machine- and human-usable format. Thus, in more practical terms, ontology describes things such as what a device name means and provides formal axioms that constrain the form and interpretation of these terms. Most ontology tools support descriptions of behaviour based on rules — hence an ontology-based approach is well suited to the challenges TOP faces.

We have chosen to base dComp around the OWL language as it is more expressive than RDF or RDF-S (i.e. provides additional formal semantic vocabularies allowing us to embed more information into our ontology) and is widely used (especially for the Semantic Web), with numerous supporting tools such as Jena [42] and inference engines such as RACER [43] and F-OWL [44]. In order to realise our vision, a set of explicitly well-defined vocabularies (i.e. an ontology) is needed to model not just the basic concept of decomposed devices, but also the communities they form, the services they provide, the rules and policies they follow, the resultant actions that they take, and of course the people who inhabit the environment along with their individual preferences — dComp provides these properties. Wherever possible, we have sought to build on existing work. The SOUPA ontology (from Ubicomp) is aimed at pervasive computing but lacks support for key TOP mechanisms such as community, decomposed functions, and co-ordinating actions (to produce higher-level meta-functionality) [45]. In addition, the current SOUPA standard has only limited support for the concept of pervasive home UPnP-based devices (on which TOP depends). However, SOUPA has a well-defined method of supporting notions of action, person, policy, and time, which dComp has adopted. Thus, most of the innovation in dComp relates to the ontology of decomposition and community — hence the name 'Decomposed Community Programming' (dComp).

The following is a summarised walk-through of the full dComp specification, which is described more fully on-line.[2] To avoid any confusion in terminology, henceforth we refer to the dComp ontology as 'the ontology' whereas the documents that describe a certain concept of entities (e.g. device, services, community) that exist in the dComp environment are referred to as 'ontology documents'. Ontology also describes a set of properties and relationships that are associated with these concepts, along with the restrictions they may have. The current version (v.1.1) of the dComp ontology consists of 10 classes (see Fig. 24.14).

---

[2] dComp ontology can be retrieved from: http://iieg.essex.ac.uk/dcomp/ont/dev/2004/05/

DCOMPDevice Class	DCOMPHardware Class	DCOMPService Class	Rule Class	Policy Class
DCOMPDevice	Hardware	DCOMPService	Rule	Policy
MobileDevice	CPU	LightsAndFittingsService	UnchangeableRule	Mode
StaticDevice	Memory	LightService	PersistentRule	
NomadicDevice	DisplayOutput	SwitchService	NonPersistentRule	**Time Class**
Light	DisplayScreenProperty	TelephoneService	Preceding	
Switch	AudioOutput	AlarmService	Device	**DCOMPperson Class**
Telephone	AudioOutputProperty	TemperatureService		
Alarm	Tuner	EntertainmentService		**Action Class**
Blind	Amplifier	AudioService	**Preference Class**	Action
Heater	**DCOMPCommunity Class**	VideoService	Preference	PermittedAction
FileRepository	Community	FollowMeService	SituationCondition	ForbiddenAction
DisplayDevice	NotJointCommunity	SetTopBoxService	CommunityPreference	Recipient
AudioDevice	PersistentCommunity	StateVariable		TargetAction
SetTopBox	TransitoryCommunity	TOPService		
Characteristic	CommunityDevice			
DeviceInfo				

Fig. 24.14   dComp ontology (v1.1).

Device Class

The main class called 'DCOMPDevice' provides a generic description of any devices. Currently DCOMPDevice has 10 sub-classes including both nuclear (traditional appliances) and atomic (decomposed) devices and remains the subject of ongoing development. The roles of most sub-classes are obvious from their names. Those which might not be obvious include 'DeviceInfo' for devices sharing some UPnP descriptions, 'Characteristic' for different mobility characteristics, and Relationships, which are defined by using the OWL object property[3] and are:

- hasDeviceInfo;
- hasHardwareProperty;
- hasDCOMPService;
- hasCharacteristic.

The main elements of a typical DCOMPDevice expression are shown in Fig. 24.15.

Hardware Class

The abstract class, DCOMPHardware, generalises all hardware that exists in a DCOMPDevice and, in the current version, has eight sub-classes along with associated properties — CPU, Memory, DisplayOutput, DisplayInput, AudioOutput, AudioInput, Amplifier, and Tuner. In order for the DCOMPDevices to work together, every DCOMPDevice on the dComp network offers services. These services are modelled by a class called 'DCOMPService', which currently contains three sub-classes, namely TOPService, LightsAndFittingsService, and EntertainmentService. Each contains sub-services — for example, the EntertainmentService class includes

---

[3]Object property denotes relations between instances of two classes (see owl:ObjectProperty).

```
<device:AudioDevice rdf:ID="TestDevice12">
<device:hasDeviceInfo>
<device:DeviceInfo>
<device:friendlyName>TestDevice12</device:friendlyName>
<device:DeviceUUID>0</device:DeviceUUID>
<device:DeviceType>urn:schemas-upnp-org:TestDevice12:1</device:DeviceType>
<device:DeviceModelURL>http://TestDevice12URL/</device:DeviceModelURL>
<device:DeviceModelNumber rdf:datatype="&xsd;double">0.0</device:DeviceModelNumber>
</device:DeviceInfo>
</device:hasDeviceInfo>
<hw:componentOf>
<hw:RAM rdf:about="#JCTestMemory2"/>
</hw:componentOf>
<serv:hasDCOMPService>
<!-- can have more than 1 service -->
<serv:AudioService rdf:about="#JCAudioService01"/>
</serv:hasDCOMPService>
<!-- 2nd service -->
<serv:hasDCOMPService>
<serv:AudioService rdf:about="#JCAudioService02"/>
</serv:hasDCOMPService>
<!-- 3rd service -->
<serv:hasDCOMPService>
<serv:AudioService rdf:about="#JCAudioService03"/>
</serv:hasDCOMPService>
```

Fig. 24.15   Typical display device expression.

AudioService, VideoService, FileRepositoryService, SetTopBoxService, and FollowMeService. The LightsAndFittingsService and EntertainmentService are mutually distinct (i.e. in mathematical terms, they do not belong to a same set). These characteristics are modelled by declaring the classes to be disjointWith[4] each other. Every service in the dComp environment is identified by a property called 'serviceID' and a class called 'StateVariable' (to represent UPnP values). The StateVariable class has three properties, namely 'name', 'value', and 'evented'. The relationship between a DCOMPService and the StateVariable is linked by an object property called 'hasStateVariable'. The relationship between a DCOMPDevice and DCOMPService is coupled by an object property called 'hasDCOMPService'.

Community Class
As dComp needs to support the notion of community (a collective), there is a class called DCOMPCommunity. In the current implementation, we model three types of community, namely SoloCommunity (for those devices not yet part of a community), PersistentCommunity (for communities with a degree of permanency), and TransitoryCommunity (for communities with a short lifetime). A DCOMPDevice can join one or more communities (a community must have at least one device). Relationship between a DCOMPDevice and a DCOMPCommunity is described using an object TransitiveProperty[5] called 'inTheCommunityOf'. A class called 'CommunityDevice' is introduced to represent all the devices in a community. These devices are identified by their deviceUUID identification. The relationship between a Community and CommunityDevice is linked by another object

---

[4] DisjointWith asserts that the class extensions of the two class descriptions involved have no individuals in common.

[5] TransitiveProperty denotes if a device X is in the community of C and the community C is a member of Community P, then the device X is also a member of community P.

TransitiveProperty called 'hasCommunityDevice'. Communities in dComp are formed by a user; thus, each community has an owner. The properties of Communities are — community ID, communityName, communityDescription, and timestamp. The relationship between a community and its owner is linked by an object type property, called 'hasOwner'. An example of the main elements in a dComp TV community is given in Fig. 24.16.

```
<com:TransitoryCommunity rdf:ID="JCTV">
<com:communityID>Tran-JCTV</com:communityID>
<com:communityName>JC TV</com:communityName>
<com:communityDescription>The first JC testing TV</com:communityDescription>
<com:timeStamp rdf:datatype="&xsd;dateTime">2004-09-06T19:43:08+01:00</com:timeStamp>
<com:hasOwner>
<person:Person rdf:about="#JC"/>
</com:hasOwner>
<com:hasCommunityDevice>
<com:CommunityDevice rdf:about="#JCMonitorCRT17"/>
</com:hasCommunityDevice>
<com:hasCommunityDevice>
<com:CommunityDevice rdf:about="#JCAudioMMS223"/>
</com:hasCommunityDevice>
<com:hasCommunityDevice>
<com:CommunityDevice rdf:about="#JC:NetGem442"/>
</com:hasCommunityDevice>
</com:TransitoryCommunity>
```

Fig. 24.16   Typical TV community definition.

Rules Class

Rules are needed in TOP for co-ordinating community actions and are supported by a class called 'Rules' that models three types of rule, namely UnchangeableRules (rules that cannot be changed), PersistentRules (rules that infrequently change), and NonPersistentRules (rules that frequently change). These rules are mutually distinct and are declared to be complementOf[6] each other. Rules have properties — ruleID and ruleDescription and an object property called 'hasRuleOwner' to link to the owner. (Note that the rule and community owners may be different people.) A class called 'Preceding' is used to represent a set of triggers that cause the co-ordinating actions to be executed. The devices in the Preceding class are identified by their deviceUUID and the service they offer. Finally, an object property called 'hasAction' binds the relationship between Rules and Actions. The main elements of a rule definition are given in Fig. 24.17.

Action, Person, Policy, and Time Class

Wherever possible we have sought to build on existing ontology work. SOUPA provides a suitable DCOMPperson, Policy, and Time ontology. Thus, these have been adopted in dComp.[7] The Action ontology document has, to some extent, been influenced by the SOUPA Action ontology. The class 'Action' represents the set of actions defined by the rules. As with SOUPA, we have two class types of action, namely PermittedAction and ForbiddenAction. The Action class in dComp is the

---

[6] ComplementOf denotes all individuals from the domain of discourse that do not belong to a certain class.

[7] For further information, refer to their Web site [46].

union of these two action classes; every co-ordinating action has its target devices. A class called 'Recipient' models target devices, which represents a set of target devices where actions take place. The members of Recipient are identified by their deviceUUID and the serviceID. Actions for the recipient are called 'TargetAction', which has two properties, namely actionName (the name of the action) and targetValue (the value for the action to be taken). A typical statement 'when the phone rings, mute the TV' could be expressed as in Fig. 24.18.

Preference Class

As the name implies, DCOMPPreference describes the preferences a person has within any given set of options. In dComp, preferences are referred as 'situated preferences', which is similar to Vastenburg's 'situated profile' concept where he

```
<NonPersistentRules rdf:ID="Rule1">
 <rule:ruleID rdf:datatype="xsd;int">00001</rule:ruleID>
 <rule:ruleDescription>Test Rule 1</rule:ruleDescription>
 <com:communityID>Tran-JCTV</com:communityID>
 <rule:hasRuleOwner>
  <person:Person rdf:about="#JC"/>
 </rule:hasRuleOwner>
 <rule:hasPreceding>
 <!-- can have more than 1 device -->
 <rule:Device>
  <dComp:DeviceUUID>uuid:Telephone01</dComp:DeviceUUID>
  <serv:hasDCOMPService>
  <!-- a device can provide more than 1 service-->
  <serv:TelephoneService>
  <serv:serviceID> Telephone</serv:serviceID>
   <serv:hasStateVariable>
      <!-- a service can have more than 1 value of state variable-->
      <serv.name>state variable 1</servname>
      <serv:value>RINGING</SERV:VALUE>
   </serv:hasState Variable>
  </serv:TelephoneService>
  </serv:hasDCOMPService>
 </rule:Device>
 </rule:hasPreceding>
 <rule:hasAction>
  <act:PermittedAction rdf:about="#TestAction"/>
 </rule:hasAction>
</NonPersistentRules>
```

Fig. 24.17   Main elements of rule definition.

```
<act:PermittedAction rdf:ID="TestAction">
 <act:actionName>Test action</act:actionName>
 <act:hasRecipient>
<device:DeviceUUID>UUID:PHLAudioMMS223</device:DeviceUUID>
  <serv:serviceID>AudioMMS223</serv:serviceID>
 </act:hasRecipient>
 <act:hasTargetAction>
  <act:actionName>Mute</act:actionName>
  <act:targetValue>Mute</act:targetValue>
 </act:hasTargetAction>
</act:PermittedAction>
```

Fig. 24.18   Main elements of an action (muting the TV).

uses situation as a framework for user profile so that the values of the profile are relative to situations [47]. The 'Preference' class represents a set of situated preferences of a person for his community. This Preference class has a sub-class called 'CommunityPreference' and an associated property called 'communityID'. To model 'person A prefers X, depending on the situation conditions of Y', another class called 'SituatedConditions' is defined that represents the set of situated conditions that the person's preferences depended on. Although a person is allowed to define his own 'SituatedConditions', dComp explicitly defines a list of pre-set situated conditions so that it forms a default template that a person can use. The Preference class has a close relationship to the Person class. To bind this relationship, an object property called 'hasPreference' is used, which links the domain of Person to the range of Preference. The relationship between the Preference class and SituationConditions class is linked by another object property called 'hasCondition'. The main elements of a Situated Condition are given in Fig. 24.19.

```
<owl1:Class rdf:ID="SituationalCondition">
<rdfs:label>SituationalCondition</rdfs:label>
</owl:Class>
<SituationalCondition rdf:ID="DuringTheWorkdays"/>
<SituationalCondition rdf:ID="DuringThe Weekends"/>
<SituationalCondition rdf:ID="WhileOutOfTown"/>
<SituationalCondition rdf:ID="WorkingFromHome"/>
<SituationalCondition rdf:ID="FriendsVisiting"/>
<SituationalCondition rdf:ID="FamilyVisiting"/>
<SituationalCondition rdf:ID="OnHoliday"/>
<SituationalCondition rdf:ID="WhenComeHomeFromWork"/>
<SituationalCondition rdf:ID="WhenComeHomeFromSchool"/>
<SituationalCondition rdf:ID="WhenAtMyOffice"/>
<SituationalCondition rdf:ID="WhenDining"/>
<SituationalCondition rdf:ID="WhenHavingLunch"/>
<SituationalCondition rdf:ID="WhenHavingBreakfast"/>
<SituationalCondition rdf:ID="WhenEasting"/>
<SituationalCondition rdf:ID="WhenPlayingComputerGames"/>
<SituationalCondition rdf:ID="WhenWatchingTV"/>
<SituationalCondition rdf:ID="AtNight"/>
<SituationalCondition rdf:ID="InTheMorning"/>
<SituationalCondition rdf:ID="AtLunchTime"/>
<SituationalCondition rdf:ID="AtTeaTime"/>
<SituationalCondition rdf:ID="Alone"/>
<SituationalCondition rdf:ID="WhenAlarmGoesOff"/>
<SituationalCondition rdf:ID="WhenSmokeAlarmGoesOff"/>
```

Fig. 24.19 Main elements of a situated condition.

24.6.5 dComp Performance

To assess the performance of dComp we compared two sets of device descriptions — the first description was structured in typical XML-based 'all-in-one' format, while the second was decomposed into smaller segments (i.e. broken up into hardware and service information), each segment being 'linked' back to the device. Both descriptions were written in OWL. For each set, we used two different quantities of devices in the test (3 and 32). A common query with 5 conditions was used for the test, with each test being run 50 times. The test was conducted using a WindowsXP, 2.08-GHz, 512-RAM machine. Four sets of tests were completed:

- 3 device descriptions in 'all-in-one' format;
- 3 device descriptions in 'decomposed' format;
- 32 device descriptions in 'all-in-one' format;
- 32 device descriptions in 'decomposed' format.

A representative example of our tests is provided in Fig. 24.20. As can be seen, we found that the decomposed device description outperformed the compact devices description for smaller domains with fewer devices. On average, queries took half the time that 'all-in-one' format descriptions took. Although we had been concerned that decomposed descriptions might not fair as well for larger domains, because of increased link following, we found that this was not the case, as the system performed as well as the 'all-in-one' descriptions, while bringing the advantages of decomposition described earlier. This we attribute to additional link-processing being counterbalanced by the processing benefits of smaller, better focused descriptions. For larger domains we found that the performance of decomposed versus the compact descriptions remained roughly the same. Both TOP and dComp represent new directions in our research and hold great promise for solving the problems of providing user creativity and privacy.

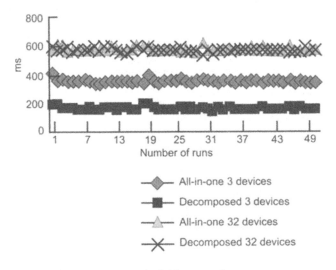

Fig. 24.20   A typical dComp performance test.

24.7   Summary and Future Directions

Both the ISL and AOFIS provide life-long learning and adaptation for pervasive devices and communities. Both techniques were evaluated by arranging for users to live in and use the iDorm for periods of up to five days. Both techniques performed well in handling human behaviour (with all the uncertainties involved) and in dealing with complex sensors, actuators, and control. The agents operated in a non-intrusive implicit manner, allowing the user to continue operating the pervasive computing device or community in a normal way while the agents learn controllers that satisfy the user's required behaviour.

In contrast, the TOP approach deliberately seeks to involve the user in the learning phase, providing explicit control of what and when the agent learns. In support of TOP, we devised the ontology dComp, which directly supports the concept of community, and collectives of decomposed devices, together with co-ordinating actions to create meta-group functionalities. We were motivated to produce such an ontology to serve our longer-term research goals, which aim to explore the development of end-user tools to allow laypeople to 'program' groups of co-ordinated pervasive computing devices, so as to become designers of their own environments. In dComp, the notion of decomposition extends to device descriptions, which are decomposed to map to separate sub-capabilities, each linked to other related descriptions. Thus, decomposed device descriptions do not necessarily have to reside in the same place, a consequence of dComp's roots being in the Semantic Web ontology, which provides firewall protection for the physical location of data servers, facilitating information retrieval via a hyperlink. dComp device descriptions can be shared or reasoned about by other applications on the network, while queries can be directed to a specific service rather than the whole device.

Contrasting these two approaches will allow us to evaluate the arguments for and against increased agent autonomy and determine when and where each is appropriate. In all the approaches, the underlying science is based on methods that are practical to implement in embedded computers.

Our work is taking a number of directions. Firstly, we are continuing to try to develop and experiment with new types of autonomous intelligent embedded agents. For example, we have projects under way looking at new type-2 fuzzy logic-based agents and new types of neuro-fuzzy agents. We are also mindful of the role that mood and emotions play in making decisions and have begun a project that is seeking to enrich the decision space of agents by adding sensed data on emotions. We have also embarked on two projects concerned with investigating developing agents at a nano-scale — one project is looking at nano agents in fluids, the other as part of smart surfaces. Our end-user programming work (TOP and ontologies) is at an early stage, but the initial results as reported in this chapter are encouraging. We anticipate future systems will require a mix of both autonomous-agent approaches (perhaps dominating low levels) and end-user programming methods (perhaps dominating higher levels). We hope our work will go some way to resolving where and when either method is most appropriate, perhaps exploring the notion of the end user's determining the levels of autonomy that the communities of devices use. Finally, to gather more realistic and meaningful results for all our research into pervasive environments, we need better data and so, with SRIF support, we have embarked on the construction of a new purpose built test bed for pervasive computing and iSpace work called the iDorm-2. The iDorm-2 is a full-size domestic flat built from scratch to facilitate experimentation with pervasive computing technology. Apart from being equipped with the latest pervasive computing appliances, and having been constructed to facilitate easy experimentation, the major advantage of the iDorm-2 is that we will be able to get much longer periods of experimentation, as people will be able to stay in the environment for weeks and months. Thus, we look forward to being able to report more interesting and useful results during 2005 now that this facility has come on-line.

References

1. Clarke G, Callaghan V, and Pounds-Cornish A. Intelligent Habitats and the Future: The Interaction of People, Agents and Environmental Artefacts. 4S/EASST Conference on Technoscience, Citizenship and Culture in the 21st Century, Vienna, September 2000.

2. Colley M et al. Intelligent Inhabited Environments: Co-operative Robotics and Buildings. 32nd International Symposium on Robotics (ISR 2001), Seoul, Korea, April 2001.

3. Chin J S Y and Callaghan V. Embedded-Internet Devices: A Means of Realizing the Pervasive Computing Vision. IADIS International Conference, Algarve, Portugal, November 2003.

4. Metcalfe R. Keynote Presentation. ACMI Conf, San Jose, CA, March 2001.

5. TINI — http://www.ibutton.com/TINI/

6. Imsys — http://www.imsys.se/

7. JStik — http://jstik.systronix.com/

8. Mini ITX — http://www.mini-itx.com/

9. Callaghan V, Clarke G, and Pounds-Cornish A. Buildings as Intelligent Autonomous Systems: A Model for Integrating Personal and Building Agents. The 6th International Conference on Intelligent Autonomous Systems (IAS-6), Venice, Italy, 2000.

10. Mozer M C. The Neural Network House: An Environment That Adapts to Its Inhabitants. In: Coen M (editor). Proceedings of the AAAI Spring Symposium on Intelligent Environments. Menlo Park, CA. AAAI Press, 1998:110–114.

11. Callaghan V et al. A Soft-Computing DAI Architecture for Intelligent Buildings. Journal of Studies in Fuzziness and Soft Computing on Soft Computing Agents, Physica-Verlag-Springer, 2001.

12. Callaghan V et al. Embedded Intelligence: Research Issues for Ubiquitous Computing. Proceedings of the Ubiquitous Computing in Domestic Environments Conference, Nottingham, September 2001.

13. Brooks R. Intelligence Without Representation. Artificial Intelligence, 1991:47:139–159.

14. Hagras H et al. A Hierarchical Fuzzy Genetic Agent Architecture for Intelligent Buildings Sensing and Control. RASC 2000 — International Conference on Recent Advances in Soft Computing, Leicester, June 2000.

15. Hagras H et al. A Hierarchical Fuzzy Genetic Multi-Agent Architecture for Intelligent Buildings Learning, Adaptation and Control. International Journal of Information Sciences, August 2001.

16. Cayci F, Callaghan V, and Clarke G. DIBAL — A Distributed Intelligent Building Agent Language. The 6th International Conference on Information Systems Analysis and Synthesis (ISAS 2000), Orlando, FL, July 2000.

17. Duman H, Hagras H A K, and Callaghan V. A Soft-Computing-based Approach to Intelligent Association in an Agent-based Ambient-intelligence Environment. 4th International Conference on Recent Advances in Soft Computing, Nottingham, 2002.

18. Duman H et al. Intelligent Association in Agent-based Ubiquitous Computing Environments. Proceedings of the 2002 International Conference on Control, Automation and System (ICCAS'02), Muju, Korea, October 2002.

19. Hagras H A K et al. Incremental Synchronous Learning for Embedded-Agents Operating in Ubiquitous Computing Environments. In: Soft Computing Agents: A New Perspective for Dynamic Information Systems. IOS Press, 2002.

20. Hagras H A K et al. A Fuzzy Incremental Synchronous Learning Technique for Embedded Agents Learning and Control in Intelligent Inhabited Environments. Proceedings of the 2002 IEEE International Conference on Fuzzy Systems, Hawaii, 2002:139–145.

21. Hagras H A K et al. Online Learning and Adaptation for Intelligent Embedded Agents Operating in Domestic Environments. In: Maravall D and Changjiu Zhou D R (editors). Fusion of Soft Computing and Hard Computing for Autonomous Robotic Systems. Physica-Verlag, 2002.

22. Holmes A, Duman H, and Pounds-Cornish A. The iDORM: Gateway to Heterogeneous Networking Environments. International ITEA Workshop on Virtual Home Environments, Paderborn, Germany, February 2002.

23. Pounds-Cornish A and Holmes A. The iDorm — A Practical Deployment of Grid Technology. 2nd IEEE International Symposium on Cluster Computing and the Grid (CCGrid2002), Berlin, May 2002.

24. Hagras H A K et al. A Fuzzy Logic-based Embedded Agent Approach to Ambient Intelligence in Ubiquitous Computing Environments. IEEE Intelligent Systems Journal, 2004.

25. Doctor F, Hagras H, and Callaghan V. A Type-2 Fuzzy Embedded Agent for Ubiquitous Computing Environments. In the Proceedings of the IEEE International Conference on Fuzzy Systems, Budapest, Hungary, July 2004.

26. Doctor F, Hagras H, and Callaghan V. An Adaptive Fuzzy Learning Mechanism for Intelligent Agents in Ubiquitous Computing Environments. Proceedings of the 2004 World Automation Congress, Seville, Spain, June 2004.

27. Genetic-Fuzzy Controller, UK Patent No 99 10539.7, May 1999.

28. Chin J S Y et al. Pervasive Computing and Urban Development: Issues for the Individual and Society. UN Second World Urban International Conference on the Role of Cities in an Information Age, Barcelona, Spain, September 2004.

29. Chin J S Y et al. Pervasive Information Systems: Issues for the Individual and Society. Springer-Verlag, 2005.

30. Berners-Lee T, Hendler J, and Lassila O. The Semantic Web. Scientific American, May 2001.

31. Chin J S Y et al. An Ontology-based Approach to Representation and Decomposition In Pervasive Home Computing Environments. Submitted to Pervasive 05.

32. Lieberman H. Your Wish Is My Command: Programing by Example. Morgan Kaufmann Press, 2001.

33. Myers B A. Creating User Interfaces Using Programming by Example, Visual Programming, and Constraints. ACM Transactions on Programming Languages and Systems (TOPLAS), April 1990:12:2:143–177.

34. Halbert D C. SmallStar: Programming by Demonstration in the Desktop Metaphor. In: Watch What I DO. MIT Press, 1993.

35. Blackwell A F and Hague R. Designing a Program Language for Home Automation. In: Kadoda G (editor). Proc of PP1G, 2001:85–103.

36. Guibert N and Girard P. Teaching and Learning Programming with a Programming by Example System. International Symposium on End User Development, Sankt Augustin, Bonn, Germany, 2003.

37. Sugiura A and Koseki Y. Internet Scrapbook: Automating Web Browsing Tasks by Demonstration. Proceedings of the 11th Annual ACM Symposium on User Interface Software and Technology, San Francisco, CA, 1998:9–18.

38. Bauer M et al. Programming by Example: Programming by Demonstration for Information Agents. Communications of the ACM, March 2000:43:3:98–103.

39. McDaniel R. Demonstrating the Hidden Features That Make an Application Work. In: Lieberman H (editor). Your Wish Is My Command: Programming by Example. Morgan Kaufmann Press, 2001:163–174.

40. Lieberman H et al. Training Agents to Recognize Text by Example. Proceedings of the Third Annual Conference on Autonomous Agents, Seattle, WA, 1999:116–122.

41. Blackwell A F and Hague R. Designing a Program Language for Home Automation. Proceedings PP1G, 2001:85–103.

42. McBride B. Jena: A Semantic Web Toolkit. IEEE Internet Computing, November/ December 2002.

43. Haarslev V and Moller R. Description of the RACER System and Its Application. Proceedings International Workshop on Description Logics, 2001.

44. Zou Y, Chen H, and Finin T. F-OWL: An Inference Engine for Semantic Web. Proceedings of the Third NASA-Goddard/IEEE Workshop on Formal Approaches to Agent-based Systems, April 2004.

45. Chen H, Finin T, and Joshil A. SOUPA: Standard Ontology for Ubiquitous and Pervasive Applications. International Conference on Mobile and Ubiquitous Systems: Networking and Services, August 2004.

46. SOUPA — http://pervasive.semanticweb.org/soupa-2004-06.html

47. Vastenburg M. SitMod: A Tool for Modelling and Communicating Situations. Second International Conference, PERVASIVE 2004, Vienna, Austria, April 2004.

Acronyms

ABS	anti-lock braking system
ACD	automatic credentials discovery
ack	positive acknowledgement
ADAM	autonomic distributed authorisation middleware
ADC	analogue-to-digital converter
ADL	activity of daily living
AGM	adaptive genetic mechanism
AI	artificial intelligence
AIM	automated intelligent modelling
AMI	ambient intelligence
AMI-C	automotive multimedia interface collaboration group
ANFIS	adaptive-neuro-fuzzy inference system
AODV	*ad hoc* on-demand distance vector
AOFIS	on-line fuzzy inference system
API	application programming interface
AROI	algorithmically detected regions of interest
ASAM	Association of Standardisation of Automation and Measuring Systems
CA	connection approved
CAN	content-addressable network
CAN	controller area network
CASPIAN	consumers against privacy invasion and numbering
CBIR	content-based image retrieval
CCA	connected component analysis
CCTV	closed-circuit television
CiA	controller area network in automation
CLI	caller line identification
CMD	command

CMOS	complementary metal-oxide semiconductor
COM	component object model
CR	connection report
CRM	customer relations management
CRT	cathode ray tube
CS	checksum
CSWL	California Software Labs
CVHS	co-operative vehicle highway system
DfT	Department for Transport
DGPS	differential GPS
DHCP	dynamic host configuration protocol
DIBAL	distributed intelligent building agent language
DLP	digital light processor
DPI	dual Purkinje image
DRAM	dynamic random access memory
DSM	domain specific modelling
DTI	Department of Trade and Industry
DWIM	'Do what I mean'
EAN	European article numbering
ECU	electronic control unit
E-P3P	Platform for Enterprise Privacy Practices
EPC	electronic product code
EPC-DS	EPC discovery service
EPC-IS	EPC information service
ERD	entity-relationship diagram
ERM	employee relationship management
ERP	enterprise resource planning
FCM	Fuzzy-C-Means
FDA	Food and Drug Administration
FIPA	Foundation for Intelligent Physical Agents
FLC	fuzzy logic controller
GA	genetic algorithm
GCMRD	gaze contingent multi-resolutional displays
GGF	global grid forum

GIS	geographical information system
GMM	Gaussian mixture model
GNSS	global navigation satellite system
GP	general practitioner
GP	genetic programming
GPRS	general packet radio service
GPS	global positioning system
GRA	generic router assist
GUI	graphical user interface
HAVi	home audio-video interoperability
HCI	human–computer interaction
HIDS	host-based intrusion detection system
HROI	human-identified region of interest
I2C	inter-integrated circuit
ICAO	International Civil Aviation Organisation
ICF	interactive content factory
ICT	information and communication technology
IDA	intelligent data analysis
iDorm	intelligent dormitory
IDS	intrusion detection system
IETF	Internet Engineering Task Force
ILSA	independent life-style assistant
IP	Internet provider
IPS	information provisioning system
ISI	Internet Sciences Institute
ISL	incremental synchronous learning
ISP	independent service provider
ISTAG	Information Society Technologies Advisory Group
ITS	intelligent transport system
JAR	Java archive
JIT	just-in-time
JPEG	joint photographic experts group
JXTA	[suite of Sun P2P protocols]
KB	knowledge base

KQML	knowledge query and manipulation language
LAN	local area network
LCD	liquid crystal display
LCOS	liquid crystal on silicon
LED	light emitting diode
LIDAR	light detection and ranging
LRUC	lorry road usage charging
LTP	local transport plan
MANET	mobile *ad hoc* network
MEM	micro-electro-mechanical
MEMS	MEM system
MF	membership function
MIMO	multi-input–multi-output
MISO	multi-input–single-output
MLP	multiplayer perceptron
MOST	media-oriented systems transport
MPEG	moving picture experts group
MSA	module specification advertisement
nack	negativeacknowledgement
NCRS	national care record system
NIDS	network-based intrusion detection system
NIS	nature-inspired system
NPC	non-player character
NR	neighbour request
NRp	neighbour reply
NSF	National Service Framework [for older people]
OECD	Organisation for Economic Co-operation and Development
OGSA	open grid services architecture
OGSI	open grid services infrastructure
OLED	organic light emitting diode
ONS	object name server
OPS	object pseudonym system
OSGi	Open Services Gateway Initiative
P2P	peer-to-peer

P3P	platform for privacy preferences
PCCR	pupil-centre/corneal-reflection
PDA	personal digital assistant
PHEN	pervasive home environment networking
PICT	pervasive information and computing technology
PKI	public key infrastructure
PROFIT	potential profit opportunities in the future ambient intelligence world
PVR	personal video recorder
QoL	quality of life
RAM	random access memory
RB	rule base
RDF	resource description framework
RDS-TMC	radio data service traffic message channel
RFID	radio frequency identification
RMSE	root mean-squared error
RNA	ribonucleic acid
RoHS	reduction of hazardous substances
ROI	region of interest
RSS	RDF site summary
RTC	real-time clock
RUC	road user charging
SAE	Society of Automotive Engineers
SC	soft computing
SCM	supply chain management
SCOOT	split cycle and offset optimisation technique
SLP	service location protocol
SMS	short message service
SNEP	sensor network encryption protocol
SNS	sensor network server
SOA	service-oriented architecture
SOAP	simple object access protocol
SOI	silicon on insulator
SPIDA	soft computing platform for IDA
SPINS	security protocols for sensor networks

STAN	simulation tool for *ad hoc* networks
STB	set-top box
STD	scaled standard deviation
SULTAN	simple universal logic-oriented trust analysis notation
SWAN	small world adaptive network
TARA	total abstract rendering architecture
TCO	total cost of ownership
TCP	transmission control protocol
TCP/IP	transmission control protocol/Internet protocol
TESLA	timed efficient stream loss-tolerant authentication
TOP	task-oriented programming
TTA	time-triggered architecture
TTCAN	time-triggered controller area network
UART	universal asynchronous receiver transmitter
UCC	Uniform Code Council
UDDI	universal description, discovery, and integration
UGVN	urban global vehicle network
UPC	universal product code
UPnP	universal plug and play
URL	uniform resource locator
USB	universal serial bus
UTC	urban traffic control
UTMC	urban traffic management and control
UWB	ultra wideband
VA	visual attention
VR	virtual reality
WEEE	waste electrical and electronic equipment
WEP	wireless equivalent privacy
WiFi	wireless fidelity
WLAN	wireless local area network
WS	Web service
WSDL	Web services description language
WS-RF	Web services resource framework
XML	extensible mark-up language

Index